D0875775

CLASSIC AND CAVALIER

CLAUDE J. SUMMERS
TED-LARRY PEBWORTH
Editors

CLASSIC AND CAVALIER

Essays on Jonson and the Sons of Ben

UNIVERSITY OF PITTSBURGH PRESS

Published by the University of Pittsburgh Press, Pittsburgh, Pa. 15260
Copyright © 1982, University of Pittsburgh Press
All rights reserved
Feffer and Simons, Inc., London
Manufactured in the United States of America

Library of Congress Cataloging in Publication Data
Main entry under title:

Classic and cavalier.

Includes index.
1. Jonson, Ben, 1573?–1637—Criticism and interpretation—Addresses, essays, lectures. 2. Jonson,
Ben, 1573?–1637—Influence—Addresses, essays,
lectures. 3. English poetry—Early modern, 1500–
1700—History and criticism—Addresses, essays, lectures. I. Summers, Claude J. II. Pebworth, Ted-
Larry.
PR2638.C55   1982   822'.3   82-1882
ISBN 0-8229-3461-2   AACR2

For
John T. Shawcross
and
Robert B. Hinman

you that have beene
Ever at home: yet, have all Countries seene:
And like a Compasse keeping one foot still
Upon your Center, doe your Circle fill
Of generall knowledge; watch'd men, manners too,
Heard what times past have said, seene what ours doe.

‡

Contents

Textual Note ‡ ix

Introduction: Classic and Cavalier: Celebrating Jonson and the
Sons of Ben ‡ xi
CLAUDE J. SUMMERS and TED-LARRY PEBWORTH

Guides, not Commanders

A Poet Nearly Anonymous ‡ 3
C. A. PATRIDES

Pindar and Jonson's Cary-Morison Ode ‡ 17
STELLA P. REVARD

Jonson and the (Re-) Invention of the Book ‡ 31
RICHARD C. NEWTON

The Language, and the Truth

The Authoritie of Truth: Jonson's Mastery of Measure and the
Founding of the Modern Plain-Style Lyric ‡ 59
RICHARD FLANTZ

The Context of Jonson's Formalism ‡ 77
SUSANNE WOODS

Words, Things, and Names: Jonson's Poetry and Philosophical
Grammar ‡ 91
MARTIN ELSKY

The Ardor, and the Passion

The Public and Private Dimensions of Jonson's Epitaphs ‡ 107
JACK D. WINNER

"A Celebration of Charis": Socratic Lover and Silenic Speaker ‡ 121
RAYMOND B. WADDINGTON

The Anxiety of Identification: Jonson and the Rival Poets ‡ 139
ROGER B. ROLLIN

The Light, and Marke unto Posterity

Circular Strategies and Structures in Jonson and Herbert ‡ 157
ILONA BELL

"To my friend G. N. from Wrest": Carew's Secular Masque ‡ 171
MICHAEL P. PARKER

Vaughan's "Amoret" Poems: A Jonsonian Sequence ‡ 193
JOHN T. SHAWCROSS

Sealed of the Tribe

"At Bottom a Criticism of Life": Suckling and the Poetry of Low Seriousness ‡ 217
THOMAS CLAYTON

Perception and Expression in Marvell's Cavalier Poetry ‡ 243
MICHAEL H. MARKEL

"A Kind of a *Christmas* Ingine": Jonson, Milton, and the Sons of Ben in the Hard Season ‡ 255
ROBERT B. HINMAN

Notes on the Contributors ‡ 281

Index to Works Cited ‡ 285

✝

Textual Note

Throughout this volume, the works of Ben Jonson are cited parenthetically in the text. The edition used is *Ben Jonson*, ed. C. H. Herford, Percy Simpson, and Evelyn Simpson, 11 vols. (Oxford: The Clarendon Press, 1925–52). The poems (cited by title or by collection and poem number) and *Discoveries* are in volume 8, Jonson's *Conversations with William Drummond of Hawthornden* (cited as *Conversations*) in volume 1. The use of *i, j, u*, and *v* has been silently modernized in all quotations, including those from works other than Jonson's.

CLAUDE J. SUMMERS
TED-LARRY PEBWORTH

✠

Introduction
Classic and Cavalier:
Celebrating Jonson and the Sons of Ben

The recent quickening of critical interest in Ben Jonson's nondramatic poetry has led to a new appreciation of his "subtle sport" and to a new willingness to read him on his own terms. His status as poet has risen steadily over the past two decades. After years of languishing in Donne's shadow, he is now recognized among the most important poets in the language. He is justly celebrated as a self-nominated arbiter of civilized values, as a public poet who articulates the "mysteries of manners, armes, and arts" in weighty judgment and broad generality, as, in fact, a thoroughgoing neoclassicist. But such a view, accurate though it is in basic outline, is at best only partial, even when buttressed with timeworn and misleading contrasts of a laborious, frigid Jonson with a gentle Shakespeare and a fiery Donne. The unqualified view of Jonson as neoclassicist neglects his frequent indulgences in emotional excess and self-dramatization, and—more positively—his ability to create poetry of individual sensation. What needs emphasis is that Jonson's carefully fashioned poetic commonwealth includes space for the personal and the private as well as for the general and the public. If Jonson is, as Arthur Marotti has characterized him, "an artistic schizophrenic, with both a Dionysian and an Apollonian side,"[1] these divergent aspects of his personality are united by the idealism that animates the contradictory impulses of his poetry: wit and didacticism, self-assertion and social vision, rage and commendation, satire and celebration.

The variety of Jonson's poetry undoubtedly reflects the contradictions of his life. Stepson to a bricklayer, he became the defender of conservative, aristocratic tradition, yet also insisted that merit and high birth are not synonymous. A felon convicted of manslaughter, he promulgated a code of ethical behavior for an age he diagnosed as corrupt and in imminent danger of social and political collapse. A gregarious man who inspired the devotion of younger poets and wits, he also made numerous enemies and prosecuted many quarrels. He asserted "the impossibility of any mans being the good Poet, without first being a good man" (*Volpone*, Dedication), yet he was described by Inigo Jones as "the best of Poetts, but the worst of men" ("To his false friend mr: Ben Johnson"),[2] and by William Drummond of Hawthornden as "a great lover and praiser of himself, a contemner and Scorner of others, given rather to losse a friend, than a Jest" (*Conversations*, 680–81). Proud of his learning and conscious of his dignity, he could nevertheless mock his physical appearance and freely reveal such idiosyncracies as that "he heth consumed a whole night in lying looking to his great toe, about which he hath seen tartars & turks Romans and Carthaginions feight in his imagination" (*Conversations*, 322–24).

The many facets of Jonson's complex personality cohere in his carefully shaped yet various canon, wherein he adopts such dramatic voices as tactful adviser, genial host, urbane commentator, scornful satirist, grieving father, and vulnerable lover. For all his multiplicity of roles, however, Jonson nearly always reveals himself as insistently and self-consciously the poet. His confession to Drummond that, "In his merry humor, he was wont to name himself the Poet" (*Conversations*, 636), both reveals his self-image and accords with his practice in the poems. But Jonson's creation of a poet-persona is not merely a self-promoting pose or simply a poetic strategy exploited deftly in such works as the verse epistles, the epitaphs on his children, "A Celebration of Charis," "My Picture left in Scotland," the Cary-Morison ode, "To Penshurst," and "On Lucy Countesse of Bedford," among many others. It is also a reflection of the idealism that unites the disparate works of his canon and constitutes one of his greatest legacies to the "Tribe of Ben."

Jonson's idealism is rooted in his unswerving conviction of the true utility of poetry, that "dulcet, and gentle *Philosophy*, which leades on, and guides us by the hand to Action, with a ravishing delight, and incredible Sweetnes" (*Discoveries*, 2398–2400). Paraphrasing Cicero, he described poetry as an art which "nourisheth, and instructeth our Youth; delights our Age; adornes our prosperity; comforts our Adversity; entertaines us at home; keepes us company abroad, travailes with us; watches; divides the times of our earnest, and sports; shares in our Country recesses and recreations; insomuch as the wisest and best learned have thought her the absolute Mistresse of manners, and neerest of kin to Vertue" (*Discoveries*, 2389–96). Of the poet, he said, "Wee doe not require in him meere

Elocution; or an excellent faculty in verse; but the exact knowledge of all vertues, and their Contraries; with ability to render the one lov'd, the other hated, by his proper embattaling them" (*Discoveries,* 1038–41). Implicit throughout Jonson's work is an abiding vision of human possibilities, a vision that poetry not only incorporates but also helps to realize. Poetry "offers to mankinde a certaine rule, and Patterne of living well, and happily" (*Discoveries,* 2386–87). And unlike wealth, beauty, and nobility, it offers the reward of immortality, as Jonson explains in his "Epistle. To Elizabeth Countesse of Rutland":

> It is the *Muse,* alone, can raise to heaven,
> And, at her strong armes end, hold up, and even,
> The soules, shee loves. Those other glorious notes,
> Incscrib'd in touch or marble, or the cotes
> Painted, or carv'd upon our great-mens tombs,
> Or in their windowes; doe but prove the wombs,
> That bred them, graves: when they were borne, they di'd,
> That had no *Muse* to make their fame abide.   (41–48)

Jonson's trust in good verses sustained him throughout the vicissitudes of his life. "*Poetry,* in this latter Age, hath prov'd but a meane *Mistresse,* to such as have wholly addicted themselves to her" (*Discoveries,* 622–24), he complained. Yet he never lost his faith in the continuity of ethical principles, in the living relevance of timeless questions about the nature of the good life, or in the ability of poetry to re-create the past and to preserve the present for the future. Thus his real audience was never limited to his own time. He offered his work to posterity, confident of its verdict. "An other Age, or juster men," he wrote, "will acknowledge the vertues of [the poet's] studies: his wisdome, in dividing: his subtilty, in arguing: with what strength hee doth inspire his readers; with what sweetnesse hee strokes them: in inveighing, what sharpnesse; in Jest, what urbanity he uses" (*Discoveries,* 786–91). Jonson's own poetry exemplifies those qualities of learning, subtlety, strength, and urbanity that he expected posterity to value. But "Saint Ben's" legacy to his poetic sons may reside almost as much in the trust in good verses as in the verses themselves. Jonson's idealistic conception of the poet-priest is certainly not original; yet he more than anyone else in the early seventeenth century exemplified in life and in poetic practice the continuity of Orpheus's direct line. As

Thomas Randolph wrote, in "A gratulatory to Mr. Ben. Johnson for his adopting of him to be his Son,"

> I am a kinne to *Hero's*, being thine,
> And part of my alliance is divine.

The fifteen essays of this volume originated as submissions to the fourth Biennial Renaissance Conference at the University of Michigan–Dearborn, "Classic and Cavalier: Jonson and the Sons of Ben," held on October 17–18, 1980;[3] the original versions of nearly all were presented there, several in abbreviated form. The collection reflects the two goals of the conference. Some of the studies presented here illuminate Jonson's accomplishment as a lyric poet, while others explore works by, and links to, his poetic "Sons," a designation broadly interpreted to include seventeenth-century poets indebted to Jonson, whether or not they were actually "sealed of the Tribe of Ben." Some of the essays are broad in scope; others concentrate on single poems or groups of poems.

Working on large canvases, C. A. Patrides, Richard Flantz, and Richard C. Newton analyze fundamental aspects of Jonson's individual achievement and trace as well key elements of his enormous influence on subsequent English poetry. Discovering in Jonson's own verse "the virtue of economy that terminates in clarity," Patrides locates the model of that economy and clarity in the lyric voice of classical Greece, where "matter depends entirely on manner." He thus redirects the emphasis on Jonson's classicism from questions of content to issues of style, and he concludes that Jonson's restrained lyricism profoundly affected English poets from Crashaw and Milton to Pope and Yeats. Flantz considers Jonson's lyric from another perspective, concentrating on the sophistication of its prosody and concluding that, through the example of his own verse as well as through his prestige as a literary arbiter, Jonson played a pivotal role in the early seventeenth century's development of *poemata*, a genre "modeled on Latinate forms and open to the native English plain-style tradition." In a richly suggestive essay, Newton argues that in the work of Jonson "we first see the impact of printing coherently assimilated." He cites Jonson's involvement in the printing of his work as the first important English instance of a vernacular poet's seeking to create and fix his corpus and individual texts as unchanging and unchangeable artifacts. The example of the 1616 folio *Workes* stimulated among Jonson's contemporaries and following generations of poets a recognition of the control made available by print transmission and, in effect, created the conditions under which literary study and systematic criticism could flourish.

Jonson's reactions to important issues in late Renaissance semantic and literary theory find treatment in the essays of Susanne Woods and Martin Elsky. Woods examines Jonson's relationship to Baconian dualism, discovering Jonson to be "the first major voice to make explicit the value of versification as an influence restraining the excesses of fantasy, and . . . the first major advocate to prefer verse forms that best accommodate the natural shapes of rational discourse to verse forms that merely convey a sensuous musicality." Placing Jonson within a linguistic tradition concerned with the referential nature of language, Elsky uses this tradition of philosophical grammar to explore the poet's evocation of names and titles to reify moral and social values.

Important poems in the many lyric modes employed by Jonson also receive careful attention. Stella P. Revard finds Pindaric matter as well as Pindaric manner in the masterful Cary-Morison ode, locating sources of approach and detail in Nemean 11 and Isthmian 8. Jack D. Winner sensitively investigates the creative tension in Jonson's epitaphs, especially the emotive power produced by the conflict between the poet's public office as celebrator of the virtuous dead and his private experience as grieving father in "On My First Sonne." Approaching "A Celebration of Charis" as an "exercise in stylistic and generic mixture," Raymond B. Waddington analyzes in detail the sequence's complexities of form, statement, and persona, concluding that "the Charis poems explore the Neoplatonic ideals of love, to find, with genuine regret, that they are unworkable." Roger B. Rollin studies the psychological complexities of Jonson's epigrams to Donne and his tribute to Shakespeare as manifestations of "a strong poet's need to come to terms with his strong contemporaries."

Of the poetic "Sons" whose works are treated in the last two sections of this volume, only three—Carew, Suckling, and Marvell—have been traditionally linked to Jonson. In a spirited essay, Thomas Clayton directs attention to Suckling's range by examining four differently representative poems. He emphasizes the seriousness lying beneath the surfaces of "natural, easy Suckling," and he defends the "poetry of low seriousness" as fundamental criticism of affectation, vanity, presumptuousness, and hypocrisy. Michael H. Markel analyzes four of Marvell's "Cavalier" poems as deliberate reactions to and expositions of "the limitations inherent in contemporary social poetry." And, revealing the true circumstances under which Carew's "To my friend G. N. from Wrest" was written, Michael P. Parker discusses the poem as an important artistic achievement in its own right and as the "crucial middle term between Jonson's initial essays in the English country-house poem and Marvell's transformation of the genre in the 1640s and 1650s."

The three "unsealed" Sons of Ben who find a place in the volume are Herbert, Vaughan, and Milton. Convinced "that Herbert's poems are often more indebted to Jonson than to Donne," Ilona Bell finds the model for one of the most important techniques in the poems of *The Temple*—"a characteristic circular strategy and structure"—in key poems of Jonson. John T. Shawcross discovers in the "Amoret" poems of Henry Vaughan's first published collection a sequential relationship that is Jonsonian rather than Donnean, and he argues that the recognition of the thirteen-poem series as a subtle narrative of a love affair "calls for praise of Vaughan's craftsmanship." And, finally, in a stirring coda, Robert B. Hinman expounds on a sympathetic relationship between Jonson and Milton and, in the process, touches nearly every English poet of the earlier seventeenth century. The "Tribe of Christ, seventeenth-century generation," Hinman concludes, comprises "spiritual members of one poetic family of whom even Milton would have been proud to honor Jonson as earthly father—and as master chef."

This brief synopsis, only a hint at the richness of subjects and treatments to be found in the essays of this volume, is of necessity largely silent on the wealth of their insights into individual poems. Neither the topics treated nor the critical and scholarly approaches employed were assigned or suggested, and the original versions of the essays were written without consultation among the authors. Many of the studies as now published have, however, profited from the exchange of ideas afforded by the Dearborn conference, and, despite their diversity, they intersect and reinforce each other in significant ways.

This collection of essays and the scholarly meeting from which it originated have profited from the generously expended time and effort of the members of the conference steering committee: Frank L. Huntley, Leah S. Marcus, Virginia Mollenkott, J. Max Patrick, and John T. Shawcross. Their insights and suggestions have been of great value, and we join the authors in expressing our thanks to them. We also gratefully acknowledge the support of Eugene

Arden, Vice-Chancellor for Academic Affairs at the University of Michigan–Dearborn, and the Campus Grants Committee.

NOTES

1. "All About Jonson's Poetry," *ELH* 39 (1972), 209.

2. This quotation from Inigo Jones and the subsequent quotation from Thomas Randolph follow the texts in volume 11 of *Ben Jonson*, ed. Herford, Simpson, and Simpson.

3. Selected papers from the first three Dearborn conferences have been published: those from the 1974 conference on Robert Herrick as *"Trust to Good Verses": Herrick Tercentenary Essays*, ed. Roger B. Rollin and J. Max Patrick (Pittsburgh: University of Pittsburgh Press, 1978), those from the 1976 conference on seventeenth-century prose as a special issue of *Studies in the Literary Imagination* 10, no. 2 (1977), ed. William A. Sessions and James S. Tillman, and those from the 1978 celebration of Herbert as *"Too Rich to Clothe the Sunne": Essays on George Herbert*, ed. Claude J. Summers and Ted-Larry Pebworth (Pittsburgh: University of Pittsburgh Press, 1980).

Guides, not Commanders

C. A. PATRIDES

A Poet Nearly Anonymous

Poetry, wrote Jonson in *Discoveries,* is "the Queene of Arts: which had her originall from heaven, received thence from the *'Ebrewes,* and had in prime estimation with the Greeks, transmitted to the *Latines,* and all Nations, that profess'd Civility" (2382–84). To grant poetry's divine origin and civilizing mission is of course to grant that poets must necessarily moralize. The notion, here crudely stated, was twice during the seventeenth century predicated with passionate conviction and in memorable terms. One formulation was ventured by Milton;[1] the other by Jonson, again in *Discoveries:*

I could never thinke the study of *Wisedome* confin'd only to the Philosopher: or of *Piety* to the *Divine:* or of State to the *Politicke.* But that he which can faine a *Common-wealth* (which is the Poet) can governe it with *Judgments,* informe it with *Religion,* and *Morals;* is all these. Wee doe not require in him meere *Elocution;* or an excellent faculty in verse; but the exact knowledge of all vertues, and their Contraries; with ability to render the one lov'd, the other hated, by his proper embattaling them. (1032–41)

If for the sake of emphasis Jonson here subordinates manner to matter or style to content, he had adequate warrant in Horace: "The very root of writing well, and spring / Is to be wise; thy matter first to know" (*The Art of Poetrie,* 440–41). Jonson was well enough aware that manner can hardly be divorced from matter. Wedded, however, they are not interchangeable, since it is manner that pierces the otherwise inert matter and animates it. "Language," as Jonson remarked, "most shewes a man: speake that I may see thee" (2031–32). Adapting a phrase from the first of his sequence of ten lyrics on Charis, it could be said that the poet's progress is not from the truth to the language but from the language to the truth; so much so, that language frequently—and in Jonson

3

habitually—itself constitutes the "truth." Style, in other words, is fundamental—and, in Jonson's case, imperative.

Jonson spoke about style on several occasions, and definitively on one. His single most important statement does not only present an argument, however. It enacts the argument, so that the language used confirms as usual the "truth" propounded:

For a man to write well, there are required three Necessaries. To reade the best Authors, observe the best Speakers: and much exercise of his own style. In style to consider, what ought to be written; and after what manner; Hee must first thinke, and excogitate his matter; then choose his words, and examine the weight of either. Then take care in placing, and ranking both matter, and words, that the composition be comely; and to doe this with diligence, and often. No matter how slow the style be at first, so it be labour'd, and accurate: seeke the best, and be not glad of the forward conceipts, or first words, that offer themselves to us, but judge of what wee invent; and order what wee approve. Repeat often, what wee have formerly written . . . . So that the summe of all is: Ready writing makes not good writing; but good writing brings on ready writing.

(*Discoveries*, 1697–1732)

As advice to aspiring authors, the statement is remarkably unexceptional. No less naïve in its generalizations than conservative in its emphases, it is also likely to mislead by the apparently mechanical approach to "good writing." But Jonson is dispensing advice not *in* so many words as *through* so many words. Positively, I am suggesting, the statement endorses solely the self-same virtue it demonstrates: the virtue of economy that terminates in clarity.

Jonson's predilection for "plainness" is writ large in his poetry, as it is in his prose, and has been studied within the context of parallel tendencies in his age.[2] But the frame of reference I would regard as crucial for his style—and through his particular style to his particular "truth"—is that of the classical tradition. For Jonson truly inhabits the centuries of Greece and Rome, more than any other seventeenth-century poet save Milton, and attests that fact, again like Milton, on countless occasions. It is evidently an understatement to aver that Jonson possessed much Greek and even more Latin. The evidence of the well-studied volumes surviving from his library—but the evidence also of his learned annotations and most particularly of his poetry—suffices to confirm his proud claim, recorded by William Drummond of Hawthornden, that he was "better Versed & knew more in Greek and Latin, than all the Poets in England" (*Conversations*, 622–23).[3] He himself declared in the prefatory note to *Hymenaei* that he was ever "grounded upon *antiquitie*, and solide *learnings*,"[4] yet in *Discoveries* warned with equal force that the Greco-Roman heritage should not be permitted to enslave:

I know *Nothing* can conduce more to letters, then to examine the writings of the *Ancients*, and not to rest in their sole Authority. . . . For to all the observations of the *Ancients*, wee have our owne experience: which, if wee will use, and apply, wee have better meanes to pronounce. It is true they open'd the gates, and made the way, that went before us; but as Guides, not Commanders.   (129–39)

The statement is immediately relevant to matter, not to manner; yet it is no less applicable to questions of style—witness the extent to which Jonson's comedies unfold, freely, under the formidable influence of Aristophanes.[5] So far as his nondramatic poetry is concerned, the contours of the classical tradition are equally clear. Jonson himself indicated that in some of his odes he put on "the wings of *Pindars* Muse" ("An Ode to James Earle of Desmond," 3). He elsewhere named Pindar yet again, but in the company of three other poets who also constitute Jonson's major predecessors in lyric poetry:

> take the *Alcaik* Lute;
> Or thine owne *Horace*, or *Anacreons* Lyre;
> Warme thee by *Pindares* fire.
>
> ("Ode to Himselfe," 42–44)

Still another poem invokes the seven poets from ancient Rome to Renaissance England who immortalized as many ladies and thereby established the tradition that encompasses Jonson's Celia and Charis: Catullus's Lesbia, Tibullus's Delia, Propertius's Cynthia, Ovid's Corinna, Petrarch's Laura, Ronsard's Cassandra, and Sidney's Stella (enumerated in "An Ode: Helen, did Homer never see," *Under-wood* 27.9–25).

Jonson's affinities with the classical tradition are impressed on any number of his poems, among them the well-known song to Celia. First used as part of *Volpone* (3.7.166 ff.) and next significantly published as one of the lyrics within *The Forrest*, the poem is a free adaptation of the celebrated fifth song of Catullus, "Vivamus, mea Lesbia":

Come my Celia, let us prove,
While we may, the sports of love;
Time will not be ours, for ever:
He, at length, our good will sever.
Spend not then his guifts in vaine.
Sunnes, that set, may rise againe:
But if once we loose this light,
'Tis, with us, perpetuall night.
Why should we deferre our joyes?
Fame, and rumor are but toys.
Cannot we delude the eyes
Of a few poore household spyes?
Or his easier eares beguile,
So removed by our wile?
'Tis no sinne, loves fruit to steale,
But the sweet theft to reveale:
To be taken, to be seene,
These have crimes accounted beene.

The Forrest provides after the song to Celia another poem "To the same." It is manifestly closer to the spirit, and partially even to the phrasing, of the Catullan original:

Kisse me, sweet: The warie lover
Can your favours keepe, and cover,
When the common courting jay
All your bounties will betray.
Kisse againe: no creature comes.
Kisse, and score up wealthy summes
On my lips, thus hardly sundred,
While you breath. First give a hundred,
Then a thousand, then another
Hundred, then unto the tother
Adde a thousand, and so more:
Till you equall with the store,
All the grasse that *Rumney* yeelds,
Or the sands in *Chelsey* fields,
Or the drops in silver *Thames*,
Or the starres, that guild his streames,
In the silent sommer-nights,
When youths ply their stolne delights.
That the curious may not know

> How to tell' hem, as they flow,
> And the envious, when they find
> What their number is, be pin'd.

Familiar though these rhythms are to us, they were for their time utterly and intentionally subversive of the predominant modes of articulation. For Jonson's accommodation of the spirit of the classical lyric to English poetry vastly enriched the latter's potential; and if his efforts are seen as no more vital than Donne's were in another direction, his influence must certainly be judged as far more lasting. In immediate relation to Jonson's diverse responses to "Vivamus, mea Lesbia," it should be insisted that its imitations during the Renaissance were so far from being confined to his practice that they embrace an impressive number of other poets, too.[6] Yet Jonson's example remains crucial, arguably instrumental as it was in conditioning the response of still another poet who never figures in the roll calls of "the Sons of Ben." We expect the poet in question to have been Lovelace or, most likely, Suckling. But he is in fact Crashaw, whose version of the Catullan poem echoes the distinctly Jonsonian rhythms both in the overall movement and in the particular sound patterns created:

> Come and let us live my Deare,
> Let us love and never feare,
> What the sowrest Fathers say:
> Brightest *Sol* that dyes to day
> Lives againe as blith to morrow,
> But if we darke sons of sorrow
> Set; ô then, how long a Night
> Shuts the Eyes of our short light!
> Then let amorous kisses dwell
> On our lips, begin and tell
> A Thousand, and a Hundred score
> An Hundred, and a Thousand more,
> Till another Thousand smother
> That, and that wipe of another.
> Thus at last when we have numbred
> Many a Thousand, many a Hundred;
> Wee'l confound the reckoning quite,
> And lose our selves in wild delight:
> While our joyes so multiply,
> As shall mocke the envious eye.[7]

If Crashaw would later be said to be affianced rather to Herbert than to Jonson, we may consider that Herbert's own debt to Jonson was not—as we shall observe shortly—of slight consequence. The Sons of Ben are clearly a variegated tribe indeed.

The achievement of Ben Jonson centers on his full cognizance that, in the classical lyric, matter depends entirely on manner. Style, that is to say, is paramount. We might consider, in the first instance negatively, that the classical lyric is not intent on elevating an exclusive image into an argument after the fashion of Ezra Pound's "In a Station of the Metro":

> The apparition of these faces in the crowd;
> Petals on a wet, black bough.[8]

Nor is the classical lyric concerned, as its Hellenistic counterpart is, to indulge in sensationalism deriving from such potentially uncontrolled excess of emotion as we may see in most poems in *The Greek Anthology*, inclusive of the verses by the third-century Peloponnesian poet Mnasalkes:

> Aristocrateia,
> You've crossed the dark stream
> Young and unwed, alas!
> Your mother's left with just
> The tears she sheds, when
> Often now she weeping lies
> Prostrate upon your tomb.[9]

The contrast with an earlier metrical inscription on a tomb is instructive:

> ⁵ Η καλὸν τὸ μνῆμα [πα]τὴρ ἔστησε θανούσ[ι]
> Λεαρέτηι· οὐ γὰρ [ἔτ]ι ζῶσαν ἐσοψόμ[εθα].

> [When Learete died her father set up a monument
> which was beauty. But we shall nevermore see her alive.][10]

The contrast, one might venture to propose, is between those exclusive modes of articulation evident also in Greek sculpture: on the one hand, the severity of the classical period that in its aspiration after an ethically oriented idealism terminates in the frieze of the

Parthenon, the Apollo of Phidias, the Discus Thrower of Myron, and—however suggestive of the incoming novel dispensation—the Hermes of Praxiteles; and, on the other, the subsequently wayward laxity that in its pursuit of "realism" encompasses the increasing turbulence so noticeable as we pass from the Aphrodite of Milos to the Victory of Samothrace and thence to the Laöcoön group. In espousing the former attitude, the classical lyric best defines its nature through any sequent provision of representative examples we may care to invoke. The ensuing eight instances, from the work of four lyric poets, might have been multiplied by drawing as well on the choric songs of Attic tragedy and, indeed, the comedies of Aristophanes. But the representative suggestiveness had been much the same, as it is in the poetry of the earliest Greek lyric poet, Archilochus:

> ἔχουσα θαλλὸν μυρσίνης ἐτέρπετο
> ῥοδῆς τε καλὸν ἄνθος,
>   ἡ δέ οἱ κόμη
> ὤμους κατεσκίαζε καὶ μετάφρενα.

[A spray of myrtle and beauty of a rose
were happiness in her hands, and her hair
fell as darkness on her back and shoulders.][11]

Again from Archilochus, with an even more impressive sense of economy:

> εἰ γὰρ ὣς ἐμοὶ γένοιτο χεῖρα Νεοβούλης θιγεῖν.

[If it only were my fortune just to touch Neoboule's hand.][12]

Sappho wrote:

> Μνάσεσθαί τινά φαιμ' ὕστερον ἀμμέων

[You may forget but

Let me tell you
this: someone in
some future time
will think of us.][13]

Next:

ψαύην δ'οὐ δοκίμοιμ' ὀράνω 'έσσα διπάχεα.

> [I could not hope
> to touch the sky
> with my two arms.][14]

Also:

τοῦτο δ' ἴσθι, διπλασίαν
κῆναν νύκτ' ἄρασθαί μ' ἄμμι γένεσθαι.

> [All the while, believe me, I prayed
> our night would last twice as long.][15]

Pindar, ever advancing from the exquisitely crafted detail to the intimation of states of mind, wrote:

ἐγκωμίων γὰρ ἄωτος ὕμνων
ἐπ' ἄλλοτ' ἄλλων ὦτε μέλισσα θύνει λόγον.

> [The light of the holiday-song
> Darts from one thought to another like a bee!][16]

Also:

τὸν μὲν ἀγάλλων θεός
ἔδωκεν δίφρον τε χρύσεον πτεροῖσίν τ' ἀκάμαντας ἵππους.

> [The God glorified him, and gave him a chariot of gold
> And winged horses that never tired.][17]

Finally, Socrates is said by Plato to have spoken thus of his lover:

Τὴν ψυχὴν 'Αγάθωνα φιλῶν ἐπὶ χείλεσιν ἔσχον·
ἦλθε γὰρ ἡ τλήμων ὡς διαβησομένη.

> [As I kissed Agathon my soul swelled to my lips,
> where it hangs, pitiful, hoping to leap across.][18]

Veritable "touchstones" of the classical lyric, these eight poems suggest but do not pronounce, and intimate but do not exhaust.

Their apparent qualities are economy to the point of telegraphic brevity, clarity to the point of obviousness, and restraint to the point of indifference. Yet their economy conceals potential fullness; their clarity, a complexity of attitudes; and their restraint, total commitment. Greek poets like Archilochus or Sappho, and Roman ones like Catullus, would have agreed with Jonson's categoric judgment that "Wee must expresse readily, and fully, not profusely" (*Discoveries*, 1962). Profusion limits—and, worse, it corrupts.

I say "corrupts" advisedly; for the moral tenor of classical lyric poetry depends on much the same ambition which underlines Jonson's poems and was to have informed his proposed grammar: "To teach . . . The puritie of Language" ("An Execration upon Vulcan," 92–93). A statement in *Discoveries* makes the point with exceptional brilliance, in that the style once again confirms the argument: "Many Writers perplexe their Readers, and Hearers with *Non-sense*. Their writings need sunshine. Pure and neat Language I love, yet plain and customary. A barbarous Phrase hath often made mee out of love with a good sense; and doubtfull writing hath wrackt mee beyond my patience" (1868–73). Jonson's endorsement of "plainness" by no means primarily reflects contemporary interests in the "plain style." His own remarks on style diverge dramatically, in that they are, in theory as in practice, moral judgments. In theory, even his nefarious wish that Shakespeare might have "blotted" a thousand lines is a reproach to be understood—if it can be understood at all—strictly in the light of the classical tradition. Hence Jonson's own practice, where "good sense" persuades not by its inherent goodness so much as by the firm clarity of its expression. For example:

> Not to know vice at all, and keep true state,
>   Is vertue, and not *Fate:*
> Next, to that vertue, is to know vice well,
>   And her blacke spight expell.
>
> ("Epode," 1–4)

The contrary is evident in Shakespeare—so Jonson was presumably inclined to argue—in that profusion encloses the potential to overwhelm the "good sense" or, in extremis, annihilate it altogether. If eventually Jonson's munificent elegy on the "Soule of the Age" was to recognize Shakespeare's supremacy, something of his earlier attitude lingered in the barbed reference to the other's "small *Latine*, and lesse *Greeke*." At issue in any case is not Shakespeare's misunderstood practice but Jonson's actual one; and, in the latter, the corruption attending the profusion of language is stamped not only on his epigrams but often on his plays, too, *Volpone*, for example, where the exhilarating hyperboles of the opening speech are meaningfully conflated with the cacophonous sounds of Nano, Androgyno, and Castrone:

> Now, room for fresh gamesters, who do will you to know,
> They do bring you neither play nor university show;
> And therefore do entreat you that whatsoever they rehearse,
> May not fare a whit the worse, for the false pace of the verse.
>
> (1.2.1–4)

Donne's response was positive. His commendatory verses on *Volpone*—pointedly phrased in Latin ("Amicissimo, et meritissimo Ben. Jonson. In Vulponem")—hail Jonson not generally because of his adherence to the cumulative wisdom of the ancients, but expressly because that adherence promised to stem the perfidious influences emanating from other quarters. The perception is vital, all the more because Donne himself remained distant from the classical tradition in poetry, but saw clearly enough how Jonson's talents might, and did, use that tradition's moral authority to great advantage.

The authority is most evident, we may now maintain, where Jonson's restraint is most palpably present. His natural predilection was for the particulars within—the monosyllabic word strategically placed, the comma intended to guide the voice, the "plain" expression calculated to suggest, the rhythm aimed to elicit a specific response—which in accumulation argue on the technical level an awesome, almost Pindaric commitment to the expertly attended detail and on the thematic level a confirmation of a manifest order or, in its absence, the intimation of that same order all the more urgent precisely because it is absent. To be sure, not all of Jonson's efforts were perfectly wrought. The elegy on the Marchioness of Winchester, for instance, extends to one hundred lines, and is one hundred lines too long. The version of Horace's *The Art of Poetrie*, also unsatisfactory, may charitably be described as versified journalism, all the more dispiriting because it is the labor of a poet otherwise fully conversant with classical poetry. But where Jonson succeeds—and he succeeds gratifyingly often—he exerts his individual talent in the direction of the classical tradition to attain the level of the nearly anonymous poet.[19]

Nearly anonymous: for Jonson temperamentally could not, and in any case should not, have altogether obliterated his self. But this is not to say that the display of self is marked in Jonson to the same degree that it is in Donne. In terms of the language each poet used—and language, Jonson reminded us, "most shewes a man"— the "masculine expression" which Carew noted in Donne is no less apparent in Jonson. The two poets shared a partiality for "strong lines." [20] Jonson could be fully as irreverent as Donne, and so he was (for example, in *The Forrest*, in the poem beginning, "And must I sing? what subject shall I chuse?"). He could also be uneconomic in utterance and splenetic in tone, and so he was (in "A speach according to Horace" and, far more virulently because much more personally engaged, in "An Expostulation with Inigo Jones"). He could also write "elegies" not only in Donne's sense of the term but in close emulation of Donne's particular manner, witness the four such poems included in *The Under-wood* (nos. 38–41), of which one is so far from being Jonson's that it may well be Donne's. [21] Yet, in spite of the several affinities between the two poets, the norm in Jonson's poetry resides in its discretion. The few religious poems he wrote are particularly delicate exemplars of this discretion, in that restraint and clarity and economy—the qualities already commended—yield rhythms quite unlike anything in Donne:

> I Sing the birth, was borne to night,
> The Author both of Life, and light.
> ("A Hymne on the Nativitie of my Saviour," 1–2)

Only Herbert was eventually to appreciate the Jonsonian approach to religious poetry, especially the stunning "simplicity" of

> Heare mee, O God!
> A broken heart,
> Is my best part:
> Use still thy rod,
> That I may prove
> Therein, thy Love.
> ("A Hymne to God the Father," 1–6)

Jonson's discretion was reinforced, in his secular poems, by his habitual predilection for firmly ordered stanzaic patterns and carefully measured single lines which themselves control the centrifugal tendencies of the given emotion. The technique appears to negate the self, but in a very particular sense asserts it all the more decisively.. It is Jonson's way of confirming the circle of the classical tradition through, not against, his individual talent.

But to conclude where a conclusion may be—and, I hope, is—singularly irrelevant: where the poets' poet is normally said to be Spenser, the same appellation should be recognized as equally merited by Jonson. Spenser's poetic practice has of course been utterly crucial for the development of English poetry; but, as it was a practice representative of a particular mode of articulation, it made Jonson's contribution all the more necessary. Individually, Spenser and Jonson had a decisive impact on numerous other poets; jointly, they affected English poetry at large.

Spenser's influence is readily identifiable because of its particularity. But Jonson's influence can be neither defined categorically nor detailed unequivocally. Our task would have been very easy had we wished solely to trace Jonson's distinct rhythms in, say, Crashaw or to observe the way Jonson's dramatic lyric "A Nymphs Passion" was transformed into Coleridge's "Mutual Passion" with an embarrassing minimum of amendment. Our task is on the contrary very difficult because Jonson's influence, extending far beyond the mundane details just enumerated, is almost—but certainly not quite—impersonal. His near anonymity was ideally suited to his ambition to accommodate the spirit of the classical lyric to English poetry; and, en route, juxtaposing "solide *learnings*" and "our owne experience," he created sound patterns violent enough to have impressed Donne, "simple" enough to have attracted Herbert, urbane enough to have allured Marvell, and variable enough to have commanded the respect of Milton. Upon consideration, I believe, Jonson's multiform poetry will also be observed to have affected Pope as much as Blake, Coleridge as much as Tennyson, and Yeats as much as T. S. Eliot. My large claims will astonish only those who are yet to discern that Jonson is to English poetry as Erasmus is to the civilization of the Renaissance: a formidable talent in himself, but also the cause why talent is in others.

NOTES

1. The celebrated passage on a poet's abilities as "the inspired guift of God," in *The Reason of Church Government* (1642), may be found in John Milton, *Selected Prose*, ed. C. A. Patrides (Harmondsworth, Middlesex: Penguin, 1974), p. 57.

2. See, especially, Wesley Trimpi, *Ben Jonson's Poems: A Study of the Plain Style* (Stanford: Stanford University Press, 1962).

3. The list of Greek and Roman writers represented in Jonson's library (see Herford, Simpson, and Simpson, vol. 11, pp. 598–600) has been dramatically expanded in "Ben Jonson's Library and Marginalia: An Annotated Catalogue," *Studies in Philology* 71 (1974), appendix, in which David McPherson cites editions from the Geneva Greek grammar to editions of Aristophanes, scholia on Euripides, *The Greek Anthology* (not the much fuller *Palatine Anthology* which was published, of course, long after Jonson), and, especially, the two volumes that between them print "virtually all ancient Greek words in verse": the editions by J. Lectius and P. de la Rivière (Geneva, 1606 and 1614).

4. *Ben Jonson*, ed. Herford, Simpson, and Simpson, vol. 7, p. 209.

5. See Coburn Gum, *The Aristophanic Comedies of Ben Jonson* (The Hague: Mouton, 1969), and Aliki L. Dick, *Paedia through Laughter* (The Hague: Mouton, 1974).

6. See Gordon Braden, "*Viuamus, mea Lesbia* in the English Renaissance," *ELR* 9 (1979), 199–224.

7. "Out of Catullus," in *The Complete Poetry of Richard Crashaw*, ed. George W. Williams (New York: Doubleday, 1970), pp. 523–25.

8. *Personae* (London: Faber, 1952), p. 119.

9. Trans. Edward Lucie-Smith, in *The Greek Anthology*, ed. Peter Jay (London: Allen Lane, 1973), p. 109 (no. 201).

10. Paul Friedländer and Herbert B. Hoffleit, *Epigrammata: Greek Inscriptions in Verse* (Berkeley and Los Angeles: University of California Press, 1948), p. 71 (no. 60); Richmond Lattimore, trans., *Greek Lyrics*, 2nd ed., rev. (Chicago: University of Chicago Press, 1960), p. 32.

11. Ernst Diehl, ed., *Anthologia lyrica graeca* (Leipzig: Teubner, 1925), vol. 1, p. 218 (no. 25); Willis Barnstone, trans., *Greek Lyric Poetry* (1962; rpt. New York: Schocken, 1972), p. 29.

12. Diehl, *Anthologia lyrica graeca*, p. 231 (no. 71); Lattimore, *Greek Lyrics*, p. 5.

13. J. M. Edmonds, ed. and trans., *Lyra graeca* (New York: Putnam, 1922–27), vol. 1, p. 236 (no. 76); *Sappho*, trans. Mary Barnard (Berkeley and Los Angeles: University of California Press, 1958), no. 60. The expansion in translation of Sappho's highly compressed single line is visible proof of one's difficulties in suggesting to the Greekless reader what "economy" actually means in Greek poetry. In his literal translation, Edmonds renders the line: "Somebody, I tell you, will remember us hereafter."

14. Edmonds, *Lyra graeca*, p. 222 (no. 53); Barnstone, *Greek Lyric Poetry*, p. 68.

15. Edmonds, *Lyra graeca*, p. 244 (no. 84a); Barnstone, *Greek Lyric Poetry*, p. 79.

16. Pythian 10.53–54, in *Pindari Carmina*, ed. Otto Schroeder (Leipzig and Berlin: Teubner, 1923), p. 260; *The Odes of Pindar*, trans. C. M. Bowra (Harmondsworth, Middlesex: Penguin, 1969), p. 23.

17. Olympian 1.87–88, in *Pindari Carmina*, ed. Schroeder, p. 87, and in *The Odes of Pindar*, trans. Bowra, p. 67.

18. Diehl, *Anthologia lyrica graeca*, p. 87 (no. 1); Barnstone, *Greek Lyric Poetry*, p. 179.

19. I adapt the phrase, but not its implications, from John Crowe Ransom's memorable essay on *Lycidas* as "A Poem Nearly Anonymous," in *The World's Body* (New York: Scribner's, 1938), pp. 1–28. My own emphasis partakes far more of the comment by L. C. Knights, ventured but in passing, that in Jonson "classical" simplicity and restraint are married to "the tones and rhythms of personal feeling." See "Ben Jonson: Public Attitudes and Social Poetry," in *A Celebration of Ben Jonson*, ed. William Blissett et al. (Toronto: University of Toronto Press, 1973), p. 181.

20. See George Williamson, "Strong Lines," in his *Seventeenth Century Contexts* (London: Faber, 1960), chap. 5.

21. The poem "probably" written by Donne is his fifteenth elegy, "The Expostulation" (*Under-wood* 39). Consult Evelyn Simpson, "Jonson and Donne: A Problem of Authorship," *Review of English Studies* 15 (1939), 274–82, and, in support of its thesis, the "internal structural evidence" provided by D. Heyward Brock, "Jonson and Donne: Structural Fingerprinting and the Attribution of Elegies XXXVIII–XLI," *Papers of the Bibliographical Society of America* 71 (1978), 519–27. I am grateful to Messrs. Pebworth and Summers for assistance with this as with other matters.

STELLA P. REVARD

Pindar and Jonson's Cary-Morison Ode

Although neither the first imitator of Pindar in English nor the only writer in the seventeenth century to modify the stanzaic form of the Greek ode for English verse, Jonson has, in "To the immortall memorie, and friendship of that noble paire, Sir Lucius Cary, and Sir H. Morison," come the closest of English poets of his time to presenting Pindaric matter in Pindaric style and so to truly emulating his great Greek original.[1] Because Jonson has englished to turn, counterturn, and stand the Greek terms strophe, antistrophe, and epode (the stanzaic pattern which many of Pindar's odes share with other Greek choral poetry), and because he has adapted some of the more striking features of the Pindaric style, critics have assumed that Pindar's contribution to Jonson's ode is largely a matter of the triple pattern of stanzas and some oddities of line length, enjambment, and splitwords.[2] No one can deny, of course, the considerable influence of Pindar's style. Seventeenth-century readers who knew Greek would recognize the Pindaric features that Jonson incorporated, for Pindar was available to readers in many editions, most particularly the excellent, annotated texts of Schmid (1616) and Benedictus (1620).[3] But even those who did not know Pindar in Greek could have recognized certain stylistic features that commentators had often remarked: his brilliant opening figures (imitated by Jonson in the opening "Infant of *Saguntum*"), his abrupt shifts in subject, his sudden leaps to the sublime. Susanne Woods has studied the characteristics of Jonson's verse in his ode, and Paul H. Fry has noted how the development of the line of argument in the strophic pattern seems to echo Pindar.[4] Certainly, the splitting of the word "twi-Lights" and the carry-over of sense from one stanza to another (even in the extreme case of splitting *Ben* and *Jonson*) are Pindaric traits, though not limited among ancient poets to Pindar.[5] It is no wonder then—with the trademarks of Pindar's style every-

17

where manifest in Jonson's verse—that few critics have gone beyond the question of Pindaric style to evaluate Pindaric content.

Yet Jonson would not have chosen the Pindaric ode as the form of his Cary-Morison poem had he not felt that Pindar's subject-matter was appropriate. Most of Pindar's victory odes concern the relationship of private virtues to the lives of public men, be they athletic victors, princes, or heroes of legend evoked in the myths of the epinicia. Moreover, Pindar's odes were renowned in antiquity and, rediscovered in the early sixteenth century, were praised during the Renaissance for their serious moral and religious content.[6] When Jonson undertook a poem that was to examine the "virtue" of two young noblemen, it was natural for him to turn to the genre that in antiquity had most eloquently celebrated the achievements of an aristocratic society. Mary I. Oates has pointed out that Jonson was attracted to Pindar's praise of public men, and that he saw himself as a bard who, like Pindar, aimed to be a spokesman for his society.[7] Therefore, he not only adopted the Pindaric style for his ode; he also used, whenever possible, such Pindaric material as the story of the Dioscuri, narrated by Pindar in Nemean 10 and adapted by Jonson in a brief, elliptical version.[8]

Jonson's imitation of Pindar goes beyond the imitation of his genre or his stylistic devices or even allusion to a "Pindaric" myth. Well versed in the victory odes that form the Pindaric corpus, Jonson makes use of these odes as specific rather than general models. His figure of the tree and, in the first half of the ode, his argument concerning the limits of achievement in human life resemble a comparable "tree figure" and a comparable argument in Pindar's Nemean 11. Within the Cary-Morison ode, his combination of praise for a living man with elegy for a dead one recalls Pindar's similar elegiac encomium in Isthmian 8, the very paradigm for poems which begin in lament and end in celebration. Throughout his own ode, moreover, Jonson reworks for his modern audience themes centrally employed by Pindar in both these odes, demonstrating how the care for human virtue that was so important in Pindar's aristocratic society had application for Jonson's new aristocratic age.

Both Nemean 11 and Isthmian 8 celebrate athletes and aristocrats, as do all of Pindar's epinicia. Both are solemn in tone, and both consider that question so often raised by Pindar: how human beings may achieve true excellence when limited and circumscribed always by their mortal nature. Nothing in the occasion of Nemean 11 prepares us for its solemn moralizing, for it was written to celebrate the prytanis of a former athlete, Aristagoras of Tenedos, as he was about to be installed in his twelve-month term of office as magistrate. The occasion is wholly celebratory. Not so, however, is it for Isthmian 8, which was written at the conclusion of the Persian wars, when Hellas was newly recovering from devastation and division and songs of celebration seemed still a little out of place. Yet both these poems look seriously at the limits the gods have placed on men, while they rejoice at what men, despite these limits, have accomplished.

Nemean 11 begins with an invocation to Hestia, the patron goddess of the festival, and an invitation to banqueting. Having called on the gods to bless Aristagoras, his family, and his city, and having celebrated his former athletic achievement in the first half of the poem, Pindar sounds a cautionary note and waxes reflective. He bids Aristagoras and all those who have achieved like excellence and prosperity through their own striving to remember that they are mortals, not gods.

> θνάτα μεμνάσθω περιστέλλων μέλη,
> Καὶ τελευτὰν ἁπάντων γᾶν 'επιεσσόμενος
>
> (Nemea 11.15–16)

[Let him remember that he possesses mortal limbs,
And that he must put on at last the garment of earth, the end for all.][9]

He then reflects that Aristagoras, though he possessed great athletic ability and as a young man won all the local contests, never achieved acclaim outside Tenedos. Because his parents held modest estimates of his powers, he was not permitted to participate in the more prestigious games at Delphi and at Olympia; therefore, although he could have won these laurels, too, he did not and so fell to lesser achievement and lesser fame than should have been his. Here Pindar poses another, but different, mortal limit to life: the limit of the unachieved, the unfulfilled excellence. Why is it, he questions, that some should achieve great deeds and become great athletes or heroes, while others, possessed of like ability, like inherited virtue, should not? Aristagoras's race was noble and had in previous generations risen to noble achievement. Some men, Pindar notes, overtax their abilities and attempt too much, while others attempt too little and fall short of achievements which strength and ancestral virtue should have made theirs. Why, Pindar puzzles, is excellent potential given to a man and then not fulfilled?

To answer this question, Pindar poses an analogy from nature, the flowering of a tree:

ἀρχαῖαι δ' ἀρεταὶ

ἀμφέροντ' ἀλλασσόμεναι γενεαῖς ἀνδρῶν σθένος ·
ἐν σχερῷ δ' οὔτ ὦν μέλαιναι καρπὸν ἔδωκαν ἄρουραι
δένδρεά τ' οὐκ ἐθέλει πάσαις ἐτέων περόδοις
ἄνθος εὐῶδες φέρειν πλούτῳ ἴσον,
ἀλλ' ἐν ἀμείβοντι. Καὶ θνατὸν οὕτως ἔθνος ἄγει μοῖρα.

(37–43)

[But ancient virtue,
In alternation, restores strength to the generations of men.
Neither the dark acres, in succession, yield harvest,
Nor the trees consent in the circuit of years, every year,
To bear flowers, sweet of scent, in like abundance,
But in alternate seasons. And so fares the fate
For mortal men.]

The flowering tree illustrates in the world of nature the same paradox that Pindar has been studying in human nature: that the ancient stock of man or plant may not attain to full yield in each generation or season. Clearly, the reason lies beyond the realm of man or nature—in the hands of the gods, who do not or will not reveal the mystery. Zeus, as Pindar notes, gives no clear sign to man to predict full season in man or tree. Men thus go forth, planning great enterprises, for mortal limbs are bound to shameless hopes. Whether these hopes will be fulfilled, man cannot know: the streams of forethought lie apart from human life (in immortal, not mortal control). Man must accept his limit, be it the ultimate limit of death or the limit of unfulfilled hope, content with the measure of things gained. The sharpest and the vainest of goads, Pindar concludes, is the mad desire for the unattainable.

The line between Pindar's ode and Jonson's is not direct, for Jonson neither translates Pindar's words nor duplicates his thought. Yet he is not unaffected by the kind of question Pindar raises about human limitation or the kind of analogy he makes with nature. Both poets begin with the same assumption, that the final limit of life, death, is unarguable and must be accepted, whether we will or not, as the ultimate measure. As Pindar reminds his athlete-hero in Nemean 11, we all possess mortal limbs and come to the same end.

Jonson begins with that assumption and draws two extreme examples of it, his opening figure of the Infant of Saguntum, whose birth and death were simultaneous, and his exemplum of the Stirrer, who, in contrast to the infant, lived too long, outliving his peers and vexing time (25–27). All mortals must close the same circle, whether briefly or at length, and the "beauty" and "justness" of the figure lies not in its short or long circumference. Some method to measure human life must be found which takes into account its quality or "virtue," not just its length.

Morison, the first of Jonson's two subjects of the ode, was a young man of excellent, though unachieved potential; dying young, he did not achieve all that he might have, for he was, like the hero of Pindar's ode, limited by circumstances outside his control. When we measure Morison, argues Jonson, we must measure him by the virtue of his character and by those acts which he in his short life did achieve, not by his unfulfilled years. Jonson contrasts him with the Stirrer, who lived four score years, but, having achieved nothing after the first score, though long lived, may be said to have died young. Though Morison was short in life, he was long in achievement. For him we must rethink our principles of measure: "For, what is life, if measur'd by the space, / Not by the act?" (21–22). Morison becomes for Jonson the perfect figure, the sphere, because in character and act, if not in the full circle of years, he was complete:

> All Offices were done
> By him, so ample, full, and round,
> In weight, in measure, number, sound,
> As though his age imperfect might appeare,
> His life was of Humanitie the Spheare.   (48–52)

Jonson argues for judging a man not only by just measure, but also by just season. We must look at what a man does at the height of his powers, when he is come into the full flower of his manhood: "Life doth her great actions spell, / By what was done and wrought / In season" (59–61). The observation on season prepares us for the analogy with nature that Jonson is about to draw. Both human and vegetative life come into season within their cycles, and what "in season" is fair is justly achieved:

> It is not growing like a tree
> In bulke, doth make man better bee;

Or standing long an Oake, three hundred yeare,
To fall a logge at last, dry, bald, and seare:
A Lillie of a Day
Is fairer farre, in May,
Although it fall, and die that night;
It was the Plant, and flowre of light.
In small proportions, we just beautie see:
And in short measures, life may perfect bee.   (65–74)

Jonson's tree-flower metaphor resembles Pindar's in the general analogy it makes between the cycles of plant and human life; it differs, however, in specific detail. Jonson considers two different cycles in nature, the long one of the tree and the short one of the flower, and argues that the tree does not because of its longer life have greater excellence than the flower, which, though ephemeral, has beauty, light, and proportion. Pindar does not separate tree and flower, but looks at the flowering tree, which differs from season to season in fullness of bloom and hence attains to greater excellence in one year than it reaches in the next. Nevertheless, both Jonson and Pindar make the flower or the abundantly flowering tree their symbol for an excellence attained briefly or only sporadically. Jonson's lily of May lasts only a day; Pindar's tree achieves full flower only in alternate seasons. Moreover, why such excellence or beauty comes so rarely or so fleetingly is a mystery locked in nature beyond human comprehension or control. Jonson may query, like Pindar, why God grants no sure sign to human beings: why the lily is perfect, but does not last, or why a young man like Morison grows to perfection and dies. But he knows that the Christian God does not disclose such mysteries. The divine is silent. Man may learn, however, by observing in the natural world a process that is much like the human: God has granted to man and nature a similar allotment. By seeing a similar, though still mysterious, design at work in both, human beings may come more easily to accept a lot which cannot be changed and thus must be accepted. Pindar urges that we accept the more modest flowering of the alternate year, Jonson that we accept beauty in small proportions, perfection in short measure. Placing their extended natural metaphors in climactic sections of their odes, both poets employ the same strategy. They test their assertions about the human world by appealing to counterparts in the world of nature, thereby setting forth and ultimately proving their assertions by analogy. Therefore, though Jonson's metaphor differs from Pindar's in detail, it is used in the same strategic way, and it makes similar statements about the connection of human and natural worlds. It becomes, then, almost a tacit compliment to the older poet.

Pindar's Isthmian 8 relates to the Cary-Morison ode not only in theme but in genre. Thematically, it goes beyond Nemean 11 in its exploration of human success and failure and ponders whether heroic achievement makes up for the tragedy of early death. In genre, it combines celebratory ode and elegy and thus achieves a perfect model for the kind of poem Jonson is attempting. Although, like most of the epinician odes, it was written to mark a specific athletic victory (that of Cleandros of Aigina), it also commemorates the end of the Persian wars in which so many Greek lives were lost, among them (most probably) the life of Cleandros's cousin, Nicocles, a boxer and former Isthmian victor. The ode focuses on these cousins, one living, one dead, and, to celebrate their different achievements, evokes the heroes of the past, most notably the short-lived Achilles, the greatest battle hero and athlete of them all, fallen in a tragic war. Hence this epinician ode, also an elegy, raises the glad choral euoi at the same time it laments ōmoi. In Jonson's time and throughout the seventeenth century, Isthmian 8, considered one of Pindar's greatest odes, was imitated and translated by many poets, among them Jonson's younger contemporary Cowley. The questions that it raises about the heroic life and the value of heroism are timeless, but had particular relevance to the Caroline society Jonson addressed in the Cary-Morison ode. Pindar spoke in his time to young aristocrats who had endured a great national ordeal, appealing to the values that had sustained Hellas once before during the great Trojan War. Jonson appeals to young aristocrats who were about to enter a time of crisis. It is no wonder that he looks back to the heroic age and a poet who reflected on its values, while reflecting also on the place of the poet and poetry in an aristocratic society.

Isthmian 8 begins, in fact, with an affirmation that the Muses are particularly necessary to society in times of crisis and grief. Pindar asks leave to summon them to celebrate the young Cleandros. Now that Hellas has been released from the threat of Persia, which hung like the great stone of Tantalus above it, there is need for the garland of poetry to be laid. In times of grief, we must not fall utterly bereft of garlands. For Pindar, poetry is at the center of a society, offering gladness in times of success, consolation in distress. It has the power not only to comfort but to renew. The young victor Cleandros becomes the focus of that renewal; his victory allows poetry to bring sweetness after hardship. The assumptions that Jonson makes about poetry are much the same. The first half of his Cary-Morison ode is spent considering the loss of the young, virtuous hero, Morison, and offering those comforts which come from viewing his short life as well lived. At the midpoint of the poem, Jonson turns away from the dead hero to consider his living friend and the grief-stricken society of nobles who remain bereft of Morison. Now, instead of offering further justification for Morison, Jonson justifies the need for songs of gladness rather than woe, for celebration of what remains behind, rather than grief for the lost. His call, like Pindar's, is for garlands and for the song of the golden Muses:

> Call, noble *Lucius*, then for Wine,
> And let thy lookes with gladnesse shine:
> Accept this garland, plant it on thy head,
> And thinke, nay know, thy *Morison's* not dead. (75–78)

At this third counterturn in his ode, Jonson turns to two other subjects: first, the merit of the society of nobles, of whom Morison was a past and Cary is a present representative, and, second, the place of the poet as the voice that honors that society. Jonson's encomium on his two young noblemen is based on those classical principles which a poet like Pindar teaches. Cary and Morison, soldiers and patriots in public life, virtuous men in private life, are joined by their friendship in a select circle of noblemen whose lives are examples to their society. There is a natural link between them and the kind of hero that Pindar celebrates in his odes, who is either an athlete whose prowess has won renown or a prince, who, as the sponsor of that athlete, also exhibits devotion to excellence. Cleandros, the victor of Isthmian 8, is a young man of great promise, whose victory has carried on a family tradition established by his dead cousin, Nicocles. He is an example of the best that the youth of Hellas has to offer, and, as a survivor, like Cary, he is the hope of the coming generation. Although Pindar lauds him and his victory directly, most of the ode is spent celebrating the value of the heroism that Cleandros and his cousin represent. For them, Pindar weaves the myth that occupies the bulk of the poem, a myth that tells how the youth of Aigina once before won renown and brought gladness and safety to Hellas in time of trial.

The myth focuses on Peleus and Achilles, two heroes of the Aeacid clan, the family said to be the ancestral founders of Aigina.

It begins with the birth from the nymph Aigina of Aeacus, a brilliant, godlike hero, who himself begets godlike sons, eminent in battle and also temperate in judgment. From him two noble heroes are sprung, the father Peleus and the son Achilles, both accomplished, but born to different fates, the father to long life and the son to early death. Pindar narrates how each in his way, through inherent nobility of character, brings safety and rescue, the one in peace, the other in war. Peleus is the means by which a conflict among the gods is settled, for Poseidon and Zeus, who have vied for Thetis, settle their quarrel by giving her in marriage to the hero Peleus, a man renowned for virtue. He is the hero of peace who wins a goddess for his wife, and Pindar celebrates their marriage. Achilles, in contrast, is the young warrior who lays down his life, but wins renown at Troy and effects the release of Helen, building the bridge of safety home for the sons of Atreus. Pindar celebrates him as a hero of war and tells how the Muses came to sing at his funeral. The one hero is lauded in dirge, the other in marriage song. Clearly, Pindar connects the father and the son with the fates of Cleandros and Nicocles—and through them speaks of the different lots that await the hero of peace and the hero of war. Peleus stands for young men like Cleandros, the happy ones who achieve eminent deeds and live to enjoy their reward. They have not thrown away their youth untested or hidden away their glory. Correspondingly, Achilles stands for the dead heroes like Nicocles, Cleandros's cousin, whose athletic triumphs are remembered with his cousin's. These dead have made their valor a memorial, and the Muses do not desert them, as they did not abandon Achilles. Even now the poet lifts his song in their memory.

When Jonson introduces a reference to the Dioscuri in the third stand, he follows Pindar's practice of using myth to elevate the status of his present-day heroes. By connecting Morison and Cary with the twins Castor and Pollux, he says that the two young noblemen are like these mythic two in virtue and accomplishment as in fate. As Pindar drew a parallel between his Aeginetan athletes and the illustrious father-son pair, Peleus and Achilles, so Jonson draws one between Cary and Morison and the Dioscuri. The mythic pairs that Pindar and Jonson choose are in themselves similar, for each contains a short-lived relative, whose death the longer-lived one is to mourn. The poet in each case draws attention to the virtue of both young men and to the tragic fate of one. Cary and Morison, the respective Pollux and Castor of the modern age, are joined in the "bright *Asterisme*" of their friendship, as the first two heroes were joined by their twin birth. Cary and Morison are like the Dioscuri in youth, in excellence, in position in society; as nobles and as soldiers, they are the epitome of their age, but one is struck down early, and they are tragically separated. Like the divided twins, one is to remain on earth, the other in heaven: "But fate doth so alternate the designe, / Whilst that in heav'n, this light on earth must shine" (95–96). Yet, while death divides them physically, it cannot dim the light of their virtue, which shall ultimately reunite them in a single constellation: "And shine as you exalted are; / Two names of friendship, but one Starre" (97–98).

Jonson emphasizes that in their friendship Cary and Morison become more like twins than other human beings. Their mutual liking first draws them to one other, and then each grows to be "the Copie of his friend" (112). Together they stand as examples of virtue to their society. Jonson describes Morison as a "perfect Patriot, and a noble friend" (46). He and Cary together scorn vain pleasure, riots, orgies, and turn their minds to "simple love of greatnesse, and of good" (102–05). The love of virtue, Jonson explains, is that which "knits brave minds, and manners, more then blood" (106), that which has made these modern "twins" leaders in the society and hence touchstones for excellence:

> You liv'd to be the great surnames,
> And titles, by which all made claimes
> Unto the Vertue. Nothing perfect done,
> But as a CARY, or a MORISON.   (113–16)

First by comparing them to the Dioscuri and then by asserting that they have become "great surnames," Jonson attempts to make Cary and Morison modern heroes. He asserts that they measure up to the great heroic types of the ancient past. As Pindar summoned Peleus and Achilles as the standard by which to measure Aiginetan youth, Jonson holds Castor and Pollux before the Caroline aristocrats. Cary and Morison, he asserts, have reached their standard, and they in turn challenge others to live up to the heroic ideal.

But Jonson does more in this ode than praise two young heroes; he also considers the role of the poet as the praiser of good men. Jonson, like Pindar before him, makes much of his active part in the ode he sings.[10] Jonson not only names himself as the framer of the ode to Morison, but also expresses the hope that he will have full share in the joys of heaven Morison now tastes. For the memory of Morison depends intimately on the poet who remembers:

And there he lives with memorie; and *Ben*

Jonson, who sung this of him, e're he went
Himselfe to rest,
Or taste a part of that full joy he meant
To have exprest.   (84–88)

In assuming this close relationship with his subject, Jonson very much follows the example of Pindar.

Pindar does not name himself directly in Isthmian 8, but he does indirectly identify himself. He declares how fitting it is for him, bred at seven-gated Thebes, to render the glory of the Graces to Aigina, since Thebes and Aigina are sister cities, descended from sister nymphs, both of whom Zeus loved. He thus closely connects himself with the ode he composes. Further, he regards it as his obligation as a bard to render the poetic garland, especially now, in time of great sorrow. One of the gifts of the Muses, as Hesiod, Pindar's fellow Boiotian and poetic progenitor, declared, is to soothe human beings in times of grief.[11] So he calls on the Muses and honors the young Cleandros. In so doing, he also fulfills a second poetic function: to remember good men and their virtuous deeds. In both the main section of the poem and in the myth, Pindar affirms that without poetry—without the golden Muses— good men could not be remembered. Achilles is his prime example. The Heliconian maidens stand about his pyre and grave, raising their loud-sounding lament. This, Pindar says, is the gift that the gods grant to the good man, that he, even though he has perished, may receive the songs of the goddesses. Pindar grants a similar boon to both the living Cleandros and the dead Nicocles, whom he hastens in the chariot of the Muses to remember.

Adopting the stance of the Pindaric bard, Jonson affirms the obligation of the poet to remember. Jonson himself bestows the poetic garland on Cary and pronounces that Morison has "leap'd the present age, / Possest with holy rage, / To see that bright eternall Day" (79–81). Jonson assumes the office of poet-priest to confer on Morison an immortality comparable to the one the Heliconian Muses in Pindar's ode confer on Achilles. This is the truth, Jonson says, "Of which we *Priests*, and *Poëts* say / . . . as we expect for happy men" (82–83). Yet Jonson goes even further; he undertakes as a poet to enroll these two men as examples to the rest of society. First, he points out how they themselves wrote their own character on their lives, "in deed . . . not in words: / And with the heart, not pen" (123–24). Accordingly, they became fair examples even to those who dared not practice good, but "were glad / That such a Law / Was left yet to Man-kind" (119–21). The poet's function is to record and so to eternize the example which the two men "wordlessly" impressed. They made rolls and records by the virtue of their lives; the poet transfers these lines of life to his own lines of verse. "They" sowed the fruits; "he," the poet (to alter the person of Jonson's final line), gets the harvest in.

Jonson prided himself on his classicism, boasting that "he was better versed & knew more in Greek and Latin, than all the Poets in England"; his emulation of ancient writers consistently involved, throughout his poetry, imitation both of classical forms and of classical values.[12] Hence his imitation of Pindar is but a single instance of a lifelong preoccupation with Roman and Greek poets. It may be that he felt, in following poets like Pindar, that he was lifting himself above the "pride" and "insolence" of his "lothsome age." In the "Ode to Himselfe," written after the failure of *The New Inne*, he deliberately assumes the stance of the classic poet and names himself with poets like Horace, Anacreon, and Pindar:

> Leave things so prostitute,
> And take the *Alcaick* Lute;
> Or thine owne *Horace*, or *Anacreons* Lyre;
> Warme thee, by *Pindares* fire. (41–44)[13]

With such poetic forebears assisting him, he proclaims that he may yet strike a "disdaine-full heate" or sing with such zeal to God or King that all should acknowledge "In sound of peace, or warres, / No Harpe ere hit the starres" (57–58). Clearly, in the Cary-Morison ode as well, he follows both in form and principle the example of poets who, like Pindar, praised the noble men of their society and so lifted both those men and themselves to the stars. As he moves, therefore, in the choral steps of turn, counterturn, and stand, Jonson means for us to attend to more than his antique melody. He calls out in a bardic voice given greater authority yet by the example of that poet of a former age who also spoke eloquently when he praised good men.

NOTES

1. Probably the first imitator of Pindar in English was a minor Elizabethan poet, John Soowthern, who took Ronsard's success with the Pindaric ode as a cue for his English

collection, *Pandora: The Musyque of the Beautie of Mistresse Diana* (London, 1584). See Robert Shafer, *The English Ode to 1660* (Princeton: Princeton University Press, 1918), pp. 46–48.

2. The editors of *The Norton Anthology of English Literature* take for granted that Jonson's debt to Pindar lies in his imitation of the "triple pattern of strophe, antistrophe, and epode, translated literally by Jonson as turn, counterturn, and stand." Also see John D. Jump, *The Ode* (London: Methuen and Co., 1974), pp. 12–14.

3. The first Renaissance edition of Pindar was printed in Venice in 1513. In Paris in 1560, Henricus Stephanus printed an edition of Pindar with facing Latin translation, which was several times reprinted. Two commentaries on Pindar appeared in the 1580s, Portus in 1583 and Aretius in 1587. Erasmus Schmid's edition of the odes (Wittenburg, 1616) and John Benedictus's edition (Saumur, 1620) contain Latin translation, notes, and commentary. For a discussion of these editions and others, see my article, "Neo-Latin Commentaries on Pindar," forthcoming in *Proceedings of the Fourth Neo-Latin Congress, Bologna*.

4. Susanne Woods, "Ben Jonson's Cary-Morison Ode: Some Observations on Structure and Form," *SEL* 18 (Winter 1978), 57–74; Paul H. Fry, *The Poet's Calling in the English Ode* (New Haven: Yale University Press, 1980), pp. 17–26. Also see Ian Donaldson, "Jonson's Ode to Sir Lucius Cary and Sir H. Morison," *Studies in the Literary Imagination* 6 (1973), 139–52; John Lemly, "Masks and Self-Portraits in Jonson's Late Poetry," *ELH* 44 (1977), 258–63; Hugh Maclean, "'A More Secret *Cause*': The Wit of Jonson's Poetry," in *A Celebration of Ben Jonson*, ed. William Blissett et al. (Toronto: University of Toronto Press, 1973), pp. 155–58; and Richard S. Peterson, *Imitation and Praise in the Poems of Ben Jonson* (New Haven: Yale University Press, 1981).

5. The practice of splitting words is not uncommon among classical poets. See Sappho, 2.3–4; 16.3–4; 31.3–4, 7–8, 11–12; Horace, *Odes* 1.2.19–20, 25.11–12; 2.16.7–8; Catullus, 11.11–12, 19–20, 22–23. Examples in other Greek and Latin poets may readily be found. My thanks to Carl Conrad, Classics, Washington University, for helping to compile the list above.

6. Zwingli, in his prefatory letter to an early edition (Basel, 1526), and Lonicer (Basel, 1528) both praised Pindar as a serious moral and religious poet. In *The Arte of English Poesie* (London, 1589), Puttenham sets Pindar's odes beside David's psalms.

7. "Jonson's 'Ode Pindarick' and the Doctrine of Imitation," *PLL* 11 (Spring 1975), 126–48.

8. *Ibid.*, 140.

9. *Pindari Carmina*, ed. C. M. Bowra (Oxford: The Clarendon Press, 1935). All translations are mine. For a discussion of Nemean 11, see Mary R. Lefkowitz, "Pindar's Nemean XI," *The Journal of Hellenic Studies* 99 (1979), 49–56.

10. For a discussion of the role of Jonson's public personality in his poetry, see Richard C. Newton, " 'Ben. / Jonson': The Poet in the Poems," in *Two Renaissance Mythmakers: Christopher Marlowe and Ben Jonson*, ed. Alvin Kernan, Selected Papers from the English Institute, n.s. 1, 1975–76 (Baltimore: Johns Hopkins University Press, 1977); also see Claude J. Summers and Ted-Larry Pebworth, *Ben Jonson* (Boston: Twayne, 1979), especially their discussion of Jonson's sense of obligation as a poet of commendatory verses (pp. 145–51).

11. Hesiod, *Theogony*, 11.78–103, ed. Hugh G. Evelyn-White (Cambridge, Mass.: Harvard University Press, 1914). Also see Pindar, "Nemea 4," 1–8.

12. On Jonson's classicism, see Summers and Pebworth, *Ben Jonson*, pp. 134–35.

13. *Ben Jonson*, ed. Herford, Simpson, and Simpson, vol. 6, pp. 492–94.

RICHARD C. NEWTON

Jonson and the (Re-)Invention of the Book

To give a text an Author is to impose a limit on that text, to furnish it with a final signified, to close the writing. Such a conception suits criticism very well, the latter allotting itself the important task of discovering the Author (or its hypostases: society, history, psyche, liberty) beneath the work: when the Author has been found, the text is "explained"—victory to the critic. —Roland Barthes[1]

For this essay on Ben Jonson and the development of the vernacular literary printed book, I had in mind three different titles: "Ben Jonson and the (Re-)Invention of the Book," "Ben Jonson and the Reification of the Work," and "Ben Jonson and the Invention of the English Classic." They express basic and interrelated themes: the discovery and rediscovery of the Book as a printed artifact, the reification of the literary artifact, and the establishment of the notion of "classic text" in English literature. Having to choose just one, I chose the one that depends most explicitly on the invention of printing, the title now situated at the top of this page. A title like this one, with its offer at wit in its typographical form, depends on transmission by print, as opposed to transmission by manuscript alone or by oral performance. As a manuscript title, if it were retained at all, its nonlinguistic, merely typographical features would surely disappear: preservation of a text accurate from copy to copy is difficult enough in manuscript tradition, but designs and figures almost inevitably blur and merge, disappearing into stereotype and bungled imitation. And, in oral performance, the special features of my title entirely vanish. There is no way of saying "(Re-)"; it just isn't speech. It is meant for print, not for performance, and only print can preserve it.[2]

The invention of print bestowed, as Elizabeth L. Eisenstein has shown, an almost incalculable legacy on Western culture, the effects of which legacy were varied, intricate, and asynchronous. Of the effects that I am interested in unraveling here, the two I have just mentioned, permanence and liberation from performance, are especially important. Every writer, perhaps, sets pen to paper with the vision of immortality; so at least those favorites of poets, the topoi of immortality, would indicate. But, from earliest antiquity, poets could not ignore the flotsam of wrecked and fragmentary texts and the jetsam of artists whose names alone had barely survived the wash of time. Before printing, all poets could hope, but none could truly expect, to survive. Preservation of the text is therefore a principal buttress of poets' immortal longings. The other buttress, equally important, is popularity, the instrument of which, before printing and the mass production of texts, was necessarily performance. To be sure, despite Augustine's quiet marvel (*Confessions* 6.3.3), Jerome could not have been the first, or even the rare, silent reader of a work in manuscript. The tangle of gloze and commentary that manuscript tradition has passed down to us gives massive testimony to centuries of silent and devoted study of texts. Before the advent of printing, however, the private study could never serve the poet's need of popularity. For, even had there been enough studiers and sufficient leisure to study, there could never have been sufficient manuscripts. To "publish" a poem, before printing, meant to send it abroad, in manuscript of course, but also in performance.

Lacking textual integrity and autonomy—impermanent, bound to performance—a manuscript, unlike a printed book, is never "complete." It may always be scraped and improved, glozed, or even obliterated. It is always the possession of its last possessor. However perfect its production, its uniqueness allows it no consistent definition of "finished." A manuscript is always at least potentially in the process of becoming (or becoming-not). And, in performance, too, a work is always in process, always being interpreted for the needs of the social group that as an audience "possesses" it. Because of both its physical and its social modes of transmission, a work in manuscript invites interpretation and reshaping. Perhaps the most striking exemplification of this is the way in which a gloze, surrounding the text, tends to become a part of the text, or at least to dwarf and dominate it. This occurs in part because the product lacks typographically fixed reference points: the most reliable way of connecting gloze with text is by simple proximity. The very scarcity that commits manuscripts to performance (and hence, inevitably, to interpretation) also promotes scholarly glozing. With few books to study, an intense devotion to a few (with the inevitable commentary) is only natural. But, with the printed book, Eisenstein notes, "The era of the glossator and commentator came to an end," as suddenly a cascade of texts cried for attention and made lifelong devotion to a handful of texts obsolete (p. 72).

Testimony to the flood of new books is common among writers: in Rabelais, in Montaigne, in Cervantes, in Marlowe, the intoxication of books is praised and damned. Living among and reading printed books, however, does not necessarily transform the writer. Writers are slow to realize the implications of printing for their art. They are slow to realize that they may write precisely for the private study, even to the exclusion of public performance.[3] And they are somewhat slow to realize that they need not submit to, indeed may actively resist, the liberty of interpretation which both performance and lifelong study legitimate. Written for the study but resistant to interpretation, printed books offer to authors two new things: completeness, an assurance of the self-contained work (neither excerpted nor glozed), and epynomity, a name attached to the work—author and authority. The known author can be "in" the work.

These promises of print certainly do not go unnoticed in the sixteenth century. The early printing of ballads and the poetic miscellanies show first attempts to make the transient permanent. And some collections, like Kendall's *Flowres of Epigrams* (1577) or Breton's *Britons Bowre of Delights* (1591), credit single authors for the work. The miscellanies, however, remain as whimsically edited and as textually chancy as manuscripts ever were.[4] And neither Kendall's nor Breton's collection is in fact the work of a single author. Sonnet sequences, like sets of eclogues, seem ideally suited for the printed book, complete and structured as they are. The thinness of the narrative structures is palpable, however, and as often as not the authors are either anonymous or pseudonymous. The authors rather pointedly avoid that very authority which print makes possible. Even Spenser first appears, in an otherwise ostentatiously "bookish" volume, as "Immeritô." The frequent pseudonymity of the sonnets, moreover, entices us to intrepretive fancies, to allegories of life and art. Pastoral poets of course by tradition write better than they know; and it is always to some extent the reader's job to do their thinking for them. So the message is clear when in *The Faerie Queene* Spenser, though now the known epic poet, retains to the end the voice and weeds of poor Colin Clout.

Despite the limitations of pastoralism and an authorial reluctance to be known (attendant on a determined amateurism), a consciousness of the meaning of print for authors slowly emerges. Early in the century, concerns for the standardization of spelling and vocabulary are voiced. Later, we find authors playing with the possibilities of print in those "figure" poems discussed by Puttenham (*The Arte of English Poesie* 2.12). Besides strictly pastoral sets and sonnet sequences, we find such authors as Googe and Gascoigne putting together collections in self-consciously "editorial" ways (*Eglogs, Epytaphes and Sonnetes*, 1563; *A Hundreth sundrie Flowres*, 1573). Spenser, though unnamed, does emerge on the scene in an "edited" text. The prefaces of countless books, moreover, display authors entangled in complicated self-definition, a task imposed on them by their appearance as authors, known by name and commercially published. Amateur or professional, they seem to writhe in shame, reluctantly enduring the scandal of publication. The result is real or pretended carelessness with the text and perpetuation of a nonauthoritative pose on the part of authors, long past the time when print has in fact begun to confer its own authority.[5]

It is not until the work of Ben Jonson, I suggest, that we first see the impact of printing on literature coherently assimilated. In Jonson's work we first find a poet appearing in texts which are decisively made for print—in texts proclaiming their own completeness, aware of their own permanence, and creative of their own context. We find in Jonson a sense of the printed text as an authorized and established object of criticism—implying, and imposing from within, its own rules for reading. Jonson establishes the printed text as the primary object of literature. Then, to aid in this project, he appropriates for his texts new sources of authority, in particular classical authority. Finally, he imbues his texts with a pervasive thematic reference to the authority and textuality that he is seeking to establish. The result of these efforts is the birth of the printed book in English literature.

Jonson in an important sense "invents" (discovers) the printed book by using the book to distinguish what is his, by asserting a propriety not generally possible in manuscripts, and, as a part of this process, by distinguishing oral performances from written texts. In his address to the readers of *Sejanus*, for instance, we are informed "that this book, in all numbers, is not the same with that which was acted on the public stage"; Jonson has purified the text by removing all that "wherein a second pen had a share." The main point here is exclusivity of authorship, although the distinction between text and performance has its implicit place. The distinction between text and performance is explicit in the masques, in the publication of which Jonson quite programmatically seeks to create, as Stephen Orgel has shown, "a work whose text was no longer dependent on its production."[6] As for the plays, Jonson cannot take sole credit for distinguishing them as texts apart from performances, but his handling of the quartos goes a long way in that direction.

Insisting that his texts are artifacts, as opposed to, say, song books or play books for future performances or aides-memoires for recalling performances past, he offers them, as we all know, as objects of criticism—that is, as objects of study and private meditation. Whether a play, for instance, is framed by commentary like that we find in *Every Man out of his Humour*, or centered on a representative critic like Crites in *Cynthia's Revels*, or simply filled up with judgers and evaluators like those in *Sejanus* and the plays after it, the characteristic mental action that Jonson seeks to invoke is instructed, critical judgment. By means of this instruction, the book creates its own context—the community of its studiers. By implication, all good studiers will judge alike, in part because of the instruction, in part because the book, unlike a manuscript, is identical for all. Thus, the immutability, or rigidity, that we sense in Jonson's work, the coercive authority, both critical and moral, to which he challenges his readers to submit, issues from (and reflectively emphasizes) his confidence in the identicalness of the copies of his texts. Printing allows the creation of a community of readers at least partly independent of any actual social community or community of class.

We might note in passing that, appropriately, we see in Jonson the portrayal of a social text that is likewise coercive in its interpretation. His dramatic commentators, of course, suggest that there is only one way to "read" the events and characters of the plays. And the characters' inflexibility, their monomaniacal pursuit of their single obsessions, suggests that univalent, relatively inflexible readings of them are correct. Speculating on the interests of someone who writes prose like Jonson's, Jonas A. Barish suggests that perhaps Jonson "is thinking . . . of a world so static that nothing in it is subject to change, [or] perhaps of a world so bewilderingly disintegrated that nothing in it seems causally related to anything else."[7] In either case, Jonson's social world seems to lack an inner dynamism, a receding horizon of cause and effect, or a hinted transcendence opening up vistas beyond the limits of the text. His world "stands still" on the intricate surface of the text, ready for our examination. It gives us the impression that we can read it forward, take it backward, or skip around in it, and find that the relation of the parts will remain the same. It has the unchanging quality of a printed book. It is "understandable" in a radical sense. Or, to put it negatively, his work discourages liberty of interpretation and the imposition of allegory.[8]

And, finally, Jonson's work seems as a whole curiously coherent and responsive to criticism, unchanging even as his readers change. Is there not among us a sense that Jonson's work is critically, self-consciously shaped, and that we are limited in what we *can* see by the closed coherence of that work? So at least a survey of most Jonson criticism would suggest. George Parfitt valiantly tries to show that Jonson, in the early stage of his reputation at least, enjoyed estimations other than that of bookish completeness, and he argues that the absence of stage tradition has reduced Jonson to the bookish version we have of him now. But even this fate—admired not loved, studied not produced—seems to fulfill a Jonsonian wish.[9] Parfitt's summary of praises easily makes the case that the reputation that has survived—the reputation for tireless art and deserving criticism—is one that from the earliest days comes closest to crossing the boundary from admiration to love. Ben Jonson clearly wishes to be known through his texts. He is in principle a textual poet, the poet of printed books, books which at once demand and teach the practice of the critic.

In his insistence on the autonomy of his texts, in his creation of his small community of critical readers, and in his confidence in the shape his texts create for reading, Jonson manifests, I believe, a profound realization of what it means to write for print: to write for an audience defined only by the limits of book distribution and the understanding of readers, rather than to perform for a few or to surrender to the whims of copyists, excerpters, and marginal glozers. We would, I think, overread the implications of print to make Jonson out a leader of the bourgeois revolution; but the exemption, at least partial, that print allows from more or less exclusive courtly or clerkly social organizations of readers (or chaotic playhouses of listeners) offers precisely that opportunity for a new audience which Jonson sought to gain, or to create, as the readers of his texts.

His apparent intention and accomplishment in seeking out, in creating, this audience is the invention of textuality for vernacular literature, that very textuality—with its presumed community of readers, coherent structure, unbroken continuity, and historical referentiality—which is so much at issue in our criticism, modernist and postmodernist, today. It is no accident that, before Jonson, the monuments of our literature are of uncertain text, fragmentary, or of uncertain structure. Think of *Beowulf*, the *Canterbury Tales*, *Sir Gawain*, Wyatt's poems, the *Arcadia*, *The Faerie Queene*, the plays of Shakespeare. That the text and coherence should be doubtful for medieval works or, perhaps, for a set of Renaissance plays offers little surprise; perhaps the social facts that obscure Wyatt's texts are also easy to see. But then we see in a work as late as the *Arcadia* how Sidney revised *away* from the relatively tight coherence of the *Old Arcadia* to the sprawling thousand-and-one-nights endlessness of the *New*. *The Faerie Queene* is certainly by definition a fragmentary work: Spenser's cavalier gesture toward "structure" in the letter to Ralegh outlines an uncompletable project that will allow him to write and write, but never to end.

Jonson's assertions of textuality, even to a "textual" certification of his name (Jonson, not Johnson), appear, I think, as a natural development of more than a century of industrious printing. The greatest accomplishment of this first hundred years or so was the presentation of classical antiquity. For the first time a writer could look to his shelves and see a collection of authors, speaking across the centuries in assuredly complete works, with voices "authorized" by the very notion of "renaissance" itself, and in texts which themselves, *because* they were printed, seemed possessed of a timeless, unchanging uniformity. An author could see on his shelves a collection established as a secular canon by humanist scholarship.[10] The appropriation of this "canonicity" was the most natural of moves for Jonson. And his attempts to do so, to "re-invent" the classical text as the English classic, are some of the most characteristic marks of his work. The inclusion of commentary and textual notes and his addresses to critics, which are part of his strategy for distinguishing text from performance, might also be considered part of his attempt to invade the domain of the classical text. This is perhaps most obvious in the annotations to *Sejanus* and a number of the masques. In the 1616 *Workes*, his translation of the Latin *opera* specifically makes the claim that Jonson as a writer is a classic.

A principal support of this claim is the clear sense of definitive order in the volume itself, in its impression of completeness. In suppressing part of his earlier work, Jonson engages in canon formation. His selection of chronological order for the plays emphasizes the *Workes* as a "study" of his career. But at the same time he covers the tracks of his development by dating even revised plays like *Every Man in his Humour* and *Sejanus* from their original performances. The result is, in effect, a study not of Jonson's development but of the unfolding in time of his timeless and unchanging talent. You might say that he presents his career not as a drama but as a masque.[11] Or he presents himself like his own social text: multiply readable and, approached from whatever direction, always the same. Jonson's success in this project is indicated by the long-standing critical opinion, only now being revised, that his career is of a piece, that Ben Jonson—unlike, say, Shakespeare— shows no "development." The culmination of this growth-as- unfolding-rather-than-development is presented in the form of a book-within-the-works, in *Epigrammes. I. Booke*, that famous "ripest of my studies, my *Epigrammes*." Curiously, that this collection is itself organized for critical study seems to have eluded critical observation until fairly recently. Now, however, critical opinion unanimously holds that it is organized in at least *some* critically self-conscious fashion.[12]

That at least up through *Epigrammes* the 1616 *Workes* is intended to show a definite order implying worthiness of study is also indicated by the physical structure of the printed volume. Each of the works through *Epigrammes* has lavished on it a separate title page and a separate dedication. And, in the table of contents, "the Catalogue," each of the works through *Epigrammes* is listed with the object of its dedication. The Catalogue also helps to emphasize the culminative position of *Epigrammes* by showing both it and *Catiline*, the final and most ostentatiously "classical" play, as dedicated to Pembroke, the only recipient of two dedications. After this listing come "The Forrest / Entertaynments / Panegyre / Masques / Barriers," a more problematic group of mixed forms, having somewhat the appearance of an appendix. The Catalogue does not quite correctly identify the actual manner in which the items appear in the volume, and in this latter section appears the only material that we can be sure was written after 1612/13. But even here Jonson's eye seems to be on the structure of the collection: he reverses the chronological order of the last two masques, so that he can end the volume not with *Mercury Vindicated* but with *The Golden Age Restored*, to suggest an almost divine completeness for the *Workes*—*Iam reddit virgo*.

Besides his implicit hinting at his "classical" worthiness for criticism and his canonization of his writings as *Workes*, Jonson of course labors throughout his writing, through allusion and imitation, to appropriate to himself the epithet "classical." So successful has he been in this attempt that no subject has dominated Jonson studies more than the issue of his classicism. A survey of that scholarship is hardly needed. I would just like to add an observation about the particular quality of his classicism, most specifically about his appropriation of the authority of the classical text to his own vernacular. What is distinctively new and textual about Jonson's classical borrowings is their specificity. That is, with remarkable frequency his allusions and sources are specifically identifiable, and their identification seems to be a natural part of our reading. Parfitt argues to the contrary that the identifications are possible but not really to the point: "Clearly there are occasions when a loan would be recognized by an educated spectator or reader, but Jonson seldom does anything to encourage such recognition, and although this diffidence may be part of his sense of writing for 'the few but fit' it is also indicative of a view of the classics as providing nourishment of a wider and richer kind than decorative or self-advertising usage could do." That his classical references are not merely "decorative or self-advertising" I hope we can agree, but Parfitt underestimates Jonson's expectation of educated readers. Everything in his work implies an audience of "learned Criticks" (*Epigrammes* 17). Parfitt correctly suggests that the use of specific classical sources, especially for his many ethical commonplaces, "may have increased Jonson's confidence that he was saying something true." [13] But the basis of this confidence is canonization of the humanist program in the printed classical text, in the commonality of culture and shared reading of identical texts which printing made possible. [14] The sheer number of almost literally translated lines, together with Jonson's evident fierce pride in them, even to the point of dramatic disaster in *Catiline*, informs all of his readers that we should hear classical texts, speaking across time, in his own.

A good contrast to Jonson is offered by the most "classical" of Elizabethans, Edmund Spenser. Characteristically, Spenser borrows details from classical myth for incorporation into schemata of his own. They generally serve a purpose different from that in their original context, when, indeed, the textual source can be ascertained. [15] By contrast, Jonson's borrowings, as Parfitt has observed, adopt not only details but the associated classical concepts themselves. At the same time, characteristically, these borrowings are verbally closer to the source than Spenser's. When a character in Jonson warns, "hee carries hey in his horne" (*Poetaster*

4.3.110), he means exactly what Horace means when he says the same (*Sermones* 1.4.34, of an angry bull). And the only way of knowing what "hey in his horne" means is to know what it means in Horace. When Jonson refers to the "painted partrich" at Penshurst ("To Penshurst," 29), we simply aren't reading all the poem until we know about Martial's *picta perdix* (3.58.15). But there are too many such examples to go on. Jonson's allusions, tied so specifically to both original form and original content, insist on themselves and tie his work to the classics, rather in the way that the classics are necessarily tied to each other by the tissue of cross-reference created by centuries of editorial work. (I refer to the inevitable cross-referencing from author to author necessary for the elucidation of obscure words and social practices unfamiliar to the postclassical reader.) Summarily, we might say that the reader Jonson has in mind is a philologist, not an allegorist. Jonson imagines a reader who in reading the classics asks, in Frank Kermode's words, "what the classic *meant* to its author and his best readers, and may still mean to those who have the necessary knowledge and skill." He imagines a reader whose readings are philological and historiographic, rather than one whose readings are accommodational, who makes the classic "signify what it cannot be said to have expressly stated," who reads allegorically.[16]

Finally, beyond the literalness both in theme and word of his classical borrowings, beyond his success in defining his writings as complete works and his insistent address of his works to studiers of books, to learned critics, Jonson thematically defines his works in terms which reflect on and intensify the impression of authority and textuality that, in their printed form, he seeks to give them. The persistent metaphors and strategies he uses to describe his art implicitly define him not so much as a poet of song and voice but as a poet of the study and of the letter. At least as much artisan as artist, Jonson capitalizes on the ambiguity of "maker" to emphasize the craft and technique of art and, hence, to emphasize the sense of finish and completeness available to a printed text. He does not, of course, claim that poetry is craft alone. On the contrary, "The state of poesie," his Lord Justice declares, is "Blessed, æternall, and most true devine" (*Every Man in his Humour* [1600] 5.3.316–17). We see in the epigram "To Clement Edmonds" that the poet has the power to immortalize and even to revive lost voices:

> CAESAR stands up, as from his urne late rose,
> By thy great helpe: and doth proclaime by mee,

They murder him againe, that envie thee.
                                                    (*Epigrammes* 110.12–14)

The poet speaks "the *Muses*"; he is "their priest" ("Epistle. To Katherine, Lady Aubigny," 100–01). But against these familiar claims of the poet-*vates* we must balance Jonson's other version of the artist, the poet-artisan. Wesley Trimpi may overstate Jonson's rejection of the traditional metaphors and figures associated with the poetry of Muses and "priests," but his account of the plain style's rejection of "commitment to past connotation" does focus our attention on the poet rather as working craftsman than as recipient of the mantle of Orpheus (p. 15). Even when he seems to be priestlike, Jonson regularly distinguishes the particular choices and individual craftsmanship peculiar to him: "Give me my cup, *but* from the Thespian well"; "And *yet* (in this t'expresse our selves more clear)" (*The Forrest* 14.11; 11.75, my emphasis in both). And, in the prelude to the "Epode" of *The Forrest*, after twenty-seven lines of rejecting traditional mythological ornaments of vatic poetry, he declares: "No, I bring / My owne true fire" (28–29). "Fire" he still has, but a fire to be defined by individual choices.

Those "individual choices" are the choices of a craftsman. Poetry is the work of an artisan; it is the province of Vulcan, as in the challenge Cupid delivers in "Why I write not of Love":

> Can Poets hope to fetter mee?
> It is enough, they once did get
> MARS, and my *Mother*, in their net:
> I weare not these my wings in vaine.
> With which he fled me: and againe,
> Into my ri'mes could ne're be got
> By any arte.   (4–10)

The abrupt stop on *arte* gives a chance for its Latin meaning—skill in joining something, combining it, working it—to connect with *net* (with perhaps a glancing pun on the etymologically related *artus*, *articulus*—joint, knot). Poetry is the work of "labour" (*Cynthia's Revels* 5.8.28). Insisting on the propriety of *Volpone*, Jonson tells us it came "From his owne hand, without a co-adjutor, / Novice, journey-man, or tutor" (Prologue, 17–18), for he is by implication the master craftsman. Moreover, he works by rule: "As best Criticks have designed, / The lawes of time, place, persons he observeth" (Prologue, 30–31). The craft of the theater is highlighted mockingly in the Horatian prologue to the folio *Every Man in his Humour* (tiring-house scars, a descending "creaking throne," "roul'd bullet heard / To say, it thunders," and so on), but his own alternative rule-based craft is the focus in the oft-quoted lines that promise "deedes, and language, such as men do use: / And persons, such as Comœdie would chuse, / When she would shew an Image of the times, / And sport with humane follies, not with crimes." Choice is craft, craft choice. Examples abound beyond quoting, and their import—that poetry is "making," in the sense not only of creating but also of "joining"—has been thoroughly absorbed, not always to his credit, by Jonson's readers from the very beginning.

This sense of art as artisanship thematically parallels Jonson's practical care for his texts. To be sure, Jonson was not unique in overseeing his own texts. In fact, when a publishing venture was entirely on the up and up, an author would usually oversee the printing as a standard obligation.[17] But the author's usual *fiction* traditionally denies responsibility for the text. Again and again writers confide that they are "compelled" to release their work, often "all togyther unpolyshed to the hands of the Prynter." Edwin Haviland Miller sums up the standard fiction this way: "The author is invariably a 'gentleman.' Unexpectedly he returns to London and 'reluctantly' gives consent to publication either out of charity [to the publisher] or out of passive acquiescence. Usually the author himself notes these facts in a preface. If he does not, the publisher swears that the gentleman does not write for money."[18] Even so aggressively professional a writer as Spenser, as I have noted, comes forth as anonymous "Immeritô" under the sponsorship of E. K., to diminish the authorial presence in the book even as he endows it with classicizing commentary. Similarly, Gascoigne introduces his *Hundreth sundrie Flowres* as writings found and imperfectly edited by another. And *The Faerie Queene*, though probably a milestone in publishing for the importance of the printed text, scrupulously avoids the arrogance of craftsmanship that would endow the text with autonomy. Spenser simply does not ask us to focus on small textual units in critical and definitive ways. That is to say, his words (we may presume) are carefully chosen, but their *choice* is not the point. How many different meanings, for instance, can we find for *stowre*, and how rarely can we settle on the "right" meaning in a particular place.[19] In Jonson, both the imagery of his plays and the ethical language of his poems pointedly seek to "define, to achieve a hard-edged effect."[20] Even when we do not *in fact* get a clear definition of Jonson's meaning, his emphasis on choice, completeness, and craft creates the impression that we do. Crites in *Cynthia's Revels* "(like a circle bounded in itself) / Contains much, as man in fullness may" (5.8.19–20). Even though we must read much of Jonson, absorbing the classical authority of his meanings before we know enough of his idea of "man" to understand what he means by "much," still the image itself, bounded and complete, implies a finished definition, just as the poem is, in printed form, a finished product.

This impression of completeness and autonomy—whether of a whole work or of an individual word, even of its spelling, or of punctuation—parallels and intensifies the impression available to the printed text of completeness, unchangeability, and autonomy. The literary work is reified as the printed text (hence my second choice of titles). It is thus released from the confines of manuscript circulation and public performance, freed to appear in a variety of contexts unpredicted by the author.[21] In part, to be sure, this unpredictable circulation can itself cause anxiety:

> When we doe give, ALPHONSO, to the light,
>   A worke of ours, we part with our owne right;
> For, then, all mouthes will judge, and their owne way.
>
> (*Epigrammes* 131.1–3)

This very fear, however, that books are commodities to be used by all purchasers as they will, is at least partially allayed by those other possibilities of print—eponymous authority, textuality, specificity, completeness, and so on—which Jonson's work realizes. In print, the author has some measure of protection from promiscuous judging. The poem remains the author's "owne right." It is protected from the arrogance of meddling copyists and editors. It no longer comes forth into the world apologetic and "unfinished," inviting the reader's mental rewriting.

In this reification of the text, Jonson finds a more or less comfortable place in a corporate enterprise. In contradiction to Jonson's special, even highly individualized, artisanship in the production both of texts and of books, there is a sense in which Jonson the individual author becomes invisible, absorbed as it were into the artifacts of his creation. As Arthur F. Marotti has said of Jonson, although "We feel we *know* him, in a way we do not know Shakespeare," there is something in his work which tends to reject individualistic poeticizing (the "auto-intoxicate" imagination "exorcised" in the dramas, in Marotti's view). Or, as I have suggested elsewhere, Jonson in some ways seeks to be known and to affirm the knowable, on the one hand, but deeply suppresses the process of our coming to know, on the other; in contrast to Donne, he conceals the workings of his imagination.[22] Parfitt's account of Jonson's classicism, to which I refer above, helps to explain how Jonson manages to be so "there" without insisting on his individuality. His classical borrowings are "an aid to articulation," for they draw on the classical commonplaces that "sum up the ethical speculations and conclusions of many men across many centuries." As a result, "Jonson's frequent use of classical expressions of such commonplaces adds to the authority and weight of his social analysis." That is to say, Jonson creates a classical texture into which his own analyses are absorbed, a texture that becomes a corporate rather than an individual ethical enterprise.[23] The book, too, by the late sixteenth century was a corporate enterprise. Book production, as a novel art, represents one of the earliest developments of an elaborated capitalism, and there quickly evolved a highly differentiated structure of labor. Printer and bookseller were rarely the same person; author and printer were the same almost never.[24] That hardly seems remarkable now, but the development from Caxton, the professional diversification, is obvious. Jonson's own insistence on his place in this professionalization of the book business marks an important step. He completely abandons the pretense of the gentleman amateur and emphasizes his professionalism in his metaphors for writing. So his avoidance of individuality of judgment and his absorption into a "corporate" classicism, in particular a book-centered classicism, metaphorically parallels, and therefore intensifies his integration into, the corporate enterprise of book production.

Jonson, as our first textual poet, as the (re-)inventor of the book, is, in a way new to English literature, possessed of his text. That is to say, he possesses his texts, and he is possessed by them. He lives in his texts in a way unprecedented because the texts themselves have an unprecedented existence. His works are defined *as* texts, in particular as "classical" texts. They as a whole amount to *Workes*. And the works themselves consistently image the craft and completeness of printed books and their attendant autonomy. This autonomous existence in a distinctive way "possesses" Jonson (our "Ben"), whom we feel we know better than Shakespeare and to the better knowledge of, specifically the better *defining* of, critical readers are tirelessly attracted. The texts' possession of Jonson is at base enabled, I think, by their possession *by* Jonson. His proprietary rights, established by his separation of texts from performance and by his insistence on texts as the products of professional enterprise and as objects of study, define them as *his* with an assurance new in literary life. In this he is distinctly ahead of his time, for authors were not to gain a legal right to their copy until 1711.[25] But with Jonson it becomes possible to talk seriously about plagiarism and textual propriety, as he does in his threat to expose "Proule the Plagiary":

> Forbeare to tempt me, PROULE, I will not show
> A line unto thee, till the world it know;
> Or that I'have by, two good sufficient men,
> To be the wealthy witnesse of my pen.
>
> (*Epigrammes* 81.1–4)

We hear of Play-wright, who stole "some toyes I'had writ," which later "past him a play" (*Epigrammes* 100.1, 4). Jonson ridicules "Old-end Gatherer" (*Epigrammes* 53) and tries to deal with the more serious challenge of "Poet-Ape":

> Poore POET-APE, that would be thought our chiefe,
> Whose workes are eene the fripperie of wit,
> From brocage is become so bold a thiefe,
> As we, the rob'd, leave rage, and pittie it.
> At first he made low shifts, would picke and gleane,
> Buy the reversion of old playes; now growne
> To'a little wealth, and credit in the *scene*,
> He takes up all, makes each mans wit his owne.
> And, told of this, he slights it. Tut, such crimes
> The sluggish gaping auditor devoures;
> He markes not whose 'twas first: and after-times
> May judge it to be his, as well as ours.
> Foole, as if halfe eyes will not know a fleece
> From locks of wooll, or shreds from the whole peece?
>
> (*Epigrammes* 56)

The conclusion of the poem reveals, in the poet's reliance on the audience's knowing the stolen from the "whole peece," the strong motive for the poet to distinguish the propriety of his text (and to seek, or create, a philologically inclined audience). A further motive, in which Jonson is not ahead of his time, is the simple need to be paid for at least the first printing or performance. Among the

"*Items*" with which he confronts "Fine Grand" are various jests, songs, poesies, charms, anagrams, and "an epitaph on my lords cock," "For which, or pay me quickly', or Ile pay you" (*Epigrammes* 73.18, 22). And, in *The Forrest*, there is a clear note of personal complaint in his praise "To Sir Robert Wroth," who

> Nor throng'st (when masquing is) to have a sight
> Of the short braverie of the night;
> To view the jewells, stuffes, the paines, the wit
> There wasted, some not paide for yet! (9–12)

It would still be long before writers would reach that stage of professionalism which could assure their rights of copy. But with Jonson and his creation of the textual object, with his reification of the work, the *possibility* of such rights emerges.

Needless to say, Jonson cannot be said to have invented this right. Rather, he can properly be seen as the focus of a trend. He cannot take credit, for instance, for the seemingly spontaneous demise of the poetic miscellany around 1604; nor can he take credit for the emergence, around 1650, of royalty payments to authors. But the end of the miscellany and its traditional association with manuscript tradition, together with the transferal of its performative bias to the increasingly popular song book (in which performance is sanctioned by the music), shows the climate in which he worked and which he helped bring to realization. The emergence of regular royalty payments would also require the reification that Jonson's work effects. In a profound way, then, Jonson's *realization* of the significance of print defines his signal importance for subsequent writers.

Of this Ben Jonson, the (re-)inventor of the book, the first English classic author, virtually all subsequent English authors can claim at least some degree of paternity. Perhaps the most immediate influence is to be seen in the moves of individual authors, or (posthumously) of their friends, to join Jonson in the canonization of "works." Harington's epigrams come forth posthumously in 1618, complete in four books. Joseph Hall issues his works in 1621. Daniel's whole works come forth posthumously in 1623, the memorable year in which the Shakespeare canon is established. We see just how powerful the idea of self-documentation in a canon may be in the *Poems* (1645) in which Milton explicitly includes his juvenilia and even "The Passion," a poem that (as he tells the reader) he left unfinished because, finding the subject "to be above the years he had, when he wrote it," he was "nothing satisfi'd with what was begun." Milton's self-documentation in the 1645 poems derives almost purely from Jonson's decision to include an incomplete poem in *The Forrest* ("Epistle. To Elizabeth Countesse of Rutland"), with a less ingenuous explanation of his reasons for the poem's incompleteness.[26]

Though it did not produce a complete works, the attempt made in 1633 to canonize the poems of Donne cannot go unnoticed. The posthumous Donne collections, and to a lesser degree the 1640 posthumous collection of Carew's poems as well, indicate a sort of halfway response to Jonson's (re-)invention of the book. Although they clearly show the intent of their collectors to build the works of their poets into the canon of English vernacular literature, the collections themselves appear to be manuscript miscellanies on the older model. That is, especially in Donne's case, they are unanalytical and textually unreliable. For Donne, this is appropriate enough because, after some early interest in writing critically related poems, he seems to have adopted an essentially nonbookish attitude toward his poetry. We note the strongly performative quality of the poems, the persistent tone of indifference to traditional and especially classical values, and of course an indifference to the preservation of the text.[27] For subsequent poets, Donne remains a model of indifference to the responsibility of being a "classic." But, in the same year that Donne's poems appear, we see the appearance of *The Temple*, perhaps the epitome of the Book. No other seventeenth-century literary book has so exercised critics in the effort to understand the mystery of its unity. Diverse critics have come to diverse conclusions, but the conviction persists that, like a Bible, *The Temple* is a Work. Certainly it seemed so to Crashaw when he published *Steps to the Temple* in 1646. The metaphorical relation between *The Temple* and *Steps* echoes Jonson's own account of the relationship between *The Forrest* and *The Under-wood:* "I am bold to entitle these lesser Poems, of later growth, by this of *Under-wood*, out of the Analogie they hold to the *Forrest*, in my former booke." Such specificity of relation between books is possible only after books have acquired the imaginative autonomy of a fixed canon.

What all these works and collections show, I think, is the triumph and transformation of what Richard I. Regosin so aptly terms "the primacy of the book" in Renaissance culture. Regosin uses this phrase to focus on the centrality of books to Montaigne's study of himself. The triumphant book in Montaigne, however, is essentially nontypographic. At the same time that Montaigne stresses reading, he "rejects the Western tradition of book learning." Using his "insistence on his lack of memory and his celebration of ignorance" as "symbolic gestures," Montaigne effects a "transformation in the use of books—from *instruction* to *exercitation*," as he "interiorizes the object of study to fix primarily, or rather exclusively, on the self." Finally, Regosin continues, "Reading and thinking, writing and self-discovery converge in the book of the self, where Montaigne is." As Regosin indicates, books are not texts for Montaigne; they are occasions for study of the self. They are not canonical; their importance is not in themselves. Similarly, Montaigne's own book, where he "is," is also not a text. It is a record of the travel of the mind. And even if, as Regosin suggests, "The *Essais* are more than a log book of progress and performance, more than a recording of physical and intellectual activity," even if "In their most profound sense they *are* Montaigne's experience, not merely the chronicle of it," they do not possess the features of a canonical book. In particular they lack a standard for or a striving after the completion of a text; there is no end point from which the author turns back an editorial and critical eye, rearranging and refining the text as he redefines himself. Far from suppressing the sense of "development," as Jonson does, Montaigne seems to revel in it. The *Essais* are a long-running performance.[28]

For contrast, we can look at Robert Burton, certainly no classical author, but one in whom the triumph of the printed book strikingly manifests itself as enabling a discourse that moves to the very edges of the dissolution of discourse. I suppose every reader tries at one time or another to make an entry to the *Anatomy* by means of Burton's enticing "analyses" of the three partitions. With the analyses, Burton stakes his claim to the coherence of his work, his claim that he has written a kind of *summa* of his subject. That the text is indeed a *summa* I think most readers fairly early conclude—not of the declared subject really, but of Everything. To a greater degree than Montaigne's "book of himself," this book of Democritus bristles with books and rumors of books, becoming, as Rosalie L. Colie blames Swift for maligning it, "an infinite digression upon an infinity of subjects."[29] What keeps it from remaining the passel of fragments it could easily be taken to be is Burton's success in conning us into the belief that it is in fact a Book. A scholastic *summa* is of course not a form of book but a form of logic, a fact unchanged by its mere transference from manuscript to print. It does not take anyone very long to realize that, despite his promise, Burton is not following a form of logic; he is just following the formal scheme of his book. But, once the book is established as the object of literature, it can have a structure of its own, and the *meaning* of the structure can then be an object of study in its own right. That is, the book itself can be an object of criticism. This is just what is suggested by the fiction that the book is Democritus Junior's revival and prosecution of Democritus Senior's "unperfect" work. Thus the work as a whole constitutes a running allusion to a book, though to a book other than the one Burton happens to be writing. The promise of the book's finally appearing holds together Burton's fundamentally explosive subject. But to read it *only* for that book is to risk the fate Johnson held out to those who read *Clarissa* for the plot. I cannot quite argue that Burton could write the *Anatomy* only within the fiction of the printed book, with the pretense to a text, but pretend to a text is exactly what he does, as the endless elaboration of the discourse, promising order at every step, dissolves all order, all points of reference, all standards of judgment, finally undermining even the idea of a text itself, leaving only the Book.[30]

For authors less radical than Burton, the text, even without the book, achieves, after Jonson, a remarkable integrity. The most striking case of this, I suppose, is Jonson's single-handed invention of the genre of country-house poem. The instant emergence of "To Penshurst" as a text to be imitated epitomizes Jonson's success in his project of becoming an English classic. In principle, Jonson's sources in Horace and Martial remain open for renewed exploitation by his imitators, yet Jonson himself is the specific source for the tradition. The thinness of the tradition might in part account for this, but, to see the difference, one need think only of the constant renewal of the sixteenth-century sonnet in Petrarch and his Italian and French successors. Before Tottel, of course, there is no printed text to become authoritative in the English sonnet, so it is perhaps only natural that, as much as he admired him, Surrey should not tie himself to the texts of Wyatt. But, even after Tottel, we cannot say that we find a canon of the sonnet. By contrast, the authority of Jonson in the forms he deals with—the epigram, the epistle, the ode, even the prefatory poem—is unquestioned. Beyond the forms, we can trace poems after Jonson to other single poems of his, even to single lines. From Jonson: "Or Scorne, or pittie on me take"; from Carew: "Give me more love, or more disdaine"; from Godolphin: "Or love me lesse, or love me more." How often successive poets work to transmute the tones of "Oh doe not wanton with those eyes" (*Under-wood* 4).[31] Having caught the trick of the imitation of texts, the "line of wit" continues as a series of closely related texts. From King: "Tell me no more how fair she is"; from Carew: "Ask me no more where *Jove* bestows"; from Godolphin: "No more unto my thoughts appeare"; from Cartwright: "Tell me no more of minds embracing minds."

That these poems find their way into books, even sometimes into works, is not the essential point. Rather, we see represented in them a new attitude toward the poem, an attitude so changed that imitation and allusion grow indistinct. Indeed, only rarely can we clearly tag a particular poem as *only* alluding, that is, existing through the reader's knowledge of another poem. Allusion is the case in Suckling's "Song to a Lute" ("Hast thou seen the Doun ith' air"). But is Herrick's "Delight in Disorder" an allusion to or an imitation of Jonson's song from *Epicoene*, "Still to be neat"? Or what of the relation of Waller's "Go, lovely rose," to Herrick's "Go, happy rose"? The problem perhaps has its analogue among the *Epigrammes*, where Jonson makes it clear that his poems do relate to one another, but where he leaves problematical ("critical") their relation; that is, he gives the task of "understanding" the Book to the reader. Herrick himself gives us a similar kind of critical work in *Hesperides* with the inclusion, in scattered places, of poems like "Art Above Nature: To Julia" and "Upon Julia's Clothes." [32] The distinctly critical problems with these collections are made possible by the authority of their texts. And it is this same authority of the text that leads us to similar attention to poems by different poets. As poets after Jonson work to absorb and transmute his work, they create what to the critical eye "reads" almost like a single text. [33]

In the poets of the "line of wit," we see Jonson's influence as immediate and easy to read. It seems to me an influence enormous and nearly overwhelming, but for the leavening counterweight of Donne. But Jonson's influence, I have been arguing, is greater than that which we see in his sons, and greater than the classicism, narrowly defined, that he passes on to the succeeding century. His greatest influence, I would argue, lies in the discovery of which his classicism is at least partially the vehicle, his (re-)invention of the book. What Jonson introduces into English literature is the "classic text."

Our literature [writes Roland Barthes] is characterized by the pitiless divorce which the literary institution maintains between the producer of the text and its user, between its author and its reader. This reader is thereby plunged into a kind of idleness—he is intransitive; he is, in short, *serious:* instead of functioning himself, instead of gaining access to the magic of the signifier, to the pleasure of writing, he is left with no more than the poor freedom either to accept or reject the text: reading is nothing more than a referendum. Opposite the writerly text, then, is its counter-value, its negative, reactive value: what can be read, but not written: the readerly. We call any readerly text a classic text.[34]

I would not call the freedom the classic text grants us "poor" or the reader of a classic text "intransitive." But Barthes's dissatisfaction with the closure of the readerly does seem to me to respond to something quite real in the classic text. In his preface to *S/Z*, Richard Howard elucidates this quality further when he characterizes the readerly experience as resistance to facing "the open text, the plurality of signification, the suspension of meaning." "How often we need to be assured of what we know in the old ways of knowing." We read in a "repressed and repressive way." Part of the blame for our repressed and repressive reading can surely be pinned on the success of capitalism in transforming readers into consumers and depriving them of productive or "writerly" capacity. A reader wholly defined by a consumerist schema is in fact "intransitive," and reading so defined is merely a referendum. But certainly there are other schemata, and not all readings are referenda. The classic text is not necessarily a tyrant. It does challenge, however, and it does demand:

> Pray thee, take care, that tak'st my booke in hand,
> To reade it well: that is, to understand.   (*Epigrammes* 1)

The means of this demand is the authority of the text, an authority of sufficient power to command its reader's willed submission to the rules of its understanding.

Our struggle to "understand" is silent. We quite literally, physically, take the book in hand—the whole object—and pore over it, turning ahead, turning back. We work to build a whole out of the parts we study; we do not expect to grasp it all in a complete performance. We read "studies," and we study them in return. With care, we will "understand." We submit ourselves to the text, and we do so believing that there *is* a "text." So submitting, so assured, we seek our own "possession of the text." In this sense, reading is not referendal, readers not intransitive. Instead, we perform a kind of contractual work, earning the text that we know to be there, taking care to understand. Such a contract is the gift, or curse, of the (re-)invention of the book, and—for English readers—of its (re-)inventor.

NOTES

1. "The Death of the Author," *Image-Music-Text*, ed. and trans. Stephen Heath, Fontana Communications Series (Glasgow: William Collins, 1977), pp. 142–48.

2. In at least some, if not most, medieval scriptoria, the two problems of inaccurate copying and oral transmission combine when copying is governed by dictation. See Elizabeth L. Eisenstein, *The Printing Press as an Agent of Change: Communications and Cultural Transformations in Early-Modern Europe*, 2 vols. (Cambridge: Cambridge University Press, 1979). See especially vol. 1, pp. 11 and 72. The two volumes are paginated as one, volume 2 beginning with page 451. I would like to express my indebtedness to, and gratitude for, Eisenstein's crucial and seminal work.

3. See William Nelson's argument for the primarily oral orientation of Renaissance literature, in "From 'Listen Lordings' to 'Dear Reader,' " *University of Toronto Quarterly* 46 (1976–77), 110–24. The strong theoretical and practical association of Renaissance literature with rhetorical performance persistently distracts our attention from the typographical object to the performance (even to our own performance, thus reinforcing liberty of interpretation). See, for instance, Richard Lanham, "*Astrophil and Stella:* Pure and Impure Persuasion," *ELR* 2 (1972), 100–15, and *The Motives of Eloquence: Literary Rhetoric in the Renaissance* (New Haven: Yale University Press, 1976).

4. Elizabeth W. Pomeroy, *The Elizabethan Miscellanies: Their Development and Conventions*, University of California English Studies, no. 36 (Berkeley and Los Angeles: University of California Press, 1973), pp. 35, 117. Pomeroy shows that the earlier miscellanies bear a similarity to and derive some characteristics from the broadside ballads (pp. 2–18).

5. For Googe, see John T. Shawcross, "The Bridge Between the Towers: Tudor Poetry, 1557–1579," forthcoming. On literary shame, see Richard Helgerson, "The Elizabethan Laureate: Self-Presentation and the Literary System," *ELH* 46 (1979), 206. On carelessness with the text, see Percy Simpson, *Proof-Reading in the Sixteenth, Seventeenth, and Eighteenth Centuries* (1935; rpt. Oxford: Oxford University Press, 1970). Simpson's examples show that the publishing industry was not organized to promote good texts.

6. *The Jonsonian Masque* (Cambridge, Mass.: Harvard University Press, 1965), p. 63.

7. *Ben Jonson and the Language of Prose Comedy* (Cambridge, Mass.: Harvard University Press, 1960), p. 77.

8. Compare Michel Butor, "The Book as Object," *Inventory: Essays by Michel Butor*, trans. Richard Howard (New York: Simon and Schuster, 1968), pp. 40–42. The understandability of things is one of the key assumptions of certain aspects of the so-called plain style. See Wesley Trimpi, *Ben Jonson's Poems: A Study of the Plain Style* (Stanford: Stanford University Press, 1962), esp. pp. 41–47. Appropriately, one of Jonson's most characteristic modes, satire, is marked by the poet's protest against "reading in" meanings beyond his intent.

9. On the coherence of the work, see D. F. McKenzie, "*The Staple of News* and the Late Plays," in *A Celebration of Ben Jonson*, ed. William Blissett et al. (Toronto: University of Toronto Press, 1973), pp. 83–84. On the early reputation, see George Parfitt, *Ben Jonson: Public Poet and Private Man* (1976; New York: Barnes'and Noble, 1977), pp. 124–41. But see as well Jonas A. Barish, "Jonson and the Loathèd Stage," in *A Celebration of Ben Jonson*, ed. Blissett et al., pp. 27–53.

10. In *The Classical Text: Aspects of Editing in the Age of the Printed Book*, Sather Classical Lectures, no. 44 (Berkeley and Los Angeles: University of California Press, 1974), E. J. Kenney notes that the printed *editio princeps* regularly became, at a stroke, "the *lectio recepta*— the text *tout court*" (p. 22). So great was the authority of the printed text that it "was absolutely standard procedure" to give it precedence and only hesitantly to advance new, even demonstrably better, manuscript evidence, often merely as a marginal comment, as if one were dealing with "the New Testament and not a pagan poet" (p. 67). On canon formation, see Ernst Robert Curtius, "Canon Formation in the Church," *European Literature and the Latin Middle Ages*, trans. Willard R. Trask, Bollingen Series 36 (New York: Pantheon Books, 1953), pp. 256–60.

11. W. David Kay highlights the importance of the *Workes* as a self-consciously shaped oeuvre by showing how Jonson used the volume to cover his tracks as he struggled for literary success. See "The Shaping of Ben Jonson's Career: Reexamination of Facts and Problems," *Modern Philology* 67 (1969–70), 224–37.

12. See, for instance, the summary essay by Edward Partridge, "Jonson's *Epigrammes:* The Named and the Nameless," *Studies in the Literary Imagination* 6 (1973), 153–98, and the discussion by Claude J. Summers and Ted-Larry Pebworth, *Ben Jonson* (Boston: Twayne, 1979), pp. 138–57.

13. *Ben Jonson*, pp. 122, 110. Parfitt argues eloquently against the notion that Jonson wears his classical learning too heavily, that he is dull, pedantic, or aggressive in his classicism; see *Ben Jonson*, pp. 104–23, and "Ethical Thought and Ben Jonson's Poetry," *SEL* 9 (1969), 123–34. With his argument, largely a reply to Edmund Wilson's longstanding challenge, I cannot in large measure agree, but its demonstration of the compatibility of English and classical thought makes the classicism a bit more appealing.

14. A little indication of a seventeenth-century learned reader's interest in Jonson's classical sources is given by James A. Riddell, in "Seventeenth-Century Identification of Jonson's Sources in the Classics," *Renaissance Quarterly* 28 (1975), 204–18. Based on the examination of a single folio, this is hardly definitive, but it is indicative nonetheless.

15. Parfitt makes essentially this point in "The Nature of Translation in Ben Jonson's Poetry," *SEL* 13 (1973), 344–59, but he omits it from the equivalent chapter of *Ben Jonson*, "Jonson and Classicism" (pp. 104–23). Compare Paul J. Alpers's account of Spenser's borrowings from Ariosto, *The Poetry of "The Faerie Queene"* (Princeton: Princeton University Press, 1967), pp. 166–79.

16. *The Classic: Literary Images of Permanence and Change* (New York: Viking, 1975), p. 40.

17. Phoebe Sheavyn, *The Literary Profession in the Elizabethan Age*, 2nd ed., rev. R. W. Saunders (New York: Barnes and Noble, 1967), p. 82.

18. *The Professional Writer in Elizabethan England: A Study of Nondramatic Literature* (Cambridge, Mass.: Harvard University Press, 1959), p. 148. The preceding quotation, from Barnabe Googe's *Eglogs, Epytaphes, and Sonnetes*, is on p. 143.

19. See Martha Craig, "The Secret Wit of Spenser's Language," *Elizabethan Poetry: Modern Essays in Criticism*, ed. Paul J. Alpers (New York: Oxford University Press, 1967), pp. 447–72. Craig's (and my) point is not of course that Spenser's words are meaningless, but that they are meaningful in surplus. As Craig notes, Spenser's fluid way with words was facilitated by loose typographical conventions. See, too, Alpers on Spenser's syntax, *The Poetry of "The Faerie Queene,"* pp. 70–106.

20. Parfitt, *Ben Jonson*, p. 94. See also Parfitt's interesting suggestions regarding the special means by which Jonson achieves this effect, in "Compromise Classicism: Language and Rhythm in Ben Jonson's Poetry," *SEL* 11 (1971), 109–23. Arguing mainly for Jonson's place in a native tradition of the plain style, Parfitt suggests (correctly, I believe) that Jonson's special plainness and "hardness" may be attributed in part to an intersection of Latin and

English syntax (119–22); this argument approaches from a different direction the observations of Barish (*Ben Jonson and the Language of Prose Comedy*, pp. 69–77).

21. See Walter Benjamin, "The Work of Art in the Age of Mechanical Reproduction," *Illuminations*, ed. Hannah Arendt, trans. Harry Zohn (New York: Harcourt, Brace and World, 1968), pp. 222–23.

22. Marotti, "All About Jonson's Poetry," *ELH* 39 (1972), 236, 211–13; Richard C. Newton, "'Ben./Jonson': The Poet in the Poems," *Two Renaissance Mythmakers: Christopher Marlowe and Ben Jonson*, ed. Alvin Kernan, Selected Papers from the English Institute, n.s. 1, 1975–76 (Baltimore: Johns Hopkins University Press, 1977), p. 179.

23. *Ben Jonson*, pp. 109–10. For some reason, Parfitt sees "articulation" and "authority" as separate, even opposed, issues, but that does not vitiate his good analysis. I speculate elsewhere on some reasons for Jonson's avoidance of individualized ethical commitments, particularly in formal verse satire: "'Goe, quit 'hem all': Ben Jonson and Formal Verse Satire," *SEL* 16 (1976), 105–16.

24. See Eisenstein, *The Printing Press*, pp. 22 and 86–88, for references (and reservations); and Miller, *The Professional Writer*, p. 139.

25. Miller, *The Professional Writer*, p. 140. Leo Kirschbaum notes only the barest number of exceptions, in "Author's Copyright in England before 1640," *The Papers of the Bibliographical Society of America* 40 (1946), 43–80. As he notes, the stationer's right had to be protected first, for "it would be foolish for stationers to pay out money to authors for manuscripts that anyone might print or reprint whenever he wishes" (p. 79). Also necessary, however, was a change in conception, from literature as a manuscript to literature as an object, after which it is not the manuscript that is sold, but the right to reproduce the object.

26. *The Complete Poetry of John Milton*, ed. John T. Shawcross, rev. ed. (Garden City, N.Y.: Doubleday, 1971), p. 78. Jonson's poem breaks off in the middle of line 93 with the "editorial" information, "The rest is lost." To tell the truth, the subject was in fact above Jonson's powers. He allowed the vatic role to carry him away, and he predicted a son for the Countess of Rutland, whose husband, by the time of the poem's publication, was widely known to be impotent.

27. On related poems, see Richard C. Newton, "Donne the Satirist," *Texas Studies in Literature and Language* 16 (1974), 427–45. The exceptional quality of the text of at least *The First Anniversary* notwithstanding, Donne almost immediately regretted having "descended to print anything in verse"; see Edmund Gosse, ed., *The Life and Letters of John Donne*, cited in *John Donne: The Anniversaries*, ed. Frank Manley (Baltimore: Johns Hopkins Press, 1963), p. 5.

28. Regosin, *The Matter of My Book: Montaigne's "Essais" as the Book of the Self* (Berkeley and Los Angeles: University of California Press, 1977), pp. 67, 92–93, 169. See the excellent study along these lines by Barry Lydgate, "Mortgaging One's Work to the World: Publication and the Structure of Montaigne's *Essais*," *PMLA* 96 (1981), 210–23.

29. *Paradoxia Epidemica: The Renaissance Tradition of Paradox* (Princeton: Princeton University Press, 1966), p. 430.

30. See Stanley E. Fish, *Self-Consuming Artifacts: The Experience of Seventeenth-Century Literature* (Berkeley and Los Angeles: University of California Press, 1972), pp. 350–52.

31. See the appreciative discussion by Philip Hosbaum, "Ben Jonson in the Seventeenth Century," *Michigan Quarterly Review* 16 (1977), 405–23.

32. Avon Jack Murphy convincingly shows Herrick to have been a good student of Jonson in organizing his poems so as to promote critical reading: "Robert Herrick: The Self-Conscious Critic in *Hesperides*," in *"Trust to Good Verses": Herrick Tercentenary Essays*, ed. Roger B. Rollin and J. Max Patrick (Pittsburgh: University of Pittsburgh Press, 1978), pp. 63–73.

33. See Gordon Braden's exemplary essay, "Herrick's Classical Quotations," in *"Trust to*

Good Verses," ed. Rollin and Patrick, pp. 127–47. Braden gives an excellent account of the literalness first of Jonson's, then of Herrick's classical borrowings, showing how Herrick takes a part of Jonson's achievement with classical borrowings and uses it to establish a textual fellowship with the classics, especially with the writings of Horace. The tissue of borrowing and close imitation in the line of wit could be similarly analyzed.

34. *S/Z,* trans. Richard Miller, preface by Richard Howard (New York: Hill and Wang, 1974), p. 4. The subsequent quotation from Howard's preface is from p. xi.

The Language, and the Truth

RICHARD FLANTZ

‡

The Authoritie of Truth:
Jonson's Mastery of Measure
and
the Founding of the Modern Plain-Style Lyric

What I am calling Jonson's mastery of measure was a major contribution to the authority not only of his own poetic voice, but also of the genre that he was helping to establish in English as a serious and valid alternative to the exhausted but insistent Italianate conventions of lyric. This alternative was the genre of short poems which Bacon had called *poemata*—"Satires, Elegies, Epigrams, Odes, and the like"—a plain-style genre modeled on Latinate forms and open to the native English plain-style tradition.[1] The establishment of this kind of lyric as a vital poetic mode worthy of study, practice, and emulation liberated English poets from the constraint to write only of love, in "ornate" or "aureate" style, and in verse forms borrowed from the Italian masters.

Jonson's lifelong devotion to the genre is well known. He published two volumes of *poemata* in his history-making *Workes* and had a third in preparation. The first of these, *Épigrammes*, he called "the ripest of my studies," and, in the first ode in his posthumous *The Under-wood*, he powerfully affirmed his sense of a lyric both visionary and beautiful in its contribution to mankind:

> Then take in hand thy Lyre,
>   Strike in thy proper straine,
> With *Japhets* lyne, aspire
> *Sols* Chariot for new fire,
>   To give the world againe:
> Who aided him, will thee, the issue of *Joves* braine.
>
> ("An Ode. To himselfe," 25–30)

Jonson endowed his poems, and the genre, with all his prestige as major playwright, laureate, and scholar, and as charismatic leader

59

of literati. But none of this would have sufficed without the effectiveness and authority of the verse itself.

His clear views about good writing were the basis of his poetic practice. "In all speech, words and sense, are as the body and the soule. The sense is, as the life and soule of language, without which all the words are dead." Jonson's "sense" is not to be understood as what post-Saussurean writers call a "signified," which is always limited by the capacity of words, as "signifiers," to formulate it. "Sense," he writes, "is wrought out of experience, the knowledge of humane life, and actions, which the *Greeks* called Ἐνκυκλοπαιδειαν. Words are the Peoples; yet there is a choise of them to be made." What Jonson affirms is the priority and primacy of the *sense* over language or any other medium which seeks to express sense; his distinction sets holistic, pre- or para-verbal cognition apart from the utterance that best approximates it. "The conceits of the mind are Pictures of things, and the tongue is the Interpreter of these Pictures. . . . Then he who could apprehend the consequence of things in their truth, and utter his apprehensions as truly, were the best Writer, or Speaker" (*Discoveries*, 1884–90, 2128–33).[2]

Truth, for Jonson, is the supreme criterion of good writing, as of good living. In all the variations and developments of his central concerns—virtue, valor, fortitude, honesty, self-knowing, centeredness, friendship, civility, the perfectible life, the true love—truth is the highest common denominator: "truth brings / That sound, and that authoritie with her name, / As, to be rais'd by her is onely fame" (*Epigrammes* 67.2–4). The "sound" of truth, however, is not guaranteed by using its "name": the best writer must "seeke the consonancy, and concatenation of Truth" (*Discoveries*, 2114–15). Jonson, then, presents himself as a champion of truth, for whom matters of sound, sequence, and structure are inextricably bound up with that correspondence to sense which gives an utterance its authority. The truest utterance of a sense will require more than words. It may require image, or gesture, or rhythm.[3]

It has often been noted how sparse Jonson's poetry is in any kind of imagery, especially in what we today call sensuously immediate imagery.[4] This is consistent with Jonson's philosophy of poetry. Imagery points to outward things; Jonson's main concern is the inward. Outward beauty is less valuable than inner virtue. And, as "the Pen [of Poetry] is more noble then the Pencill [of Picture]" (*Discoveries*, 1514–15), a poetry based on sound, rhythm, and words can be more noble, and more expressive of the mind, than a poetry based on images.

What Jonson chooses as most fit to utter his sense is that which is the most basic property of poetry as a verbal art: its marriage of diction and versification. Diction is the choice of words, versification their structuring across lines of verse and stanzas, their patternings of sound, their rhythm. The sense that reaches us through all these addresses simultaneously our senses, emotions, intellect. Together with our intellectual apprehension of word meanings, significances of comparisons, antitheses, balancings, recurrences, allusions, and with our emotional responses to these, we apprehend and respond to tone and rhythm. If, as cognitive psychology is teaching us today, language and logical distinctions are functions of the left hemisphere of the brain, music and rhythm functions of the right, poetry can be a medium through which both hemispheres function unitively and simultaneously. What reaches us is more than thought: it is what Jonson called *sense*, a movement of concern, of feeling which incorporates judgment and valuation.[5]

Many aspects of Jonson's diction and versification have been studied in detail.[6] Of all the sounded features of verse, rhythm is his forte, and his mastery here is primarily a mastery of measure. Verse rhythm is a function of measure. Measure, in a line of English verse, can be understood as the product of duration (also called quantity) and accent (also called stress). In prosodic studies, long neglect of quantity derives from the correct perception that quantitative meters were never significantly absorbed into English versification, and from the incorrect conclusion that quantity is therefore not an important factor in verse rhythm. Jonson's strongest and most characteristic poetry makes various use of quantity, of the duration or length of syllables or vowels, in the production of rhythms which help to carry what we have spoken of as the sense beyond the words. The kind of use I want to focus on here, and the one that I feel is responsible for some of his most powerful poetic effects, may be called quantitative augmentation of emphasis on metrically unaccented syllables.

To speak of metrically unaccented syllables implies the existence of an underlying metric norm, an accentual norm such as the "iambic," which had already dominated English verse during the sixteenth century and had been explicitly described by Gascoigne and "naturalized" most thoroughly by Sidney. Jonson, one of whose major objections to Donne's poetry was his "not keeping of accent" (*Conversations*, 48), achieved some of his most impressive results not by violating the accentual meter but by using the fact that a long syllable in an unaccented position may receive an augmentation of emphasis when this is appropriate to the sense.

In "An Epistle to Sir Edward Sacvile," for example, we find a pair of vivid conceits, both indignantly attacking a self-indulging skepticism that denies our power to "know, / Looke to, and cure" our faults:

> Can I discerne how shadowes are decreast,
> Or growne; by height or lownesse of the Sunne?
> And can I lesse of substance? When I runne,
> Ride, saile, am coach'd, know I how farre I have gone,
> And my minds motion not? or have I none?
> No! he must feele and know, that will advance.
>
> (*Under-wood* 13.118–123)

The conceits are Plutarch's,[7] but it is Jonson's rhythm that carries the conviction, the emotion, the growing energy, the anger that such truth is denied, and the sense—when we reach the second conceit—not only of motion but also of the many varieties of physical traveling to which the motions of the mind may be compared. How much is compressed into the long but rapid fourth line quoted here, and how vigorous are the concluding assertions! Or, in "An Epistle to Master John Selden," consider the lines that convey a marveling (and critically acute) admiration at the latter's scholarly achievement in his historical study of English forms and degrees of rank, *Titles of Honour*. Specifically, the admiration here wonders at the quantity of detail and the quality of method concentrated in a single work:

> What fables have you vext! what truth redeem'd!
> Antiquities search'd! Opinions dis-esteem'd!
> Impostures branded! and Authorities urg'd!
> What blots and errours, have you watch'd and purg'd
> Records, and Authors of! how rectified
> Times, manners, customes! Innovations spide!
> Sought out the Fountaines, Sources, Creekes, paths, wayes,
> And noted the beginnings and decayes!
>
> (*Under-wood* 14.39–46)

These lines also imitate the concentration and the energetic qualities they describe and admire. How can their mastery of measure be described?

Traditionalists might want to say that in the most powerful lines Jonson uses spondees as well as iambs. A rough scansion on such a basis—using a dot to mark weak or unaccented syllables, an ictus to mark the strong or accented—might look like this:

    ´   ´ | .   ´ | ´ .| . ´ |. .   ´ |

Ride, saile, am coach'd, know I how farre I have gone,

   . ´| ´ ´| . ´ |. ´ |. ´ |

And my minds motion not? or have I none?

   ´ ´| .   ´ |

No! he must feele

    ´   ´ | .   ´ | .   ´|. ´| .   ´ |

Times, manners, customes! Innovations spide!

    ´   ´| .   ´ | .   ´ | .   ´ | ´   ´ |

Sought out the Fountaines, Sources, Creekes, paths, wayes

But such scansion would undermine the notion of the pentameter norm by allowing the arbitrary introduction of a sixth or seventh stress. An alternative might be to apply the notion of relative accent, based on the idea of four degrees of speech stress.[8] Here, marking degrees of accent, graduating from weak to strong with numbers from 1 to 4, we might scan as follows:

   3   4 | 1   3 | 4 3| 1   3 | 1 1   3 |

Ride, saile, am coach'd, know I how farre I have gone,

  1   2| 3   4| 1   3 | 2   3 |3 4 |

And my minds motion not? or have I none?

  4   3| 1   3 |

No! he must feele

   3   4 |1   4 |1   3 | 1 2|1   3 |

Times, manners, customes! Innovations spide!

  2   3 | 1 4 | 2   4|1   4 | 3   4 |

Sought out the Fountaines, Sources, Creekes, paths, wayes

This scansion shows how the pentameter norm is retained throughout, and how, within it, except for the inversions permissible at the beginning of a line or after a caesura (and one anapest, at the end of the first of the lines above), each foot is iambic. But, although such scansion helps to describe how these lines are read, it does not account for or explain the role of duration or quantity in what happens as we read.

What does happen is that unaccented syllables which can be read

as long sometimes receive augmented emphasis: "Ride," "minds,"
"I" (in "know I," and "have I none"), "he," "Times," "sought," and
"paths." And, when this happens, it often produces even greater
emphasis on the metrically accented syllable that follows. In the
lines above, this happens most significantly in the stresses on "motion," "none," perhaps "he" (which might also have been read as
uninverted: "No! he"), and "manners." The effect, in almost all
these cases, is a rhythmic mimesis of energetic sense. A notation
system that hopes to convey something of how this works must
therefore indicate quantity as well as accent. In the system I propose, the upper markings, for accent, will be dot and ictus; the
lower, for quantity, will use mora and dash for short and long.
While a more sophisticated method could use the relative stress
notation in the upper line, this system allows for more immediate
visibility of the measure:

Ride, saile, am coach'd, know I how farre I have gone,

And my minds motion not? Or have I none?

No! he must feele

Times, manners, customes! Innovations spide!

Sought out the Fountaines, Sources, Creekes, paths, wayes.

In such notation, the appearance of a long, unaccented syllable
(marked ‒) will always suggest the possibility that quantitative augmentation is being activated. One proviso: we are speaking of syllables which can be pronounced as long. Some English syllables are
always long, like "strength," where, though the vowel is short, the
consonants produce the length, or like "saile," where the vowel (a
diphthong) is long; others, however, like "I," may be long or short
depending on the context. What we are attempting to do is to
explain Jonson's intuitive practice, not rules he deliberately
followed.[9]

Although in the examples above it is the *sense* that gains direct
affective/expressive precision by means of quantitative augmenta-

tion, the technique also works interestingly for *meaning*. In the second stand of the Cary-Morison ode, for example, there is a line that cannot be read both meaningfully and metrically unless we give the necessary augmentation of emphasis to a monosyllabic word which is in an unaccented position. Jonson, here, is calling on his reader (on himself?) to consider his (your? my?) life:

> Repeat of things a throng,
>
> | ◡ ◜ | ◡ ◜ | — ◜ |
> To shew thou hast beene long,
>
> Not liv'd; for Life doth her great actions spell,
>
> By what was done and wrought,
>
> In season.   (*The Under-wood* 70.57–61)

The contrast, in the marked line, distinguishes "being" from "living." The line is one we must all misread at first, for not until we read "Not liv'd" do we realize that this "beene" is predicateless, attributeless, not an auxiliary. But when we return, augment the "beene," and, still keeping accent, pronounce "long" as accented and at a necessarily higher pitch, we find that we can hear an apt and sardonic characterization of the really long and essentially empty way of being that Jonson contrasts to a well-lived life. We can hear the sense the lines aim at.

Quantitative augmentation can also suggest *more* meaning, as it does in the first two feet of "To Heaven":

> | ◜ ◡ | — ◜ |
> Good, and great GOD, can I not thinke of thee,
>
> But it must, straight, my melancholy bee?   (*The Forrest* 15)

Here the first foot is inverted, and augmentation occurs on "great" in the second foot. "Great" is thus sounded with emphasis almost equal to that given "Good," while "GOD," the accented syllable after "great," receives even stronger stress, greater length, and higher pitch. The stress pattern across the comma/caesura sets up a powerful ambiguity of mutually enriching meanings heard simultaneously: one as it were ignoring the comma, reading "Good" and "great" as two distinct, though related, attributes of God; the other posing "Good" and "great GOD" in apposition, as two distinct ways of naming the essentially unnameable Deity. The combined effect expresses reverential wonder.

And, in the very center of this poem, after that amazing couplet (13–14) where the preceding meditation suddenly breaks through to an awed and grateful realization of God's immediate presence, the poignant line that is already reacting to the sensation of the imminent withdrawal of this sense of presence gains its intensity from two powerful quantitative augmentations:

> Where have I beene this while exil'd from thee?
>
> And whither rap'd, now thou but stoup'st to mee?
>
> Dwell, dwell here still: O, being every-where,
>
> How can I doubt to finde thee ever, here?   (13–16)

The unaccented "Dwell" and the "O" are augmented, raising the accented "dwell" and the "be" of "being" to a higher pitch of sound and emotional intensity in a moving mimesis of a stage of devotion.[10]

The effects of augmentation are more than local. They can be structural. In "On My First Sonne," for example, the first two lines have almost identical closing measures:

> Farewell, thou child of my right hand, and joy;
>
> My sinne was too much hope of thee, lov'd boy.

(Epigrammes 45)

But the measures of the first four feet make these two lines very different. The first, with its eight long syllables, is more solemn and extended, befitting an apostrophe that characterizes the essence of the dead son as the speaker feels it; the second line is shorter, its feeling ("My sinne . . .") being less comprehensive than that of the first. And the feeling modulates in the next pair of lines, as the penultimate comma advances one foot into the line:

Seven yeeres tho' wert lent to me, and I thee pay,

Exacted by thy fate, on the just day.

The first foot here is not unmetrical. An unaccented position may occasionally be filled by two shorts making up one long. We have already seen this strategy of substituting an anapest for an iamb in line 121 of the epistle to Sacvile. It is a strategy Jonson uses rarely and judiciously. Here, Jonson could have written "Sev'n," using elision as he does in the following foot; his choice not to elide extends the duration of the foot, impressing on us a sense of the speaker's feeling about the duration of the period he refers to. And, in both lines, the effect of the augmentation on the second-to-last syllable ("thee" and "just") seems to suggest some ambivalence about the notions expressed by the augmented words.[11]

In the exquisitely evocative fifth line of the poem—

O, could I loose all father, now. For why

—the length of the unstressed "O" gains it added emphasis; the accented "could," though short, takes a very strong stress in consequence, as if precipitating an outburst of emotion, the "loosing" or venting of the bereaved father's anguish. The measure, then, supports this reading of "loose," but does not rule out the meaning "lose." The imagined letting go (loosing) into an outburst of confused, irrational grief could go to the extreme of the father's wish never to have been a father at all.[12] When we come to "For why" at the end of the line, still reading under the influence of what precedes it, we tend to read it, even before the absence of a comma sends us to the run-on sequel, as part of the cry of anguish, as the "WHY?!" of absolute grief. If we are reading the poem with a sense of its mimesis of an inner drama, we can imagine the speaker inwardly uttering this heartfelt cry, then hearing the word he has uttered—"why"—a word that he then recognizes as belonging to the realm of rational discourse. And, if reason has reappeared, let reason answer.

Reason's answer is a question that nullifies the original "why," but does not erase it or its anguish from the poem or the experience it presents. The answer is a commonplace of Christian/Stoic wisdom, but here it is lyric. Its measure stands in absolute contrast to that of the preceding line. Its tone is solemn, steady, harmonious. And, although it runs on from "For why," it can also be read as an independent statement, uttered by the new voice that has made itself heard at the moment of transition in the utterance of the "why":

$$| \; \smile \; \diagup \; | \; \smile \; \diagup \; | \; \smile \; \diagup \; | \; \smile \; \diagup \; | \; \smile \; \diagup \; |$$

Will man lament the state he should envie?

If we have been attending to the drama, the line resounds with the conviction of winning through to something, though here, as in "To Heaven," there will be a falling away from the moment of transcendence in the center of the poem.

The line we have just considered is an almost perfect normative line of measure. Such a line would have perfect coincidence of accent and quantity throughout—no caesurae, no dieresis—and would be a complete sense unit, beginning- and end-stopped. In iambic pentameter, it would scan thus:

$$| \; \smile \; \diagup \; | \; \smile \; \diagup \; | \; \smile \; \diagup \; | \; \smile \; \diagup \; | \; \smile \; \diagup \; |$$

Such lines hardly occur in actual verse, but the meter, recurring in lines of differing measures, sets up something like an expectancy for them, so that, when an almost normative line occurs after several lines of varying measures, it achieves a kind of heightened aesthetic stasis. Something like this happens in the central lines of both of the poems we have last looked at:

$$| \; \smile \; \diagup \; | \; \smile \; \diagup \; | \; \smile \; \diagup \; | \; \smile \; \diagup \; | \; \smile \; \diagup \; |$$

Where have I beene this while exil'd from thee?

$$| \; \smile \; \diagup \; | \; \smile \; \diagup \; | \; \smile \; \diagup \; | \; \smile \; \diagup \; | \; \smile \; \diagup \; |$$

Will man lament the state he should envie?

The rhythmic stasis at the center, enhanced in both poems by suggestive and harmonious sound-recurrences—"this while / exil'd"; "Will man / lament"—corresponds with a rare identification of the individual consciousness with a universal truth. This identification cannot, however, be maintained. Both poems move into renewed meditation on the particular case, meditation which, though informed now by participation in transcendence, focuses precisely in the pained awareness of the necessary separation from it. In "To Heaven," it is the fallen man, the human "son" deprived of the constant sense of the presence of the divine "Father," who contemplates his state; in "On My First Sonne," it is the bereaved father. From that center of transcendence, both poems move through varying rhythms, departing again from the measural norm, to a closure that never fully returns to the stasis at the center.

Measure as a structuring principle can also serve very witty irony, as in the first quatrain of that highly complex epigram, "On Lucy Countesse of Bedford":

This morning, timely rapt with holy fire,

I thought to forme unto my zealous *Muse*,

What kinde of creature I could most desire,

To honor, serve, and love; as *Poets* use.

(*Epigrammes* 76.1–4)

Here the conventional notion of a poet writing well only when possessed by a "furor" is subverted not only by the sense of what follows—a representation of an act of highly rational consideration and planning—but also by the calm rhythms, the modulations around almost normative lines. This poem is simultaneously a true compliment to a lady and a revolutionary anti-Petrarchan manifesto. Sidney questioned certain Petrarchan conventions and also the concept of the "poet's fury"; in his sonnets Shakespeare subverted the Petrarchan tradition, both in principle (by addressing the sonnets to a young man and then to a dark lady) and in many individual sonnets (in 130, for example, "My mistress' eyes are nothing like the sun").[13] And, though both Sidney and Shakespeare introduced plain-style rhythms and diction into their lyrics, both worked primarily *within* the Italianate convention. Jonson's sonnet, unlike theirs, appears in a sequence of epigrams; here the sonnet form, one Jonson rarely used, is another device to carry the poem's epigrammatic sense. The poem exposes Petrarchan methods: here Jonson does explicitly what the Petrarchan sonneteers do covertly. They too "forme a creature" out of their ideals, but they claim to discover those qualities in some actual—though usually pseudonymic and somehow also ethereal—beloved. Jonson constructs such a "creature" out of his own less ethereal ideals, and only at the end, in an Astrophilian one-liner, clinches the poem by attributing all these characteristics to an actual, contemporary, living lady, not to a beloved, who is named in this last line not by her first name, which would be too stellar in this context, but by her titled name, Bedford.

The urbane wit of this epigram, carried by its calm, almost normative measures, gives us the sense that, though he satirizes Petrarchan poetics, Jonson values the qualities he mentions and believes that the countess possesses them. One may even feel, on reading this poem among others addressed to Lucy of Bedford by Jonson, Donne, and other contemporaries, that the countess would have appreciated not only the compliment to herself but also the nature of the programmatic anti-Petrarchan act this poem accomplishes.

The examples we have looked at so far show something of how Jonson's mastery of measure operated to create that "new charter" which Douglas Bush says Jonson gave to English poetry.[14] In lyric, this meant opening the range of concerns short poems could deal with and establishing a new minimum requirement for good poems: sense ("the life and soule"), a store of learning, decorum, and mastery of diction and versification in the plain style.

To set a minimum poetic norm is not to limit oneself to it. It is to re-create the ground of decorum. Jonson, creating a plain-style norm whose authority rested on the "consonancy, and concatenation of Truth," could call on the resources of the higher style when he needed them, as in his opening to the Cary-Morison ode:

> Brave Infant of *Saguntum*, cleare
> Thy comming forth in that great yeare,
> When the Prodigious *Hannibal* did crowne
> His rage, with razing your immortall Towne. (1–4)

He could also write of love, despite his disclaimer in the opening poem of *The Forrest*, and of female beauty, balancing perceptions of perfection with images of tenuity; and affirming the ideal and idyllic as a possible dimension of actual experience, sometimes through an exquisite control of measure. Consider the marvelous play of quantity and accent in the alternating meters of "A Celebration of Charis," which mark "Her Triumph" in a technical achievement sensitively noted by L. A. Beaurline:[15]

| ◡   ◡   ´ | ◡   ◡   ´ | ◡   ◡   ´ |
Have you seene but a bright Lillie grow,

| ◡ ´ | ◡   ´ | ◡   ´   ◡ |
Before rude hands have touch'd it?

| ◡   ◡   ´ | ◡   ◡   ´ | ◡   ◡   ´ |
Have you mark'd but the fall o'the Snow

| ◡ ´ | ◡   ´ | ◡   ´   ◡ |
Before the soyle hath smutch'd it?   (21–24)

In the interesting alternations of anapestic and hypercatalectic iambic lines that mark most of this stanza, almost all accented syllables are long, unaccented syllables short. In the closing line all the syllables in the first three anapests are long, and the line concludes with an additional iamb, in which the accented syllable is also long:

| •   •   ´ | •   •   ´ | •   •   ´ | ◡   ´ |
O so white! O so soft! O so sweet is she!   (30)

Here the measure, even more than the copula, insists that every projection of sensible beauty mentioned in the stanza "is she."

The establishment of a plain-style norm, then, meant that poems no longer had to depend on elevated style, or on love or beauty as subjects, to be considered good poems. This allowed for a more functional use of elevated language, and for treatments of love by choice rather than necessity. Henceforth a poet's elevated flights could be taken as appropriate to his concern rather than as essential to the demands of an ornate norm. The new lyric—for how could these *poemata* not be called lyric, with their fusings of rhythm, sound, verse melody, line patterning, stanza patterning, word meanings, allusions, figurations, images of speakers and their concerns?—reached beyond the court and the coteries to a larger cultural community, which it helped to form and define.

John Donne was also a pioneer of this genre, and a stronger poet than Jonson in his own mannerist style. But he developed fewer verse forms than Jonson, did not publish his *poemata*, and finally opted out of poetry. Donne wrote some brilliant lyrics and was indeed, as Jonson saw, the first poet in the world in some things. Donne was the extravagant outrider; Jonson, first in English in many things, was much more the weighty figure at the center in the founding of the modern English plain-style lyric. His verse had the "sound" and "authoritie" of Truth, and, because its mastery was comprehensive and central in range of concern and in control of lyric components, it was appreciated not only by readers but also by poets, who saw it as worthy of emulation.

Jonson's is a lyric of serious concern. This idea does not preclude playfulness, wit, role playing;[16] it implies that the *sense* it seeks to utter is serious, that it is a *concern*, if we use this word to name that totality of feeling which incorporates valuations and seeks to articulate or influence the way things are. The lyric of serious concern is simultaneously a subgenre of lyric and a mode to express concern—both an artistic and a communicational mode. It is not "pure poetry." As a plain-style form, its diction and rhythm rest on those of speech—and speech, as distinct from prose or ornate poetic diction, is that in which intonation and gesture accompany words to transmit sense or concern. As activity, it mediates, contemplates, praises, persuades, pleads, blames, complains, laments whatever it conceives, wishes, imagines, always somehow relating to some reality outside the poem.

To the extent that we see Ben Jonson as a founder of the modern plain-style lyric in English and of the modern lyric of serious concern, we may want to say that his line (*"Japhets* lyne"?) extends not only, and not primarily, to Cavalier paths, but to many diverse ways, that among his significant "Sons" are to be numbered poets like Herbert, Milton, Marvell, and—since a list would fill pages—that his poetic project was the original of Wordsworth's more explicit reprise of it (with a move, of course, to different spheres of concern) two centuries later.

Perhaps the source of Jonson's authority is his commitment to and identification of the concerns of poetry and of life. In both, as I have said, truth was for him the supreme criterion. And in both, for this truth to exist, measure—ethical and prosodic—is what matters as a minimum, necessary, or enabling condition. Good poetry need not yet be sublime, and most of Jonson's is not. Sublimity is not the only goal of good poetry; rather, it is a rare achievement. Jonson has achieved that, too, in a poem like "Eupheme," but that is another topic. His poetic authority, however, rests on his entire corpus of *poemata* or modern plain-style lyrics, most of which exhibit his mastery of prosodic measure, several instances of which we have examined. Jonson could have been writing about his vision of poetry (and his words can be read as a description of his own poetic achievement) when he used one of his favorite conceits relating measure to life in the continuation of the lines I have already quoted from the second stand of the Cary-Morison ode:

for Life doth her great actions spell,
By what was done and wrought
In season, and so brought
To light: her measures are, how well
Each syllab'e answer'd, and was form'd, how faire;
These make the lines of life, and that's her ayre.   (59–64)

NOTES

1. Wesley Trimpi invokes Bacon's distinction, explained in *The Advancement of Learning*, between "Poesy *Narrative, Dramatic*, and *Parabolical*" and such *poemata*; see the invaluable *Ben Jonson's Poems: A Study of the Plain Style* (Stanford: Stanford University Press, 1962), pp. 191–92. Trimpi's study relates Jonson's practice in his *poemata* to classical plain-style theories and principles. A necessary supplement to this, which insists also on Jonson's absorption of native plain-style traditions, is George Parfitt's "Compromise Classicism: Language and Rhythm in Ben Jonson's Poetry," *SEL* 11 (1971), 109–21.

2. Jonson lifted this last passage from the opening of Sir John Hoskyns's *Direccōns for Speech and Style . . . exemplified . . . out of [Sidney's] "Arcadia"* (1591). Geoffrey Shepherd, who notes the borrowing in the excellent introduction to his edition of Sidney's *An Apology for Poetry* (Manchester: Manchester University Press, 1973), interprets it in terms of the notion of a "double speech," first internal and then external (p. 59); this notion points in the direction of my distinction between the pre- or para-verbal cognition and the utterance.

3. Such a sense may even be communicated without words, by music, the plastic arts, or dance. Compare Jonson's address to audience and dancers in *Pleasure Reconcil'd to Vertue*, in *Ben Jonson*, ed. Herford, Simpson, and Simpson, vol. 7:

> Then, as all actions of mankind
>   are but a Laborinth, or maze,
>   so let your Daunces be entwin'd
>   yet not perplex men unto gaze.
> But measur'd, and so numerous too,
>   as men may read each act you doo.
> And when they see the Graces meet,
>   admire the wisdom of your feet.
> For Dauncing is an exercise
>   not only shows the movers wit,
> but maketh the beholder wise
>   as he hath powre to rise to it.   (261–72)

4. See especially Parfitt, "Compromise Classicism"; Trimpi, *Ben Jonson's Poems*; Judith Kegan Gardiner, *Craftsmanship in Context: The Development of Ben Jonson's Poetry* (The Hague: Mouton, 1975), pp. 19–20; and Arthur F. Marotti, "All About Jonson's Poetry," *ELH* 39 (1972), 208–37. I find illuminating Marotti's drawing Jonson's dramatic and nondramatic verse together for consideration and his consequent positing of "two kinds of verse Jonson composed—the first a poetry of explosive imagery and perverse imagining, the second a

poetry of more visible control, imagistically spare, prosodically tight, and intellectually lucid" (209). The *poemata* considered here are primarily verse of the second kind.

5. For a pioneering application of recent findings in cognitive psychology to the study of literature, see Earl Miner, "That Literature Is a Kind of Knowing," *Critical Inquiry* 2 (1976), 487–518. My holistic use of the term *concern* is based on Donald Ferguson, "The Nature of the Musical Image," *Centennial Review* 9, no. 1 (1965), 115–34. Ferguson explains how music can, through *tone* and *rhythm*, convey an "image" of such concern. My contention is that rhythm and verse-melody function similarly in poetry, and that this was understood by Jonson, expressed in the passage from *Discoveries* on "sense" and "words," and practiced, as an informing principle, in most of his *poemata*.

6. See works cited in note 4, and Thomas Greene, "Ben Jonson and the Centered Self," *SEL* 10 (1970), 325–48. On Jonson's rhythm, see Felix Emmanuel Schelling, *Ben Jonson and the Classical School* (Baltimore: Modern Language Publications, 1898); John Hollander's discussions of Jonson's enjambments, especially those in *Vision and Resonance* (New York: Oxford University Press, 1975) and in his introduction to his edition of *Ben Jonson* (New York: Dell, 1961); and the very detailed study by Hubert M. English, Jr., "Prosody and Meaning in Ben Jonson's Poems," Ph.D. dissertation, Yale University, 1955, which develops a method of prosodic analysis much more complex than mine and more oriented to considerations of semantic effects.

7. See *Ben Jonson: Poems*, ed. Ian Donaldson (Oxford: Oxford University Press, 1975), p. 151 n.

8. As developed by George L. Trager and Henry Lee Smith, Jr., in *An Outline of English Structure*, Studies in Linguistics, Occasional Papers, no. 3 (Norman: University of Oklahoma Press, 1951). And see John Thompson, *The Founding of English Metre* (London: Routledge and Kegan Paul; New York: Columbia University Press, 1966), esp. pp. 6–7 n.

9. Jonson's sense of length and shortness of syllables is expressed in *The English Grammar* (chap. 3, pp. 468–69); he later speaks of the *"carelesnesse"* of English poets in disregarding *"Quantitie of Syllabes"* and of his own determination to attempt more *"Artificiall"* rhythms (chap. 6, pp. 500–01). Jonson says that the topic is larger than he can deal with in the context of his chapter and promises a fuller treatment "in the heele of the booke"; this promise, however, is not kept.

10. Whether the word "still" is read as "always" or "a little while longer" the effect is the same. The plea is a recognition that what has just been experienced cannot be experienced constantly. For a poetic expression of extreme senses of the presence and the absence of the Divine, see George Herbert's "The Flower."

11. For discussions of this ambiguity, see Gardiner, *Craftsmanship*, pp. 47–48.

12. This ambiguity, which has had readers opting for one reading or the other, is lost in texts where the spelling is modernized.

13. For Sidney, see the *Apology:* on the lyric, p. 137; on divine inspiration, p. 130; and *Astrophil and Stella*, Sonnets 6, 15, 74; for an ingenious discussion of Shakespeare's strategy in this context, see Richard Lanham, *The Motives of Eloquence: Literary Rhetoric in the Renaissance* (New Haven: Yale University Press, 1976).

14. "Jonson, the first great English theorist and practitioner of neoclassicism, the first really direct, learned, deliberate, and single-hearted heir of antiquity, gave poetry a new charter through his dynamic assimilation of the main tradition of the past." I believe this assessment to be valid, especially with regard to the modern plain-style lyric, though Douglas Bush himself sees Jonson's nondramatic poetry as "a minor part of a dramatist's output." I have quoted from *English Literature in the Earlier Seventeenth Century, 1600–1660*, 2nd ed. (Oxford: Oxford University Press, 1962), pp. 107–108.

15. In "The Selective Principle in Jonson's Shorter Poems," *Criticism* 8 (1966), 64–74.

Beaurline's demonstration that in these lines Jonson used quantity as a principle of versification triggered my recognition of Jonson's measural techniques, especially that of augmentation. My scansion and analysis differ from Beaurline's, however.

16. I posit this as an alternative to the view of Lanham, who opposes the "serious" and the "rhetorical" as two mutually exclusive motivations for poetry (*The Motives of Eloquence*).

SUSANNE WOODS

The Context of Jonson's Formalism

Ben Jonson's elegant formalism is without question among his greatest, most characteristic poetic accomplishments and perhaps the single most influential aspect of his poetic practice.[1] However else one might define that formalism, one important feature is surely Jonson's practice and advocacy of what Coleridge called the "translucence" of man's rational faculty through the ordering process of poetic form.[2] Jonson's insistence on formal verse structures—for example, the balance of couplets or the received traditions of ode or epigram—has usually been viewed either as a later-blooming Renaissance classicism, as Wesley Trimpi suggests, or as an early anticipation of Restoration neoclassicism. In noting how Jonson was admired by Dryden's generation, for instance, Herford and Simpson comment that if Jonson had "been born two generations later . . . he would have found himself in a society at some points more intellectually akin than his own."[3] In fact, Jonson's formalism was as much a response to the "new philosophy" that "cals al in doubt" as were the metaphysical speculations of Donne and his followers or the meditations of the religious poets or of Robert Burton and Thomas Browne. The very strength of the formalist heritage that Jonson bequeathed to Herrick and Carew, to Lovelace, and to Dryden himself, suggests that it was a particularly timely and effective response to what was perceived as the breakdown of an essentially unified world view.[4] I would like to emphasize Jonson's formal approach to verse as a response to his time and especially to his immediate literary tradition and contemporary intellectual climate.

Jonson's immediate tradition was the mostly unitary world view of the English Renaissance. A heritage of medieval cosmology and the Thomist-Aristotelian devotion to connecting categories, that view depended on hierarchies and correspondences to present the ordered abundance of God's network of creation. When Richard Hooker, in service to the new English church, reaffirmed natural law's basis in the causal interconnections of God's creation,[5] he relied on a longstanding intellectual tradition that was shortly to be challenged by the new science.

Another immediate, but shorter-lived tradition in Renaissance culture was the mostly unitary perception of literary style. Although the Middle Ages provided the model for an interlocking universe, medieval thought did not provide a common model for the inseparability of matter and manner, of substance and style. The rhetoricians of the twelfth and fourteenth centuries, including such Englishmen as John of Garland and Geoffrey of Vinsauf, followed in the general European mainstream when they made clear distinctions between what were called the "Arts of First Rhetoric" and the "Arts of Second Rhetoric." First rhetoric referred to matters of substance, particularly to topics, evidence, and rhetorical organization. Second rhetoric referred to certain of the less substantive colors of rhetoric and to versification. Although poetry was considered a legitimate branch of general rhetoric the verse by which it was usually recognized was considered the least of its elements.[6]

One characteristic of Renaissance humanism was to reject such distinctions and to insist, instead, on the necessary interconnection between style and substance. Reviving and even extending the principles of decorum established by Cicero and Quintillian, such English humanists as Sir Thomas Elyot and Roger Ascham affirmed the inseparability of manner and matter. In his 1531 *Boke named the Governour*, for example, Elyot proclaimed the substantive magnificence of eloquence:

Lorde God, what incomparable swetnesse of wordes and mater shall [a student] finde in the saide warkes of Plato & Cicero: wherein is joyned gravitie with dilectation: excellent wysedome with divine eloquence: absolute vertue with pleasure incredible: & every place is so infarced with profitable counsaile joyned with honestie: that those thre books be almoste sufficient to make a perfecte and excellente governour.[7]

Similarly, although Ascham's 1570 *Scholemaster* indirectly acknowledged a danger in style pursued for its own sake, it reaffirmed the humanist conviction that matter and manner are inseparable:

Ye know not, what hurt ye do to learning, that care not for wordes, but for matter, and so make a devorse betwixt the tong and the hart. For marke all aiges: looke upon the whole course of both the Greeke and Latin tonge, and ye shall surelie finde, that, whan apte and good wordes began to be neglected, and properties of those two tonges to be confounded, than also began, ill deedes to spring: strange maners to oppresse good orders, newe and fond opinions to strive with olde and trewe doctrine, first in Philosophie and after in Religion: right judgement of all thinges to be perverted, and so vertue with learning is contemned, and studie left of: of ill thoughtes cummeth perverse judgement: of ill deedes springeth lewde taulke.[8]

As a practical matter, however, the old distinctions between content and form remained a feature of the discussion of poetry in the later Elizabethan age. Puttenham divides his great work on English poetics into "Book I: of Poets and Poesie" and "Book II: of Proportion Poetical."[9] Again we see verse structures and versification—the usual forms of poetry—relegated to the less substantive and by implication less important branches of poetics. This view is most clearly stated by Sir Philip Sidney:

Now, for the out-side of it [that is, the externals of poetry] which is words, or (as I may tearme it) *Diction*, it is even well worse. So it is that honny-flowing Matron Eloquence, apparelled, or rather disguised, in a Curtizan-like painted affectation: one time with so farr fette words, that may seeme Monsters: but must seeme straungers to any poore English man. Another tyme, with coursing of a Letter [alliteration] as if they were bound to followe the method of a Dictionary: an other tyme, with figures and flowers, extreamlie winter-starved.[10]

The inseparability of matter and manner on which Elyot and Ascham had been so insistent began, therefore, to break down almost immediately. And the return to an older view of the relation of language and ideas occurred just when the old analogical view of the universe was dissolving. Ben Jonson's response was to insist more emphatically than his predecessors on the importance of formal restraint as the proportionate, and proportioning, reflection of the inseparability of good matter and good manner. In particular, his insistence on balanced and decorous verse structures represented a uniquely important incorporation of and response to new ideas most familiarly outlined by Sir Francis Bacon. While distrustful of fiction generally and of the arts of eloquence specifically, Bacon's ideas had some curious implications for the importance of form to poetry. A brief review of these implications will establish the context of Jonson's formalism and suggest its unique departure from previous attitudes toward eloquence and the arts of second rhetoric.

Bacon's warning against the pursuit of eloquence for its own sake, though conventional in its basic import, helped establish the inductive, analytical attitudes with which the new science approached reality. "The first distemper of learning," says Bacon in a familiar passage from *The Advancement of Learning*, arises "when men studie words, and not matter . . . for wordes are but the Images of matter, and except they have life of reason and invention: to fall in love with them, is all one, as to fall in love with a Picture."[11] Although Bacon goes on, with his usual sense of balance, to acknowledge that appropriate eloquence is decorous and useful, he continues to assume the separability of substance and style. For Bacon, as for most who have assumed that separability, substance takes precedence over style, and attraction to words for their own sake constitutes a futile and fantastical passion. Like the Book of God's Word and the Book of God's Works, words and substance are treated as generally distinct. Their synthesis was a brief and uneasy one, and in Bacon's writings they separate into a concern for the relation between nature and art that was to affect Donne and Herbert, Jonson and Herrick, and indeed most of the better seventeenth-century poets at least until the 1640s and 1650s, when Thomas Hobbes codified many of the implications of Baconian dualism.[12] It may well be that Spenserian style foundered not so much because of the lesser talents of Spenser's followers (such as Giles and Phineas Fletcher), as because the cheerful syncretism that allowed his variety and abundance gave way to a more analytical frame of mind.

A Baconian question that particularly concerned Ben Jonson was the relation of poetry to human learning. Sidney had claimed that poetry, by combining precept with example, triumphed over the other humanities, history and philosophy. Bacon keeps these categories, but his emphasis is very different: "The Parts of humane learning have reference to the three partes of Mans understanding, which is the seate of Learning: HISTORY to his MEMORY, POESIE to his IMAGINATION, AND PHILOSOPHIE to his REASON."[13] Bacon defines "Poesie" as "a part of Learning in measure of words for the most part restrained: but in all other points extreamely licensed: and doth truly referre to the Imagination: which beeing not tyed to the Laws of Matter; may at pleasure joyne that which Nature hath severed: & sever that which Nature hath joyned, and so make unlawfull Matches & divorses of things."[14]

"Poetry" may therefore be taken to refer to verse, or it may be taken to refer to fiction generally, as Sidney and Jonson both tended to use the term.[15] Poetry may therefore refer either to an external manner of communication or to an essential mode of dealing with nature. Bacon goes on to make that double reference explicit when he states that "poesie"

> is taken in two senses in respect of Wordes or Matter; In the first sense it is but a *Character* of stile, and belongeth to Arts of speeche, and is not pertinent for the present. In the later, it is (as hath beene saide) one of the principall Portions of learning: and is nothing else but FAINED HISTORY, which may be stiled as well in Prose as in Verse.[16]

There is an important paradox here. For Bacon, as for most who see style and substance as separate entities, substance is much more valuable than style. But Bacon succeeds in implying that, in the case of poetry, the reverse may be true. He begins, of course, by noting that "poesie" is, on the one hand, only a "*Character* of stile." On the other hand, insofar as poetry is "one of the principal Portions of learning," which may in fact "be stiled as well in Prose as in Verse," it allows for unnatural fantasy. As a result, what is apparently the most superficial aspect of poetry, its verse, may be its most valuable aspect. For when Bacon says that poetry "is a part of Learning in measure of words for the most part restrained," he surely refers to the fact that what he calls poetry is usually written in verse, and order and restraint are undoubted values throughout *The Advancement of Learning*. When he adds that poetry is "in all other points extremely licensed," he surely means its imaginative and fictional qualities, of which he does not wholly approve.

Bacon's rhetorical distinctions between matter and manner hearken back to the arts of first and second rhetoric. What is new is Bacon's implicit evaluation. Although verse "belongeth to the Arts of Speeche," it provides at least formal regulation of the licenses of fantasy and so deserves attention and respect not conceded to other merely stylistic features of rhetoric.

Ben Jonson, in his theory and practice and in their subsequent influence on generations of poets, is the first major voice to make explicit the value of versification in restraining the excesses of fantasy, and he is the first major advocate to prefer verse forms that best accommodate the natural shapes of rational discourse to verse forms that merely convey a sensuous musicality.[17] Jonson's 1619 *Conversations with William Drummond of Hawthornden* remain our best record of his stated opinions. The relaxed, sociable context for the views Drummond recorded may have produced less temperate judgments than Jonson offers in the more contemplative *Timber, or Discoveries*, but both sources support a coherent vision of the role of verse in the pragmatic, inductive, and analytical world of early seventeenth-century dualism. While his *Discoveries* generally offer more comprehensive, detailed evidence of Jonson's opinions, the *Conversations* suggest that in practical discussions of poetics and poetic techniques he emphasized versification. Versification is the subject with which the *Conversations* begin and one which returns throughout. Specifically, Drummond's notes begin with Jonson's reaction to the verse treatises of Campion and Daniel and continue with his praise of the couplet.

Daniel specifically condemned the couplet, on the grounds that, in "long and continued Poems," couplets become "very tyresome, and unpleasing, by reason that still, me thinks, they runne on with a sound of one nature, and a kind of certaintie which stuffs the delight rather than intertaines it." [18] His preference was for stanzas of "alternate or cross rhyme," largely because such rhyme contributes to a metricality more subtle and complex than that permitted by the rhyme of couplets or by the lack of rhyme in the blank verse that Campion preferred. Jonson, on the other hand, announced to Drummond

that he had ane intention to perfect ane Epick Poeme intitled Heroologia of the Worthies of his Country, it is all in Couplets, for he detesteth all other Rimes, and he had written a discourse of Poesie both against Campion & Daniel especially this Last, wher he proves couplets to be the bravest sort of Verses, especially when they are broken, like Hexameters and that crosse Rimes and Stanzaes (becaus the purpose would lead him beyond 8 lines to conclude) were all forced.   (*Conversations*, 1–11)

Jonson's advocacy of the couplet rests primarily on the premise that manner, including form, must follow matter, and not the reverse. He answers Daniel directly, preferring the couplet because his "purpose" (that is, the semantic content of the verse, its "matter") can best be served by a verse form that has no artificial termination. The standard ottava-rima stanza frequently used for both narrative poetry and epigrams would not, for example, serve Jonson because he might need more than eight lines to make his statement, or because his narration would not fit into eight-line units, or perhaps because he would need fewer than eight lines, as he does in many of his epigrams. By contrast, couplets provide measure and restraint without artificially overriding the content of the statement. Similarly, Jonson rejects a stiff formality in favor of more natural, graceful, and subtle rhythms. Couplets are approved "especially when they are broken, like Hexameters." Jonson grants the need for mid-line pauses and run-on lines, of which he was himself a master, in order to prevent the formal advantages of the couplet's rhyming and balance from degenerating into boring and artificial repetition.

Overall, Jonson approves formal restraint that accommodates itself naturally and pleasantly to the nature and content of the English language. His famous comment that John Donne "for not keeping of accent deserved hanging" is typically overstated, since Jonson also esteemed Donne "the first poet in the World in some things" (*Conversations*, 48–9, 117–18). But Jonson's insistence on care with accentuation in a line of verse testifies to his belief in restraint. Jonson does not misread Donne; he recognizes, as we do more approvingly in this century, that Donne stretches the limits of what is appropriate for the by then well-established accentual-syllabic verse model, and that in doing so he challenges verse as a mechanism for restraining the perhaps dangerous excesses of the poetic imagination. At the same time Jonson, like Daniel, rejects the artificial attempt to impose restraints of classical quantitative verse on English. "Abram Francis in his English Hexameters was a Foole," Jonson announced to Drummond (*Conversations*, 53–54). This, along with his rejection of Thomas Campion's advocacy of classical meters in English, suggests Jonson's recognition that accentual-syllabic verse is a natural abstraction from the English language, whereas verse based on conventions of syllabic quantity is not.

Throughout the *Conversations* Jonson sees versification in service to the exposition of rational thought. In that service it is potentially much more than mere ornament; it is an agent for clarity, as well as for restraint in a fantastical medium, and as such it can be so much a part of the content that the usual separation between "rhyme" and "reason" disappears. That sometimes this can happen, but sometimes it does not, is perhaps the gist of another of Jonson's statements, also reported by Drummond: "that Verses stood by sense without either Colour's or accent, which yett other tymes he denied" (*Conversations*, 79–80).

To some extent this view of verse as integral to idea is a reaffirmation of the earlier Renaissance (and Ciceronian and Horatian) view of proper eloquence: that when decorum is served, when art labors to serve nature, then style and substance conjoin. There are differences, however. For one thing, Jonson and his contemporaries saw the synthesis of style and substance as more fragile than it had appeared to their near predecessors. They did not have Elyot's or Ascham's faith that to labor for eloquence is also to labor for wisdom. In paraphrasing Quintillian in *Discoveries*, for example, Jonson disparages those "wits" who "labour onely to ostentation; and are ever more busie about the colours, and surface of a worke, then in the matter, and foundation: For that is hid, the other is seene" (691–94). Like Bacon, who insists that all learning be applied "to use, and not to ostentation," Jonson emphasizes the primacy of rational content over affective presentation. Also like Bacon, Jonson apparently sees versification both as an elegant color of rhetoric and as an appropriate restraint on the fantasy and passion that are elemental to poetry. When it is merely the former, it is as dangerous as all other forms of ostentation. He goes on to say in *Discoveries*, perhaps in response to the "musicality" of Campion and Daniel, that

poets there are, that have no composition at all; but a kind of tuneing, and riming fall, in what they write. It runs and slides, and onely makes a sound. Womens-*Poets* they are call'd: as you have womens-*Taylors*.

> *They write a verse, as smooth, as soft, as creame;*
> *In which there is no torrent, nor scarce streame.*

You may sound these wits, and find the depth of them, with your middle finger. They are *Cream-bowle*, or but puddle deepe.   (710–18)

Jonson's own mastery of versification as a means to clarity and restraint has long been noted and is immediately observable in the *Epigrammes* and in such famous testimonies to civilized values as we find in "To Penshurst." The latter is both praise and example of the art that hides art and of the balanced variety that joins art and nature. Jonson's couplets sound each other, but he avoids monotony through his masterful use of mid-line pauses and run-on lines, which of course proceed just so far as the "purpose" of his discourse demands. It is not that the versification of a poem such as "To Penshurst" avoids being pleasing; on the contrary, Jonson's elegant euphonies and rhythmic balances exist in their own right. But they also inform (and are informed by) the substance of the poem. Like the abundance of the Sidneys' park and streams and the generosity of their hospitality, the poem has its own sensuous delights:

> Then hath thy orchard fruit, thy garden flowers,
>   Fresh as the ayre, and new as are the houres.
> The earley cherry, with the later plum,
>   Fig, grape, and quince, each in his time doth come.
>
> (39–42)

The reasoned use of all these delights gives them value and indeed sustains the pleasure. Mere abundance—whether of flora or of the phonological patternings verse allows—leads to an overgrown or overblown excess and stifles rather than liberates the senses as well as the spirit.

Rhyme is an example of a stylistic feature that may be overused or used inappropriately. For some of the humanist advocates of classical measures in English, rhyme was a barbaric version of rhythm (the common etymology was recognized). They thought that it provided an artificial measure based on the rhyming return of like-sounding syllables, which ignored the true weight and natural harmony of syllabic relationship. Although Jonson dismissed classical quantitative measures for English verse, he could rail nonetheless against ostentatious rhyming, in the delightful "Fit of Rime against Rime":

> Wresting words, from their true calling;
> Propping Verse, for feare of falling
>   To the ground.
> Joynting Syllabes, drowning Letters,
> Fastning Vowells, as with fetters
>   They were bound!   (7–12)

In this poem Jonson wishes for the inventor of rhyme "joints tormented," "Cramp's for ever," and even further malediction:

> Still may Syllabes jarre with time,
> Still may reason warre with rime,
>   Resting never.   (52–54)

Of course, in this poem the inadequacies of rhyme are revealed by means of rhyme; in this poem reason does not, and therefore need not, war with rhyme. Even the most despised feature of versification, displayed even in apparent excess, may therefore reveal and illustrate substantial truth.

For Jonson versification is a bastion against the fantastical excesses of mere display. His famous feud with Inigo Jones, through which a number of Jonson's ideas were defined and transmitted to his partisans, grew from Jones's insistence on the primacy of magnificent visual artifice in the masque. Jonson, on the other hand, demanded the primacy of substantive poetic language, as the sarcasm of "An Expostulation with Inigo Jones" makes clear:

> O Showes! Mighty Showes!
> The Eloquence of Masques! What need of prose
> Or Verse, or Sense, t'express Immortall you?
> You are the Spectacles of State! Tis true
> Court Hieroglyphicks! & all Artes affoord
> In the mere perspective of an Inch board!
>
> . . . .
>
> Pack with your pedling Poetry to the Stage,
> This is the money-gett, Mechanick Age!
> To plant the musick where noe thought can teach
> Sense, what they are! Which by a specious fyne
> Terme of the Architects is called Designe!
>
> (39–44, 51–56)

Jonson's respect for the inherent rationality of language, including poetry and its verse, is more than just a rhetorical device. Jonson frequently insists that speech by nature has rational content which must be controlled and understood, even as it sometimes points to the ineffable. As opposed to the meaningless ostentation of which Jonson accused Jones, the formal ordering of speech in verse was for Jonson an agent of clarity when it set out to serve idea more than sound, and an agent for truth when it served recognition rather than excess. As such, the poetic mode of learning may be imaginative, but, properly revealed and restrained by verse, it is as valuable as history and philosophy. Jonson is the first major poet to extend and affirm absolutely Sidney's claim that poetry transcends history and philosophy by reuniting form and substance.

The extent of Jonson's claim for the ordering power of verse may be seen in the Cary-Morison ode. Here Jonson's versification is a principal means of revealing how order and proportion inhere as essential in the universe, despite the devastating appearances of such apparently dominant disjunctions as untimely death. In this poem the measure of verse symbolizes and partakes of a renewed and transcendent vision of the orderly position of man in a frightening, apparently alien universe. Although Morison died young, the importance of his life lies not in its apparent duration; it lies rather in the proportion of his actions and their correspondence with an ideal of virtue:

> All offices were done
> By him, so ample, full, and round,
> In weight, in measure, number, sound,
> As though his age imperfect might appear,
> His life was of Humanitie the Spheare. (48–52)

At the very center of this first true Pindaric ode in English, in measures kept by couplet-rhyming lines often unequal in length, Jonson directs his life and art toward a fusion of style and substance, a fusion of what Elyot had called "excellent wysedome with divine eloquence."

> Goe now, and tell out dayes summ'd up with feares,
> And make them yeares;
> Produce thy masse of miseries on the Stage,
> To swell thine age;
> Repeat of things a throng,
> To show thou hast beene long,
> Not liv'd; for Life doth her great actions spell,
> By what was done and wrought
> In season, and so brought
> To light: her measures are, how well
> Each syllab'e answr'd, and was form'd, how faire;
> These make the lines of life, and that's her ayre. (53–65)

Here, at the poem's formal center, Jonson abstracts, addresses, and centers himself, to tell how the due proportion of verse, naturally presented, provides the model for joining gravity with elegance, restraint with pleasure, or, as he puts it in musical terms of meter and tune, "lines" with "ayre." This stanza summarizes Jonson's response to Baconian dualism, a response that affirms the use of form for pleasantly revealing the unparaphrasable truths proper to the "part" of "humane learning" known as "poesie." At the same time it provides an example of that response, of form embodying and revealing substance. Here verse restrains, or rather proportions, imaginative vision, even as it provides the pleasures we associate with mere "characters of style." Here verse is at one and the same time essence and accident, matter and manner, substance and style. Throughout the Cary-Morison ode, Jonson affirms as literally true the unifying and eternizing value of verse.[19]

Jonson's formalism may be a heritage of Renaissance humanist classicism and it may anticipate some of the values of Restoration writers, but it is more particularly his contribution to the evolution of early seventeenth-century attitudes he shared with Bacon and his contemporaries. Jonson's formalism may derive in part from his understanding and appreciation of classical models, in part from his own unquestionable skills as a manipulator of verse form. But also, and more important, it avows an attempt to unite the apparently disparate and to assert the unity and primacy of the coherent substance of true art. As such, Jonson's formal versification is itself a statement in the history of ideas, as well as a monument to artistic skill.

NOTES

1. Jonson's formalism has been amply discussed. See, for example, *Ben Jonson*, ed. Herford, Simpson, and Simpson, vols. 1 and 2; Wesley Trimpi, *Ben Jonson's Poems: A Study of the Plain Style* (Stanford: Stanford University Press, 1962); George Parfitt, *Ben Jonson: Public Man and Private Poet* (New York: Barnes and Noble, 1976), chaps. 5 and 6; and Joseph H. Summers, *The Heirs of Donne and Jonson* (New York: Oxford University Press, 1970), chap. 1. For the influence of Jonson's formalism on subsequent poets, see Summers, and Earl Miner, *The Cavalier Mode from Jonson to Cotton* (Princeton: Princeton University Press, 1971).

2. In "The Statesman's Manual" (1815), Coleridge defines a "symbol" as "above all characterized by the translucence of the eternal in and through the temporal," and he perceives symbolism as the characteristic artistry of the imagination mediating between idea and object. Despite the philosophical changes from Renaissance to Romantic, this is remarkably similar to Jonson's idea of poetic form.

3. Trimpi, *Ben Jonson's Poems*, pp. 40–41 and passim; *Ben Jonson*, ed. Herford, Simpson, and Simpson, vol. 1, p. 120. At another point Herford and Percy Simpson refer to Jonson as "ultra Elizabethan" (vol. 2, p. 121), an attitude that continues to be popular—see, for example, Gabriele B. Jackson, *Vision and Judgment in Ben Jonson's Drama* (New Haven: Yale University Press, 1968), pp. 7–11. A recent assumption that Jonson's character shows more affinities with a later era is evident in J. B. Bamborough, *Ben Jonson* (London: Hutchinson University Library, 1970), pp. 170, 174–75.

4. Standard discussions of that unified world view include A. O. Lovejoy, *The Great Chain of Being* (Cambridge, Mass.: Harvard University Press, 1936), and C. S. Lewis, *The Discarded Image* (Cambridge: Cambridge University Press, 1963). Its decline in the earlier seventeenth century is a commonplace, described, for example, by Basil Willey, *The Seventeenth Century Background* (London: Chatto and Windus, 1934), especially in chapters 2 ("Bacon and the

Rehabilitation of Nature") and 4 ("The Heroic Poem in a Scientific Age"); by Marjorie Hope Nicholson, *The Breaking of the Circle* (Evanston, Ill.: Northwestern University Press, 1950); and by John Hollander, *The Untuning of the Sky* (Princeton: Princeton University Press, 1961). Most recent critics tend to reaffirm this commonplace, albeit in more trendy terms. See, for example, Michael McCanles, *Dialectical Criticism and Renaissance Literature* (Berkeley and Los Angeles: University of California Press, 1975). An exception is Russell Fraser's idiosyncratic *The Dark Ages and the Age of Gold* (Princeton: Princeton University Press, 1973), p. 265: "In the seventeenth century the skepticism or tolerance which is the nourishing of art yields to the conviction that we can come to enabling conclusions. The essential displacement is anterior to Shakespeare, whose magnitude conceals but does not repair the infectious optimism mining all within. That optimism is something new under the sun. Certitude denotes it." To see the Baconian analytical technique as an optimistic belief in certainty suggests that Fraser takes a nineteenth-century view of scientific optimism, but there is little in the earlier seventeenth century to anticipate logical positivism.

5. *Of the Laws of Ecclesiasticall Politie* (London, 1594), Book 1.

6. For a useful summary of the tradition that most directly affects England, see W. F. Patterson, *Three Centuries of French Poetic Theory* (Ann Arbor: University of Michigan Press, 1935), vol. 1, pp. 3–12. See also Traugott Lawler, *The Parisiana Poetria of John of Garland* (New Haven: Yale University Press, 1974).

7. Book 1, chap. 11, sig. F^v.

8. Book 2, "Imitatio," sig. o2^v.

9. *The Arte of English Poesie* (1589).

10. *The Defense of Poesie* (1595), sig. K4.

11. *The Twoo Bookes of Sir Francis Bacon, of the proficiencie and advancement of Learning, divine and humane* (London, 1605), Book 1, pp. 18^v–19, sigs. E3^v–E4.

12. Most explicitly in his "Answer" to William Davenant's "Preface" to *Gondibert: An Heroick Poem* (London, 1651), pp. 71–88. See, for example, page 78: "Time and Education begets experience; Experience begets memory; Memory begets Judgement, and Fancy; Judgement begets the strength and structure; and Fancy begets the ornaments of a Poem."

13. *Advancement*, Book 2, p. 7, sig. Bb3.

14. Ibid., Book 2, p. 17^v, sig. Ee^v.

15. Sidney, *Defense of Poesie*, sigs. C3v–C4: "Verse being but an ornament and no cause to Poetry: sith there have beene many most excellent Poets, that never versified, and nowe swarme many versifiers that neede never aunswere to the name of Poets." See also Jonson's comment that he "thought not Bartas a Poet but a Verser, because he wrote not Fiction" (*Conversations*, 58–59).

16. *Advancement*, Book 2, p. 17^v, sig. Ee^v.

17. To a certain extent the role of verse as an element of restraint, and as a purveyor of feeling, was recognized throughout the short history of English versification, from George Gascoigne in 1575 to Samuel Daniel in 1603. See Gascoigne, *Certayne Notes of Instruction* (London, 1575); particularly note his rejection of poetic license, his insistence on natural patterns of accent in lines of verse, and his discussion of the proper (that is, decorous) use of verse forms. See Daniel, *Defence of Ryme* (London, 1603), sig. G4: "All verse is but a frame of words confinde within certaine measure."

18. *Defence of Ryme*, sig. H6–H6^v.

19. For a more detailed discussion, see Susanne Woods, "Ben Jonson's Cary-Morison Ode: Some Observations on Structure and Form," *SEL* 18 (1978), 57–74.

MARTIN ELSKY

Words, Things, and Names:
Jonson's Poetry and Philosophical Grammar

Most of the interest in the language of Ben Jonson's nondramatic
works has been devoted to placing him in the Renaissance history
of style or to examining his humanist view of language as an instrument of social and moral judgment.[1] While such issues are of integral importance to Jonson's use of language, critical interest in them
has not sufficiently examined their foundation in a larger tradition,
namely, the tradition concerned with the relationship between
words and things, the Renaissance semantic theory, which, derived
from Aristotle, philosophically describes the referential nature of
language. My contention is that Jonson was profoundly concerned
with this fundamental linguistic issue of the period, an issue associated in England primarily with Bacon and his followers, though
Jonson came to the problem of words and things from a humanistic
rather than a scientific point of view.

The ultimate source of Jonson's understanding of how words
refer to things is the opening passage of *De interpretatione*, where
Aristotle connects language to reality through the soul: "spoken
sounds are symbols of affections in the soul, and written marks
symbols of spoken sounds. But what these are in the first place
signs of—affections in the soul—are the same for all; and what
these affections are likenesses of—actual things—are also the
same."[2] For Aristotle the structure of language reflected the
metaphysical structure of reality as reason perceives reality and
translates that perception into words. Aristotle's semantic theory
later underwent complex elaboration in the medieval philosophical
analysis of language variously known as philosophical, speculative,
or modistic grammar, which explains the referential nature of language: the ontological natures of things *(modi essendi)* are perceived
by corresponding faculties of the mind *(modi intellegendi)*, which,
through the *modi significandi*, express those perceptions as words. In

91

this schema of the relationship between mind, language, and reality, medieval philosophical grammar showed special interest in the relationship of the parts of speech to the ontological status of their referents: nouns, for example, signify being through the mental faculty that perceives being, while verbs signify becoming through the mental faculty that perceives becoming.[3]

It has been argued that Renaissance humanists systematically expunged philosophical grammar from the curriculum as well as from grammar textbooks. Terence Heath has shown how humanists rejected the view of medieval speculative grammarians that the rules governing language can be ontologically deduced, and how, instead, they proposed that the norms of language are not defined by philosophy, but determined by usage and convention.[4] Jonson seems to agree with the humanist position when he quotes Quintillian in *Discoveries:* "*Custome* is the most certaine mistresse of language" (1926). However, even though the humanists did of course react against the elaborate apparatus of scholastic philosophy in medieval speculative grammar, it is clear that several important Renaissance thinkers, including Vives and Scaliger, continued the tradition of philosophical grammar.[5] It is also clear that Jonson knew their work, because he quotes them in *Discoveries* and in *The English Grammar* (which itself, however, shows no interest in philosophical grammar). That speculative grammar was known in England is also suggested by Bacon's reference to it in *De augmentis scientarium* and by Wilkins's reference to medieval and Renaissance philosophical grammarians in his *Essay Towards a Real Character, and a Philosophical Language.*[6]

One of the ways in which language reflects reality, according to the principles of philosophical grammar, inheres in the ability of words to name things in accordance with their metaphysical natures; the mind that allocates words to things therefore acts with philosophical knowledge. Virtually the same idea is repeated in John Hoskyns's *Direccōns for Speech and Style* (c. 1599), which Jonson quotes verbatim in *Discoveries:*

The conceits of the mind are Pictures of things, and the tongue is the Interpreter of those Pictures. The order of Gods creatures in themselves, is not only admirable, and glorious, but eloquent; Then he who could apprehend the consequence of things in their truth, and utter his apprehensions as truly, were the best Writer, or Speaker. Therefore *Cicero* said much, when hee said, *Dicere rectè nemo potest, nisi qui prudenter intelligit.* (2128–35)[7]

Through Hoskyns, Jonson refers to the world of things, "the order of Gods creatures," as an "eloquent" language in itself, to be reflected in human language in turn made eloquent by the mind's apprehension of the order of things. Eloquence is thus justified through recourse to the Aristotelian basis of philosophical grammar. Although neither Hoskyns nor Jonson was interested in the elaborate technical details of medieval speculative grammar, the Aristotelian concept of the relationship between mind, language, and reality, was for both of them the theoretical underpinning of the humanist concern with eloquence.

However, Renaissance thinkers who continued the tradition of medieval philosophical grammar modified it significantly because of their deep concern with language as a social medium, "the Instrument of Society," as Jonson quotes Vives (1882–83), or the vehicle of the moral perception of human behavior in society. This is especially so in Jonson's case. As a result, humanist notions of the relationship between mind, language, and reality reflect the belief that the reality named in language is social and moral, rather than metaphysical, and that the ability to name this reality depends on the ethical condition of the mind assigning words to things. "*Language* most shewes a man," Jonson quotes Vives again, because it is "the Image of the Parent of it, the mind" (2031–33). Words, then, not only name moral and social things in the external world; they also indicate the quality of mind that speaks them. For Jonson, as for other humanists, the problem of *res et verba*, considered as both a semantic and a stylistic concept, has moral and social implications.

Jonson is particularly interested in the social and moral implications of Vives's humanist version of the Aristotelian connection between mind and language. In this respect Jonson's most important ancient predecessor is Seneca, who represents at least one source of humanist interest in the social and moral context of language, and whom Jonson quotes: "Wheresoever, manners, and fashions are corrupted, Language is. It imitates the publicke riot. The excesse of Feasts, and apparell, are the notes of a sick State; and the wantonnesse of language, of a sick mind" (954–58). (The analogy between language and apparel, which recurs throughout *Discoveries*, is particularly relevant to the humanist image of language as the garment of thought.) For Jonson such social and moral consequences of the Aristotelian semantic theory are inescapable, since, for him, as for most humanists, language cannot exist apart from society, whose moral condition it reflects. Jonson's view of

language as utterance emerging from the minds of speakers underlies his social understanding of language: words do not exist apart
from speakers, and speakers do not exist apart from society. The
moral quality of the words speakers utter is finally determined by
the ethical conditions of their minds, which can only be nurtured
by a good society.

Moreover, because the matter of language is so often in Jonson's
poetry the moral order embodied in a social order, eloquence rests,
then, on the ability of the morally sensitive mind to transform the
moral order into a linguistic order through the decorous fitting
together of *res et verba*. In this way language becomes the "Image"
that reflects the moral capacity of its "Parents," the mind. Only the
moral condition of the mind can guarantee an accurate correspondence between the moral order and the mind's ideas of that order.
A dysfunction of this process—the result of a morally corrupt
mind—manifests itself in what Hoskyns called, as Jonson quotes
him, "Negligent speech," or misappareled thoughts, which "dis-
credit the person of the Speaker" as well as his "reason and judgement" (2151–53).

I would like to suggest that this view of language generates at
least some aspects of Jonson's poetic language, as well as his view of
the function of the poet. That is, for Jonson the poet's office is to
maintain the proper connection between words and things in a
social world that habitually subverts that connection through de-
ceit, flattery, and cunning, each an abuse of language that distorts
the referential link between words and the things they name. The
Aristotelian correspondence between mind, language, and reality
becomes the basis for judging the right word for the right thing in a
kind of ethical semantic decorum. And, where the state of social
reality makes that decorum difficult, as Jonson thought it did in
seventeenth-century England, only the moral poet's unimpaired
mind can preserve the proper reference of words. In this sense,
Jonson translates philosophical grammar into a theory of poetic
diction.

Jonson's concern with the moral and social dimensions of verbal
reference is most evident in poems constructed to redefine highly
charged words denoting moral qualities applied to another person.
For instance, *The Under-wood 26* is an ode addressed to a young man
recently wounded in battle. For his eagerness to return to the field,
Jonson calls him "High-spirited friend" in the poem's almost epis-
tolary opening line. Jonson praises the young man's behavior in
battle with military words like "honour" and "valour," but he

warns him that his reckless desire to return to the battleground is nothing more than the urge to act with a "covetous hand" that "Must now be rayned," as Jonson morally fixes the meaning of honor and valor in an aphorism: "True valour doth her owne renowne command / In one full Action." Going beyond that one action would violate the very meaning of the word "valour," Jonson here suggests, as he ethically readjusts his young friend's limited understanding of the word.

In the end the poet asks the young man to think, instead, on the meaning of his action, to reach a higher plane of moral existence than that achieved by the action itself: "'Tis wisdome, and that high, / For men to use their fortune reverently, / Even in youth." The reintroduction of words like "high wisdome" and "reverently" harks back to the poem's opening address to the poet's "High-spirited friend," converting that congenial, almost familiar salutation into an appellation of moral significance. The entire poem hinges on the opening address identifying the friend, only to rename him in the end by urging him to follow a more significant model of social behavior. The poet's self-proclaimed role here as spiritual physician is thus coextensive with his linguistic role as the provider of a significant moral referent, or *res*, to a socially familiar phrase, or *verbum*.

Jonson's ode to his "High-spirited friend" is characteristic of his attempts to focus his poetry on someone's ethical being. In the process, Jonson often draws attention to the poet's ethical relationship to the person he writes about, an important theme aptly illustrated in the epigram "To William Camden" *(Epigrammes 14)*. For Jonson, Camden is a subject to whom a poet may properly affix words bearing laudatory ethical attributions, because their reference is secured by the moral and intellectual personality of Camden. As a result, the poem comprises a series of nouns and adjectives naming Camden's moral being in a manner particularly appropriate to a man who is himself a namer of public essences; Jonson credits him as one "to whom my countrey owes / The great renowne, and name wherewith shee goes," referring of course to Camden's *Britannia*.

Many of the naming nouns and adjectives Jonson applies to Camden have their etymologies in Augustan, Virgilian Latin ("grave," "name," "faith," "authoritie"), as well as in words of English origin with strong classical associations ("things," "weight"). The quality of the poet's moral being, which enables him to identify Camden's, is likewise associated with Roman origins: Jonson notes his "pietie," a virtue he most likely learned from Camden himself, his humanist teacher. The poet's subject, the poet's word, and the poet himself are all connected with classical ethical ideals. Etymologies here secure the moral nature of both the poet and his subject in the common medium of classical ethical institutions. In this sense, the moral reference of the poet's *verba* to the *res* of Camden's moral being is a dimension of humanist history, as Camden's naming of Britain is, too, an act of the historical understanding. As the repository of unchanging ethical ideals for emulation in Renaissance England, classical antiquity also provides linguistic institutions (diction based on classical etymology or on English equivalents of Augustan words) which stretch across centuries, guaranteeing the linguistic connection of an English *verbum* and the *res* to which it refers, by defining the word, its referent (Camden), and the mind that assigns one to the other (the poet's "pietie").

The "Ode. To Sir William Sydney, on his Birth-day" *(The Forrest 14)* also locates the connection between words and their referents in history, this time in the history of the Sidney family; the word that names William is here the Sidney family name. Jonson defines for William the kind of behavior that will enable him to live up to what "will be exacted of your name," thus teaching him how to "live in honor, as in name."[8] The moral significance of the Sidney name is defined by the honorable life and actions of the Sidney family; young Sidney's understanding of the poet's advice will ensure that the name can be properly applied to him, that he, too, can give the name a legitimate referent, that he shall not prove like those who bear noble names and titles unmatched by noble deeds, and who therefore die rather than live by their names. Jonson transforms Sidney's congenial birthday gathering into a social ritual of moral significance: the naming of Sidney. He exhorts the young man to become the embodiment of an ethically conceived semantic decorum, his name and essence corresponding perfectly. The poet enjoins his *res*—William's social and moral behavior—to unite with the *verbum*, his name, that properly signifies that behavior.[9]

Jonson's view of the Sidney name typifies his calling on representative English contemporaries as models of the proper union of name and referent. For instance, Jonson praises Sir Henry Nevil *(Epigrammes 109)* as a subject proper to his poetic muse because Nevil's virtuous deeds "make" and therefore match his fame, title, and name. In all probability, Jonson acquires this interest in names from his teacher, William Camden; on several occasions, both in

Britannia and in *Remaines Concerning Britaine*, Camden explains the origins and etymologies of British names, almost always including in his remarks some reference to Plato's *Cratylus*.[10] However, whereas Jonson uses Latin etymologies to connect English words to Roman social and ethical institutions, he shows little interest in the Platonic understanding of etymology: setting aside Plato's major concern in the *Cratylus*, Jonson is not particularly concerned with the aboriginal roots by which words—outside of any social context—reveal their intrinsic relationship to the things they signify. Nevertheless, Jonson does share Plato's and Camden's thesis that the name (or, perhaps more important, a noble title) of a person in some way reveals his essence—for Jonson, a moral or social essence. By reminding people of their names and titles, Jonson reminds them of their obligation to live up to, and provide examples of, the social and moral ideals represented by those names, so that, as Camden commands, "wee faile not to be answerable to [our names], but be Nostris nominis homines."[11]

In this way, Jonson fulfills his obligation as a humanist poet actively engaged in the affairs of his society, advising and correcting it. But as Hugh Maclean has pointed out, Jonson replaces the humanist poet's office as poet-counselor to princes with that of poet-counselor to members of the ruling and learned classes.[12] This is nowhere more evident than in the many poems addressed to nobles and intellectuals. As a result, many of Jonson's poems are marked by the appearance of important English names, a matter he draws attention to in "To all, to whom I write" *(Epigrammes 9)*, and in his dedication of the *Epigrammes* to the Earl of Pembroke. For Jonson, a name may variously represent ideals associated with a renowned family, a title defined by a place, or simply a reputation one has earned, and it is particularly in these associations of names that the moral and social implications of Jonson's Aristotelian view of words' relationship to things are most evident. It is more than just a flashy tour de force, for instance, that Jonson's funereal praise describing Margaret Ratcliffe's virtues *(Epigrammes 40)* emanates acrostically from the letters of her name. The acrostic expresses an almost ritual identification of name and moral nature perceived and celebrated by the poet.

In fact, in some of the *Epigrammes*, Jonson portrays himself as having an almost magical power over the names of people he addresses. For instance, in one of the two epigrams addressed "To Person Guiltie" *(Epigrammes 38)*, Jonson's power over his subject lies in his discretion to withhold or reveal his subject's name: "Be-

leeve it, GUILTIE, if you loose your shame, / I'le loose my mod-
estie, and tell your name." In "An Epistle to Master John Selden"
(Under-wood 14), Jonson enunciates his poetic office as the praiser of
names. Though he "confesse[s]" that "I have too oft preferr'd / Men
past their termes, and prais'd some names too much," he explains
that " 'twas with purpose to have made them such," in an example
of *laudando praecipere.*[13] The nature of the poet's relationship not
only to his subject but to his patron is for Jonson a matter of the
relationship names bear to the moral content to which they refer. In
"An Epistle to Sir Edward Sacvile" *(Under-wood 13)*, Jonson proclaims that a patron must be someone the poet would feel proud to
acknowledge; Jonson "Should shame / To have such doe me good, I
durst not name." Similarly, patrons should avoid the poet who
possesses nothing but a name. Just as the poet must beware of
rendering the name he praises empty because the person named
does not live up to the moral reality ascribed to that name, so, too,
the patron must not seek an empty name to bestow his favor on.

In the epistles to Selden and Sacvile, the word *name* retains its
classical association with the idea of reputation (for Jonson, moral
reputation). In this sense, a name is the sign of the moral essence of
a person, and, when it is good, it is the poet's duty to preserve and
celebrate the essence signified by the name. Such is the case in "To
William Earle of Pembroke" *(Epigrammes 102):*

> I doe but name thee PEMBROKE, and I find
> It is an *Epigramme*, on all man-kind;
> Against the bad, but of, and to the good:
> Both which are ask'd, to have thee understood.

Here the celebration of Pembroke's name renders it the generic
name of virtue itself, a technique characteristic of Jonson's poetry.
To name Pembroke is to pronounce the generic name of goodness,
just as to name a morally corrupt patron—or, for that matter, any
morally depraved person—would be to pronounce the generic
name of a vice. Even worse is either to be so morally corrupt as to
have only a privative moral nature, and therefore to be nameless, or
to have a name that signifies the opposite of one's being, both of
which possibilities are realized in the title character of the epigram
"On the Townes honest Man" *(Epigrammes 115)*.

Jonson explicity discusses his interest in the moral dimension of
generic names in *Discoveries*, when, borrowing from Erasmus, he
puzzles that people are offended by his poems that "tax vice gener-

ally" without mentioning any specific person or name.[14] Jonson is both angry and amused. He suggests that those who object to such poems name themselves as the specific manifestations of the vices generically named in the poems: they "publish that on [their] owne forehead, which [they] saw there noted without a title." Playing on "title" as the name of both a person and a poem, Jonson thus constructs the following analogy: as a title, at the head of a poem, names that poem, so Jonson's poem, on the heads of his detractors, becomes their title, naming the vice they admit to by seeing offense in the poem. In this way, they supply the specific name (their own) as the species of vice generically named in the poem and *its* title (2304–45). The same naming process appears in poems like "On Sir Voluptuous Beast" *(Epigrammes 25)* and "To Censorious Courtling" *(Epigrammes 52)*, as well as in poems praising virtuous individuals, whose proper names become the generic names of virtues. Jonson makes the members of the aristocracy the archetypes of civilized behavior, as they take their places in the vocabulary of a philosophical language turned social and moral. As nouns name metaphysical being in *grammatica speculativa*, names in Jonson's poems signify moral condition, just as they do for Jonson's teacher, Camden.

Accordingly, the climax of the Cary-Morison ode *(Under-wood 70)* occurs in the last triad, when Jonson announces Cary and Morison as "Two names of friendship." Their surnames become explicit, generic names of friendship, as they themselves embody that universal:

> You liv'd to be the great surnames,
> And titles, by which all made claimes
> Unto the Vertue. Nothing perfect done,
> But as a CARY, or a MORISON.

The ethical nature of Cary and Morison, signified by their names, becomes itself a language as "Each [is] *stiled*, by his end, / The *Copie* [in the stylistic and rhetorical sense] of his friend" (emphasis added). Moreover, Cary and Morison take on the "force" of "faire example" and so become "a Law / . . . left . . . to Man-Kind; / Where they might read, and find / *Friendship*, in deed, was written, not in words." In Cary and Morison, the perfect union of name and deed approaches the status of the ideal language of hieroglyphs.

References to people as if they were pages in a book, or as if they were language itself, are part of a metaphoric strand that runs through much of Jonson's poetry. Jonson "stiles" (playing perhaps on the Latin *stilus)* Don Surly "a most great foole" *(Epigrammes 28).* Likewise, Jonson praises Sir Henry Goodyere *(Epigrammes 86)* for "making thy friends bookes, and thy bookes friends," metamorphosing friends into books to be read and studied as a source of the knowledge of virtue. Perhaps the same metaphor lies behind Jonson's compliment to Benjamin Rudyerd *(Epigrammes 122),* when he says, "I need no other arts, but studie thee." The personal qualities of an exemplary figure are identified with language in a more potent manner in Jonson's epigram "To Mary Lady Wroth" *(Epigrammes 105).* Jonson pays an elaborate compliment to Lady Wroth by imagining what would happen if all the written records of antiquity were lost, "All historie seal'd up, and fables crost [out]," so that no "mention" were left "of a *Nymph,* a *Muse,* a *Grace."* Not only the charms but even the very names of the classical goddesses could be restored in the person of Lady Wroth, who, possessing their graces, would also "make a-new" their names. Lady Wroth is a compendium of classical "historie" and "fable" because, like them, she contains in her person the "treasure" of the golden age, "th'age before." As such, she is *"Natures Index,"* in a phrase that not only intends "index" to mean nature's "sign" of itself but plays on the word's meaning as a summary of a book's contents. In Latin, *index* can also mean a book's title, as in *index libri.* That is, Lady Wroth contains in her own being the names of the classical deities, as if she were a printed book. She appears here metaphorically as language itself endowed, as announced by the vatic poet, with almost cosmic powers of creation, or re-creation, through the power of names.

Similarly, in the "Epistle. To Katherine, Lady Aubigny" *(The Forrest 13),* Jonson plays the poet-priest celebrating Lady Aubigny's family name and heritage on the occasion of the impending birth of her child. Jonson praises "your name, and goodnesse of your life" in a world of dissembling that debilitates language by making it "almost a danger to speake true / Of any good minde, now." In a world that misrepresents the connection between word and thing, Jonson the poet presents himself as one of the few morally unimpaired minds that can properly match name and referent. It is an act of moral—and linguistic—courage that Jonson bids Lady Aubigny "see / In my character, what your features bee." Jonson here plays on "character" taken in the sense that Theophrastus wrote characters: Lady Aubigny is an exemplar of virtue. But he also refers to a "character" as both a letter of the alphabet and a hieroglyphic emblem: like the perfectly congruous connection between the hieroglyphic sign and its referent, the letters of Jonson's verse create a morally just connection between *res et verba* in praising Lady Aubigny's name, since, unlike the fraudulent "painting" of the social world, his verse truly does contain the moral reality Jonson ascribes to it, matching as it does her "vertue" to her "great title." [15]

The sentiment is particularly poignant, since Jonson thinks of his moral stance in naming Lady Aubigny as a way of naming himself as well. To be identified as one "at fewd / With sinne and vice" is to be "in this name" (that is, of poet, social critic) and, as such, to be "given out dangerous" by those who "For their owne cap'tall crimes . . . *indite* my wit" (emphasis added). The lies of the poet's enemies constitute an inversion of the poet's language, which names things according to their natures. The Cary-Morison ode, the epigram on Lady Wroth, and the epistle to Lady Aubigny all portray exemplary English nobles as embodiments of a perfect language come alive, a language in which name and referent decorously unite, perceived, celebrated, and perpetuated by the ethically clear mind of the poet.

The philosophical background of Jonson's understanding of language, rooted in Aristotelian semantic theory and its continuation in medieval and Renaissance philosophical grammar, places him in intellectual kinship with Bacon, himself a major force in the seventeenth-century survival of philosophical grammar. That is, both Bacon and Jonson were searching for an ideal language in which mind, words, and reality might each mirror the other perfectly, an ideal language Bacon thought to be expressed, as he understood it, in the "congruous" relationship between sign and referent embodied in the Egyptian hieroglyph (*De augmentis* 6.1). Considering Jonson's deep concern with the distortion of the proper relationship between *res et verba*, it is not surprising that he greatly admired Bacon; he refers to him three times in *Discoveries* (915–23, 932–37, 2090–95), twice as a master of eloquence and once as a reformer of language concerned with those "distempers of learning" which damage the relationship of words to things, though Jonson does not seem to grasp just how devastating Bacon's critique of language actually was. It is of course ironic that one of the most important proponents of the humanistic view of language should muster the authority of the figure most associated with the attack on that view as a major impediment to the advancement of learning. But, whatever their obvious differences, however diverse their viewpoints, both Bacon and Jonson were deeply interested in a

similar issue: whereas Bacon was concerned with the scientific repercussions of the abuse of the relationship between *res et verba,*
Jonson was concerned with its moral and social repercussions.

Admitting that their views were of course by no means identical,
I have tried to suggest that Jonson and Bacon responded, in their
different ways, to a cultural and linguistic malaise that was, ever
more intensely, to occupy the minds of linguistic theorists in the
seventeenth and eighteenth centuries. Still, Jonson's was a conservative position in the debate over *res et verba.* Bacon and his
followers for the most part gave up the possibility of words' close
correspondence to things, in any spoken language. They sought
correspondence instead in an invented, artificial "philosophical"
language of written signs modeled on hieroglyphs and ideograms
which altogether circumvent the use of words and thereby avoid
the idols of the marketplace. Jonson, on the other hand, tried,
against what he thought to be tremendous odds, to hold words and
things together in a poetic language modeled on spoken language.
In fact, if one can distinguish in Jonson's poetry between a lexical
level of language—the level at which individual words refer to
things—and a syntactical level of language, carried by the rhythmic
patterns of speech uttered in a social context, then it is only in the
intersection of the two that real language can exist for Jonson.
However, it was the particular social context of Jonson's day that
portended ethical subversion of language's referential function, and
it is the feeling of this threat of corruption that gives moral urgency
to Jonson's muscular attempt to hold words and things together.

Jonson could not say with la Primaudaye's equanimity, undis-
turbed by anxiety or qualification, that words are "the markes and
paintings . . . of . . . things . . . and . . . thoughts . . . for if we
have no wordes and names to make [things] knowen by, we must
alwayes have the things themselves present, that wee may point at
them with the finger, which is impossible." [16] Instead, Jonson's
anxiety over the coming apart of words and things did not long
precede the scattered, solipsistic voice of Democritus Junior, a
voice no longer securely anchored in a sense of moral and social
reality. Democritus Junior's speech was to reflect a "roving
humour," a "running wit, an unconstant, unsettled mind" that can
scarcely name itself, and that envisions a world of moral names
without referents. Declaring that "We may peradventure usurp the
name, or attribute it to others for favour, as Carolus Sapiens, Phi-
lippus Bonus . . . etc., and describe the properties of a wise man,
as Tully doth an orator, Xenophon Cyrus," he asks, "But where

shall such a man be found?" It is in such a world that "honesty is accounted folly; knavery, policy"; in this world flourish "such shifting, lying, cogging, plotting, counterplotting, temporizing, flattering, cozening, dissembling" [17] perversions of language and mind that Jonson sought to prevent.

NOTES

Research for this paper was supported in part by a grant from The City University of New York PSC-CUNY Research Award Program.

1. See especially Wesley Trimpi, *Ben Jonson's Poems: A Study of the Plain Style* (Stanford: Stanford University Press, 1962), and George Parfitt, *Ben Jonson: Public Poet and Private Man* (New York: Harper and Row, 1977). See also the essays by Susanne Woods and Richard Flantz in this volume.

2. *"Categories" and "De interpretatione,"* trans. J. L. Akrill (Oxford: The Clarendon Press, 1963), p. 43.

3. For a survey of medieval grammatical theory, see G. L. Bursill-Hall, *Speculative Grammars of the Middle Ages* (The Hague: Mouton, 1971).

4. "Logical Grammar, Grammatical Logic, and Humanism in Three German Universities," *Studies in the Renaissance* 18 (1971), 9–64. For the excision of philosophical grammar from Renaissance grammar textbooks, see W. Keith Percival, "The Grammatical Tradition and the Rise of the Vernaculars," in *Current Trends in Linguistics*, vol. 13, *The Historiography of Linguistics*, ed. T. A. Sebeok (The Hague: Mouton, 1975), pp. 231–75.

5. See Julius Caesar Scaliger, *De causis linguae latinae* (Lyons, 1540), sigs. (:)iiij^r–(:)vii^r; Vives attacks philosophical grammar in *In pseudo-dialecticos*, but draws on its precepts in *De censura veri*, in *Opera omnia*, ed. G. Mayans (Valencia, 1782–90), vol. 3, pp. 142–48. For an overview of Vives's views on language, see Eugenio Coseriu, "Zur Sprachtheorie von Juan Luis Vives," in *Festschrift zum 65. Geburtstag von Walter Mönch*, ed. Werner Dierlamm and Wolfgang Drost (Heidelberg: Kerle, 1971), pp. 234–55.

6. *The Works of Francis Bacon*, ed. James Spedding, Robert Leslie Ellis, and Douglas Denton Heath, 7 vols. (London: Longmans, 1857–74), vol. 4, pp. 438–40; John Wilkins, *An Essay Towards a Real Character, and a Philosophical Language* (London, 1668), p. 297. For the persistence of philosophical grammar in the Renaissance, see two essays by Vivian Salmon, review of *Cartesian Linguistics* by Noam Chomsky, *Journal of Linguistics* 5 (1969), 165–87, and " 'Philosophical' Grammar in John Wilkins' Essay," *Canadian Journal of Linguistics* 20 (1975), 131–60.

7. For the passage Jonson quotes from Hoskyns, see *The Life, Letters, and Writings of John Hoskins, 1566–1638*, ed. L. B. Osborn (New Haven: Yale University Press, 1937), p. 116.

8. Lisle Cecil John shows how the facts of William Sidney's sometimes violent life elucidate the seriousness of Jonson's admonition, in "Ben Jonson's 'To Sir William Sidney on his Birthday,' " *Modern Language Review* 52 (1957), 168–76. See also Claude J. Summers and Ted-Larry Pebworth, *Ben Jonson* (Boston: Twayne, 1979), pp. 170–71.

9. The subject of naming in Jonson's poetry has also been discussed by Edward Partridge, "Jonson's *Epigrammes*: The Named and the Nameless," *Studies in the Literary Imagination* 6 (1973), 153–98, and by Helen Marlborough, "Herrick's Epigrams of Praise," in *"Trust to Good Verses": Herrick Tercentenary Essays*, ed. Roger B. Rollin and J. Max Patrick (Pittsburgh: University of Pittsburgh Press, 1978), pp. 159–69.

10. See *Britain*, trans. Philemon Holland (London, 1637), p. 23, and *Remaines Concerning Britaine* (London, 1614), pp. 46–53. (On page 36, Camden refers to a view of language based on Aristotelian semantic theory.) See also "A posthumous Discourse. . . . By Mr. *Camden*," in *Camden's Britannia, . . . with large additions and improvements. Published by Edmund Gibson.* (London, 1695), col. 189.

11. *Remaines*, p. 53. For Camden's remarks on the representation of moral ideals in Christian names, which "stir men up to the imitation of them whose names they bare," see page 48.

12. "Ben Jonson's Poems: Notes on the Ordered Society," in *Essays in English Literature from the Renaissance to the Victorian Age, Presented to A. S. P. Woodhouse*, ed. M. MacLure and F. Watt (Toronto: University of Toronto Press, 1964), pp. 56–57.

13. See Summers and Pebworth, *Ben Jonson*, p. 123. The concern with naming that Jonson expresses in the epistle to Selden (61–86) fits the poem's occasion: it was first printed in Selden's *Titles of Honour* (London, 1614), whose subject is the meaning and origin of ancient and modern noble titles. Selden's attitude toward names and titles is similar to Jonson's: "*He that is* . . . *both* discended *from truly Noble Parentage, and withall* following *their steps, or adding to their Name, is the* Gentleman *that may lawfully glorie in his Title*" (sigs. b4ʳ–b4ᵛ).

14. Attacking vice generically was an issue much discussed in the satire of the period. See, for example, Jacques's observation, in Shakespeare's *As You Like It* (2.7.70–87), that those who complain about his satirical remarks identify themselves as worthy of them.

15. In their discussion of the poem, Summers and Pebworth point out that Jonson plays on his similarity to Lady Aubigny (*Ben Jonson*, pp. 164–65); both are untouched by the "debased world" in which they live: "The personal experience of the poet establishes his credentials, and inasmuch as it is an exemplum of lonely virtue, it reflects the very qualities Lady Aubigny comes to embody in the course of the poem which mirrors the beauties of her mind."

16. *The Second Part of the French Academie*, trans. T. B[owes] (London, 1594), p. 98. In the same passage, la Primaudaye rejects any language based on the same hieroglyphic signs that Bacon was to find so necessary a generation later.

17. Robert Burton, *The Anatomy of Melancholy*, ed. Holbrook Jackson (1932; rpt. New York: Random House, 1977), pp. 17, 76, 65.

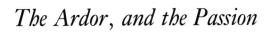

The Ardor, and the Passion

JACK D. WINNER

The Public and Private Dimensions
of Jonson's Epitaphs

In the dedication of *Volpone*, Ben Jonson portrays himself as fulfilling
"the offices, and function of a Poet." This fundamentally public
definition of his vocation accounts for the social orientation of much
of his verse; to cite one example, it results in his concern in *Epigrammes* with "leading forth so many good, and great names . . . to
their remembrance with posteritie" (Dedication, 18–21). To view
the poet as someone responsible for certain "offices" and "functions" argues that the poet accrues duties he must discharge and
suggests further that his role involves primarily social experience.
Jonson's poetry vindicates this argument, since the bulk of it employs forms—satires, complimentary epigrams, verse epistles—
which allow him, as he describes it in the dedication of *Volpone*, to
"effect the businesse of man-kind." But, if this attitude helps to
explain the formality of structure and tone in much of Jonson's
poetry, it also suggests the possibility for conflict when the poet
must deal with an inherently private experience in what he views as
the public forum of poetry. In Jonson's epitaphs, a social form that
constitutes a subgenre of *Epigrammes*, we find such a phenomenon.
Most of the epitaphs respond to the poet's sense of his office by
publicly celebrating the virtuous dead in poems distinguished by
their polished surfaces and emotional control. When Jonson comes
to meditate on the deaths of his own children, however, he cannot
so easily sustain the perspective of the public mode, and, particularly in "On My First Sonne," the personal depth of the experience
strains against the poet's sense of his office. By approaching this
poem through the other epitaphs in *Epigrammes*, we can define a
pattern that generally obtains in the epitaphs and then explain how
Jonson's divergence from this pattern contributes to the distinction
of "On My First Sonne." [1]

Jonson has received much praise for his epitaphs, beginning with that of his nineteenth-century editor William Gifford, who esteemed him "the best writer of epitaphs that this country ever produced."[2] Jonson's success as a writer of epitaphs certainly derives in part from his suggestive restraint, one in which he quickens relatively sparse diction and generalized statements with graceful, often songlike cadences. The tone of these poems is self-assured, the poet's presence unobtrusive, almost impersonal, his attention directed to praising the life and achievements of the deceased. Here he concentrates not so much on addressing the emotional complications brought by death as on designing an artful compliment that serves as a memorial to his subject and as a consolatory pattern that gives form to the emotions of his audience. A good example illustrating this point comes in the three poems Jonson wrote on the death of Sir John Roe (*Epigrammes* 27, 32, and 33). According to the account Jonson gave Drummond of Hawthornden, Roe was a close personal friend who, in his mid-twenties, died of the plague in Jonson's arms. But the poems do not relate much about the friendship shared by the two men; nor do they to any significant extent explore the poet's emotional response to Roe's death. The first concludes simply, with an ideal Christian response to death: "Oh happy state! wherein / Wee, sad for him, may glorie, and not sinne." The propriety of the sentiment—that, when a pious man dies, good Christians should rejoice because he will now enjoy eternal blessedness—combines with the use of the plural pronoun to displace emphasis on the two men's personal relationship in favor of a more ceremonial, more public statement. Thus, although the poem does not prompt us to question its sincerity, neither does it capture the immediacy of emotion that one might expect, given the circumstances of Roe's death.

In epitaphs on persons whom Jonson probably knew less well than Roe, the tendency to formality becomes even more marked. Drawing skillfully on the conventions of the funeral elegy, Jonson creates poems that are touching yet distant and that convey emotion more through suggestive technique than through direct statement. In poems such as those on Margaret Ratcliffe, Salomon Pavy, and the elusive Elizabeth, L. H., Jonson's masterful reworking of the commonplaces that provide a rationale for death not only helps to generalize the experience voiced in the poems, but also renders the poet's voice impersonal. Indeed, the poet's craftsmanship and his willingness to subjugate his personality to the formal design of these poems make their self-conscious artistry the highest tribute he can pay to the deceased. The poems, in other words, perfectly fulfill the poet's duty of "leading forth . . . good and great names."

Always quick to comment on the artistic principles that inform his poetry, Jonson includes in his elegy on Lady Jane Pawlet an indication of his preferred method of praising the dead: "who doth praise a person by a new, / But a fain'd way, doth rob it of the true" (*Under-wood* 83.37–38). These lines echo those in which Jonson insists that his *Epigrammes* follow "the old way, and the true" (*Epigrammes* 18), and they underline the importance he places on circumscribing invention within the rigors of tradition. Among his epitaphs, we can locate this fidelity to tradition in two sources. The first source is, of course, Jonson's familiarity with the classics, particularly *The Greek Anthology* and Martial's epigrams, an easy familiarity that surely enhanced his talent for composing such lines of resonant simplicity as that which concludes his epitaph on Margaret Ratcliffe: "Earth, thou hast not such another."[3] But, if one purpose of the epitaph is to praise, another is to offer consolation to the friends and the family of the dead person, and here Jonson turns to the rich tradition of Christian consolation that developed in sixteenth-century England. Works such as Thomas Wilson's extremely popular *The Art of Rhetorique* offered various schemes for accounting for death, and these soon worked their way into poetic expression, as the epitaphs and elegies appearing in *Tottel's Miscellany* testify.[4] Not surprisingly, for almost every consolatory sentiment in Jonson's epitaphs we can find an analogue in works such as Wilson's and Tottel's. Hence the pleasant conceit that ends Jonson's epitaph on Salomon Pavy—"But, being so much too good for earth, / Heaven vowes to keepe him"—reflects a common sentiment that Wilson, too, covers: "GOD at his pleasure hath taken them both to his mercie, and placed them with him, which were surely over good to tarie here with us."[5] The very familiarity of sentiments such as this accords with Jonson's purpose in most of the epitaphs of *Epigrammes:* to offer public praise, which distinguishes the individual as it firmly anchors the poem's sentiments in a conventional wisdom available to all.

If Jonson contents himself with reshaping commonplace attitudes toward death, he bestows freshness on his epitaphs through his virtuosity of technique. The conventions for elegiac poems in the late sixteenth century, as A. L. Bennett points out, "had more to do with the ordonnance and the consolatory sentiments expressed than with the form [rhyme and meter] of the verse."[6] Jonson's epitaphs reflect the freedom of form available to the writer of epitaphs, and his felicitous choices in rhyme, meter, and diction at times invest his epitaphs with lyric qualities. (It is worth noting that his epitaphs often resemble his songs in meter, as in his fondness for octosyllabic and headless iambic tetrameter lines.) But Jonson also draws on technique to accent formality. For example, his "Epitaph on Margaret Ratcliffe" (*Epigrammes* 40) is not only an acrostic; it also unfolds in four quatrains rhyming in a pattern of *a b b a*, only to return in the seventeenth line to rhyme back to the first. The explanation for the use of such an elaborate scheme appears in Jonson's epitaph on Sir John Roe, where he offers his lines as "better ornaments" than "scutcheons." As ornaments, the epitaphs pursue not heightened emotional response but beauty of form appropriate to the life of the subject. In contrast to the supple iambic pentameter couplets that set the norm in *Epigrammes*, then, the varied patterns of the epitaphs aspire rather to conspicuous than to concealed art.

In a number of the epitaphs Jonson displays his talent for modulating emotion through a poem's structure. His epitaph on the child actor Salomon Pavy (*Epigrammes* 120), for example, derives its delicacy of tone in part from its alternate three- and four-stress lines:

> Weepe with me all you that read
> This little storie:
> And know, for whom a teare you shed,
> *Death's* selfe is sorry. (1–4)

The verse form merits attention because it blends so well with the occasion: writing on the death of a child, Jonson composes his "little storie" in short lines. The use of the word "storie," with its connotations of a conscious design, further identifies the poem as an artifact rather than a spontaneous outpouring of emotion. The care with which Jonson allows his "storie" to unfold gradually disengages the reader from intense involvement with the subject, in part because it is in reality a little drama. The poem opens with a series of personifications—Death, Nature, Heaven—and then launches into a witty conceit based on the boy's acting career:

> And [he] did act (what now we mone)
> Old men so duely,
> As, sooth, the *Parcae* thought him one,
> He plai'd so truely. (13–16)

The theatrical trappings help to neutralize the possibly tragic over-
tones of the young boy's death. The reader, at first invited to
participate actively in the mourning, now assumes the more distant
role of a spectator.

In the course of shaping his ingenious central metaphor, Jonson
neatly integrates a number of commonplaces of the funeral elegy.
In a few lines he commends both the boy's personal and his physical attributes ("grace and feature"), gives an account of his activities
(that he was an actor), establishes the time of his death ("scarse
thirteene"), and finishes with the previously mentioned, consolatory explanation of his demise: "But, being so much too good for
earth, / Heaven vowes to keepe him." The poem's diction also
reveals a familiarity with the conventions: the epithet, "the stages
jewell," appropriately adapts a popular expression—pearls and
jewels being numerous in funeral literature—to the boy's career.
These commonplaces do not intrude on the poem, but they do
contribute to the recognition of the poem as an artifact. Likewise,
the speaker's own presence in the poem almost escapes notice.
After the hortatory "weepe with me," he remains in the background. Nor is the reader given much opportunity to grieve. Instead, the life of Salomon Pavy and its metaphorical elaboration
occupy our attention. An overemotional response, either the poet's
or the reader's, would disturb the subtle interplay of wit and
solemnity that the poem seeks. Consequently, the epitaph achieves
dignity through its restraint while it offers consolation through
its wit.

The poem on Salomon Pavy defines the mean for Jonson's
approach in the epitaph. His speaker tends to contain emotion
rather than to generate it and to pay tribute to the dead rather than
to mourn them. This artistic distance derives much of its effect
from such consciously formal style as we see in the opening of the
"Epitaph on Elizabeth, L. H." (*Epigrammes* 124): "Would'st thou
heare, what man can say / In a little? Reader, stay." The poet's
reference to himself as "man," rather than "I," frames the voice of
this poem as a collective expression not of personal emotion but of
more general feeling. The word "little" also recalls the "Epitaph on
S. P." and, as in that poem, indicates the author's concern with
pregnant brevity. Here, however, it also translates into a metaphor
for both the woman and the poem: to borrow from Jonson's Cary-
Morison ode, "in short measures, life may perfect bee."

The sense of little prevades the poem, even down to its headless
iambic tetrameter couplets. Working within the short line, Jonson

imparts dignity to it through subtle manipulation of rhythm, as in the second line, where the punctuation demands a lingering pause on both "reader" and "stay." "Stay" literally arrests the reader and asserts the poet's command over the poem's technique and emotive force. In fact, the emotion is articulated primarily through the self-consciousness of style. The deft antithetic parallelism of the two couplets commending Elizabeth's beauty and virtue expresses the poem's general concern:

> Under-neath this stone doth lye
> As much beautie, as could dye:
> Which in life did harbour give
> To more vertue, then doth live. (3–6)

Each statement stresses the fullness of the woman's life—"as much," "to more"—and reflects a preoccupation with developing the underlying trope of *multo in parvo*. The compliment adopts an affective form: as the woman's life was, so the poem will be.

Jonson's refusal to divulge Elizabeth's full name and the suggestiveness of his language concerning his reasons for this omission have piqued the curiosity of more than one reader.[7] But this reticence simply accentuates the poem's overall reticence. That is, the poem exists in a state curiously detached from emotion, its development focusing on the final summing up, which, significantly, works at two levels: that of the woman's death (there is no suggestion of an afterlife) and that of the formal artifact of the poem, opening in its final line into a complete iambic tetrameter that "fulfills" the previous seven-syllable lines—"Fitter, where it dyed, to tell, / Then that it liv'd at all. Farewell" (11–12). The syntactic isolation of "Farewell" underscores its finality and, at the same time, provides relief, releasing the reader from the attention summoned in the earlier "stay." The entire thrust of the epitaph announces it as an artistic construct. The precise balance of the commands "stay" and "farewell" finds a matching balance in parallel constructions. Like the "Epitaph on S. P.," this poem recognizes no personal relationship between the poet and his subject; in both, Jonson makes the reader aware of an artistic presence standing behind the poem, without delineating that figure's character.

These poems also lack that corona of deeply felt religious belief that we might expect from an epitaph. The poem on Elizabeth, L. H. recognizes no existence beyond the grave, completely shutting off a Christian metaphysical perspective. Although the "Epitaph on

S. P." dwells on an afterlife, the poem becomes so involved with mythological machinery—the Fates, Zodiac, and Parcae—that it loses specifically Christian associations. Even in the epitaph on his daughter (*Epigrammes* 22), Jonson softens the impact of the trauma by coloring her ascent to heaven with mythological shadings: she rises, "plac'd amoungst [Mary's] virgin-traine," in a Christian apotheosis. When Jonson pauses to examine the personal ramifications of death, as he does most dramatically in the epitaph on his son, he pushes the poem in a different direction, one that generates a tension absent from the epitaphs in the public mode. Presented with a moment of personal suffering, the poet responds by using the conventions simultaneously as a bulwark to his grief and as a means to question the effectiveness with which such traditional commonplaces can console in time of loss. But even in "On My First Sonne," perhaps his most personal poem, Jonson refers to himself primarily as a poet, and the experience rendered there is inextricably involved with this fact.

Like the "Epitaph on S. P.," "On My First Sonne" (*Epigrammes* 45) draws much of its power from a daring conceit, here the play on the word "poet" as "maker." The striking difference in the two poems comes from the tone the speaker creates. Where the "Epitaph on S. P." indulges in a playful but decorous wittiness, "On My First Sonne" employs a more austere wit to delve into the mysteries of death and paternal love. In the first quatrain the poet introduces semantic ambiguities that reverberate throughout the poem:

> Farewell, thou child of my right hand, and joy;
>   My sinne was too much hope of thee, lov'd boy,
> Seven yeeres tho'wert lent to me, and I thee pay,
>   Exacted by thy fate, on the just day.

The disturbing collocation of "joy" and "sinne" posits the poem's major oppositions and anticipates later contrasts. The phrase "child of my right hand" at first seems only a thoughtful play on the boy's name, Benjamin (literally, "son of the right hand");[8] but the sense of right as "conforming with justice" echoes ironically in the phrase, "the just day," as the idea of the "right" nudges that of the "just." In the same vein, the note of submission in "I thee pay" is checked by the force of "exacted," which loses its theological connotations by virtue of its subject—the impersonal "thy fate."

Critical discussions of this poem have rightly centered on the conflict between the poet's love for his son and his love for God.[9] In this reading the father's "sinne" arises from his earthly expectations for his son, rather than from his "hope" for him in the spiritual context of the boy's return to God. While I do not disagree with this approach, I should like to refocus it to define the conflict as opposition between the public poet and the private man. In other words, the tumultuous emotions that arise naturally from the death of the poet's son do not necessarily offer a subject appropriate for exploration in the public circumstances of a poem. While he remains loyal to an authentic expression of feeling, Jonson must submit that feeling to the demands of his own sense of literary propriety.

The crux of the poem's ambivalence resides in the word play of line five, when the poet briefly gives full vent to his feelings: "O, could I loose all father, now." The line invites two readings. First, it expresses a wish to lose, or surrender, the feeling of a father, because of the grief the relationship entails. But it also pleads to loose, or unleash, the powerful emotion that the poem has thus far restrained. The latter meaning pinpoints the struggle the father undergoes, attempting to channel his grief into traditional consolatory patterns, but never quite accepting them as adequate. Furthermore, Jonson complicates the contrast between the logic of divine providence and the feeling involved in human relationships by drawing on consolations that are not always logically consistent. In the first quatrain we find two consolatory sentiments whose import does not entirely square, and, examining Jonson's reworking of traditional elements, we can see how he transmutes conventional sentiments into a poignant statement on the human condition.

Thomas Wilson, addressing a woman whose two sons have recently died, gives a Christian context to the classical theme of life as a loan: "God lent you them two for a time, and tooke them two againe at his time. . . . He is very unjust that boroweth and will not paie againe but at his pleasure." In this scheme, the mourner who refuses to acknowledge his indebtedness emerges as insensitive to the largesse of a beneficent God. But, in Jonson's epitaph, whatever comfort such a reasonable proposition may afford becomes entangled in the larger question of the poet's "sinne." That is, his willingness to admit his culpability in his son's death adapts another conventional idea to his own life. As Wilson explains, death may be God's retribution for mankind's sin: "wee may by all likenesse affirme, that they were taken away from us for our wretched sinnes, and most vile naughtinesse of life." [10] Blaming himself rather than mankind, Jonson movingly captures one of the most common reactions to death—that a lapse in the survivor directly implicates him in the cause of death. Moreover, Jonson clouds the distinction between a generous, lending God and a righteous, judging one. By placing these two conventional sentiments in such proximity, Jonson effectively dramatizes the human confusion that can arise when one gropes for an intellectually logical account of an experience that is emotionally illogical. Where drawing on only one of the consolations might have quietly resolved the matter of the boy's death, drawing on both brings out their possible insufficiency.

The father's effort to find solace in a persuasive explanation of his son's death thus becomes the central drama in the poem. After trying to assume responsibility for his son's death, which he first sees as a punishment for his sin, the poet turns to a gentler interpretation, to construe his son's life as a "loan" that he must now pay. Yet neither of these rationalizations quite satisfies, since they lead into the abrupt, impassioned exclamation, "O, could I loose all father, now." In fact, Jonson does not "loose" his feelings; instead, he tests yet another familiar consolation—that he should envy his son for so soon escaping the "worlds and fleshes rage" and for avoiding the misery of aging. As Wilson phrases it, "what folly is it to sorrowe that, for the which they joye that are departed? They have taken now their rest, that lived here in travaile. . . . They have chosen for sicknesse, health: for earth, heaven: for life transitorie, life immortall." [11] This argument too falters, however, because Jonson casts it in the tentative form of two questions, rather than in positive, declarative statements. As a result, this point in the poem finds him yet unable to resolve the congeries of emotions he experiences.

We can understand Jonson's indecision more fully if we recall that as a public poet, the "teacher of things Divine" he describes in the dedication of *Volpone*, he must account for his son's death within an orthodox Christian framework; consequently, he begins by invoking traditional, accepted responses to death. On the other hand, such orthodox doctrine does not obviate the private emotions that spring from him as a man. Only in the final quatrain does he arrive at a resolution of his conflict:

> Rest in soft peace, and, ask'd, say here doth lye
> BEN. JONSON his best piece of *poetrie*.

For whose sake, hence-forth, all his vowes be such,
   As what he loves may never like too much.

Much has been made of Jonson's conceit on poesis—the poet as a maker of things—in which he conflates as his creations both his poetry and his son. What has passed unnoticed is that Jonson very literally makes his son here, since he gives him an imaginary response to deliver from the grave. To use language that Jonson would use, he "feigns," makes a "piece of poetrie," of the scene of his son's reciting these words, and through this fiction he arrives at the only consolation that can accommodate his grief.

For his working out of this final consolation, Jonson may have found a point of departure in Montaigne's essay, "Of the Affections of Fathers to Their Children." Toward the end of the essay Montaigne raises the point that some writers value their works as they do their children. There are even those, he argues, who place a higher value on their literary productions than on their children; this thought may have caught Jonson's attention: "There are few men given unto Poesie, that would not esteeme it for a greater honour, to be the fathers of *Virgils Aeneidos*, than of the goodliest boy in *Rome*, and that would not rather endure the losse of the one than the perishing of the other. For, according to *Aristotle, Of all workemen, the Poet is principally the most amorous of his productions and conceited of his Labours*." [12] Jonson collapses Montaigne's distinction when he puns on "poesis," but Montaigne's essay provides an interesting perspective from which to view the pun's operation in the poem. Earlier in the essay Montaigne muses that intellectual "products," since they issue from the mind and, therefore, allow the author to be both father and mother, represent an achievement nobler than mere biological offspring. [13] By "making" his son in his poem, however, Jonson becomes both a biological and a poetic father; what he cannot do simply as a man—for he can neither return his son to life nor find consolation for his son's death in traditional religious comforts—he can do as a poet, re-creating his son in the epitaph and thereby discovering a way to accommodate his feelings. And, significantly, Jonson does not allude to the boy's mother, as he does in the epitaph on his daughter. More than a brilliant and moving pun, Jonson's conceit stands as a complex response to "fathering," in both a biological and a literary sense. In this light, too, the distinction in the final line between "loving" and "liking" gains in significance, for it suggests that among "what he loves" we can place his poetry, in which he here admonishes himself to moderate his "hope"—to be neither too amorous nor too conceited of his labors.

Just as Jonson moves from consideration of himself as a biological father (who has lost his son) to the discovery of himself as a poetic father (who now makes his son), the poem moves away from the troubling issues that the first eight lines raise. If Jonson's resolution of his predicament helps to make "On My First Sonne" one of his best pieces of poetry, it does not settle the poem's underlying nervousness. Even in the final quatrain the play on "peace/piece" and the quibble on "love" and "like" provoke our awareness of the poet's self-consciousness. Although Jonson does not allow the poem to lose its sense of direction, its impulses do not entirely coalesce. The word play in which he engages bifurcates rather than crystalizes meaning; instead of holding conflicting views in suspension, it underscores their incompatibility. The use of conventional consolatory figures creates a similar effect, as I have pointed out. Rather than assuage the poet's grief, they indicate the limitations of conventional wisdom as an anodyne for human suffering. But Jonson avoids confronting these issues directly. On the whole, the disruptive elements of "On My First Sonne" remain below the surface. The symmetric, three-part structure, the adherence to a linear process of thought, the introduction of the familiar requiescat in pace and hic jacet in the final lines—all these features help to stabilize the poem.

If we approach "On My First Sonne" from the perspective of a private occasion treated in public circumstances, we see that Jonson retreats from a theological to a literary framework to give form and meaning to the poem's experience. As a corollary to this movement, he shifts from speaking simply as a man to speaking specifically as a poet. As a man, Jonson seems unable to sustain the proper Christian resolve in the face of personal tragedy, but he cannot admit that such wisdom is inapplicable to his personal circumstances, unless he would violate the responsibilities of his office. To understand the strain between public and private that surfaces in "On My First Sonne," we should remember the social duties implicit in Jonson's definition of the poet's office: "The Study of [poetry] . . . offers to mankinde a certaine rule, and Patterne of living well, and happily; disposing us to all Civill offices of Society" (*Discoveries*, 2386–88). The pattern of Jonson's epitaphs reveals, I believe, his predisposition for poetry that comes within the bounds of a "Civill office." Secure in treating those experiences that clearly fulfill a social function, Jonson reveals a certain discomfort when he strays from this end; and he draws on this discomfort to produce the unsettling features of "On My First Sonne."

Ultimately, the understated power of "On My First Sonne" resists analysis, but the kind of tension I have discussed becomes more apparent when we restore the poem to its context in the *Epigrammes*. Throughout the collection we encounter a presence who very insistently discourses on his vocation and his approach to it, and who constructs for us a life that revolves largely around this status. *Epigrammes* begins with the request that the reader "understand" (*Epigrammes* 1), reminds him that "I a *Poet* here, no *Herald* am" (*Epigrammes* 9), distinguishes Jonson from such contemporaries as Weever and Davis (*Epigrammes* 18), assumes the duty England "should have done" by creating a "worke [that] shall out-last common deeds" (*Epigrammes* 60), and pauses on numerous occasions to discuss the strategies of the poet's craft. In the poems of praise that make up roughly half the collection, and to which the epitaphs belong, the emphasis falls on rewarding the worthy and presenting the virtuous as models of ideal social behavior. As Jonson tells William, Earl of Pembroke, those who "hope to see / The commonwealth still safe, must studie thee" (*Epigrammes* 102). Into this civic consciousness most of Jonson's epitaphs fit comfortably. It is only when we arrive at the epitaph on his daughter and then at "On My First Sonne" that we sense a personal dimension lacking in other epitaphs. Precisely because the public mode dominates the *Epigrammes*, the touching response to the private occasions that these two poems evoke especially concentrates their emotional impact. By drawing our attention to his dual role of father and poet, Jonson takes on a demanding poetic responsibility, and his delicate, skillful response to both public and private demands profoundly enhances the artistry of these two poems.

NOTES

1. Although individual epitaphs have been discussed at length, little treatment has been given to the group. Wesley Trimpi remarks that "There is not a great deal that can be said about them as a whole"; see *Ben Jonson's Poems: A Study of the Plain Style* (Stanford: Stanford University Press, 1962), p. 180. Claude J. Summers and Ted-Larry Pebworth prove more helpful, finding throughout the epitaphs a subtle tension in which Jonson's intellectual response to death "is often countered by an emotional response which complicates the intellectual acceptance of death," *Ben Jonson* (Boston: Twayne, 1979), p. 152.

2. Ben Jonson, *The Works*, ed. William Gifford, rev. Francis Cunningham, 9 vols. (London: Chatto and Windus, 1875), vol. 8, p. 156.

3. For a discussion of Jonson's epitaphs and *The Greek Anthology*, see John M. Major, "A Reading of Jonson's 'Epitaph on Elizabeth, L. H.'," *Studies in Philology* 73 (1976), 78–79, 82–86.

4. See Douglas L. Peterson, *The English Lyric from Wyatt to Donne* (Princeton: Princeton University Press, 1967), pp. 62–71.

5. Thomas Wilson, *The Arte of Rhetorique*, ed. G. H. Mair (Oxford: The Clarendon Press, 1908), p. 68.

6. A. L. Bennett, "The Principal Rhetorical Conventions in the Renaissance Personal Elegy," *Studies in Philology* 51 (1954), 107.

7. After considering the most likely candidates for identification with her, John M. Major concludes, "No identification of 'Elizabeth, L. H.' is possible" ("A Reading," 78). For other discussions of the poem, see Howard S. Babb, "The 'Epitaph on Elizabeth, L. H.' and Ben Jonson's Style," *JEGP* 62 (1963), 738–44; O. B. Hardison, *The Enduring Monument* (Chapel Hill: University of North Carolina Press, 1962), pp. 124–26; Ossi Ihalainen, "The Problem of Unity in Ben Jonson's 'Epitaph on Elizabeth, L. H.'," *Neuphilologische Mitteilungen* 80 (1979), 238–44.

8. Summers and Pebworth point to a further significance, referring to the naming of Benjamin in Genesis 35:16-20: "The biblical child is given two contrasting names: his mother Rachel, dying in childbirth, calls him Ben-oni, child of sorrow; his father Jacob names him Benjamin" (*Ben Jonson*, p. 154).

9. For discussions approaching the poem through its Christian sentiments, see Summers and Pebworth, *Ben Jonson*, pp. 153–55; Trimpi, *Ben Jonson's Poems*, pp. 182–83; L. A. Beaurline, "The Selective Principle in Ben Jonson's Shorter Poems," *Criticism* 8 (1966), 64–74; Francis Fike, "Ben Jonson's 'On My First Sonne'," *Gordon Review* 11 (1969), 205–20; W. David Kay, "The Christian Wisdom of Ben Jonson's 'On My First Sonne'," *SEL* 11 (1971), 125–36; and J. Z. Kronenfeld, "The Father Found: Consolation Achieved through Love in Ben Jonson's 'On My First Sonne'," *Studies in Philology* 75 (1978), 64–83.

10. *The Arte of Rhetorique*, pp. 75, 68–69.

11. Ibid., pp. 70–71.

12. *The Essayes of Michael Lord of Montaigne*, trans. John Florio, 3 vols. (New York: Everyman, 1921), vol. 2, p. 88. The italics are Florio's. It is not at all unlikely that Jonson would be familiar with the work around the time of his son's death. The first edition of Florio's translation appeared in the same year (1603) as the death of his son. Furthermore, Jonson knew Florio and esteemed him enough to present him with an inscribed copy of *Volpone*, addressing him as a "Loving Father, & worthy Freind [sic]" (see *Ben Jonson*, ed. Herford, Simpson, and Simpson, vol. 1, p. 56).

13. Ibid., p. 85.

RAYMOND B. WADDINGTON

†

"A Celebration of Charis": Socratic Lover and Silenic Speaker

Criticism of Jonson's "A Celebration of Charis" came of age with Wesley Trimpi's book, *Ben Jonson's Poems*. Placing the sequence against the general background of the Neoplatonic *discorsi d'amore*, Trimpi argues that the question of the poems is that of the old lover, particularly as it is developed in Castiglione's *The Courtier*. As Judith Gardiner remarked, Trimpi "provides the indispensable context for the series."[1] Since the appearance of Trimpi's study, the learnedness, the intellectual seriousness, and the coherent design of Jonson's sequence have been accepted without dispute; but the actual interpretation of the sequence remains remarkably fluid: How seriously does "Ben" attempt to live up to the Neoplatonic ideal of the old lover? How does he "revenge" himself on Charis? Is Ben accepted or rejected as Charis's lover? Is Charis satirized as a shallow coquette, no different essentially from the grossly sensual lady who has the last word, or does she represent a reasoned mean between the poet's unworldly idealism and the lady's cynical realism?[2] Most of the differences of interpretation arise from questions of tone and emphasis, which themselves result from the variety of forms, modes, and styles employed in the ten-poem sequence. This poetic variety is an issue that Trimpi's book does not address. Committed to demonstrating that Jonson is a "plain-style" poet, Trimpi's discussion levels distinctions in the series: "By using the tone and simplicity of the plain style, he can give even the worn comparisons of conventional love poetry a passionate plainness rarely equaled in English literature."[3] But "A Celebration of Charis" is actually an exercise in stylistic and generic mixture.

The dominance of such mixture is established by the title of the sequence, "A Celebration of Charis in ten Lyrick Peeces," with its interplay of public ("Celebration") and private ("Lyrick") modes. A celebration, as its etymology proclaims, requires an audience and a

121

public setting, whereas the idea of a group of love poems devoted to a single woman gives us a lyric structure analogous to the sonnet sequence. Poems 1 through 4 address an unspecified audience, carrying out the literal notion of celebration. In 5 through 8, the poet speaks directly to Charis; the first three of these pieces are strictly private and amatory, without a fictive audience. Poems 9 and 10 are, like the eighth, given a court setting, but they introduce two new speakers, Charis herself answering the poet in 9 and, in 10, the unnamed lady commenting on Charis's speech, thus converting the recurrent monologic form to actual *diologhi d'amore*.

The first poem, "His Excuse for loving," is a prefatory argument introducing the themes and topics of the sequence itself: "If you then will read the Storie, / First, prepare you to be sorie" (13–14). The "Storie," the succeeding nine poems, Jonson has organized in three groups of three. Formally, each set of three poems is completed by one that deviates markedly from the prevailing poetic vehicle, the couplets of headless iambic tetrameter which Jonson employs in eight of the ten poems (including "His Excuse"). Number 4, "Her Triumph," and number 7, "Begging another," differ most conspicuously from the dominant, tetrameter couplets because they are songs, written in three stanzas, the last two of which exactly repeat the rhyme scheme and metrical pattern established in the first stanza of each poem. While number 10, "Another Ladyes exception," does use the couplet medium, the difference in length is striking. The preceding couplet poems, ranging in length from twenty-four to fifty-six lines, average thirty-six lines; but this last poem, almost abrupt in its brevity, consists of only four couplets.

Although the employment of the tetrameter couplet as the predominant verse form might seem to effect uniformity in the sequence, the converse is true: these poems, chameleonlike, take on a considerable variety of hues. Judith Gardiner and Sara van den Berg, the two critics who have analyzed form and style most precisely, agree that "A Celebration" is thoroughly mixed.[4]

Generic reference and stylistic interplay within larger literary structures function, Rosalie Colie has reminded us, as something like a shorthand system of metaphor, evoking in allusions the values, attitudes, and assumptions encoded by the genres.[5] So it is with Jonson's sequence. "His Excuse for loving" responds—like Donne's "The Canonization"—to a voiced or anticipated criticism; it asserts the proposition and establishes the terms for debate. The first half of the poem not only advances the argument of propriety in action, the old man presenting himself as lover, but underscores the ambivalent qualifications of this particular actor, with his combination of immortal ability and fallible humanity. "Poëts, though divine, are men" (5); and the divinity of his talent, "the Language, and the Truth" (10), is held in uneasy balance with human emotions, "the Ardor, and the Passion" (11). Gardiner has skillfully analyzed the firm control of this poem, its rhetorical and metrical balance, its careful matching of positives and negatives, the shifts of tone achieved by small stylistic variants within the deliberately ordered structure. But the second poem, "How he saw her," immediately proves the enormous adaptability of the tetrameter couplet. Gardiner notes "a light, flippant tone conveyed through a sing-song use of meter";[6] here feminine rhyme (stupid/*Cupid*) signals comic intention, just as it does later in poems 5, 8, and 9. While prosodic modulation alters the tone to comic, it is the narrative, Ben's attempted usurpation of Cupid's role, that effects the click of generic identification, causing the allusion to fall into place.

"How he saw her," a creative pastiche of the Anacreontic Cupid poems, seems to draw on at least four of the *Anacreontea*.[7] Three and possibly four other poems in "A Celebration" are adapted from specific Anacreontic sources. Perhaps on the authority of Jonson's example in these poems, the iambic tetrameter couplet becomes the form by which Anacreon is both translated and spiritually evoked in seventeenth-century English.[8] If, as Trimpi has argued persuasively, the behavioral model invoked by Ben is Socrates, the ideal lover described by Alcibiades in the *Symposium*, interpreted by Ficino's *Commentary*, and amplified by Bembo's speech in *The Courtier*, a counterpersona has, from the beginning, lurked concealed in the very verse form:

> By the women I am told
> 'Lasse *Anacreon* thou grow'st old,
> Take thy glasse and look else, there
> Thou wilt see thy temples bare;
> Whether I be bald or no
> That I know not, this I know
> Pleasures, as lesse time to try
> Old men have, they more should ply.[9]

Gordon Braden observes that the speaker of the Anacreontic poems "is intelligible mostly as a convergence of repeated clichés: he is old and usually broke, fond of dancing and roses and young boys and girls, and especially liquor, . . . given to observing that we know nothing about the future and little about anything else and advocating a philosophy of the 'present moment.' "[10] For Jonson's purposes, Anacreon's value as a counter to Socrates lies in his being an old lover who is not only, like Ben, a poet, but one committed to "the Ardor, and the Passion," without a care for "the Language, and the Truth." Just as the form of "His Excuse" creates a palimpsest with the portrait of the Socratic lover sketched on the Anacreontic canvas, so "How he saw her" gives us a latent, double image, the inversion of the first. The Anacreontic surface and furniture of the poem should not disguise the fact that the action itself is Socratic. Ficino entitles a chapter of his *Commentary*, "Socrates was the true Lover and was like Cupid";[11] thus, however grotesque the outcome, by trying to become Cupid, Ben seeks to emulate the ideal.

The pattern of mixed thematic genres continues in number 3, "What hee suffered." Whereas the situation derives from Anacreon 33, in which a laughing Cupid wounds the defenseless speaker with an arrow, the generic mind-set is Petrarchan. In contrast to the Anacreontic aggressiveness of the preceding poem, the poet here must helplessly accept the cruel dominance of Charis in phrasing that is a catalogue of Petrarchan clichés: "suffered," "scornes," "prouder Beauties," "hurt me more," "kneeling yeeld," "repented," "fate," "Pittie," "revenge." His comic humiliation as a man drives Ben "To revenge me with my Tongue, / Which how Dexterously I doe, / Heare and make Example too" (24–26).

Astonishingly, his revenge is to acknowledge "Her Triumph" by creating the celebration he initially promised. In assuming his role as divinely favored poet, he regains his lost manhood to the extent of proclaiming his identity through his art—"Which how Dexterously I doe, / Heare"[12]—thereby, as her creator, converting her triumph into his own. No longer the comic sufferer of number 3, Ben presents Charis as if she were the spectacle of an Inigo Jones masque: as his words celebrate the beauty and the wonder, they interpret the significance of her image. The poem, on the witness of its commentators, is the most triumphantly mixed form in the sequence. Trimpi regards it as "a curious mix of classical and Renaissance sources," adducing Ovid, Plato, Spenser, Ficino, Martial, and Jonson's own dramatic works. To Gardiner the mode is "Ovidian transformation," but van den Berg, defining the style as Demetrius's "charis," finds a generic and rhetorical range; Paul Cubeta perceives a Spenserian style, and Anne Ferry detects

Marlovian pastoral. Since such varying accents are not likely to be reconciled satisfactorily, it may be more helpful to focus on the function of resonant, stylistic inclusiveness. As Ferry concludes, "Jonson's speaker is preeminently a poet who adopts the role of lover for literary effects which his readers, assumed to share his poetic inheritance as they share his 'duty' to appreciate 'such a sight,' are expected to recognize." [13]

That the audience may fail in appreciation and the poet in his aspiration to divinity, is the implication of "His discourse with Cupid." The opening poem of the middle group, in some obvious ways it repeats the gestures of "How he saw her," its parallel in the first set. Again Anacreontic and Socratic models interplay through the source material of Anacreon 16 and the connotations of *diologhi d'amore* in title and structure; like number 2, the discourse is a Cupid poem in tetrameters, and, once again, it is a narration of a past event. But a shift in audience indicates an internal transition from celebration to lyric, from the unspecified public, whom he addresses in 1 through 4, to Charis herself, to whom he speaks in 5 through 8. Ben relates to Charis his "late Discourse" with Cupid, who, " 'Mongst my Muses finding me, / Where he chanc't your name to see" (7–8), identified Charis with Venus: "Sure, said he, if I have Braine, / This, here sung, can be no other / By description, but my Mother!" Since in the "Storie" the only piece self-consciously presented as a poem and the only song thus far is "Her Triumph," which does name Charis through the pun on "grace" (17), it follows that Cupid has discovered the preceding poem. [14] This supposition is confirmed by his enumeration of details—face, hair, eyes, and brows—from the blazon of number 4's second stanza.

Cupid, however, either misreads "Her Triumph" or simply refuses to accept Ben's interpretation of his own poem. For the Neoplatonic concept of Divine Beauty emanating through the particular beauty of Charis's face (4.17–20), [15] Cupid substitutes "So, [hath] *Anacreon* drawne the Ayre / Of her face" (5.14–15), trivializing to fantasized sexual attractiveness the serious values that Ben invested in Charis. The process of poetic degradation that began with the comic rhyme by which Cupid announced his discovery (other/Mother) continues as Cupid literally substitutes a redaction of Anacreon 16.15–29 for Ben's third stanza, thereby rendering Ben's marvelous pastoral transmutation of the garden-of-the-face metaphor as a trite compilation of poeticisms for complexion, lips, chin, and neck. With Cupid's naming of Anacreon, the clash of behavioral models for the aged lover becomes fully overt for the first time in the sequence. Significantly, Ben concedes poetic defeat. He does not object on aesthetic grounds to the rewriting of his celebration as Anacreontic cliché; he simply rebuts Cupid's misinterpretation of Charis, doing so by direct statement, not by poetic assertion:

> All is *Venus:* save unchaste.
> But alas, thou seest the least
> Of her good.
> . . . .
> For this Beauty yet doth hide
> Something more than thou hast spi'd.
> Outward Grace weake love beguiles:
> Shee is *Venus*, when she smiles,
> But shee's *Juno*, when she walkes,
> And *Minerva*, when she talkes. (5. 42–44, 49–54)

Ben's distinctions about "Outward Grace" and "weake love" are well taken; but the allusion to the Judgment of Paris ominously suggests the fallibility of weak lovers. By surrendering his claim to poetic divinity, the human Ben gains ascendance; hereafter in the middle group, his poetic skill will serve the weaker love.

We see the consequence in the remainder of this set, which shows the abuse of Ben's poetic art. After the unlocated setting of the first five poems, "Clayming a Second kisse by Desert" enters the world with a thump, placing Charis and her admirers in the milieu of the court at Whitehall. Charis, having permitted Ben "a Morning kisse," is challenged to guess "What my Muse and I have done" (5), as he amuses her with praise at the expense of the other court ladies. "If love has become a game," Gardiner notes, "so too has poetry." [16] Clearly the equation of language and truth has been discarded, since this poet will say anything to achieve his desire. The conclusion of number 6 repeats the action of number 3, its parallel in the first group, by announcing the following song: "Guesse of these, which is the true; / And, if such a verse as this, / May not claime another kisse" (34–36). The parallelism of the two sets is designed for contrast; rather than the poetic gold of "Her Triumph," "Begging another, on colour of mending the former," is debased currency. Trimpi considers it "as beautiful of its kind as 'Her Triumph,'" [17] but we need to reflect on the implications of that kind. It is a "kiss poem," a genre most notoriously associated with Johannes Secundus, whose image could be described as that of a sixteenth-century Anacreon. Indeed, Jonson's specific model might be some one of the *Basia* such as this:

> A Kiss I begg'd, and thou didst joyn
>   Thy Lips to mine;
> Then, as afraid, snatch'd back their Treasure,
>   And mock'd my pleasure;
> Again my Dearest! for in this
> Thou onely gav'st Desire, and not a Kiss. [18]

Jonson's own opinion of the kind can be inferred from "Hedon's Song" in *Cynthia's Revels* (4.3.242–53), a parodic "kiss poem" which serves as "an outstanding example of effete court poetry." [19]

The style that Ben employs for "Begging another" decidedly differs from that of Secundus or Hedon. It gives us yet another notable mixture—an abrupt, dramatic opening, the simulation of the tone and rhythms of realistic speech, the vigorous, relentless pseudologic applied to love persuasion:

> For *Loves*-sake, kisse me once againe,
>   I long, and should not beg in vaine,
> Here's none to spie, or see;
>   Why doe you doubt, or stay?   (7.1–4)

Juxtaposed on a repeated song stanza, all of this suggests too unmistakably the amatory manner of John Donne. [20] Whereas the bee simile (5–6) reduces the famous closing couplet of "Her Triumph" to the merely sensual and cynical, the conclusion of "Begging another" seems to hit at a particular Donnean locus:

> Joyne lip to lip, and try:
>   Each suck [the] others breath.
> And whilst our tongues perplexed lie,
> Let who will thinke us dead, or wish our death.   (15–18)

Interwined tongues replace Donne's twisted eye-beams; Jonson perplexes, while Donne claims to "unperplex." But the motionless posture of the grotesquely self-absorbed couple, "like sepulchral statues," appears the same to onlookers. Jonson may have read "The Extasie" much as Pierre Leguois later did, for here Ben abuses poetic art to aid love of the weaker sort.

"Urging her of a promise," the opening poem of the final set, calls attention to itself by replicating features of numbers 2 and 5, its predecessors in the first two sets. Like number 2, it begins as a narration of past events to an unspecified general audience, but, at line 13, it shifts to the formula of number 5, a present-tense, direct address to Charis herself. The affinity with 5, "His discourse with Cupid," is underscored in the reference to "discourse" in line 1 here; as in both 2 and 5, there is an early instance of feminine rhyme (expected/effected) to establish comic tone. "Urging her" further aligns it with the rhetorical persuasion of the immediately preceding poems; but, whereas 6 and 7 are persuasions to kiss, this is a persuasion to speak, an effort to make Charis "tell / What a man she could love well" (3–4). Despite the fact that the persuasion is largely effected by Ben's urbane, teasing pretense that Charis is a frivolous coquette, the shift from kisses to speech suggests renewed concern for language and truth, rather than the ardor and passion that dominated the middle group, a redirection which the address to a general audience also emphasizes. In the last of the poems spoken by Ben, this deliberate echo of forms and themes introduced in the first and second groups of the sequence evinces an attempt to return to the belief enunciated in "His Excuse," the possibility that both sides of Ben's nature—language and truth, ardor and passion—can be held in balance through his role as lover. A similar balance, new to the sequence, is struck by Ben's concern to make Charis speak her man. Until this point Ben has projected the emotional solipsism typical of the sonneteer-lover—describing his feelings, interpreting events, and explaining Charis from his perspective—but now he tries to move out of this vacuum of idealized fantasies, whether Neoplatonic or sensual, to see what Charis thinks and feels and needs.

Prodded by Ben's importunities, Charis answers in "Her man described by her owne Dictamen"; the last word of the title punningly repeats Ben's final imperative: "*dictamen*," "speak a man." [21] As the usual comic implication of the initial feminine rhyme (ease me/please me) cues us, Charis has determined to have her revenge on Ben, gently mocking his excesses by describing a beautiful young man who is, almost feature for feature, the analogue to the ideal of feminine beauty evoked in 4 and 5. Richard Peterson has observed that Charis also draws details of description from Anacreon 17, directions to a painter for the portrait of a boy, the companion piece to Anacreon 16, directions for painting the portrait of a woman, on which Cupid relied in number 5.[22] Anacreon 17 follows a familiar blazon structure: first, beauties of the face—hair, forehead, eyes, cheeks, and lips—then beauties of the body—neck, breast, arms, stomach, and thighs. Although the general organization of Charis's speech is similar, the resemblance is compellingly close only in the description of the hair, black tipped with gold.[23] Thereafter Charis increasingly parts company with Anacreon. Whereas he anatomizes the boy's body with considerable suggestiveness, she specifies only the harmony of the body's proportions and movements. The Anacreontic model is limited to physical beauty; it does not consider the qualities of character and behavior with which Charis concludes her prescription. Trimpi seems entirely correct in postulating Castiglione's descriptions of the ideal courtier as the prototype for this section of the poem.[24] The organizational principle here is a value hierarchy graduating from least to most important features; movement away from physical characteristics—which are chosen for their teasing unlikeness to Ben—denotes a parallel shift from the comic to the serious, from raillery suiting the occasion to a projection of an ideal differing little from Ben's own: "And from baseness to be free, / As he durst love Truth and me" (51–52).

While most critics concede that the qualities of character and behavior described in lines 34 to 56 are not negligible, and that the real-life Ben Jonson would have valued them, Arthur Marotti complains that they "do not particularly excite her imagination."[25] By this he apparently means that the language and analogies of this section become abstract and general, in contrast to the concrete imagery of the preceding physical description. But there are obvious reasons for this. Rather than through imagery, the excitement of the speaker is revealed through a shift to paratactic sentence structure:

> Nor o're-praise, nor yet condemne;
> Nor out-valew, nor contemne;
> Nor doe wrongs, nor wrongs receave;
> Nor tie knots, nor knots unweave;
> And from basenesse to be free. (47–51)

The run-on sentence structure is reinforced by the intense, rocking-horse rhythm of the passage, the heavy use of short mono- or duo-syllabic words, the insistent patterns of sound repetition. All of this conveys a rising involvement and excitement that contrasts vividly with the amused leisureliness of the physical description. Literally carried away, Charis becomes a rhapsode in her vision.

Charis ends her speech by affirming her commitment to its totality: "Such a man, with every part, / I could give my very heart; / But of one, if short he came, / I can rest me where I am" (53–56). What I would regard as pejorative interpretations of Charis frequently spring from two closely related misreadings of this passage. First, there is the assumption that Charis intends the bawdy play on "part" that "Another Ladye" actually makes in the final poem. Second, there is the presumption that Charis has accepted Ben as her lover, and that "rest me where I am" means, as Anne Ferry puts it, "she concludes that she may after all choose to 'rest' with her sexually satisfying lover." Ferry thinks that "The last joke argues for the supremacy of physical fact over disembodied fancy, and therefore of fat, old 'Ben' over the youth mythologized in Charis' description as a Petrarchan lover. . . . She is made to prefer the actual, living poet because as a flesh-and-blood man he 'for love may die' in the punning sexual sense, whereas the literary lover perpetuated as an ideal image can never 'die.' "[26] To assert that Charis "prefers" the reality to the ideal simply distorts the literal sense of the passage. But what is the evidence for the belief that Charis has taken Ben as a lover, finding him "sexually satisfying"?

In poem 2, Ben ineptly attempted to wound Charis with Cupid's arrow, whereupon—rather like Minerva with the Gorgon shield—she threw a glance that turned him to stone— a transparent allegory expressing her imperviousness to Eros. The behavior in number 3 is purely Petrarchan; Ben's lot as lover is the pain of frustration and abasement. In number 5, he insists that "All is *Venus:* save unchaste"; numbers 6 and 7 try first to charm and then to beg a second kiss from Charis, because the "Morning kisse" he did receive was unsatisfactory, "but halfe a kisse." Finally, what causes Ben to nag Charis into speaking is a collective anxiety of the courtiers: "untill she tell her one, / We all feare she loveth none." In short, the evidence provided by the story indicates that, with the exception of the occasional, chaste kiss, Charis has given Ben very little satisfaction and remains perfectly content to continue that way. It therefore seems extremely unlikely that she would undercut the plainspoken vehemence of her own description of an ideal man's inner qualities for the sake of a tired double entendre. It is not Charis who makes that witticism, but the unnamed Lady of the next poem. The relation between poems 9 and 10 neatly repeats the one that we have seen between numbers 4 and 5. Just as Cupid defames Ben's Neoplatonic celebration by reading it as Anacreontic praise of the earthly Venus, so the Lady degrades Charis's celebration of "Her man" by restating it as an expression of plain lust. Although there are distinct differences between Ben and Charis, in large ways they are alike—both idealists yearning to express the truth but finding, to their frustration, that language is an imperfect instrument for communicating it to a debased world, which of course includes themselves.

Charis's speech is the poem that seems closest in mode to the playfully serious *discorsi* of *The Courtier*, and, as the Lady deconstructs the meaning of Charis's text, so, too, she replaces it with a countergenre, completing the pattern of giving the third poem in each set a different form. Although "Another Ladyes exception" is written in couplets of the pervasive, headless iambic tetrameter, it is far too short (eight lines, as opposed to the average thirty-six), lacking in narrative content, barren of imagery, and sharp in tonal bite to pass as Jonsonian *Anacreontea*. Instead—as the setup and punchline structure and the emphasis on brevity and point would suggest—it is a satiric epigram very thinly disguised as Anacreontic lyric. Since the key phrase from the last line, "one good part," is a quotation from *Epigrammes* 69, "To Pertinax Cob," it would be perfectly accurate to call it a Jonsonian epigram. It differs from a regular epigram, of course, by its adaptation to the fictive requirements of the sequence. The poet does not skewer his satiric object speaking in his own voice; the dramatic speaker exposes herself as the satiric target. Jonson uses the generic reference as a metaphor, evoking through it the attitudes, values, and entire moral perspective of the satiric epigrams. Possibly, too, he follows the epigrammatic technique of naming only those individuals who are somehow praiseworthy ("Charis" and "Ben"), reducing the satiric object to type label. "Another Ladyes exception" places her in the gallery of corrupt or degenerate aristocrats and court hangers-on— "Sir Voluptuous Beast," "Fine Lady Would-bee," "Court-worme," "my lord Ignorant," and the like—who populate the satiric epigrams.

As we have seen, then, the expectation of mixed genre and mode, implanted in a general title combining "Celebration" and "Lyrick," is richly fulfilled. Primarily, Jonson plays off the form of englished Anacreontics against the fictive structure of Neoplatonic discourse, but he varies this at key points with stanzaic song forms. The Anacreontic form is deployed in a variety of modes, ranging from

Petrarchan lyric to satiric epigram. And, even though Jonson disdains the sonnet as a procrustean form, he constantly exploits the reader's expectations of the conventional structure, movements, and actions of a sonnet sequence.

Just as "A Celebration" presents a thorough generic mixture, so it also presents a corresponding range of stylistic modulation and interplay. Most conspicuous, perhaps, are the styles of the three poems in deviate form: the mellifluous, high and low "Elizabethan" style of "Her Triumph"; the exaggeratedly tortuous, "Metaphysical" style of "Begging another"; and the chiseled, epigrammatic spareness of "Another Ladyes exception." But the stylistic and tonal range of the Anacreontic poems is also considerable. By and large, Jonson does not achieve these effects through mingled levels of diction; only in "Her Triumph," which embraces both the consciously poetic ("rideth" and "enamour'd") and the homely, unselfconsciously prosaic ("smutch'd," "the bag o' the bee"), are we strongly aware of a mixed vocabulary. His most persistent devices are inconspicuously technical ones: variation in metrical pattern, cadence, and caesura, variation in the kind and deployment of rhetorical devices, tropes, and schemes, changes in sentence structure and in the relation of thought unit to couplet unit and metrical pattern.

Jonson uses these generic mixtures metaphorically to project the thematic oppositions and pairings that his better critics have discerned in the sequence—the clashes between the ideal and the real, between pastoral innocence and courtly sophistication, between virtue and pleasure, between the divinity of the poet and the fallibility of the man, and the correlations between language and truth, ardor and passion. Underlying his systematic reliance on genre to embody meaning is the conviction that poetic kinds, modes, and styles are not the product of random or arbitrary invention and evolution; rather, they are expressions of cultures, ways of life, and individual characters. For Ben, therefore, the issues completely revolve around his decision to become the aged lover; and all the themes are subsumed in the characters of the two old lovers, Socrates and Anacreon, who provide mirror images of the meaning of that role, just as in Ben's vision of Charis her human behavior is understood through rival mythic prototypes, usually Venus and Minerva.

In choosing to measure the experience of Ben as an old lover against the polarity embodied by Socrates and Anacreon, Jonson has found an appropriateness more personal than his mere ambivalence to the ways of life which they represent.[27] Physically, he greatly resembles them. The fictive self-portrait that Jonson persistently intrudes into the nondramatic poetry remains highly consistent:

> fat and old,
> Laden with Bellie, and doth hardly approach
> His friends, but to breake Chaires or cracke a Coach.
> His weight is twenty Stone within two pound;
> And that's made up as doth the purse abound.
>
> (*Under-wood* 56.8–12)

Whether Ben demands acceptance as he is—"Let me be what I am, as *Virgil* cold; / As *Horace* fat, or as *Anacreon* old" (*Under-wood* 42. 1–2)—or acknowledges that another course would have been preferable—"It is not growing like a tree / In bulke, doth make man better bee" (*Under-wood* 70.65–66)—the details remain constant: he is old, prodigiously fat, gray-haired, homely, and fearsomely bearded. "My Picture left in Scotland" presents the paradigmatic statement explaining why "Love is rather deafe than blind," as the "she, Whom I adore" allows Ben's appalling physical presence to erase the sound of his eloquence:

> she hath seene
> My hundred of grey haires
> Told seven and fortie years,
> Read so much wast, as she cannot imbrace
> My mountaine belly, and my rockie face,
> And all these through her eyes have stopt her eares.
>
> (*Under-wood* 9.13–18)

This is the same portrait, and the same dilemma, on which "A Celebration" turns, from Ben's own pun on "weight" (1.12) to Charis's reference to "cherish[ing] too much beard, / And mak[ing] *Love* or me afeared" (9.23–24).

In the *Symposium*, Alcibiades states that he will praise Socrates "in a figure which will appear to him to be a caricature": "I say, that he is exactly like the busts of Silenus, which are set up in the statuaries' shops, holding pipes and flutes in their mouths; and they are made to open in the middle, and have images of gods inside them. I say also that he is like Marsyas the satyr. You yourself will not deny, Socrates, that your face is like that of a satyr."[28] Like those hollow busts of Silenus, Socrates is grotesquely ugly without; but, Alcibiades asserts, looking within his mind, one finds "divine and golden images" of fascinating beauty. Trimpi has pointed out that the absurd, comic caricature of Ben as aged lover in the second lyric draws on this tradition of the Silenic Socrates:[29]

> So that, there, I stood a stone,
> Mock'd of all and call'd of one
> (Which with griefe and wrath I heard)
> *Cupids* Statue with a Beard,
> Or else one that plaid his Ape
> In a *Hercules*-his shape.　　　　　　　　　　　(27–32)

Jonson's own notes to the masque *Oberon* (1611) confirm that he knew the myth of Silenus not only from the *Symposium* but from various classical and modern sources,[30] giving particular emphasis to Virgil's *Sixth Eclogue*, which makes Silenus a philosopher and singer of mysteries. The eclogue thereby importantly extends the beauties-within paradox to a context where Silenus is not identified with Socrates.

Although the learned notes to *Oberon* do not acknowledge it, Jonson also knew, from his own copy of the Estienne edition, that Anacreon claimed identification with a nonphilosophic Silenus: "Old I am, and therefore may / Like *Silenus* drink and play." [31] Given the scanty but salient physical traits of the poet—old, gray and balding, endlessly thirsty—the association with the conventional figure of Bacchus's drunken tutor seems inevitable. Therefore, in whichever model of the aged lover Ben chooses to follow, Jonson can perceive his own Silenic image.

In the *Symposium*, Alcibiades goes on to relate that he has been affected by the speeches of Socrates more strongly than by hearing Pericles and the other great orators. Finally, describing the correspondence between the man and his speech, he circles back to his initial metaphor:

his words are like the images of Silenus which open; they are ridiculous when you first hear them; he clothes himself in language that is like the skin of the wanton satyr—for his talk is of pack-asses and smiths and cobblers and curriers, and he is always repeating the same things in the same words, so that any ignorant or inexperienced person might feel disposed to laugh at him; but he who opens the bust and sees what is within will find that they are the only words which have a meaning in them, and also the most divine, abounding in fair images of virtue, and of the widest comprehension, or rather extending to the whole duty of a good and honourable man. (221D–222A)

Trimpi has neglected to discuss the extension of the Silenus metaphor from Socrates the lover to Socrates the speaker; were he to have done so, the ramification of his own argument would have exploded his assumption that "A Celebration of Charis" is written in the plain style. Noting the "great impression" that the Socrates-Silenus analogy made on Renaissance writers, Erich Auerbach explains:

It offers a concept of Socrates' personality and style which seems to give the authority of the most impressive figure among the Greek philosophers to the mixture of genres which was a legacy of the Middle Ages. . . .
. . . a "Socratic" style meant to them something free and untrammeled, something close to ordinary life, and indeed, for Rabelais, something close to buffoonery . . . in which at the same time divine wisdom and perfect virtue are concealed. It is as much a style of life as a literary style; it is, as in Socrates (and in Montaigne too), the expression of the man.[32]

Having elected to emulate Socrates the lover in "A Celebration," Jonson, good classicist that he is, really has no choice but to let Ben work out his amatory destiny in mixed genres and styles. Style and persona, through Socratic tradition, are inextricably related; just as the Silenic style is a reflex of the Socratic speaker, his natural voice, so that style certifies in itself the authenticity of its speaker.

By introducing into the sequence the second Silenus, Anacreon the lover, Jonson does enormously complicate the reference points—mythological, generic, and stylistic—by which we are to understand the whole. The Silenic satyr masks of the two old lovers look the same but mean the opposite. Anacreon is what he appears; with Socrates, however, the inner man is the inverse of the physical exterior, which must be read for its hidden significance. In combination the two present a puzzle like one of the "perspectives" or "turning pictures" that contemporary poets found endlessly fascinating: Which Silenus is Ben—Socrates or Anacreon? Following the stylistic correlation supplies one answer. "No glasse renders a mans forme, or likenesse, so true as his speech," Jonson writes in *Discoveries* (2033–35), quoting Vives.[33] But this direct equation of man and speech only works for those who know the literary traditions involved. Socrates's words, violating every decorum, are ridiculous when one first hears them, Alcibiades explains; it is only when one appreciates the character of the speaker that their beauty becomes apparent. Conversely, the poetic style of Anacreon, whose satyr mask exactly expresses his character, is praised by Henri Estienne for its flowery smoothness and ease, regularity and limpidity.[34] Beautiful without and ugly within. It is suggestive, therefore, that for all its Anacreontic allusiveness, "A Celebration" seldom presents straightforwardly Anacreontic poetry. Instead, mixed style and genre prevail.

Like the Silenic double portrait, the mixed poetic character of the sequence serves to project, implicitly but eloquently, the thoroughly mixed nature of its protagonist: "Poëts, though divine, are men." Trimpi maintains that, playfully but seriously, the Charis poems explore the Neoplatonic ideals of love, to find, with genuine regret, that they are unworkable. Perhaps it should be argued as well, however, that the reference point defined by the mixed style lies as much in Socrates the man as in the comedy of Socrates the lover. And the man for whom self-knowledge was a way of life might well have approved the candor and objectivity with which the poet Ben Jonson scrutinizes the mixture of his own life.[35]

NOTES

1. See Wesley Trimpi, *Ben Jonson's Poems: A Study of the Plain Style* (Stanford: Stanford University Press, 1962), and Judith Kegan Gardiner, *Craftsmanship in Context: The Development of Ben Jonson's Poetry* (The Hague: Mouton, 1975), p. 97 n. Claude J. Summers and Ted-Larry Pebworth extend Trimpi's position, arguing that "the importance of neoplatonism to Jonson's love poetry can hardly be overestimated." See *Ben Jonson* (Boston: Twayne, 1979), p. 180.

2. Paul M. Cubeta, " 'A Celebration of Charis': An Evaluation of Jonsonian Poetic Strategy," *ELH* 25 (1958), 163–80, is the only substantial study predating Trimpi's. Since then we have had G. T. Weinberger, "Jonson's Mock-Encomiastic 'Celebration of Charis,' " *Genre* 4 (1971), 305–28; Arthur F. Marotti, "All About Jonson's Poetry," *ELH* 39 (1972), 208–37, especially pp. 230–35; Richard S. Peterson, "Virtue Reconciled to Pleasure: 'A Celebration of Charis,' " *Studies in the Literary Imagination* 6 (1973), 219–68; Sara van den Berg, "The Play of Wit and Love: Demetrius' *On Style* and Jonson's 'A Celebration of Charis.' " *ELH*, 41 (1974), 26–36; S. P. Zitner, "The Revenge on Charis," *The Elizabethan Theatre*, vol. 4, ed. G. R. Hibbard (Hamden, Conn.: The Shoe String Press, 1974), pp. 127–42; Gardiner, *Craftsmanship*, pp. 97–108; R. V. LeClercq, "The Reciprocal Harmony of Jonson's 'A Celebration of Charis,' " *Texas Studies in Literature and Language* 16 (1975), 627–50; Anne Ferry, *All in War with Time: Love Poetry of Shakespeare, Donne, Jonson, Marvell* (Cambridge, Mass.: Harvard University Press, 1975), pp. 130–33, 157–63; and Summers and Pebworth, *Ben Jonson*, pp. 187–91. I have been unable to see Zitner's essay.

3. *Ben Jonson's Poems*, pp. 234–35.

4. In *Craftsmanship*, Gardiner finds a "multiple form" and an "oscillation" of voices which present a virtual anthology of amatory styles (pp. 107–08). Van der Berg wishes to limit the sequence to a single style, *charis*, the graceful style described by Demetrius of Phalerus; but this is a mixed style, ranging from elegance to wit to coarseness. See also Summers and Pebworth, *Ben Jonson*, pp. 188, 190.

5. *The Resources of Kind: Genre-Theory in the Renaissance* (Berkeley and Los Angeles: University of California Press, 1973), esp. pp. 114–28.

6. *Craftsmanship*, pp. 98–103; quotation, p. 103.

7. See Anacreon 13, 28, 30, and 31. I give the numbering used by J. M. Edmonds, ed., *Elegy and Iambus with the Anacreontea*, vol. 2, Loeb Classical Library (London: Heinemann, 1931). The numbering in Henri Estienne's 1554 *editio princeps* is helpfully tabulated with that of modern editions by Gordon Braden, *The Classics and English Renaissance Poetry: Three Case Studies*, Yale Studies in English, no. 187 (New Haven: Yale University Press, 1978), p. 256. Braden's is the most suggestive account of the Renaissance Anacreon (see pp. 196–232, 255–58). Also see, Cubeta, " 'A Celebration of Charis,' " p. 167, and van den Berg, "The Play of Wit and Love," p. 31, who note in passing the Anacreontic element in lyrics 2 and 3.

8. Of Anacreon's translators, Thomas Stanley follows Jonson precisely in employing couplets of headless iambic tetrameter; Cowley uses the regular tetrameter couplet. Herrick's Anacreontic poems are frequently written in headless tetrameter couplets. In Lovelace's "The Grasshopper," indebted to Anacreon 34, iambic tetrameter alternates with pentameter. Peterson ("Virtue Reconciled to Pleasure," p. 221 n.) calls attention to William Browne's unpublished lyrics in Anacreontic couplets.

9. "The Old Lover XI," *The Poems and Translations of Thomas Stanley*, ed. G. M. Crump (Oxford: The Clarendon Press, 1962), p. 80. Edmonds, no. 7.

10. Braden, *The Classics and English Renaissance Poetry*, p. 207.

11. As Trimpi has remarked (*Ben Jonson's Poems*, p. 217).

12. Van den Berg notices the pun in "Dexterously" ("The Play of Wit and Love," p. 32). Compare *Epigrammes* 45, "On My First Sonne,": "child of my right hand."

13. Trimpi, *Ben Jonson's Poems*, pp. 218–20; quotation, p. 218. (The rhetorical formula also owes something to Anacreon 46.) Gardiner, *Craftsmanship*, p. 107; van den Berg, "The Play of Wit and Love," p. 32; Cubeta, " 'A Celebration of Charis,' " p. 170; and Ferry, *All in War with Time*, pp. 130–32; quotation, p. 133.

14. Line 7, " 'Mongst my Muses finding me," alludes to the multiple sources of inspiration for the song; it does not necessarily mean "composing many songs," as Trimpi (*Ben Jonson's Poems*, p. 220) and Peterson ("Virtue Reconciled to Pleasure," p. 235) assume.

15. See Trimpi, *Ben Jonson's Poems*, pp. 219–20.

16. *Craftsmanship*, p. 104. "Love poems are lies," Marotti infers ("All About Jonson's Poetry," p. 234).

17. *Ben Jonson's Poems*, p. 221.

18. Trans. Stanley, p. 123.

19. Marotti, "All About Jonson's Poetry," p. 234.

20. Cubeta has noted a Donnean "tone of voice" (" 'A Celebration of Charis,' " p. 174). Weinberger points to "The Extasie" as the model for the concluding stanza; however, he sees the resemblance as nonparodic, reading the poem as a "looked-for balance" between "frustrated Platonism" and "utter carnality" ("Jonson's Mock-Encomiastic 'Celebration of Charis,' " pp. 316 and 318).

21. In "Virtue Reconciled to Pleasure," Peterson finds an elaborate play on *Dictamnum*, the herb dittany, but misses the obvious (pp. 362–63).

22. Ibid., p. 260.

23. "Limn me thus the lad I love: / Sleek and shining make his hair, / Dark beneath, sun-bright above, / And let the love-locks free as air / Lie as they will, disordered, there" (Edmonds, *Elegy and Iambus with the Anacreontea*, p. 43). Possibly moved by the example of Benson's edition of the Shakespeare *Sonnets*, Stanley changes the gender to feminine in his translation.

24. *Ben Jonson's Poems*, pp. 222–24.

25. "All About Jonson's Poetry," p. 235.

26. Ferry, *All in War with Time*, p. 162. Peterson, greatly exaggerating the Homeric dimension of the sequence, argues that Charis accepts Ben as a lover, but keeps the relationship secret. They are both virtuous and discreet (see "Virtue Reconciled to Pleasure," pp. 259–67).

27. Marotti discusses Jonson as "an artistic schizophrenic, with both a Dionysian and an Apollonian side" ("All About Jonson's Poetry," p. 209).

28. *Symposium* 215B, trans. Jowett, rev. Moses Hadas (Chicago: Henry Regnery, 1953).

29. *Ben Jonson's Poems*, pp. 216–18.

30. *Ben Jonson*, ed. Herford, Simpson, and Simpson, vol. 7, pp. 341–56, and vol. 10, pp. 525–26.

31. Trans. Stanley, p. 92 (Edmonds, no. 47). Jonson's copy of Anacreon is described by David McPherson, "Ben Jonson's Library and Marginalia," *Studies in Philology* 71, no. 5 (1974), 77, no. 142.

32. *Mimesis*, trans. Willard Trask (Garden City, N.Y.: Doubleday-Anchor, 1957), p. 246.

33. Ferry misapplies this passage to "A Celebration" (*All in War with Time*, pp. 150–61).

34. See Braden, *The Classics and English Renaissance Poetry*, pp. 201–05, 208–09.

35. For a similar use of Socratic model and Silenic, mixed style, with which Jonson was also familiar, see R. B. Waddington, "Socrates in Montaigne's 'traicté de la phisionomie,' " *Modern Language Quarterly* 41 (1980), 328–45.

ROGER B. ROLLIN

✝

The Anxiety of Identification: Jonson and the Rival Poets

> . . . strong poets can only read themselves.
> —Harold Bloom[1]

For Satan, Milton's "rival poet and dark brother,"[2] "to be weak is miserable / Doing or Suffering." That "rare Arch-Poet JOHNSON"[3] would surely have agreed. His credo, after all, was:

> He that is round within himselfe, and streight,
>   Need seeke no other strength, no other height;
> Fortune upon him breakes her selfe, if ill,
>   And what would hurt his vertue makes it still.
>
> ("To Sir Thomas Roe," *Epigrammes* 98)

Yet Satan knew that to be strong also could be to be miserable, often more miserable. Even a strong poet may have to retreat from "the wolves black jaw, and the dull Asses hoofe" ("An Ode. To himselfe," 36), only to find that, when he does take lyre in hand and strike in his proper strain, his own poetic sons may snicker at their father's "presumption" and "immodest rage."[4]

In addition to thankless poet-sons, the strong poet must deal with those potential rivals, his brother poets: "*Nothing* in our Age . . . is more preposterous, then the *running Judgements* upon *Poetry,* and *Poets;* when wee shall heare those things commended, and cry'd up for the best writings, which a man would scarce vouchsafe, to wrap any wholesome drug in; hee would never light his *Tobacco* with them" (*Discoveries* 587–92). Eventually the poet who himself commended and cried up for the best writings the works of a Benjamin Rudyerd (*Epigrammes* 121), a Christopher Brooke (*Ungathered Verse*

139

20), even a King James (*Epigrammes* 4), must confront a John Donne, a William Shakespeare.

"We need," says Harold Bloom, "to stop thinking of any poet as an autonomous ego, however solipsistic the strongest of poets may be. Every poet is a being caught up in a dialectical relationship (transference, repetition, error, communication) with another poet or poets."[5] For Jonson that dialectical relationship was not only with the safely dead—a Martial or a Horace—but with the danger-ously alive or but recently deceased. One of the mind's strategies for coping with such relationships can be verbal aggression—direct or indirect, conscious or unconscious; for example, fantasizing Donne hanged, and worse, forgotten; portraying Donne as a burnt-out blasphemer and heretic; ranking Donne as "the first poet in the World"—"in some things," an evaluation that may be read as mere hyperbole, faint damnation, or balanced criticism (*Conversations*, 48–49, 120–22, 117–18).

Another of the ego's defenses in the dialectic with the rival is displacement, of which *Epigrammes* 96, "To John Donne," provides a convenient example. Here Jonson manages to turn a compliment to his dark brother to his own credit by portraying *himself* as a poet-hero: "Who shall doubt, DONNE, where I a *Poet* bee, / When I dare send my *Epigrammes* to thee?" Donne is acknowledged to be a poet as well as a critic, "That so alone canst judge, so'alone dost make," and it is his stature as a poet, presumably, that gives Donne his "best authoritie." But it is his judiciousness *as critic* that receives Jonson's emphasis. Donne is portrayed as the king of critics, ca-pable of sealing one's title as poet by putting his imprimatur on but a single epigram. Yet Jonson's approach to him is brisk to the point of imperiousness: "Reade all I send." The poem ends as it began, barely concealing self-congratulation, rebuking those "that for claps doe write," celebrating those who would win the approbation of rigorous critics like Donne: "A man should seeke great glorie, and not broad." Thus a tribute to a brother poet provides Jonson with an opportunity for "intruding himself or his image into his writ-ing," a practice E. Pearlman has enabled us to appreciate as a form of "creative egotism."[6] "To John Donne" becomes another of Jonson's poems to himself, an exercise in ego-reinforcement as well as a handsome encomium. The poet's breezy self-confidence makes the supposedly formidable Donne into something of a straw critic. Far from a potential threat to Jonson's identity as a poet, he seems to exist to confirm it, and this sense of inner security, of the well-defined self, manifests itself in the epigram's clarity and control.[7]

The case is altered when Jonson approaches Donne primarily as poet, in *Epigrammes* 23. For Bloom the sublimation of aggressive instincts "is central to writing . . . poetry," [8] and, as Freud indicated, the varieties of sublimation of which the human mind is capable are wonderful. In Jonson's short poem of supposed affirmation, for example, denial is everywhere present. The Donne who could not keep accent is hailed as "the delight of PHOEBUS, and each *Muse*." This generous compliment to one who would perish for not being understood (*Conversations*, 196) is followed by another, regarding which, to this day, there is no interpretational consensus: "Who, to thy one, all other braines refuse." William B. Hunter, assuming Jonsonian consistency, is, nonetheless, tentative: "perhaps, Who reject all other brains in favor of yours." Hugh Maclean glosses "refuse" as "add to it," implying that Donne's brain is the sum total of brains. Of the thirteen significations listed in the *OED* for "refuse" (all of which entail rejection), Maclean's is not one. His gloss belongs to another verb entirely, "re-fuse," meaning "to fuse or melt again." Robert M. Adams raises the possibility of "the idea of welding (re-fusing) lesser minds to a greater," but adds that the verb "could imply a reproach against Donne's obscurity" or "a notion of egotism." [9] Ambiguity need not be symptomatic of ambivalence, of course, but the possibility that Jonson is indeed ambivalent toward Donne increases as the poem's problems mount. The cause of these problems could be temporary incompetence or carelessness, but a more persuasive explanation lies in Pearlman's theory that it is ambivalence toward power and power figures around which "the crucial psychological themes in Jonson's life and work are keyed." [10]

At least three years had passed between the time Jonson wrote "Whose every worke, of thy most earely wit, / Came forth example and remaines so, yet," and his alleged assertion to Drummond that Donne had written "all his best pieces err he was 25 years old" (*Conversations*, 121–22). Both the poetic statement and the reported remark admit of ambiguity: Was Donne a prodigy, or was he one of those wits who "never performe much, but quickly"? "They are, what they are on the sudden. . . . They are wits of good promise at first, but there is an *Ingeni-stitium*: They stand still at sixteene, they get no higher" (*Discoveries*, 684–90). Context is of little assistance, for the statement Drummond recorded appears amid an account of those verses of Donne's which Jonson "hath by heart"; however, it is shortly followed by allusions to Donne's obscurity and folly (*Conversations*, 118–120, 125–127, 135–137).

The reader who has been baffled by the second line of Jonson's epigram on Donne will not likely be illuminated by his third: Donne is "Longer a knowing, then most wits doe live." Does this mean: "Your poetry will endure longer than the very life-spans of most wits"? Or does it mean: "It takes longer to understand your work than most wits have to live"? In either case the compliment is at best lefthanded, implying either Donne's "obscurenesse" or the prospect of his limited rather than enduring fame. What follows, however, is a line of straightforward, conventional hyperbole: "And which no 'affection praise enough can give!" The conjunction "and" here may lend credence to Ian Donaldson's interpretation that Donne has practiced his art longer than most wits survive.[11] Nevertheless, readers' bafflement concerning the intentions of this practitioner of the plain style suggests that the problem is in Jonson, not in his audience.

Moreover, problems continue to arise, as compliments which, in other encomia, come trippingly from Jonson's tongue here stumble over syntax and semantics: "To it, thy language, letters, arts, best life, / Which might with halfe mankind maintayne a strife." Hunter's gloss provides the clause with the absent verbal, "Add to it."[12] But the question remains: What is the referent of "it"? Could it be "wit," four lines above and in another clause? And what is meant by the announcement that Donne's best life (since taking holy orders? the sum of his good parts?) might maintain a strife with half of mankind? Are we to picture Donne as a genius-champion against whom half of the human race would make fair odds? And what would be the cause of such a strife, anyway?

The questions are raised—not to be answered—but to suggest that, in "To John Donne," either Jonson is parodying his meta-physical friend, or, as is more likely, he has gotten himself into trouble and knows it: "All which I meant to praise, and, yet, I would; / But leave, because I cannot as I should!" It needs no excursion into psychoanalysis to infer that, when an accomplished poet flounders about in so conventional a form, the causes are likely to be more than artistic ones. One such cause might be Jonson's creative egotism, capable of sublimating unconscious aggression when the subject is his rival *critic* (which Donne actually was not, of course), incapable of doing so when the subject is Donne the rival *poet*. The epigram then in part confirms what Pearlman has so persuasively argued: that the aggressiveness, even the violence, of Jonson the man is a vital factor in the creativity of Jonson the author, in his failures as well as in his successes.

The more psychological distance Jonson can put between himself and his rivals, the easier it may be for him to sublimate his aggressiveness in poetry. Another case in point is "To the Reader" (*Ungathered Verse* 25), Jonson's poem on Shakespeare's portrait in the First Folio. This epigram seems to have posed as few problems for the poet as it has for readers. Its compliment to "gentle Shakespeare" is unqualified by obfuscations or double meanings, and the reasons for this are not far to seek: the poem's addressee is the folio's reader, *not* Shakespeare or his shade; its subject is *not* the rival himself but an engraving of his features; and finally, the role Jonson adopts is more that of personal friend and art critic than that of man of letters: "the Graver had a strife / With Nature, to out-doo the life." Ironically, the problem faced by Droeshout will also be the problem faced by Jonson himself in his poem to Shakespeare's memory: As the engraver is doomed to fail in his attempt to capture Shakespeare's genius, so imposing his own art on Shakespeare will (as shall be suggested below) prove to be Jonson's noble undoing. For just as, according to Jonson, the reader can only find the real William Shakespeare in "his Booke," so will the reader find in Jonson's ambitious poem, not so much William Shakespeare, as William Shakespeare Jonsonized.

Jonson's ambivalence toward Shakespeare is so well documented by himself as to require only mention here. In *Discoveries*, compliments concerning Shakespeare's person—"honest, and of an open, free nature"; "I lov'd the man, and doe honour his memory (on this side Idolatry)" (656, 654–5)—are intermixed with praise for his literary talent—"excellent *Phantsie;* brave notions, and gentle expressions"(657–58)—but also with criticism regarding that talent's lack of judgment and discipline. Such juxtapositions are understandable. Jonson, after all, may be the last writer in the world to distinguish between attacks on his art and on his person. And, while the line between evenhanded judgment and ambivalence can be a fine one, Drummond's accusation that Jonson was "a contemner and Scorner of others, given rather to losse a friend, than a Jest, jealous of every word and action of those about him" (*Conversations*, 681–82), does not go without confirmation elsewhere. It is a psychological commonplace that ambivalence frequently goes hand in hand with envy. For envy is a state of mind involving both "elements of admiration and hopefulness" and "feelings of resentment and injured deprivation." Likewise, envy is linked to aggression, specifically, and, generally, to "the vicissitudes of narcissism."[13]

Jonson's narcissism can hardly be in doubt, even (one suspects) to himself. That he was "a great lover and praiser of himself" (*Conversations*, 680) could be taken as merely Drummond's snideness, the result of a visiting literary lion's projecting the criticism leveled against his own verses—that they "smelled too much of ye schooles" (110–13)—onto the verses of his poet-host. But Jonson's admirer, James Howell, reiterates Drummond's judgment and quotes another admirer, Thomas Carew, in support.[14] Carew's own reluctant admonishment of Jonson for his egotism and ambition—"thy owne tounge proclaimes thy ytch of praise"[15]—has been seconded by not a few readers of Jonson's "An Ode. To himselfe."

Thus, when Jonson is faced with writing a poem to Shakespeare the *author*, it is understandable that there should surface that ambivalence toward power which Pearlman shows to be so characteristic of the author and the man. Compounded of aggressiveness and ambition, of narcissism and envy, that ambivalence is part of what makes Jonson a strong poet, if sometimes a less than successful one (as in the case of the epigram to the poet Donne). On the other hand, envy can foster a "mobilization of aggression," resulting in "a manageable state of the ego which at once defends against depression, preserves narcissism and self-esteem, and avoids the excessive reaction of the paranoid position. Envy can thus be seen as having a coping aspect which may serve adaptive ends."[16] It will be suggested here that Jonson's eulogy of Shakespeare is indeed a product of envy channeled into just such "adaptive ends," making the poem considerably more than the "Insolent, Sparing, and Invidious Panegyrick" to which Dryden objected.[17] The adaptation, however, is only partially accomplished. For all its greatness, the poem is flawed by conceptual and structural peculiarities symptomatic of Jonson's difficulty in coping with what might be regarded as his Shakespeare syndrome. The extent to which he does cope with it seems to be determined by the extent to which the process of identification can take place. That process emerges as early as the poem's title, one of Jonson's most elaborate and effusive.

The title refers to Shakespeare as "*my* beloved" (*Ungathered Verse* 26), a phrase Jonson applies to no other subject of a poem of his. At the level of rhetoric, the phrase simply signifies strong personal feeling. From a phenomenological perspective on the poem as a whole, the sense of possessiveness and proprietorship (often characteristic of envy)[18] that it conveys sets the psychological stage for an exercise in identification. It is worth noting, therefore, that Jonson opens his tribute by firmly *dis*associating himself from those who might envy Shakespeare: he is "thus ample" to his author's "Booke, and Fame," he says, out of no malicious intent, no desire to make others envious of Shakespeare's reputation. Beginning a tribute thus with an apologia would be unremarkable—were it not that this particular effusion will go on for a full sixteen lines.[19] Such displacement—attributing to others the envy one feels oneself but must resist—is a routine defense against anxiety. Moreover, at least four other unconsious strategies for coping with envy are present in some form in Jonson's eulogy: *"idealization," "confusion," "devaluation of the object"* (like envy-incitement, implicit in the poem by its conspicuous denial), and *"devaluation of the self."*[20]

"Confusion" can serve unconsciously to counteract guilt associated with envy, and Jonson's elegy, for all its well-known felicities, is confused. It moves by fits and starts, changing addressees, persons, and subjects—Wesley Trimpi has even suggested a quite reasonable rearrangement of four lines[21]—as if indirection and changing direction are the only ways Jonson can get where he must go. "I confesse," he says, as if the hyperbole were being extracted from him, "thy writings to be such, / As neither *Man*, nor *Muse*, can praise too much." Then, as if anticipating that the sincerity or validity of his praise might be questioned, he reaffirms it—" 'Tis true"—then affirms it a third time by an appeal to vox populi— "and all mens suffrage."

Much protest leads to more. Jonson's uneasiness apparently impels him to take another tack, apologizing—not for ambivalence, of course—but for indecision: "But these wayes / Were not the paths I meant unto thy praise." Are "these wayes" the compliments hyperbolical of lines 3 to 5? Ben Jonson, he goes on to imply, is hardly some know-nothing whose praises ring hollow, "For seelist Ignorance on these may light, / Which, when it sounds at best, but eccho's right." Nor is he a mere Bardolator who, praising everything, "doth ne're advance / The truth." Certainly he is no Machiavel of letters, with "crafty Malice" overpraising in order to "ruine" by evoking ironic readings: "These are, as some infamous Baud, or Whore, / Should praise a Matron. What could hurt her more?" Ben Jonson's reputation for integrity, he implies, authenticates his praise. Yet this same Jonson frankly confessed to John Selden, "I have too oft preferr'd / Men past their termes, and prais'd some names too much" ("An Epistle to Master John Selden," 20–21). His justification, "But 'twas with purpose to have made them such," is of interest, carrying with it the idea of the poet as maker not only of poems but of men. And when one is out to remake men the fact that they are dead can be a convenience. Being illustrious, or safely deceased, Shakespeare, Jonson argues, is invulnerable to suspect praise and to any need of it. It is curious that this very deadness of Shakespeare, which is implied in the poem's title but obscured by the familiar-address form of the first fourteen lines, seems, by coming to the fore again in lines 15 and 16, to free Jonson (temporarily) of his indecision: "I, therefore will begin." [22]

Sixteen lines of denial, focusing as much on the praiser's mind as on the memory of the praised, weaving a circuitous route from a beloved friend to women who sell love, give way at last to plain epithets, remarkable for their prescience—"Soule of the Age!"—and for their generosity—"The applause! delight! the wonder of our Stage!" The poet, however, appears to be on the verge of performing a greater wonder, nothing less than his subject's resurrection: "My *Shakespeare*, rise." But what promises to be Jonson acting as Messiah to Shakespeare's Lazarus turns out to be more a revision of mortuary arrangements: "I will not lodge thee by / *Chaucer*, or *Spenser*, or bid *Beaumont* lye / A little further, to make thee a roome." The implied fiction of this stunning compliment—that Jonson is responsible for Shakespeare's interment in Holy Trinity Church rather than in Westminster Abbey—is yet another interesting example of Jonson's self-dramatizing tendency. These lines do, however, facilitate a graceful modulation to a handsome tribute based on the convention of the immortalizing power of poetry—"And art alive still, while thy Booke doth live"—and on Shakespeare's superiority to three rival playwrights. (Though *not* to the logical fourth, the author of *Volpone*.)

That Lyly, Kyd, and Marlowe are said to have had "great, but disproportion'd *Muses*" implies that Shakespeare is the Compleat Poet whose five essential qualities Jonson would delineate in *Discoveries*. The luster of this tribute, however, has been dimmed for generations of readers by the famous reference to Shakespeare's want of classical learning. In *Discoveries*, Jonson stipulates that, of the five requisites of the true poet or maker, two are "*Imitation*, to bee able to convert the substance, or Riches of an other *Poet*, to his owne use" (2467–69), and "that, which wee especially require in him . . . an exactnesse of Studie, and multiplicity of reading" (2482–84). Everything we know about Jonson suggests that in this passage he means the close reading and imitation of classical as well as native authors.

The conventions of the encomium do not, however, require the wholesale importation of unvarnished truth (much less creativity theory) into the praise of the subject, especially not if the praise itself could thereby be compromised. Why then was "small *Latine*, and less *Greeke*" apparently irresistible to Jonson? Obviously the reference offers a transition from the moderns/Shakespeare comparison to the ancients/Shakespeare comparison—except that a poet of Jonson's skill would have available to him a score of such devices, not one of which need ever raise a single question in any reader's mind. On the other hand, if the purpose here is to honor Shakespeare for succeeding artistically without recourse to imitation (an exception to his theory that must have been troublesome to Jonson), nothing dictates that it be put so that it implies the subject's transcendence of his own education, an implication that takes away even as it gives.[23] Nothing, that is, except feelings of ambivalence.

The ancients/moderns compliment is, in addition, so constructed as to make Jonson once more the resurrection and the life—though again he declines the miracle. He will *not* "call forth" the ancients, perhaps because it would be such a noisy business: Aeschylus, Euripides, and Sophocles thunder, and even Shakespeare's buskin shakes the stage. For the cognoscenti, Jonson's pun would recall Robert Greene's slur on Will "Shakescene" (in *Groat's-worth of Wit*). Other readers of the First Folio would receive an impression of these tragedians' power—or of their bombast. There may be ambiguity as well in Jonson's tribute to Shakespeare as a writer of comedy: his work is said to compare favorably with the products of "insolent" and "haughtie" civilizations and with those produced "from their ashes" by imitative drudges. The rhetoric is at least potentially reductive: if X is favorably compared with negatively characterized Y and Z, the comparison can become faintly odorous. Again the point is that Jonson is not under compulsion here: it would be easy enough for so accomplished a poet to say "Your comedy surpasses the great achievements of Old Comedy and New" in language both graceful and memorable, but he does not, seemingly cannot, do so.

Subsequent context, thirteen lines of straightforward and undeniably generous compliment, might be thought to banish such squint suspicion. Worth noting, however, is the fact that these tributes are issued *indirectly*, not to Shakespeare but to "*Britaine*." It is as if shifting from the second-person familiar to the third person allows Jonson more psychological space. The creative egotist in him must be free, it seems, to award to his rival the artistic immortality for which he himself has worked and hoped: "He was not of an age, but for all time!" With the advantage of hindsight, such praise seems merely apt; but in the 1620s it must have seemed either hyperbolical or touchingly ample that a poet who could mock himself as "*Cupids* Statue with a Beard" ("A Celebration of Charis," "How he saw her," 30) should endow his rival with dignity by association with the gods of poetry and eloquence.

Another effect of psychological distancing is that it actually can enhance possibilities for identification. Identification, of course, is a complex process involving far more than merely seeing resemblances between oneself and another or putting oneself in another's place. As Norman N. Holland has explained, identification has to do with the very structure of the ego. It entails an "internal matching" of one's "adaptations" (conscious modes of coping with reality) and one's "defenses" (unconcious modes). It involves both "introjection" and "projection," that is, mentally "taking in" from the other "certain drives and defenses" and "putting into" the other characteristics that actually are one's own.[24] The unconscious stratagem that controls much of the latter half of Jonson's poem can be seen as an attempt to cope with his Shakespeare syndrome by absorbing both admiration and envy into identification: Jonson projects into Shakespeare qualities like learning and skill at imitation, which he knew himself to possess but which were wanting in his rival.

The outcome of this strategy is the portrayal of Shakespeare as the *poeta* or maker Jonson would profile in *Discoveries*.[25] There Jonson affirms that the true poet is endowed with "Nature" or a "goodnes of naturall wit" (2410 ff.), our "genius" or "native talent." That Shakespeare was one of those who was able "by nature, and instinct, to powre out the Treasure of his minde" (2412–13) Jonson grants unequivocally: "Nature her selfe was proud of his designes . . . she will vouchsafe no other Wit."

As to the extent to which nature was one of Jonson's strong suits, both his contemporaries and subsequent readers have disagreed. Donne couples Jonson's *ingenium* with his *labor*, Herrick's ode to Jonson refers to his "wits great over-plus," and Godolphin writes admiringly of Jonson's "most proportioned wit / To nature." On the other hand, while they do not deny Jonson's genius, Carew, Fane, Randolph, and Waller tend to emphasize his study, imitation, and exercise.[26] Since the seventeenth century it has been possible to snigger at a poet who "wrott all his [verse] first in prose, for so his master Cambden had Learned him" (*Conversations*, 377–78), but it is to take away little from Jonson to acknowledge that he fell short of Shakespeare when it came to "naturall wit." His compliment to Shakespeare's "Nature" is not, then, patently projective or introjective but an authoritative confirmation of a consensus.

"Art," in Jonson's *Discoveries*, is that which alone can lead the true poet "to perfection" (2495). As James D. Redwine has noted, Jonson conceives of art as the sum of the poet's genius, learning, discipline, and decorum.[27] Drummond, of course, remembered Jonson as charging "That Shaksperr wanted Arte" (*Conversations*, 50), a judgment consciously or unconsciously reversed but a few years later:

> Yet must I not give Nature all: Thy Art,
>   My gentle *Shakespeare*, must enjoy a part.
> For though the *Poets* matter, Nature be,
>   His Art doth give the fashion.

In *Discoveries*, Jonson would write of gentle Shakespeare, "His wit was in his owne power; would the rule of it had beene so too" (660–61).

Since the occasion would permit Jonson to pass silently over the question of Shakespeare's art, the most simple if not elegant explanations for the contradiction between Jonson's eulogy and his *Discoveries* would be a change of mind, hypocrisy, or carelessness. But, if a great deal about human beings besides beauty is in the eye of the beholder, and if the process of identification does indeed have more to do with ego-reinforcement than with facts, then what may be happening here is that Jonson increasingly is projecting upon his image of Shakespeare his own idealized self-image. What could more effectively lessen Jonson's anxiety about his rival's higher reputation than to make Shakespeare into a maker much like himself, a poet who fulfills the requisite of "Exercise," who is wont to "bring all to the forge, and file, againe; tourne it a newe" (*Discoveries*, 2452–53)? Flying in the face of most of the evidence and of contemporary opinion, Jonson transforms Shakespeare into a poet who "must sweat" and "strike the second heat / Upon the *Muses* anvile." It is a classic example of the principle of cognitive dissonance in operation: Whatever fails to fit a comfortable conception must be *made* to fit.

But, while dissonance may be reduced, neither it nor its attendant anxiety has been eliminated entirely. There is a trace of nervousness, for example, in the passage's parenthetical affirmations: yes, Shakespeare's lines are "living"; yes, Shakespeare did remake himself (as Jonson is remaking Shakespeare) when he brought forth all those verses "like a Beare, and after form'd them with licking" (*Discoveries*, 2450–51). Envy that may resurface as just if hyperbolical criticism in "Would he had blotted a thousand" (650) and "hee flow'd with that facility, that sometime it was necessary he should be stop'd" (658–59), here becomes the defensive projection of "For a good *Poet's* made, as well as borne. / And such wert thou."

In mid-line the form of address shifts again to the third person, but the theme is still the act of making, and the controlling conceit is the parallel between procreation and poetic creation. Reversing the terms of the famous line from the epigram "On My First Sonne"—"here doth lye / BEN. JONSON his best piece of *poetrie*"—Jonson invites readers to look upon the works of the First Folio as Shakespeare's progeny. In the course of doing so, he adds two new thoughts and reiterates a third. First, the style is the man: "Looke how the fathers face / Lives in his issue"—or as Jonson would proclaim in *Discoveries*, "*Language* most shewes a man: speake that I may see thee" (2031–32). Second, like the bricklayer-poet Jonson, Shakespeare had to have been one who labored at his trade, like a smith whose work's reworking displays all the "exercise" that went into it: "the race / Of *Shakespeares* minde, and manners brightly shines / In his well torned, and true-filed lines." Third, as true poetry is instructive, offering "to mankinde a certaine rule, and Patterne of living well, and happily; disposing us to all Civill offices of Society" (*Discoveries*, 2386–88), so in Shakespeare's lines "he seemes to shake a Lance, / As brandish't at the eyes of Ignorance." That is, like Jonson he is an aggressively ethical poet, among those "wisest and best learned [who] have thought [Poesy] the absolute Mistresse of manners, and neerest of kin to Vertue" (*Discoveries*, 2394–96). With such a Shakespeare, even one created by a pun, identification is possible for Jonson; with the Shakespeare who "Many times . . . fell into those things, could not escape laughter" (*Discoveries*, 661–62), it is not.[28]

In the elegy's climactic nine lines, Jonson shifts his rhetorical mode back to celebratory direct address—"Sweet Swan of Avon!"—and to two new variations on his resurrection theme. Now, however, the metamorphosis is imagined without any suggestion of Jonson's own agency. This change could indicate that, as a result of the identification process going on in the poem, Jonson has been able to work through his combined admiration and envy of Shakespeare to achieve both ego-integration and -reinforcement. Not that the process has been completed, however: after all, Jonson, too, could be thought of as a poet who took "flights upon the bankes of *Thames*" and had won favor in the eyes of *"Eliza,* and our *James!"* Nor is it likely that the Jonson who would be apotheosized by Donne, Herrick, Carew, and others would be incapable of envisioning himself "in the *Hemisphere* / Advanc'd, and made a Constellation there!" and invoked to revivify a darkened and "drooping Stage." Nevertheless, despite its conventionality and despite the fact that for the controlling swan-star conceit Jonson has plagiarized his ode prefaced to Hugh Holland's *Pancharis* (*Ungathered Verse* 6), the apotheosis concludes the poem in a blaze of glory, on a note of celebration of this "Starre of *Poets*" that is unqualified by ambiguity or ambivalence.[29]

Identification with "a good and whole object" can strengthen the ego and enable it "to preserve its identity" and a sense "of possessing goodness of its own."[30] Whether the eulogy "cured" Jonson of his Shakespeare syndrome may, on the basis of his observations in *Discoveries*, be doubted, but poetry therapy is not the issue here. Of more interest is the possibility that the four poems under discussion offer insights into Ben Jonson's creativity,[31] plus a more general possibility: that Bloom's radical theory could be extended to include an "anxiety of identification" arising out of a strong poet's need to come to terms with his strong contemporaries. But, whereas the Oedipal rivalry is the psychological foundation of Bloom's theory, the basis for an anxiety of identification would be that other significant emotional factor in the early development of personality, sibling rivalry. Bloom theorizes that, in the high English Renaissance, the anxiety of influence has not yet become "central to poetic consciousness," which seems to be borne out not only by his example of Shakespeare, but also by the case of such poets as Donne and Jonson.[32] "Father Jonson" does not appear to be the threat to his "Sons" that Milton, according to Bloom, would become to his successors. Quite the contrary, Jonson can be, on the one hand, the "dear Ben" whose follies a Carew deferentially enumerates and, on the other hand, the "Saint *Ben*" a Herrick can whimsically but reverently invoke.[33]

Nor does artistic sibling rivalry appear to be endemic to the age. For the seventeenth century shows, besides a host of mainly conventional commendatory poems to fellow poets, such glories as a Carew rising to magnificence to commemorate a Donne, a Cowley soaring to near sublimity to honor the memory of a Crashaw. Anxiety of identification seems, then, more likely to emerge in the case of great creative egotists like Ben Jonson. That such poets have always existed and have always had to come to terms with their poet-siblings, their dark brothers, through poetry or outside of it, is the possibility that dost tease us out of thought.

NOTES

1. *The Anxiety of Influence* (New York: Oxford University Press, 1975), p. 19.

2. Ibid., p. 23.

3. Robert Herrick, "Upon Master Ben. Johnson. Epigram," *The Complete Poetry of Robert Herrick*, ed. J. Max Patrick (New York: Norton, 1968).

4. Sir John Suckling, "A Sessions of the Poets" (29), *The Works of Sir John Suckling*, ed. A. H. Thompson (New York: Russell and Russell, 1964). Thomas Carew, "To Ben. Johnson. Upon occasion of his Ode of defiance annext to his play of the new Inne" (24), *The Poems of Thomas Carew*, ed. Rhodes Dunlap (London: Oxford University Press, 1957).

5. *Anxiety*, p. 91.

6. "Ben Jonson: An Anatomy," *ELR* 9 (1979), 374. For his helpful comments on my work, I wish to express my gratitude to Professor Pearlman, whose brilliantly revisionary essay I did not see until after this paper had taken shape.

7. To my colleague, Professor John Idol of Clemson University, I am indebted for the observation that similar clarity and control mark Jonson's poems to Sir Francis Beaumont (*Epigrammes* 55), Josuah Sylvester (*Epigrammes* 132), and Sir Thomas Overbury (*Epigrammes* 113)—none of them, it is safe to assume, perceived by Jonson as true rival poets. Jonson's handling of the convention of the panegyric in such cases sharpens the contrast with the epigram to Donne and the eulogy to Shakespeare.

8. *Anxiety*, p. 115.

9. *The Complete Poetry of Ben Jonson*, ed. William B. Hunter, Jr., (Garden City, N.Y.: Doubleday, 1963), p. 12 n. Hugh Maclean, ed., *Ben Jonson and the Cavalier Poets* (New York: Norton, 1974), p. 7 n. Robert M. Adams, in *The Norton Anthology of English Literature*, 4th ed., comp. M. H. Abrams et al. (New York: Norton, 1979), p. 1220 n.

10. "Ben Jonson: An Anatomy," p. 382.

11. *Ben Jonson: Poems*, ed. Ian Donaldson (London: Oxford University Press, 1975).

12. *The Complete Poetry*, p. 12 n.

13. W. W. Meissner, *The Paranoid Process* (New York: Jason Aronson, 1978), p. 77. E. Glover, *On the Early Development of the Mind* (London: Imago, 1956), cited in Meissner, p. 74. Karl Abraham, *Selected Papers of Karl Abraham* (New York: Basic Books, 1954), cited in Meissner, p. 76.

14. James Howell, *Epistolae Ho-Elianae, The Familiar Letters of James Howell (1737)*, ed. Joseph Jacobs (London: D. Nutt, 1890–92), vol. 1, pp. 403–04, quoted in MacLean, ed., *Ben Jonson and the Cavalier Poets*, p. 423.

15. "To Ben. Iohnson" (26), *The Poems*, ed. Dunlap.

16. Meissner, *The Paranoid Process*, p. 77.

17. In "Ben Jonson on his beloved The Author Mr. William Shakespeare," *The Elizabethan Theatre*, ed. G. R. Hibbard (Waterloo, Canada: Archon, 1974), vol. 4, pp. 29–30, T. J. B. Spencer points out that, although the context of this phrase from "A Discourse concerning

the Original and Progress of Satire" is unclear, Dryden is at the very least comparing Jonson's poem to such a panegyric.

18. Meissner, *The Paranoid Process*, p. 74.

19. In *The Poetry of Ben Jonson* (New York: Barnes and Noble, 1969), p. 126, J. G. Nichols notes that Jonson "winds into his subject deliberately slowly." More in accordance with my own view is Wesley Trimpi, who, in *Ben Jonson's Poems: A Study of the Plain Style* (Stanford: Stanford University Press, 1962), observes that "such introductions are common in [Jonson's] poems, but this one is long and awkwardly connected to the rest of the poem" (p. 149). Trimpi also remarks on the elegy's syntactical obscurity (p. 150) and "structural looseness," which indicate, "perhaps, an indecisive attitude toward the subject himself" (p. 151). Spencer observes: "It must be admitted that these first sixteen lines express Jonson's personal preoccupations with ignorance, prejudice, and envy" (in *The Elizabethan Theatre*, ed. Hibbard, p. 32).

20. Melanie Klein, *Envy and Gratitude: A Study of Unconscious Sources* (London: Tavistock, 1957), pp. 63–65.

21. *Ben Jonson's Poems*, p. 151.

22. In *Ben Jonson* (Boston: Twayne, 1979), Claude J. Summers and Ted-Larry Pebworth make a somewhat similar observation about these lines: "This expansive new beginning releases the energy restrained in the cautionary introduction" (p. 199).

23. Between the poem's encomiastic form and the tendency of some critics to sentimentalize the complex relationships between strong brother poets, "small *Latine*, and lesse *Greeke*" has been rationalized as, at worst, a Jonsonian kindness to the educationally handicapped. Spencer, however, has called attention to the fact that Dryden was not the only seventeenth-century reader discomfited by such phrases: "The editor of Richard Brome's *Five New Plays* (1659) wrote a preface [including] Jonson's poem on Brome (who had been his amanuensis). 'We have here prefixt *Ben Johnson's* own testimony to his Servant our *Author;* we grant it is (according to *Ben's* own nature and custome) magisterial enough; and who looks for other, since he said to *Shakespear—I shall draw envy on his name* (by writing in his praise) and threw in his face—*small Latine and less Greek*.' " See *The Elizabethan Theatre*, ed. Hibbard, p. 30.

24. Norman N. Holland, *5 Readers Reading* (New Haven: Yale University Press, 1975), pp. 204–05. Norman N. Holland, *The Dynamics of Literary Response* (New York: Oxford University Press, 1968), p. 278. Also see Melanie Klein, "On Identification," *New Directions in Psycho-analysis*, ed. Melaine Klein et al. (New York: Basic Books, 1955), p. 311.

25. Herford, Simpson, and Simpson date *Discoveries* after the elegy to Shakespeare and the fire of 1623, but it is most probable that Jonson had developed his conception of the ideal poet long before he reached his fifties. See *Ben Jonson*, vol. 11, p. 213.

26. See Donne's "Amicissimo, et meritissimo Ben. Jonson. In Vulponem" (13), in *The Complete Poetry of John Donne*, ed. John T. Shawcross (Garden City, N.Y.: Doubleday, 1967); Herrick's "An Ode for him" (14), in *The Complete Poetry*, ed. Patrick; Carew's "To Ben. Johnson" (29–46), in *The Poems*, ed. Dunlap; Sidney Godolphin's "On Ben Jonson" (3), in Maclean, ed., *Ben Jonson and the Cavalier Poets*. Also see Mildmay Fane's "He who began from brick and lime," Thomas Randolph's "Answer to Mr. Ben Jonson's Ode, to Persuade Him Not to Leave the Stage," and Edmund Waller's "Upon Ben Jonson."

27. *Ben Jonson's Literary Criticism* (Lincoln: University of Nebraska Press, 1970), pp. xiii–xiv.

28. As Spencer puts it, here "it is Jonson's own activity that he attributes to Shakespeare" (p. 37). This is a variation on what Spencer sees as Jonson's tendency to turn Shakespeare "into a kind of sparring partner, whom he could make use of in order to justify his own rather solemn and laborious critical position" (p. 23). See *The Elizabethan Theatre*, ed. Hibbard.

29. Although Spencer sees the poem as another indication of "Jonson's lack of sympathy with Shakespeare's genius" (*The Elizabethan Theatre*, ed. Hibbard, p. 40), he is not moved to

inquire much further into the matter. Indeed, he takes some pains to apologize for it. For Spencer, the eulogy is really only a kind of advertisement, with "something of the flavour of a blurb, designed to sell a book; the panegyric is at times wild, only this side of absurdity. It is not intended to impress us as being well-considered, and in this respect it compares unfavourably with the thoughtful paragraph in Jonson's notebooks" (p. 39). The poem is, after all, only a fiction, designed more to delight than instruct: "It is primarily a literary composition, entertainingly making use of literary conventions. It is full of clever adaptations of Latinate words and thoughts." It is, in sum, "a poem and not an *affidavit*" (pp. 39–40).

Spencer concludes his useful essay, one of the very few that actually attempts to come to grips with Jonson's poem, by trying to sort out his own feelings about "Jonson's lack of sympathy with Shakespeare's genius": "I find the partial antipathy excusable, when I remember what mutual dislike has been nourished by great literary contemporaries" (p. 40). Unlike most commentators on the great eulogy, Spencer senses in it a strong poet's struggle with his text and with his subject.

30. Klein, *Envy and Gratitude*, p. 25.

31. Since this essay attempts to focus as much as possible on one particular aspect of Jonson's creativity, it has not endeavored to deal with Edmund Wilson's well-known analysis of Jonson as an anal-erotic psychological type, in "Morose Ben Jonson," *Ben Jonson: A Collection of Critical Essays*, ed. Jonas A. Barish (Englewood Cliffs, N.J.: Prentice-Hall, 1963), pp. 60–74, affirmed by Norman N. Holland, *Psychoanalysis and Shakespeare* (New York: McGraw-Hill, 1966), pp. 137–38. To do so has in fact become unnecessary, thanks to Professor Pearlman's work (see n. 6 above).

32. Bloom, *Anxiety*, p. 11.

33. See Carew's "To Ben Johnson," in *The Poems*, ed. Dunlap, and Herrick's "His Prayer to Ben. Johnson," in *The Complete Poetry*, ed. Patrick.

The Light, and Marke unto Posterity

ILONA BELL

✝

Circular Strategies and Structures in Jonson and Herbert

> Sure he that made us with such large discourse
> Looking before and after, gave us not
> That capability and godlike reason
> To fust in us unused.   *—Hamlet* 4. 4. 36–39

*G*eorge Herbert has *always been* solidly allied with Donne and the "metaphysicals," not with Jonson and the Sons of Ben.[1] John Roberts's complete bibliography of Herbert lists 171 references to Donne, but only 12 to Jonson, and those are for the most part asides rather than extended comparisons.[2] Although Jonson's influence on Herbert has rarely been considered or discussed, I have lately come to believe that Herbert's poems are often indebted more to Jonson than to Donne. Herbert shares Jonson's concern for the book, for the poem as written and constructed rather than spoken, for poetic form and meaning joined as one through the creation of the poem itself.[3] I am particularly interested in one aspect of this common concern: a characteristic, circular strategy and structure, "looking before and after," which I believe Herbert owed to Jonson. If he did, the comparison will complicate some of our most cherished assumptions about both Jonson and Herbert.

Recent criticism of *The Temple* has stressed Herbert's uncertainty and self-correction rather than the clarity and simplicity emphasized by earlier critics. Hence it can help us to recognize that, like Herbert's, the strategy of Jonson's poems is more corrective and demanding than we may have realized. Jonson's poems, especially the epigrams, create an impression of polished lucidity, only to disclose at their ends surprising, unexpected complexities that send the reader circling back to reinterpret and reconsider the entire poem. At the same time, Jonson's judgments remain more clearly

157

centered and more avowedly controlled than Herbert's. Thus Jonsonians can in turn help Herbertians to discover that reconsideration can be an essential corrective that reveals a complex structural coherence and yields a balanced, judicious assessment. There is now widespread belief in the validity of "mistaken" or "correcting" responses to *The Temple*.[4] Yet I believe that Herbert's self-corrections, like Jonson's overarching judgments, often circle back on themselves, enabling us to discover in retrospect an ultimate, more trustworthy point of view. And it is here, I think, that Herbert resembles and learned from Jonson.

Although it is impossible to prove that Herbert knew Jonson's poetry, it seems likely. Jonson published his collected works in 1616, just about the time Herbert was beginning to write poetry seriously. Since Herbert was then a fellow in classics at Trinity College, Cambridge, he had every reason to read and appreciate Jonson, who was clearly the greatest classical poet of the time. The circular strategies and structures I will examine seem closely related to Jonson's classicism, to his characteristic strategy of allowing the past to impinge on the present, of seeing his subjects as anachronistic reincarnations of ancient grace.[5] Although Herbert's classicism is less visible in *The Temple*, his immersion in biblical typology also encouraged him to imagine the present as a repetition and re-exploration of ancient grace.[6] As the past impinges on the present and the present hearkens back to the past, Jonson's and Herbert's poems become circular rather than dramatic, progressively retrospective rather than developmental.

Like Jonson in "To the Reader," the first of the *Epigrammes*, Herbert pauses in the "Dedication" of *The Temple* to discuss the proper way to read and judge his poems. The parallels are striking and characteristic. Both poets adopt a retrospective point of view and a circular poetic structure to demonstrate the intricacy of simplicity, a characteristic Jonson's best poetry shares with Herbert's. I wish to examine Herbert's "Dedication" first, since we are presently more accustomed to retrospective revision in *The Temple*, and since this dedication announces its own strategies and defines our involvement more clearly.

Dedication

Lord, my first fruits present themselves to thee;
Yet not mine neither: for from thee they came,
And must return. Accept of them and me,

And make us strive, who shall sing best thy name.
Turn their eyes hither, who shall make a gain:
Theirs, who shall hurt themselves or me, refrain.[7]

Herbert's petition seems to have been written in retrospect, after *The Temple* was completed, for the poems have already acquired an independent existence, a voice separate from the poet's. The dedication addresses God, but the final couplet refers to us and the danger that we will seriously misread the following poems. The experience of reading sounds as difficult and hazardous as the experience of writing. In fact, Herbert seems to think that each reader makes the poems anew, for better or worse, for he puns on the final rhymes of the poem: "make a gain" and "refrain." To profit, to make a gain, we must "make" the poem "again," afresh. Herbert also seems to pun on the original meaning of poet, *vates* or "maker," thereby inviting the reader to become "cocreator" of the poem.[8] Should we refuse to take our responsibility seriously, should we simply echo the words as if they were a static "refrain," Herbert would just as soon have us "refrain" or desist.

Thus the conclusion should send us circling back to read the dedication once again, armed with the expectation that we will in fact "make a gain," that we will advance beyond our initial response. On rereading, we basically share Herbert's own retrospective point of view. Now the circular structure and the punning conclusion alert us to further, analogous ambiguities in the opening lines: "Lord, my first fruits present themselves to thee; / Yet not mine neither: for from thee they came, / And must return." On first reading, we may naturally assume that the poems, given by God to the poet, must return whence they came. But, if the poems return to heaven, how are we to judge them, as the final lines suggest that we should? Only, it seems, if the whole process begins again, if God returns the poems and then turns our eyes thither. This possibility is suggested by the studied ambiguity of lines 1 to 3. "For from thee they came, / And must return," could mean "from thee they came, and *to* thee they must return"; but it could as easily mean "from thee they came originally, and *from thee* they will return once again." The second possibility, though less obvious, is reinforced at every stage of the poem. At the outset, "first fruits" imply other fruits to follow, and, at the end, Herbert's plea, "Turn their eyes hither, who shall make a gain," recalls the pivotal verb, "return," suggesting that the whole process begins over again. But the sentence that follows holds the key: "make us strive, who shall sing best thy name." If Herbert is suggesting, and nothing else makes as much sense, a singing contest between his "first fruits," his poems, and himself, we must imagine the poet rereading his poems when they return and discovering where they were originally inspired by God and where marred by his own human fallibility. In retrospect, from a distance, the poet sees his creations more objectively; he can thus criticize them when they deserve to be criticized, and he can learn from them when they contain a transcendent point of view. Thus writing and reading intertwine continually, more intricately and variously: the poems that follow, Herbert warns us, should be read as they unfold, then be reread from a perspective that can only be attained after the poems are completed.

It is now perhaps easier to understand why Herbert worries so openly and intensely about our capacity to understand, to make a gain, both to profit and to make the poems vital and viable once again. To read *The Temple* well, we must be able to decide when the poem prevails because it is divinely inspired, and when the poet sings best because, finding his first fruits inadequate, he suggests an alternative, critical point of view. Herbert's poetry requires active discernment and careful judgment. His dedication is designed not only to describe the poet's complicated relation to his poems but also to instruct us: to "make us strive, who shall sing best thy name." Thus I would say that Herbert's poems are writerly at the outset, readerly at the close.[9]

If we now look at Jonson's first epigram, "To the Reader," we should see clear parallels between Herbert and Jonson, for it is precisely this combination of simplicity and difficulty that makes the structure and language of *The Temple* resemble Jonson perhaps even more than Donne. Jonson shares Herbert's desire for the pointed clarity of a single trustworthy interpretation that makes "a gain." At the same time, he expects us to choose the "best" interpretation from the complex alternatives and demands posed by reconsideration; he expects us to read and thus make "again."

> To the Reader.
> Pray thee, take care, that tak'st my booke in hand,
> To reade it well: that is, to understand.[10]

Jonson's conscious awareness of "my booke," the object he has created and now released to the reader, recalls Herbert's vision of his poems as "first fruits," as independent products of the poet's mind and God's inspiration. This first epigram is one of the simplest poems imaginable, or so it seems. The words are all monosyllables, until the last word, "understand," which is hardly a rarity. "Take," one of the most basic and familiar verbs in English, appears twice in the first line. The syntax is equally direct. There are no inversions. The phrases are short, and they follow a natural progression. A simple idea, "take care," is followed by a simple clarification, "To reade it well," which is itself spelled out by an even more direct explication, "that is, to understand." Like Herbert, Jonson seems to write spontaneously, as he would have spoken, and this casual impression, combined with Jonson's gracious, almost courtly tone, immediately establishes a direct, comfortable relationship between poet and reader. However, when we reach the end of the epigram, we discover that Jonson's purpose is more pointed and precise, his tone more stern and anxious, than we first assumed. There is a warning here, and a fear, that cannot be dismissed.

Although "To the Reader" does not itself present a terribly intricate interpretative challenge, I do not think it simply commands the reader's willed submission. Jonson worries, and wants us to know, that as we read on our responses will be fraught with difficulty and potential error. In fact, if we now read "To the Reader" again, we no longer find it quite so simple or casual. In retrospect, Jonson's plea, "Pray thee, take care," sounds less gracious, more forbidding. Even the casual repetition of "take care" in "tak'st my booke" seems more studied, more like a sophisticated play on words calculated to make us reassess our response and Jonson's meaning. For "take" has many meanings, including one, "if you take my meaning," which we might easily overlook until we reach Jonson's pointed, final reminder: we must grasp his book with the intellect, if we are to understand it.

Since "To the Reader" is so short, it is not as notably circular in structure and strategy as Herbert's "Dedication." Yet Jonson's conclusion also surprises us into discovering—and warns us to remember—that words, even the most unassertive, forgettable words, can convey multiple meanings, which only go to show "what man can say in a little" ("Epitaph on Elizabeth, L. H."). Like *The Temple*, Jonson's *Epigrammes* must be constantly reread to be read well.

If we can judge from these introductory poems, and I think Jonson and Herbert hoped we would, these two poets share a vision of their poems as both experiential and retrospective. Though

Jonson only hints at complexities and dangers which Herbert specifies, "To the Reader" and "Dedication" both suggest, by their very
existence, that their respective poets anxiously perused the whole
book after the individual poems were completed. We know that
Jonson did in fact do so in seeing the poems into print, and we have
good reason to believe that Herbert also prepared his collected
poems for publication.[11] The experience of redaction following the
experience of writing has led both poets to consider and worry
about the experience of reading and, thus, to make the experiences
of writing and reading the subjects of these and other poems. They
both simplify their language to encourage clear, careful judgments:
Herbert says "sing best," "make a gain"; Jonson says, "reade it
well." Knowing that readers are sure to have difficulty understanding, simplicity and clarity being qualities of mind as well as
qualities of poetry, Jonson and Herbert acknowledge the distance
between the reader's first impression and the poet's considered
judgment. Consequently, and this is my main concern, they create
circular poetic structures, so that the point, the surprising epigrammatic punch of the conclusion, will send the reader circling
back to consider alternative interpretations, to discover that reading
well means considering and selecting the best of all possible readings and rereadings.

"To the Reader" may seem too brief and simple to bear the
weight of my comparison with Herbert's "Dedication," but many
of Jonson's best epigrams explore and confirm the very issues
and strategies we have noticed in the first epigram. "On Lucy
Countesse of Bedford," one of Jonson's most brilliant and justly
famous poems, is probably the best example (*Epigrammes* 76). The
poem begins as an amusing little tale about the process of writing
poetry, but it becomes a serious study of the process required to
read Jonsonian poetry. At the outset, Jonson playfully, presump-
tuously sits down to instruct his "zealous *Muse*" about the "kinde of
creature I could most desire, / To honor, serve, and love; as *Poets*
use."[12] Yet the urbanity, the wit, the subtlety of the poem fully
emerge only at the end, when the poem moves from the writerly to
the readerly: "Such when I meant to faine, and wish'd to see, / My
Muse bad, *Bedford* write, and that was shee." It turns out that the
Countess of Bedford is both the ideal "kinde of creature" Jonson
wished to create and the real woman actually described in the
poem's impressive list of virtues. This duality raises questions
which threaten the apparent clarity and finality of the conclusion.
Did Jonson begin his morning, "timely rapt with holy fire," be-

cause he already had the countess in mind? Or did he, setting out to write a poem about an ideal woman, fail to produce a poem until he decided to describe Lucy, whom he had actually seen and already admired? We have no way of knowing. One suspects the former, but the dramatic structure of the poem captures and sustains both possibilities. The muse seems to lead us outside the poem to the real Lucy, but Jonson immediately turns back to the poem. "Shee" is Lucy, but "that" refers to the written word, *"Bedford,"* which returns to the title and the process of writing that follows. Thus the end of the poem is essentially inseparable from the beginning, for Jonson has only to follow the muse's instructions to have his title ready made. The final turn of wit emerges when Jonson leads us back to the beginning and sets us reading the poem once again, playing with all the twists and turns of feigning and meaning, in the many senses of both words. On rereading, we see both what Jonson "meant" or intended and what the poem "meant," once written; we see both what Jonson wished to feign, to fashion or form, and what he wished to feign, to pretend or dissemble.

In "On Lucy Countesse of Bedford," circular structure is dramatically appropriate, since Jonson only began to write the poem, he says, when the experience it describes was already over, when he, as writer, could see his own meaning from several points of view. Yet I think this kind of structural circularity, with all the resulting intricacies of meaning that emerge only on rereading, is absolutely characteristic of Jonson's epigrammatic imagination. Many of the satirical epigrams work in precisely this way. For example, in "On some-thing, that walkes some-where" (*Epigrammes* 11), the desire to reread and reexamine Jonson's ghostly creation is all but guaranteed by his punning conclusion. "Good Lord, walke dead still." In "On court-worme" (*Epigrammes* 15), the syllogistic structure also turns full circle:

> All men are wormes: But this no man. In silke
>   'Twas brought to court first wrapt, and white as milke;
> Where, afterwards, it grew a butter-flye:
>   Which was a cater-piller. So't will dye.

The final joke is on us when we reread the opening phrase in light of what follows.

Jonson finds this structural circularity irresistible, even when his point of view is present rather than past. "To William Roe" (*Epigrammes* 128), for example, is a valediction—wishing Roe a success-

ful voyage abroad—that begins in the present and turns toward the
future. At the outset, Jonson describes Roe setting out, "Countries,
and climes, manners, and men to know, / T[o] 'extract, and choose
the best of all these knowne, / And those to turne to bloud, and
make thine owne." [13] Jonson then introduces the image of a circle,
which, much like the compass in Donne's "A Valediction: Forbidding Mourning," prophesies a safe and certain return:

> May windes as soft as breath of kissing friends,
>   Attend thee hence; and there, may all thy ends,
> As the beginnings here, prove purely sweet,
>   And perfect in a circle always meet.
> So, when we, blest with thy returne, shall see
>   Thy selfe, with thy first thoughts, brought home by thee.

The entire circle will presumably be retraced and enriched upon
Roe's happy return, but we can sample the benefits of retrospective
rediscovery now, by seeing the beginning of the voyage and the
poem in light of Jonson's ending.

By emphasizing the distinct, independent value of Roe's "first
thoughts," Jonson sends us circling back to reexamine their expression at the beginning of the poem. Roe will "extract, and
choose the best of all" he sees abroad, Jonson suggests, because his
judgment and discrimination are infallible. Yet, when Roe returns,
his friends will say he "came backe untouch'd," meaning that he has
returned both unharmed and unchanged. Thus Roe must already
embody the best that is known by all the countries and men he will
encounter. As in "On Lucy Countesse of Bedford," Jonson's full
meaning emerges only on rereading, when we can understand the
ideal in terms of the actual, when we can reassess the beginning in
terms of the ending. It is Jonson's particular genius to make the
return to a starting place seem like a dramatic discovery. The end of
the poem is already in the past, though it has not yet taken place,
because the future essentially returns and remakes the present
when it is past. Indeed, the poem ends with a projection into the
future of "this voyce" inspired to sing of Roe as an exemplar of the
past, "that good AENEAS." Jonson's most successful poems are,
like Roe's thoughts, "perfect in a circle always meet;" they continually embrace fresh alternatives because he balances intricacy
through circularity.

To see just how characteristic this strategy is, we might consider
a couple of poems where circularity is present but less prominent.

Unlike the surprising epigrammatic stroke that concludes and reopens "On Lucy Countesse of Bedford," the conclusion of "To Penshurst" does not cast the entire poem in a new light. Nevertheless, Jonson's judicious summary does inspire rereading: it encourages us to look back at the initial comparison between Penshurst and other more showy houses. It also asks us to recall all the intervening observations that have embodied and enriched Jonson's judgment. "Inviting a friend to supper" (*Epigrammes* 101) is even less strategically circular, but the conclusion exalts and practices retrospective reconsideration:

> But, at our parting, we will be, as when
> We innocently met. No simple word,
>> That shall be utter'd at our mirthfull boord,
> Shall make us sad next morning: or affright
> The libertie, that wee'll enjoy to night.

The invitation, to be confirmed, Jonson promises, by the evening's experiences, will be reaffirmed when the evening is over. By looking forward to the next morning, Jonson can already look back on and certify advantages which are still forthcoming. The circle is only beginning.

Perhaps even more clearly than the poems that are themselves more intrinsically circular, "To Penshurst" and "Inviting a friend to supper" explain why circular structures and strategies appeal to Jonson's imagination. As a poet of consummate judgment, Jonson must both anticipate and reassess the experiences he describes. His authority depends on the multiplicity of perspectives, the looking back to look forward, that classicism encourages and circularity creates. And this observation is equally true for Herbert, I believe, for, like Jonson's, many of Herbert's most subtle and successful poems have circular structures which juxtapose earlier, more naïve points of view against subsequent critiques and more valid discoveries.

Poems like "Affliction (I)" and "The Collar" begin after experience has ended, forcing us to assess Herbert's first thoughts in light of his ultimate conclusions. Like the title and first line of "On Lucy Countesse of Bedford," their beginnings announce their conclusions: "When first thou didst entice to thee my heart, / I thought the service brave"; "I struck the board, and cry'd, No more." What makes these poems intriguingly Jonsonian is that, despite the initial, retrospective point of view, we cannot quite discern or fully understand the poet's final judgment until we reach the surprising epigrammatic punch of the conclusion that sends us circling back to reassess what we have just read. Thus, at the end of "The Collar," we learn to perceive within the speaker's own words thoughts that he has not acknowledged, and that we cannot discern, until his outburst has reached its surprising conclusion: "At every word, / Me thoughts I heard one calling." On first reading, we are caught up in the speaker's rebellion. We must reread the whole poem, with the conclusion in mind, to discover the simple solution of God's voice calling at every word, saying, "Not so, my heart: but there is fruit, / And thou hast hands." [14]

"The Flower" also illustrates Herbert's penchant for circular structures at once retrospective and progressive. The opening image of flowers, "Quite under ground . . . Where they together / All the hard weather / Dead to the world, keep house unknown," has been directly inspired by the speaker's final discovery:

> These are thy wonders, Lord of love,
> To make us see we are but flowers that glide:
> Which we once can finde and prove,
> Thou hast a garden for us, where to bide.

Though the split between reading and rereading is less violent than in "The Collar," rereading is still essential, for we obviously cannot know that the beginning echoes and continues the conclusion until we have read the end of the poem. And, in retrospect, when we are familiar with the whole story, Herbert's language reverberates more deeply. When all is said and done, we can see (as can the speaker) that the image of flowers "dead to the world" embraces both the desperation he once felt and the "unknown" revivification he now recognizes. The more we read about the long, cold, wintry periods of God's absence, the more intense and precious seem God's *returns*. As in "The Collar," Herbert has structured "The Flower" so that our experience reenacts the speaker's own discoveries, which perhaps explains why Herbert's language fluctuates from the general (stanzas 1 and 3) to the intensely personal (stanza 2, 4–6), only to include us again most insistently at the end: "we are but flowers that glide." On first reading, confused, inexperienced, unenlightened, "We say amisse, / This or that is." On rereading, we return from the knowledge of the end to a new, more complex view of the beginning, and the cycle begins again, "fresh" and "sweet and clean." Now we can see where the speaker is mired in his own errors and where we "can finde and prove" God's presence. In fact, the very mention of "returns" recalls all the "turns" and "returns" of Herbert's "Dedication," both the warning that we may hurt ourselves and the more positive injunction to "make a gain" and to make again.

Of course, Jonson and Herbert do not hold a monopoly on circular poetic structure. The form becomes very popular, for example, among the Romantics. Still, this characteristic strategy does forge a new alliance between Jonson and Herbert, because this particular concept of circularity is alien to Donne. Even when Donne uses the image of a circle, his argument moves forward dramatically, masking or moving beyond what has gone before. The famous image of the compass in "A Valediction: Forbidding Mourning" is completely self-contained and definitive. Because it gives a more concrete, satisfying account of the lover's relationship, it supersedes the earlier, more general images of the departing soul, the trepidation of the spheres, and the gold beaten to airy thinness. Although these images are ingeniously connected, they function dramatically to reveal the progress in the speaker's developing thoughts. Similarly, in "A Valediction: Of Weeping," the first image of tears as coins is literally shattered by the lady's grief, and the speaker must "quickly make" a new, more consoling metaphor to banish all thought of the image that has just failed. Though the circular images that end both valedictions, like that at the end of "To William Roe," promise the speaker's safe return, this reassurance is not translated into poetic structure.

Even when Donne chooses a circular poetic form, as in "A nocturnall upon S. Lucies day, Being the shortest day," he does not use circularity to include the reader in the process of discovery, as Herbert and Jonson do. The poem begins, " 'Tis the yeares midnight, and it is the dayes," and it ends, coming full circle. "This houre her Vigill, and her Eve, since this / Both the yeares, and the dayes deep midnight is." Yet the speaker is buried in his own grief, "the grave / Of all, that's nothing," and he recalls the past only to perpetuate his original loss. Thus in returning to the beginning of the poem, he creates a "deep" and unalterable stasis, "Of the first nothing, the Elixer grown." Repetition becomes a ritual ("let mee call / This houre her Vigill") that precludes regeneration and reinterpretation. The poem remains a dramatic utterance, mired in misery, isolated from other "lovers, for whose sake, the lesser Sunne . . . is runne / To fetch new lust." The poem ends where it has begun, but it does not begin again where it has ended.[15] In

Donne's poems, circular forms and circular images do not become structural strategies to explore—or to encourage us to explore—the complexities of rewriting and rereading. Donne's poems are either retrospective or progressive, but they are not both. I do not mean to suggest, of course, that Donne's poems do not merit or require rereading. What I do suggest is that a return to the beginning of a poem, a reassessment of the speaker's "first thoughts" in light of his conclusion, is not intrinsic or necessary to the structure and meaning of Donne's poems, as it is so often to Jonson's and Herbert's.

For both Jonson and Herbert, the poem is not ultimately a dramatic performance, as it was for Donne, but a written construct, which can be read and reread and misread and made again because it can be read from so many different points of view. Unlike Donne, Jonson and Herbert pause to observe and try out and prescribe the process of writing and reading, choosing puns and circular poetic structures to define this process, to juxtapose the ideal against the actual, to capture the turnings and returnings of all the poet meant and all the poem means, once it is written and reread. Jonson and Herbert have both suffered, as they both feared they would, from our expectation of simplicity and clarity. Yet I think our current understanding of Herbert's emphasis on variation, self-correction, and retrospection in *The Temple* can help us understand the intricacy of Jonson's simplicity. At the same time, our understanding of Jonson's balanced, centered judgment should help us understand the retrospective clarity that can emerge from Herbert's circularity. Jonson was already a poet widely respected and published when *The Temple* was only a glimmer in Herbert's future. If Jonson and Herbert indeed share this penchant for retrospective judgments and circular structures, it is likely that Jonson taught Herbert to see its remarkable potential for looking before and after.

NOTES

1. George Williamson, *The Donne Tradition: A Study in English Poetry from Donne to the Death of Cowley* (Cambridge, Mass.: Harvard University Press, 1930), is typical. "Of all the Metaphysicals," he says, "Herbert is in some ways most like Donne," (p. 98). Joseph Summers, *The Heirs of Donne and Jonson* (Oxford: Oxford University Press, 1970), is much more willing than most other critics to associate Jonson and Herbert (pp. 88 and 89).

2. *George Herbert: An Annotated Bibliography of Modern Criticism, 1905–1974* (Columbia: University of Missouri Press, 1978). The boldest comparisons of Jonson and Herbert are

made-by Josephine Miles and Hanan C. Selvin, "A Factor Analysis of the Vocabulary of Poetry in the Seventeenth Century," in *The Computer and Literary Style: Introductory Essays and Studies*, ed. Jacob Leed (Kent, Ohio: Kent State University Press, 1966), pp. 116–27, and by Paul Cubeta, "Ben Jonson's Religious Lyrics," *JEGP* 62 (1963), 96–110.

3. For those perceptions, and indeed for many helpful suggestions, I am indebted to the readers and participants of the conference at Dearborn, who seemed remarkably willing to associate Jonson and Herbert. See, for example, the essays Patrides and Newton contribute to this volume.

4. Stanley E. Fish, *The Living Temple: George Herbert and Catechizing* (Berkeley and Los Angeles: University of California Press, 1978), p. 27. Other pertinent books on Herbert include Joseph Summers, *George Herbert: His Religion and Art* (Cambridge, Mass.: Harvard University Press, 1954); Arnold Stein, *George Herbert's Lyrics* (Baltimore: Johns Hopkins Press, 1968); Coburn Freer, *Music for a King: George Herbert's Style and the Metrical Psalms* (Baltimore: Johns Hopkins University Press, 1972); and, above all, Helen Vendler, *The Poetry of George Herbert* (Cambridge, Mass.: Harvard University Press, 1975). Thomas M. Greene, "Ben Jonson and the Centered Self," *SEL* 10 (1970), 325–48, describes the relation between the image of the circle and the moral qualities in Jonson's poems and plays. He concludes that "on the whole the circles of the lyric verse shrink toward their center, toward the Stoic individual soul, self-contained, balanced, at peace with itself even in isolation."

5. For this connection between circularity and Jonson's and many others' classicism, I would like to thank the editors of this volume.

6. For discussions of Herbert's debts to the classics and biblical typology, see, respectively, Mary Ellen Rickey, *Utmost Art: Complexity in the Verse of George Herbert* (Lexington: University of Kentucky Press, 1966), and Barbara Lewalski, *Protestant Poetics and the Seventeenth-Century Religious Lyric* (Princeton: Princeton University Press, 1979).

7. Quoted from *The Works of George Herbert*, ed. F. E. Hutchinson (Oxford: Oxford University Press, 1941; rev. 1945). Interpretations of Herbert's "Dedication" are rare. Robert's *Bibliography* has no listings.

8. Jonson explains the etymology in *Discoveries* and uses the pun quite self-consciously in "On My First Sonne." See Wesley Trimpi, *Ben Jonson's Poems: A Study of the Plain Style* (Stanford: Stanford University Press, 1962), pp. 182–83.

9. For a discussion of the terms "writerly" and "readerly," see Roland Barthes, *S/Z*, trans. Richard Miller (New York: Hill and Wang, 1974). The terms are also used by Richard Newton in the essay printed in this volume.

10. For obvious reasons, detailed readings of "To the Reader" are also rare. Bruce Smith, "Ben Jonson's Epigrammes: Portrait-Gallery, Theater, Commonwealth," *SEL* 14 (1974), 101, gives the poem more attention that most have devoted to it. Claude J. Summers and Ted-Larry Pebworth, *Ben Jonson* (Boston: Twayne, 1979), p. 140, describe the importance of the conclusion most compellingly.

11. See J. Max Patrick, "Critical Problems in Editing George Herbert's *The Temple*," in *The Editor as Critic and the Critic as Editor*, ed. Murray Krieger (Los Angeles: Clark Memorial Library, 1973), pp. 3–40.

12. My reading of this poem is deeply indebted to Anne Ferry. See *All in War with Time: Love Poetry of Shakespeare, Donne, Jonson, Marvell* (Cambridge, Mass.: Harvard University Press, 1975), pp. 142–49. Trimpi also discusses Jonson's self-consciousness about conventions of love and poetry (*Ben Jonson's Poems*, pp. 140–41).

13. See, especially, Summers and Pebworth, *Ben Jonson*, pp. 148–49. For a reading quite different from mine, see Trimpi, *Ben Jonson's Poems*, pp. 174–75.

14. For a more detailed examination of these points, see my article, "The Double Pleasures of Herbert's *Collar*," in *"Too Rich to Clothe the Sunne": Essays on George Herbert*, ed.

Claude J. Summers and Ted-Larry Pebworth (Pittsburgh: University of Pittsburgh Press, 1980), pp. 77–88.

15. For a somewhat different response to the conclusion, see James L. Spenko, "Circular Form in Two Donne Lyrics," *English Language Notes* 13 (1975), 103–07.

MICHAEL P. PARKER

"To my friend G. N. from Wrest":
Carew's Secular Masque

Despite the upsurge of interest in the English country-house poem
during the past twenty-five years, critics have largely ignored
Thomas Carew's two contributions to the genre, "To Saxham" and
"To my friend G. N. from Wrest." The neglect of "To Saxham" is
attributable in part to Carew's patterning of his poem on "To
Penshurst"; despite its occasionally ingenious conceits and felicitous phrasing, we might argue that "To Saxham" can be dismissed
as no more than a good imitation of a Jonsonian original. But the
poem to G. N. from Wrest is a different piece altogether. Composed in late 1639 or early 1640, Carew's poem diverges consciously from the Jonsonian model.[1] For Jonson, Penshurst not
only mirrors the larger social and moral hierarchy but is an integral
part of that hierarchy: the incident of King James's impromptu visit
to the Sidney estate establishes that duty to sovereign, duty to
dependents, and duty to self are complementary and inseparable.
In "To G. N. from Wrest," however, Carew abandons the Jonsonian ideal of the ordered cosmos. The primary attraction of Wrest
is its isolation from the macrocosm: the sovereign has come to
represent a threat to the ideals of the country house, rather than
their fulfillment. Employing techniques borrowed from the court
masque, Carew invests the congenial company gathered at Wrest
Park with the mythology traditionally reserved for the monarch
and his immediate circle. In a number of respects, "To G. N. from
Wrest" foreshadows the treatment and themes of "Upon Appleton
House." Carew's piece represents the crucial middle term between
Jonson's initial essays in the English country-house poem and Marvell's transformation of the genre in the 1640s and 1650s.

   To appreciate Carew's poem, it is necessary to have some knowledge of Wrest Park, its proprietor, and his circle of friends. Unfortunately, a scholarly blunder in the early twentieth century has

until now impeded such investigation. In the detailed history of Wrest Park in *The Victoria History of the County of Bedfordshire*, M. R. Manfield remarks that the manor and the title of earl of Kent passed to Anthony de Grey, an aged and obscure Leicestershire clergyman, on the death of his cousin Henry in 1631.[2] In fact, Henry de Grey did not die until the close of 1639, and it is undoubtedly during the residence of Henry and his fascinating countess, Elizabeth Talbot, that Carew visited Wrest.[3] Rhodes Dunlap, editor of the standard edition of Carew's poetry, perpetuates the error of the *Victoria History;* only the general excellence of his commentary appears to have prevented subsequent editors and critics from rectifying his mistake.[4] The error is of significance, however, since it deterred Dunlap from pursuing the clues to the remarkable cultural life that flourished at Wrest Park during the 1630s.

Wrest Park had been in the possession of his family for almost three hundred and fifty years when Henry de Grey, eighth earl of Kent, succeeded to the title in 1623.[5] The family fortunes, ailing for over a century, greatly improved with Kent's marriage in 1601 to Elizabeth Talbot, granddaughter of the redoubtable Bess of Hardwick and, with her two sisters, coheiress to the vast Shrewsbury land holdings. The de Greys were in constant attendance at court during the reign of James I, maintaining a house in Whitefriars; in 1617 Lady Kent succeeded the countess of Roxborough as chief lady-in-waiting to Queen Anne. With the accession of Charles I, however, the earl and countess appear to have lost what influence they commanded at court. In 1627 Kent resisted the king's attempt to extract a forced loan from the nation; as one of the so-called Refusers, he was stripped of the lord-lieutenancy of Bedfordshire, a position he had held since 1621.[6] Although the earl regained his office by December 1629 and occasionally thereafter attended important court ceremonies—the baptism of the duke of York in 1633 and the Garter installation the following year—from the late 1620s, he and his wife retired more or less permanently to Wrest Park.

Retirement from London, however, did not entail abandoning all courtly pleasures: Wrest became the gathering place for many of the most brilliant men and women of the Caroline period. From 1628, the jurist John Selden was a constant house guest of the de Greys and may have acted as legal adviser to the family.[7] The relationship between Selden and his hosts was intimate, to say the least. John Aubrey reports that the "Countesse, being an ingeniose woman and loving men, would let him [Selden] lye with her, and

Elizabeth, Countess of Kent, by Paul van Somer.
Courtesy of the Tate Gallery.

her husband knew it. After the Earle's death he maried her. . . . I remember my Sadler (who wrought many years to that Family) told me that Mr. Selden had got more by his Prick than he had done by his practise." [8] Although Selden's biographers have traditionally discounted Aubrey's steamy relation (on what ground is unclear), the jurist's contemporaries wrote of the connection in a vein that corroborates the account in *Brief Lives*. In an anonymous parliamentary satire of the 1640s (Osborn MS. PB VII/30 in the Beinecke Library at Yale University), the royalist author snipes at "Grave Mr Selden, who doth now repent / He ever searcht ye Antiquities of Kent." Both Selden and the countess, it should be noted, were in their sixties at the time the satire was written. Selden was not the only writer to find the company at Wrest Park congenial. Samuel Butler served as a page in the countess's household sometime during the late twenties or early thirties; there, Aubrey reports, Butler "employed his time much in painting and drawing, and also in Musique," and may have met the miniaturist Samuel Cooper under the countess's auspices.[9] Sir John Suckling also appears to have known the de Greys well. In a 1639 letter to Selden, he inquires after the countess's health and remarks the esteem he holds for her "conversation." [10]

The company of poets and wits apparently whetted Lady Kent's literary aspirations, although her own efforts were on a more modest scale. She was the authoress of *A Choice Manuall of Rare and Select Secrets in Physick and Chyrurgery*, which went through nineteen seventeenth-century editions, and of *A True Gentlewoman's Delight, wherein is contained all manner of Cookery*, a collection of recipes perhaps got up with the aid of the French-trained cook she had inherited from Lord Montague.[11] Although the society at Wrest had a strong literary coloring, life there does not seem to have been so learned as to exclude all else. In a letter from Wrest dated January 21, 1638/39, Madam Ann Merrick writes her friend Mrs. Lydall to discuss the latest plays, to ask what cut of sleeve is currently in vogue at court, and to lament the impending Scottish campaign, "lest all the young gallants should go for soldiers, and the ladies should want servants to accompany them." [12] The evidence, though slim, suggests that the family and guests at Wrest Park pursued a lively round of cultural activities. Such a surmise is supported by the countess's family ties to the two most important aristocratic patrons of art and literature in early seventeenth-century England: one of her two sisters married William Herbert, third earl of Pembroke, the other Thomas Howard, second earl of

Arundel. The de Greys' not altogether friendly relations with their wealthy brothers-in-law may, in fact, have spurred the countess to literary hobnobbing. Financially unable to compete with Arundel and Pembroke in reedifying country seats or acquiring choice objets d'art, the earl and countess contented themselves with cultivating the friendship of the choice wits of the age.

The most prominent literary figure associated with Wrest Park, however, is Thomas Carew. "To my friend G. N. from Wrest," probably his last poem, is also one of his best. Although Carew again employs many of the country-house topoi that he used in "To Saxham," he organizes them according to an utterly different structural principle borrowed from the court masque. Stephen Orgel describes how, in Jonson's hands, the masque "separated into two sections. The first, called the antimasque, . . . presented a world of disorder or vice, everything that the ideal world of the second, the courtly main masque, was to overcome and supersede." [13] The physical structure of the Jacobean and Caroline stage underlined the cosmic implications of the conflict: by means of machinery, the antimasque figures were customarily banished to "hell," the space beneath the stage, when the deities of the main masque descended from the "heavens" above it. The shift from order to disorder was conveyed not only through the dramatic action but through the use of "scenes"—architectural and landscape tableaux painted on curtains or shutters. In "To G. N. from Wrest," Carew translates the vertical geography of the masque into a horizontal frame. The three regions of the stage—"heavens," stage proper, and "hell"—are echoed in the poem by the three regions of the hall, the garden, and the world outside the estate, respectively. As in the masque, the drama stems from the poet's efforts to unite the first two regions as he separates them from the third. Carew integrates hall and garden by dissolving the architectural frame of the house; he divides the unified estate from the disorder of the external world by elevating another barrier, the moat, into an encompassing zodiac. Wrest, "i' th' center plac'd," becomes a world in its own right.

Carew's structural innovation is illuminated by a comparison with "To Penshurst." Jonson presents the Sidney estate in terms of the natural and social hierarchy: he begins with the four elements, works his way up the scale through beasts and men, and concludes with the king—God's anointed—and God himself. The first half of "To G. N. from Wrest" reproduces the Jonsonian structure through geographical movement. The poet proceeds from the world outside the estate through the meadows to the house and its inhabitants. From the hall, however, he retraces his steps through the grounds to the moat; in the final movement, the poet again reverses his path, bringing the tutelary gods of the garden into the house itself through the emblematic marriage of Ceres and Bacchus. This peripatetic progress, which foreshadows the speaker's mental and physical perambulations in "Upon Appleton House," echoes the regular alternation between order and disorder in the tableaux of the court masques. With the poet's "beating of the bounds," Wrest is closed off from the ruder world outside; the daimonic forces of the estate are released, and the gods emerge from the landscape to mingle with men.

While other country-house poems address an estate itself—Penshurst, Saxham, Appleton House—or the estate's owner—Sir Robert Wroth, Sir Lewis Pemberton—Carew writes this poem from inside Wrest to the world outside, to the G. N. (perhaps Gilbert North) of the title. As the poet describes it, that external world is not appealing:

> I Breathe (sweet *Ghib:*) the temperate ayre of *Wrest*
> Where I no more with raging stormes opprest,
> Weare the cold nights out by the bankes of Tweed,
> On the bleake Mountaines, where fierce tempests breed,
> And everlasting Winter dwells; where milde
> *Favonius*, and the Vernall windes exilde,
> Did never spread their wings: but the wilde North
> Brings sterill Fearne, Thistles, and Brambles forth.   (1–8)

"Bankes of Tweed" and "the wilde North" undoubtedly allude to the unsuccessful military expedition of 1639, in which Charles I sought to bring the convenanting Scots to heel. In Carew's mention of the hardships of the campaign and the sterility of the landscape, it is difficult to overlook an oblique criticism of the king's imprudent Scottish policy—criticism that the presence of the opposition leader Selden at the de Grey estate would make all the more pointed.[14] The retrospective viewpoint provided by the pleasures of the "temperate ayre" of Wrest renders the horrors of the border country striking. Carew builds up the disparate details of his experience—the "raging stormes," "cold nights," "bleake Mountaines," "fierce tempests"— into a fully realized, almost fantastic description of the realm of "everlasting Winter."

The technique is painterly: in fact, Carew's landscape closely resembles the tableau designed by Inigo Jones for the first scene of *Salmacida Spolia*, the last masque of the Caroline period. Performed on January 21, 1639/40, during the month in which Carew may have added final touches to his poem, Davenant's masque opens with

a horrid scene . . . of storm and tempest; no glimpse of the sun was seen, as if darkness, confusion, and deformity, had possest the world, and driven light to heaven, the trees bending, as forced by a gust of wind, their branches rent from their trunks, and some torn up by the roots: afar off was a dark wrought sea, with rolling billows, breaking against the rocks, with rain, lightning and thunder.[15]

Davenant retains a belief in the power of royal example to tame discord and to put a permanent end to political unrest. In the final song of *Salmacida Spolia*, an address to the monarchs, the chorus proclaims:

> All that are harsh, all that are rude,
> Are by your harmony subdu'd;
> Yet so into obedience wrought,
> As if not forc'd to it, but taught. (5–8)

In "To G. N. from Wrest," however, Carew abandons this faith in monarchs to seek a solution in a more limited sphere. In *Salmacida Spolia*, the opening landscape of darkness and confusion is dispelled by divine intervention:

the scene changed into a calm, the sky serene, afar off Zephyrus appeared breathing a gentle gale: in the landskip were corn fields and pleasant trees, sustaining vines fraught with grapes, and in some of the furthest parts villages, with all such things as might express a country in peace, rich, and fruitful. There came breaking out of the heavens a silver chariot, in which sate two persons, the one a woman . . . representing Concord; somewhat below her sate the good Genius of Great Britain. (2. 313)

The change of scene in Carew's poem is no less dramatic: as in the masque, the wintry landscape cedes to a bucolic vision of peace and plenty. But the transformation is effected, not by deus ex machina, but through the poet's physical retreat to a private estate—to "here," at Wrest. The de Greys' country seat contrasts with the bleak northern mountains in every respect—in its warmth, in its light, but especially in its fertility.

Carew's transition, theatrical in its suddenness, departs from the technique of gradual intensification that Jonson employs to distinguish the Sidney home from the surrounding landscape. Whereas Jonson portrays Penshurst as a working estate, replete with farmers, clowns, and grazing stock, Carew describes Wrest in a manner usually reserved for an earthly paradise such as Eden or "Loves Elizium":

> Here steep'd in balmie dew, the pregnant Earth
> Sends from her teeming wombe a flowrie birth,
> And cherisht with the warme Suns quickning heate,
> Her porous bosome doth rich odours sweate;
> Whose perfumes through the Ambient ayre diffuse
> Such native Aromatiques, as we use
> No forraigne Gums, nor essence fetcht from farre.   (9–15)

Jonson's "better markes, of soyle, of ayre, / Of wood, of water" (7–8) undergo exuberant expansion; as G. R. Hibbard remarks, Carew depicts Wrest in "terms appropriate to a court beauty."[16] Indeed, the personification inverts the topographical blazon that Carew so often employs in his lyrics: it is not hard to connect the "Arromatick dew" and "Balmy sweat" that the poet celebrates in "Upon a Mole in Celias bosome" with the Ovidian luxurance of the earth at Wrest. Carew's description of the grounds at Wrest, however, is no mere purple patch; the passage provides a neat transition between the opening rejection of the military life in the northern hills and the introduction of the theme of good housekeeping. The portrayal of the estate as a *locus amoenus* intensifies the reader's sense of Wrest's isolation from the bleak external world; insistence on the use of only "native Aromatiques," an echo of the "native sweets" celebrated in "To Saxham," anticipates the themes of economy and self-sufficiency that govern the treatment of the house proper.

The first architect of Wrest, Carew asserts, "built a house for hospitalitie" (24). The audible similarity between "house" and "hospitality" posits a like relation between the concepts the words represent: Wrest indeed seems completely devoted to the "ancient and laudable" tradition of housekeeping that the Stuart monarchs had vainly tried to revive during the first decades of the century.[17] If Carew's account of the earl's openhanded hospitality is accurate, the de Greys were among the last to practice a dying custom; by the 1630s, Lawrence Stone observes, "most noblemen had adopted a more modest manner of rural living."[18] Feasting in the hall at Wrest recalls the similar passage in "To Penshurst," but Carew orchestrates the details very differently. At the Sidney's "liberall boord," all gradations of rank are laid aside; there, no guest comes

> but is allow'd to eate,
> Withoute his feare, and of thy lords owne meate:
> Where the same beere, and bread, and selfe-same wine,
> That is his Lordships, shall be also mine.   (61–64)

Jonson's insistence on sharing the "lords owne meate" perhaps glances at the snub administered him by the earl of Salisbury, who once invited him to dine, but seated him at a lower table.[19]

If Jonson's account of the freedom of Penshurst is not merely literary embellishment, Carew's description of the meal at Wrest displays a marked shift in social mores. The guests are carefully segregated by rank, and the poet presents them in descending social order. This hierarchy is subtly underlined by the progression from positive to superlative degree in the adjectives modifying the foods on which the banqueters dine. The tenants, servants, and neighbors, seated at "large Tables," eat "wholesome meates"; the women, household officers, and neighbors of the better sort dine on "daintier cates"; at the summit of the social hierarchy,

> Others of better note
> Whom wealth, parts, office, or the Heralds coate
> Have sever'd from the common, freely sit
> At the Lords Table, whose spread sides admit
> A large accesse of friends to fill those seates
> Of his capacious circle, fill'd with meates
> Of choycest rellish, till his Oaken back
> Under the load of pil'd-up dishes crack.   (39–46)

The earl's "capacious circle" is the emblem of the convivial society of aristocrats and commoners that Carew celebrates at Wrest. Though hardly democratic, this inner circle does recognize the claims of "wealth" and "parts"; Selden, whose father was of yeoman stock, could never have found entrée at Wrest if it did not. To this small group belong not only the "choycest" viands but the freedom of the estate. The modern reader may blanch at the inequities on which this freedom is based; to Carew, however, the careful distinctions preserved in the hall at Wrest reflect a stable, smoothly functioning society. In a period of increasing social rigidity, the generosity of the de Greys was striking; by the 1630s, housekeeping of this sort was largely a thing of the past.[20] The poetic emphasis is on the sense of fellowship that the communal meal symbolizes. All those linked to the earl by ties of love or duty can be sure of a place at his board.

The readiness of the de Greys to fulfill the responsibilities adhering to their social rank is reflected by the architecture of Wrest Park—or, rather, by the lack of architecture.[21] Carew brackets the central scene of feasting in hall with two passages of negative definition in which the claims of "reall use" balance those of "outward gay Embellishment." The very phrasing of the alternatives forecasts the way the beam will fly: the simple solidity of "reall use" outweighs the polysyllabic fussiness of its opponent. Instead of elaborate but unused fireplaces, Wrest offers "cheereful flames"; in place of "Dorique" and "Corinthian Pillars," the house boasts a "Lord and Lady" who "delight / Rather to be in act, then seeme in sight"; instead of antique statuary, "living men" throng the hall (25–34). In Carew's design, the two passages describing false architecture function as antimasques. In a movement that parallels the climactic dramatic incident of the court masque, the unmasking that reveals the revelers' true identities, the poet calls forth the realities—fire, lord and lady, men—that in other houses remain frozen in architectural disguises. The poet banishes the perverted emblems of hospitality to evoke the spirit of hospitality itself.

Employing negative definition to make his point, Carew draws what seems a forced dichotomy between elaborate architecture and good housekeeping; the one, after all, does not necessarily preclude the other. On a limited income, however, a large expenditure on building could entail retrenchment in other areas of consumption.[22] The de Greys' failure to remodel Wrest may in fact have been due to economic considerations: although the countess's personal fortune augmented it, the earl's income was not large.[23] While G. R. Hibbard reads Carew's rejection of "Dorique" and "Corinthian" pillars as an attack on the neo-Palladian architecture introduced into England by Inigo Jones, more recent research indicates that such an intent is unlikely.[24] Examples of English Palladian architecture were few and far between in 1639; the cultured and widely traveled Carew, moreover, was hardly the man to attack them. It is more likely that the poet has made a virtue of necessity, and that his depreciation of elaborate architecture is an attempt to salve his hosts' vanity rather than an artistic manifesto. That the de Greys' vanity needed salving is, of course, only speculation. Nevertheless, the fact that the earl's two brothers-in-law, the earls of Pembroke and Arundel, were among the few English noblemen engaged during this period in large-scale rebuilding or artistic acquisition suggests that familial rivalry between the countess and her two sisters may have in part determined the course of Carew's poem. Lady Kent had taken legal action against her brothers-in-law in 1630, alleging that they had shortchanged her in the division of the Talbot inheritance; it is unlikely that the bad blood arising from the suit had entirely abated with the 1635 settlement in Lady Kent's favor.[25] Carew's immediate audience among the household at Wrest may have read the attack on Corinthian pillars as a subtle glance at Pembroke's embellishment of Wilton, the reference to a hall thronged with statuary as an allusion to the marbles that lined the main gallery of Arundel House.[26] The de Greys might conceivably have grown incensed at artistic display financed with income they regarded as rightfully theirs. Although the precise identities of Carew's satiric targets have been lost with time, the moral point of his satire remains clear. The poet praises the decision *not* to build, and the old-fashioned homeliness of Wrest becomes, paradoxically, a negative monument to the owner's virtue.

Aesthetic considerations, however, are as influential as personal concerns in determining Carew's poetic procedure. Negative definition is a complex strategy. By describing architectural embellishment in detail—"carved marble," "sumptuous" mantels, pillars, statues, "Piramides," and "Exalted Turrets"—the poet captures the devices of the enemy. Each detail is specifically named, each excoriated in turn: the itemized list functions as ritual exorcism in which the poet expels every lurking expectation from the reader's mind. But the device functions in the opposite way as well. Most readers would be surprised to learn that Carew gives no description at all of the house at Wrest; in remembrance, the proscribed details of the "prouder Piles" fuse with the description of the festivities in the hall to create a much grander vision of Wrest than reality would warrant. By evoking, then dismissing, these visually striking forms of misdirected architecture, Carew effectively dissolves the boundaries between the house and the garden that surrounds it. The spirit of good fellowship flows out from the hall to embrace the estate; the gods of grove and field enter into the moral economy that centers on the lord and his guests. The house as a self-contained architectural fabric disappears, unimportant to the larger structure.

The entry into the garden is marked by another series of negative definitions. In a passage that balances the exorcism of the pillars, mantels, and statuary, Carew dismisses fashionable garden ornaments of the type that Pembroke recently installed at Wilton.[27] The de Greys' estate boasts no "Effigie" of Amalthea's horn, no stone statue of Ceres, and no "Marble Tunne" carved with the figure of Bacchus, since

> We offer not in Emblemes to the eyes,
> But to the taste those usefull Deities.
> Wee presse the juycie God, and quaffe his blood,
> And grinde the Yeallow Goddesse into food.　　　　(65–68)

Again, the rhetorical device produces a double effect. The detailed visual imagery evokes the deities in concrete form; transcending that form is the appeal to another sense to confirm the reality of the experience. The high-spirited sacramental parody, which recalls the transformation of gore into wine in Carew's verses welcoming the king to Saxham, insists on the real presence of the gods at Wrest. Carew quite literally presses the pagan deities into the service of the rites of hospitality: nature and the gods who rule it impart their conjoined power to the human inhabitants of the estate through the communal meal.

In the passages of the poem that deal with the house and housekeeping, Carew denounces art which separates man from nature. Within their estate, the de Greys achieve a perfect integration of the natural and human worlds; no art interferes with the process. But the statement is deceptive in its simplicity. The housekeeping of the de Greys evinces more skill than any amount of architectural embellishment. In subordinating display to use, they practice an art that caters to all the senses, rather than to one. In its total effect, their art becomes indistinguishable from nature.

Carew demonstrates the proper application of art in the lively description of the moat surrounding the estate, a passage that provides the second focal point of the poem:

> Yet we decline not, all the worke of Art,
> But where more bounteous Nature beares a part
> And guides her Hand-maid, if she but dispence

Fit matter, she with care and diligence
Employes her skill, for where the neighbor sourse
Powers forth her waters she directs their course,
And entertaines the flowing streames in deepe
And spacious channells, where they slowly creepe
In snakie windings, as the shelving ground
Leades them in circles, till they twice surround
This Island Mansion, which i' th' center plac'd,
Is with a double Crystall heaven embrac'd,
In which our watery constellations floate,
Our Fishes, Swans, our Water-man and Boate,
Envy'd by those above, which wish to slake
Their starre-burnt limbes, in our refreshing lake,
But they stick fast nayl'd to the barren Spheare,
Whilst our encrease in fertile waters here
Disport, and wander freely where they please
Within the circuit of our narrow Seas.   (69–88)

The theory that art is the "Hand-maid" of nature is utterly conventional: Carew blazes no critical trails here. The syntax of the sentence, however, redefines the simple distinction that the poet seems to make. Amid the wealth of modifying phrases and clauses, the precise antecedent of the repeated "she" is lost. The confusion is singular in Carew's oeuvre and probably should not be attributed to shoddy craftsmanship. Instead, Carew graphically indicates that at Wrest art and nature have become indistinguishable: their interdependence is so perfect as to transcend the facile rules that still hold in the world outside. The sinuous windings of the sentence, moreover, answer another purpose as well, for they nicely recreate the scene that they describe. "Serpentine" or "snaky" is an epithet commonly applied to the natural movement of streams; in the genre of the country-house poem, one can cite the "serpent river" in "To Sir Robert Wroth" (18), or the "snake" that curls in "wanton harmless folds" through the meads surrounding Appleton House.[28] The "snakie windings" of the river at Wrest, however, are directed by art; they are designed to surround the estate in the circles of the double moat, isolating it completely from the external world. The happy conjunction of epithet and topography assumes emblematic significance: the serpent turning back on itself is a common Renaissance image of eternity or perfection.[29] The poet emphasizes this conquest of time in his characterization of the encircling moat as another "Crystall heaven," replete with its own cast of constellations. The moat both reflects and surpasses the circle of the zodiac. The contrast between "fertile waters" and "barren Spheare," in its return to the polarities introduced in the opening lines of the poem, boldly reaffirms the superiority of Wrest to the larger but bleaker world outside. The reanimated signs of the zodiac, whose procession marks the change of the seasons, mix in lively confusion in the "narrow seas," freeing Wrest from the ordained temporal cycles that regulate less happy climes.

Although William A. McClung views this episode as a "pretty but somewhat purposeless *divertissement*,"[30] the transformation of the moat into a new zodiac signals an important shift for Carew and for the whole genre of the country-house poem. The aquatic free-for-all in the outer "circles" of the moat constitutes a masque of the natural world that complements the human celebration of the "circle" around the earl's table within. The renovation of the zodiac, moreover, forms the basic conceit of Carew's one masque, *Coelum Britannicum;* in "To G. N. from Wrest," the conceit is transferred from the public setting of the court to the private world of an estate. Eternity, the demigod whose appearance concludes *Coelum Britannicum,* no longer extends his protection solely to the court; the mythological regalia that traditionally invest the monarch have found a new and safer home. While the king and court pursue military adventures in the bleak northern hills, Carew strives to preserve the Caroline ideal of peace and plenty that he helped to create in his masque. In attempting to isolate Wrest from the impending political struggle, Carew echoes, on a smaller scale, his advice in the epistle to Aurelian Townshend, given some seven years earlier, that England steer clear of the embroilments of the Thirty Years' War. This separation of the estate from the turmoil outside looks forward to Marvell's celebration of Appleton House as "heaven's center, Nature's lap, / And paradise's only map" (767–68). The "Island Mansion" of Wrest, "i' th' center plac'd," could merit the same description.

By demarcating the boundaries of Wrest, Carew releases the daimonic powers within. The natural forces of fertility and abundance, described in the introduction to the estate, assume vital, anthropomorphic form. In the grove bordering the moat,

> On this side young *Vertumnus* sits, and courts
> His ruddie-cheek'd *Pomona, Zephyre* sports
> On th'other, with lov'd *Flora,* yeelding there
> Sweetes for the smell, sweetes for the palate here.   (93–96)

Carew presents the deities as actually present: no disclaimer, such as Denham's "quick Poetic sight," mediates the vision. The paired couples are mythological emblems of autumn and spring, respectively; in pictorial tradition, Vertumnus and Pomona are crowned with fruits, while Flora, attended by the blossom-garlanded Zephyr, wears a robe embroidered with flowers.[31] In their complementary arrangement, the couples recall the allegorical figures that often flanked the proscenium in Jones's masque designs. For *Salmacida Spolia,* Jones created a frieze on which were painted, among others, "Commerce, with ears of corn," and "Felicity, with a basket of lilies," figures meant to express the benefits that the masque both celebrates and aims to effect. Carew's deities play a like role, but they also assume a tutelary function. Zephyr and Flora, Vertumnus and Pomona, are the guardians of Wrest, stationed at the estate's border to mark the gentle extremes of the perpetual summer that reigns within.

The moment of intense vision fades as Carew again turns to his correspondent. But, while the deities are no longer visible, their influence continues to be felt:

> But did you taste the high & mighty drinke
> Which from that Fountaine flowes, you'ld cleerly think
> The God of Wine did his plumpe clusters bring,
> And crush the Falerne grape into our spring;
> Or else disguis'd in watery Robes did swim
> To *Ceres* bed, and make her big of Him,
> Begetting so himselfe on Her: for know
> Our Vintage here in *March* doth nothing owe
> To theirs in Autumne, but our fire boyles here
> As lustie liquour as the Sun makes there. (97–106)

What begins as a celebration of Wrest's water supply shades, without warning, into a paean to the estate's home-distilled spirits—the "lustie liquour" that "our fire boyles here." The consummation of Ceres and Bacchus crowns the series of fertility images that runs throughout the poem; the fruit of their union, brought forth with the aid of a little mechanical midwifery, is a drink that surpasses the most prized of classical vintages. Again, the activity emphasizes the estate's independence of seasonal time: like the "suns within" of Saxham, the kitchen fires of March at Wrest re-create the mild southern autumn. The blurred geography of the scene—is it set in the garden or in the house cellars?—and the conflation of miracle and technology underscore the integration of the human and natural worlds of the estate into a unified, divinely favored whole.

The secular masque Carew composes for the de Greys culminates in the marriage of Ceres and Bacchus. The marriage also provides a fitting climax to Carew's poetic quest for the "Paradise within" ("A deposition from Love," 8). In Carew's lyrics, the adverb "there" invariably designates an unattained spiritual or physical ideal, "here" the disappointing reality that the poet is compelled to accept.[32] But in this last poem, and only in this last poem, the signification of the two adverbs is reversed: the poet at last achieves the ideal for which he has so long searched "here," on a private estate in Bedfordshire.

A sense of personal fulfillment suffuses the envoi of "To G. N. from Wrest"; with pointed brevity, the poet contrasts his own lot with that of his addressee:

> Thus I enjoy my selfe, and taste the fruit
> Of this blest Peace, whilst toyl'd in the pursuit
> Of Bucks, and Stags, th'embleme of warre, you strive
> To keepe the memory of our Armes alive.   (107–10)

The opposition sets the retired against the active life, peace against war. The verbs reinforce the polarity. In contrast to the sensual relaxation of the poet, who can "enjoy" and "taste the fruit" of his hours, G. N. must "strive." The participial modifier, "toyl'd," suggests not only exhaustion but entanglement. G. N. is a prisoner of his own activity; the poem implicitly invites its addressee to relinquish his fruitless pursuits to share the "blest Peace" that, in a matter of three years, would survive only on isolated country estates like Wrest. The image of the chase—"th'embleme of warre"—may well comment on the actual political situation at the time Carew was writing. The Treaty of Berwick, which ended the Scottish campaign, was a makeshift agreement that resolved none of the religious and political questions behind the dispute; sensible observers realized that it was only a matter of time before war erupted again in earnest. In G. N.'s effort "To keepe the memory of our Armes alive," the poet glances both at the recent military failure and the threat of more serious conflict to come. The view of England that Carew sketches in the last lines of the poem is even darker than the stylized bleakness of the opening landscape would lead one to expect.

The magic circle that Carew traces encompassed a select company that did not endure the coming winter. Henry, eighth earl of Kent, died during the night of November 20/21, 1639; Edward Nicholas related on December 12 that the countess "so much laments the death of her husband that Mr. Selden cannot comfort her."[33] Selden and Lady Kent moved permanently to her house in Whitefriars soon after. The title and Wrest Park passed to a distant cousin, Anthony de Grey, the eighty-three-year-old parson of Aston Flamville in Leicestershire. Thomas Smith reported to Sir John Pennington that the new earl "is a minister, and has divers daughters, some married to farmers and some to mercers, who will be much troubled to know how to carry themselves like ladies."[34] The succession of an aged clergyman with Puritan sympathies broke up the cultured circle at Wrest; almost overnight, the estate moved from the golden age to the more practical world of Jane Austen. Thomas Carew did not long outlive the transition, dying in March 1640. In Clarendon's words, "after fifty Years of his Life spent with less Severity or Exactness than it ought to have been, He died with the greatest Remorse for that Licence, and with the greatest Manifestation of Christianity, that his best Friends could desire."[35]

Unlike their illustrious brothers-in-law, the earl and countess of Kent are scarcely remembered today. The de Greys played no crucial role in the politics of the period. They assembled no lasting collections of objets d'art, as did Arundel; they constructed no architectural monument to their glory, as did Pembroke at Wilton. Their chief accomplishment was to gather at Wrest a coterie of writers and intellectuals and to provide a congenial atmosphere in which their protégés could work and unwind—quiet accomplishments no less important for the arts and letters in Caroline England than those of Arundel and Pembroke. Aside from the scattered bits of information given by Aubrey and contemporary correspondence, "To G. N. from Wrest" is the only surviving testimony to the de Greys' interests and hospitality. Since those interests were primarily literary and social, Carew's poetic tribute to the conviviality of Wrest is a fitting memorial.

The masquelike elements Carew employs in "To G. N. from Wrest" suggest the central position the de Greys and their estate had come to hold in the poet's own system of values. Through their proper ordering of Wrest, the earl and countess re-create, on a limited scale, that golden age when the gods feasted and visited with men. As befits a lord and lady who "delight / Rather to be in act, then seeme in sight" (31–32), the de Greys relinquish the center stage in the poem to the deities—Vertumnus and Pomona, Zephyr and Flora, Ceres and Bacchus—whose presence at Wrest is both the proof and the fruit of the proprietors' virtue. The celebration of peace and plenty, the expulsion of false forms of order, and the use of scenic tableaux and a detailed iconographic program echo *Coelum Britannicum* and the series of Jonsonian masques that preceded it. In "To G. N. from Wrest," however, Carew translates these themes and techniques to a less ambitious, more personal sphere.

The innovations Carew brings to the country-house poem prefigure the transformations the genre would undergo in the hands of Marvell. The comprehensive vision of social harmony that Jonson expresses in "To Penshurst" becomes, in "To G. N. from Wrest," an ideal attainable only by a chosen few; Carew associates the country-house poem with the ideal of rural retirement that became increasingly prominent in English poetry during the 1630s. In "Upon Appleton House," Marvell simultaneously intensifies the significance of this vision and restricts its scope even further. Like Wrest, Appleton House becomes a world complete in itself, detached from outside disorder. Unlike the de Greys, however, the Fairfax family retires for a higher end, and their retreat is only temporary: In the course of time, the young Maria will emerge from the demiparadise and turn the lessons she has learned there to "some universal good" (741). Carew's poem from Wrest lacks this meditative, at moments almost messianic, strain. The speaker of Carew's poem is a gregarious reveler rather than a haunter of meadows and woods; his emphasis falls on the pleasures of society rather than on those of solitude. But, in spite of their differences, the two poems share much—a new emphasis on the role of the poet, the isolation of the estate from a larger hierarchy, the playing with masque conventions—that distinguishes them from "To Penshurst." The line of development seems clear. Carew's retirement on the eve of civil war anticipates the retreat of the Fairfaxes and their poet from the frustrations and disappointments of interregnum politics ten years later. It was on estates such as Wrest and Nun Appleton, removed from the immediate conflicts of midcentury, that the ideals of Charles I's court would bear their last, late fruit.

Granted some latitude in definition, "To G. N. from Wrest" might be dubbed Carew's "Secular Masque": "secular" in the sense that it celebrates a private family rather than the public, semidivine persons of the monarchs, and "secular" inasmuch as the poem addresses the question central to so much Cavalier verse—how to escape the ravages of time. Like Dryden's "Secular Masque," Carew's poem constitutes a farewell, in part disillusioned, in the main elegiac, to a court and a culture whose time was past. And as Dryden's verses, presumably the last he wrote, sum so well his entire career, so the poetic and personal concerns of Thomas Carew coalesce in "To G. N. from Wrest." Abandoning the court in which he spent so much of his life and the elusive "Celia" on whom he spent so much of his verse, the poet finally discovers what Jonson might call his "center" in a new setting and in a different genre. The "secure repose" and "steadfast peace" for which Carew yearns in lyrics like "An Eddy" and "A Rapture" are realized at last in the attainment of "Wrest."

NOTES

1. For the dating of the poem, see *The Poems of Thomas Carew with His Masque "Coelum Britannicum,"* ed. Rhodes Dunlap (Oxford: The Clarendon Press, 1949; rpt. 1970), pp. xli–xlii. All citations of Carew's poetry follow Dunlap's edition.

2. "Flitton cum Silsoe," in *The Victoria History of the County of Bedfordshire*, ed. H. Arthur Doubleday and William Page (Westminister: A. Constable, 1904–14), vol. 2, p. 327.

3. G. E. Cokayne, in *The Complete Peerage of England, Scotland, Ireland, Great Britain, and the United Kingdom* (London: St. Catherine, 1910–59), vol. 7, pp. 173–74, and the *Dictionary of National Biography*, hereafter cited as *DNB*, concur in placing Henry's death on November 21, 1639; the former cites his will and two contemporary notices to confirm the date. The burial register of Flitton Parish records the following entry for November 28, 1639: "The right Honorable Lord Henry Grey, Earle of Kent; he died upon Wednesday night beeing the 20th day of November." Reprinted in F. G. Emmison, ed., *Bedfordshire Parish Registers*, (Bedford: County Record Office, 1938), vol. 18, B-65.

4. In view of the earl's death in November 1639, Dunlap's tentative dating of the poem to March 1640 should probably be revised to the summer or autumn of the preceding year.

5. Because two of the sixteenth-century earls of Kent held their title only de jure (the fourth earl of Kent declined the peerage, "by reason of his slender estate"), the numerical sequence of the various earls is hopelessly confused. I follow Cokayne in designating Henry de Grey, who held the title from 1623 to 1639, the eighth earl.

6. Thomas Birch, ed., *The Court and Times of Charles I* (London: Henry Colburn, 1848), vol. 1, p. 241; letter of June 15, 1627, to the Reverend Joseph Mead. A number of peers who refused to help collect the loan were removed from local office; see Conrad Russell, *Parliaments and English Politics, 1621–29* (Oxford: The Clarendon Press, 1979), pp. 332–33.

7. "John Selden," *DNB*, vol. 17, pp. 1150–62.

8. *Brief Lives*, ed. Oliver Lawson Dick (London: Secker and Warburg, 1949; rpt. 1950), p. 271.

9. Ibid., p. 45. Although Aubrey's notes are ambiguous concerning Butler's meeting with Cooper, Edmund Gosse believes that it came through the countess ("Samuel Butler," *DNB*, vol. 3, p. 526).

10. The letter is reprinted in *The Works of Sir John Suckling: The Non-Dramatic Works*, ed. Thomas Clayton (Oxford: The Clarendon Press, 1971), pp. 150–51.

11. "Elizabeth de Grey," *DNB*, vol. 8, pp. 624–25; Lawrence Stone, *The Crisis of the Aristocracy, 1558–1641* (Oxford: The Clarendon Press, 1965), p. 560.

12. *Calendar of State Papers Domestic, 1638–1639*, p. 342; hereafter cited as *CSPD*.

13. *The Illusion of Power: Political Theater in the English Renaissance* (Berkeley and Los Angeles: University of California Press, 1975), p. 40.

14. The earl himself paid a fine rather than accompany the king on the expedition, although the cause may have been ill health rather than opposition to royal policy (*CSPD, 1638–1639*, pp. 621–22).

15. *The Dramatic Works of Sir William D'Avenant*, ed. James Maidment and W. H. Logan (Edinburgh: William Paterson, 1872–74), vol. 2, p. 312. Subsequent references to Davenant's works are given parenthetically in the text.

16. "The Country House Poem of the Seventeenth Century," *Journal of the Warburg and Courtauld Institutes* 19 (1956), 167.

17. Between 1614 and 1627, the government issued no fewer than nine proclamations ordering gentlemen in London to return to their country estates to "keepe hospitality." That eight of the nine proclamations were issued in the months immediately preceding Christmas suggests royal authorities' concern not only to remind the gentry to attend to their Hilary Term responsibilities but to head off a crush at the court's annual Christmas festivities. The texts of the proclamations are reprinted in R. R. Steele, ed., *A Bibliography of Royal Proclamations of Tudor and Stuart Sovereigns and of Others Published Under Authority, 1485–1714*, in *Biblioteca Lindesiana* (Oxford: The Clarendon Press, 1910), vol. 5.

18. *The Crisis of the Aristocracy*, p. 187.

19. William A. McClung, *The Country House in English Renaissance Poetry* (Berkeley and Los Angeles: University of California Press, 1977), pp. 9–10.

20. Stone, *The Crisis of the Aristocracy*, p. 187. If Carew's account is accurate, the earl was also singular in taking his meals in the hall; as early as the fourteenth century, it had become customary for the lord and his family to dine in the great chamber or parlor, relinquishing the hall to the servants and household officers; see Mark Girouard, *Life in the English Country House: An Architectural and Social History* (New Haven: Yale University Press, 1978), pp. 46–47. Yet the practice of the entire household's dining in the hall during the warm summer months apparently survived on some estates well into the 1700s (Girouard, p. 136); perhaps Carew's poem describes this custom.

21. Almost no information remains on the character of the manor house at Wrest Park. McClung, supplementing the work of Sir Nikolaus Pevsner, suggests that it was probably a fifteenth-century structure with sixteenth-century additions (*The Country House in English Renaissance Poetry*, p. 111 n.).

22. The Sidneys confronted precisely this choice between remodeling and "keeping hospitality" at Penshurst some thirty years earlier. In "Jonson, Lord Lisle, and Penshurst," *ELR* 1 (1971), 250–60, J. C. A. Rathmell draws on the correspondence between Lord Lisle and his wife to suggest that Jonson's celebration of the bounty of Penshurst is a gentle exhortation to dissuade the family from embarking on a building project that undoubtedly would embarrass them financially. "To my friend G. N. from Wrest" differs from Jonson's poem inasmuch as the de Greys had already made the decision not to build before the time of the poem's composition.

23. See Stone, *The Crisis of the Aristocracy*, appendix 8c. In 1641 the de Greys received less than £1100 in gross annual rents. In Stone's stratification of the peerage into eight income levels, the earl of Kent is included in the lowest group. Edward Nicholas, writing to Sir John Pennington on December 12, 1639, reported that the earldom was worth only £500 a year (*CSPD, 1639–1640*, p. 158).

24. "The Country House Poem," p. 167. McClung discounts this hypothesis (*The Country House in English Renaissance Poetry*, pp. 99–103).

25. Cokayne, *The Complete Peerage*, vol. 7, p. 174. Cokayne cites brief parts of the bill of complaint filed by the countess; the complete deposition, however, remains unpublished. David Berkowitz of Brandeis University, who is working on a biography of Selden, informs me that he has been unable to locate the file in the Public Record Office. He adds that the suit "was undoubtedly embarrassing to Selden, who had been aided by Herbert and was on excellent terms with Arundel, who was soon to grant him an annuity and had been instrumental in changing the king's hostility to Selden" (letter of July 24, 1979, to the author). William Herbert, third earl of Pembroke, died on April 10, 1630; Lady Kent amended her suit to include his brother and heir, Philip, as well as her sister Mary.

26. For an account of the Herbert brothers' rebuilding of Wilton, see John Summerson, *Architecture in Britain, 1530–1830*, 5th ed. (Harmondsworth, Middlesex: Penguin, 1970), pp. 142–44; and see Roy Strong, *The Renaissance Garden in England* (London: Thames and Hudson, 1979), pp. 147–65. The famous gallery of statues at Arundel House is depicted in the portrait of the earl by Daniel Mytens.

27. Wilton did in fact possess a statue of Bacchus (Strong, *The Renaissance Garden*, pp. 149–52); the gardens of Arundel House in London contained 32 statues, 128 busts, and 250 other assorted fragments in the mid-1630s (Strong, p. 170). Both gardens were innovative in their use of sculptural ornament.

28. Lines 632–33. All citations of Marvell's poetry follow *Andrew Marvell: The Complete Poems*, ed. Elizabeth Story Donno (Harmondsworth, Middlesex: Penguin, 1972).

29. Edgar Wind, *Pagan Mysteries in the Renaissance*, 2nd ed. (New York: Barnes and Noble, 1968), p. 266. Wind notes the emblem as commonly illustrated "by the serpent biting its own tail, but known also in the form of a circular loop on the serpent's back."

30. *The Country House in English Renaissance Poetry*, p. 145.

31. Vincenzo Cartari, *Le imagini . . . degli dei*, intro. Stephen Orgel (Venice, 1571; rpt. New York: Garland, 1976), pp. 262, 267–68. Although Carew may have consulted Cartari or some other mythological handbook, it is just as likely that he drew his descriptions from the major classical sources themselves: for Vertumnus and Pomona, *Metamorphoses*, 14. 623 ff., and Propertius, 4.1; for Zephyr and Flora, Ovid's *Fasti*, 5.193 ff.

32. A partial catalogue of poems in which Carew employs this distinction would include "A Rapture," "To my Mistresse in absence," "Upon a Ribband," "On a Damask rose," and "A prayer to the Wind." For a full discussion of this issue, see Paula Johnson, "Carew's 'A Rapture': The Dynamics of Fantasy," *SEL* 16 (1976), 148.

33. *CSPD, 1639–1640*, p. 158; letter to Sir John Pennington.

34. Ibid., p. 128; letter of November 28, 1639.

35. *The Life of Edward Earl of Clarendon, Lord High Chancellor of England and Chancellor of the University of Oxford* (Oxford: The Clarendon Press, 1759), vol. 1, p. 36.

JOHN T. SHAWCROSS

‡

Vaughan's "Amoret" Poems: A Jonsonian Sequence

Despite the efforts of E. L. Marilla to raise the evaluation of Vaughan's secular poems, they seem to have attracted few readers and even less scholarly attention.[1] Marilla argued primarily that the "secular verse is characterized by craftsmanship that is distinctly similar to and but little less skillful than that of the religious poetry."[2] Yet, while the religious poems are praised, the secular poems are condemned. Only James D. Simmonds has championed Marilla's position in print. In his *Masques of God*, he calls the secular poems a "cool, deliberative statement and reasoned argument rather than passionate ardors and hyperbolical enthusiasm."[3] He finds a variety of form, meter, imagery, and language, and at times "an awkwardness in development of thought and in the handling of the complex stanzaic patterns" which "too often produces a heavy, turgid effect." Perhaps. But there is more going on, at least in the 1646 *Poems*, than has been set forth to date, and, to my way of thinking, what is going on calls for praise of Vaughan's craftsmanship.

I propose that Vaughan's 1646 *Poems*, which number thirteen, constitute a sequence, and that, aside from the very different sonnet sequences of the Elizabethans, the force behind it is the Jonson to be seen in "A Celebration of Charis in ten Lyrick Peeces."[4] There are no love-poem sequences, let it be noted, in Donne's canon, or in Cherbury's (despite the series of Lady Diana Cecil poems), Herrick's, Carew's, Waller's, Suckling's, Lovelace's, Marvell's. Habington's *Castara*, owing sustenance to Jonson, is an elaborate series of sequences, and Cowley's *The Mistress*, owing style to Donne, qualifies as a series of related poems. But it is Jonson's sequence, put together from poems written at various times, that supplies the literary fountainhead. It depicts the progress of an affair with lacunae between the individual poetic

193

narratives (though they are easily filled in) and with Petrarchan complications, turned as a result of evaluating the affair from the woman's point of view. The ten titles help the reader follow the progress of the affair and interpret the poems. There are varying verse forms in poems 4 and 7, giving a sequence of three in iambic tetrameter couplets, one in stanzas, two in iambic tetrameter, one in stanzas, and three in iambic tetrameter.[5] The sequence mocks Petrarchan narrative and imagery and revels in sexual double entendre and some supposedly autobiographical lines (like "Of your Trouble, *Ben*, to ease me, / I will tell what Man would please me"). Vaughan's sequence is more ambitious, more crafted, and more "sincere." It rebuffs the Donnean form of love plea, rejection, and sour grapes (in a way different, of course, from that of Carew or Suckling) as the lover alters through the influence of the woman and her point of view. It is more firmly autobiographical, and it reverses Jonson's ambiguities by employing them toward the beginning of the sequence, not primarily at the end. Jonson starts with sympathy-evoking lines:

> Let it not your wonder move,
> Lesse your laughter; that I love.
> Though I now write fiftie yeares,
> I have had, and have my Peeres.

He ends with a woman's ridicule of the game of love:

> What you please, you parts may call,
> 'Tis one good part I'ld lie withall.

Vaughan begins bathetically and in Donnean language:

> When we are dead, and now, no more
> Our harmles mirth, our wit, and score
> Distracts the Towne; when all is spent
> That the base niggard world hath lent
> Thy purse, or mine . . .
> Wee'le beg the world would be so kinde,
> To give's one grave, as wee'de one minde.

But he ends exaltedly:

> So there againe, thou'lt see us move
> In our first Innocence, and Love:

And in thy shades, as now, so then,
Wee'le kisse, and smile, and walke agen.[6]

Marilla discerned in the 1646 *Poems* a continuity of theme, from rejection of the author's initial overtures through a succession of changes in Amoret's attitude and, finally, to marriage and a peaceful reminiscence of the courtship. The poems, nonetheless, have not been read as a sequence and have therefore been found lacking as individually successful poems. What few comments have been printed see no context for a poem beyond what is on its surface, and this has led to negative evaluation.[7] A verse epistle introduces the sequence, followed by a poem entitled, "Les Amours," and the first poem in which Amoret is named. Next are two "non-Amoret" poems, then three more Amoret poems, then two more poems, and, finally, two Amoret poems and "Upon the Priorie Grove." The pattern of "non-Amoret" and Amoret poems is 2, *1*; 2, *3*, 2; *2*, 1.[8] Simmonds's analysis of Vaughan's poems, including those under discussion here, stresses Vaughan's employment of balance and symmetry. We see structural balance and symmetry in this sequence in the placement of those poems specifically referring to Amoret. As sequence, all the poems impinge on Amoret; as sequence, they demand awareness of the lacunae in the love affair being depicted through the continuity of theme and the continuity of imagery. Each poem requires analysis in terms of itself and its relationship to the sequence. So little has been published on any one of the poems that detailed explication is necessary. The sequence tells the story of the reversal of a disrupted love affair, which indeed may have existed at first more in the poet's hopes than in reality. The individual poems become steps away from despair and rationalization to arguments which wear the loved one down—his guilt, his loss, his love, his contemplated life without her—until she, as if guilty, repents and opens the way leading ultimately to marriage and serenity.

The first poem is the verse epistle "To my Ingenuous Friend, *R. W.*," which divides into two halves. Lines 1 to 28 indicate the poet's and his noble friend's harmless mirth in carousing and running up debts. Postulating a time when they will have put such crass matters behind them through death, the poet says that they will beg burial in one grave since they have been of one mind. Thus equally will they proceed to the Elysian Fields, where their spirits will meet others like themselves. In poetry of the period, however, such burial was usually sought for the lover and his beloved, as in

Donne's "The Relique," a form of the bed-grave image. The implication is that the poet has found only man to be of his mind and, by unexpressed analogy, woman to be only bodily. This Donnean attitude, as expressed in "Loves Alchymie," is further reinforced by Donnean phrases: the clauses "When we are dead," which begins the poem, and "When I am dead," which opens Donne's "The Dampe"; the reversal of the idea of "Wee'le beg the world would be so kind," which contrasts those of the mundane world in "The Canonization," who invoke the lovers in their heaven to "Beg from above / A patterne of your love!" The first half of the verse epistle relates the "ancient love" of R. W. and the poet, a love based on compatibility of mind; it plays on a comparison between the friendship of men and the sexual love of man and woman. The souls of the poet and R. W. will meet and proceed to the Elysian Fields, once "Freed from the tyranny of clay." The first half moves through death to a rebirth and from the concerns of the world (the outer view) to spiritual or mental union (the inner view).

The second half, lines 29 to 56, balances the first by indicating whom they will meet who are "More of thy Genius, and my mind." First, such spiritual or mental union leads to forgetfulness of the outer world of perjured love and bodily things. Lines 43 to 50 specifically concern male-female bodily love, which is "unhappy" because murdered (as in Donne's "The Apparition") "by some perjur'd face." Lethe will allow the poet's spirit no longer to be vexed in death by the "inconstant, cruell sex." The second half moves from their souls' rebirth, when they meet Ben Jonson and Thomas Randolph and when they dismiss the past alongside the stream that can subdue all sorrow, to potential birth into a new life. Lines 51 to 56 discuss the pregnancy of their souls, "bigge with delight / Of their new state." Only now will last thoughts appear; now will their souls have come to rest with "all sense and cares" drunk away. The intoxicating liquors of the world with which the poem began have been replaced at the conclusion by the waters of Lethe. The two halves of the poem directly correspond, in reverse. And, whereas the pints drunk in the Moon or the Star (rooms of the Globe Tavern) apparently lead to assignations upstairs, where the "calm whisperers" await payment, the draughts of Lethe negate care, since they do away with "all sense"—that is, bodily appetite and gratification of the senses. Whereas the worldly of part one proceed to the skies (the Moon, the Star, the upstairs chambers), the spiritual of part two are already in the Elysian Fields. Reversals of imagery are everywhere in the two halves of the poem. The basic reversal, however, is the use of materials of "love" poems (like Donne's) to express a state where love in a sexual sense is missing. The heaven after death envisioned by the poet becomes one of stasis, of the present only; it contrasts with the view of the mutable, earthly heaven of sexual love built on concepts of the past and the future.

The verse epistle concludes with a couplet, "So they that did of these discusse, / Shall find their fables true in us." Again, it is Donne in the background, where the poet of "The Relique" would have the age taught "What miracles wee harmless lovers wrought." The summary couplet indicates the kind of solace that the thwarted lover has allowed himself, rationalization. The fables that have discussed the spirits of the dead allege their nonbodily concerns and oneness. And R. W. and the poet will illustrate this "truth" well. The union of two such minds in this peculiar form of coition will beget "delight of their new state." Throughout the poem we should have been remembering the double meaning of "die" as sexual intercourse, for contrast with this kind of love-death. The fables concern the meeting of minds without bodily implications; yet the poet dwells on this subject because he has apparently fallen in love with one who has, he says, proved inconstant and lied about her love for the poet or her lack of love for him. The fables he alludes to have therefore also discussed man's constancy and woman's fickleness (a staple of Renaissance love lyrics), and again their "truth" is "proved" in the poem. But this is only the way the poet sees the situation. Surely man's "harmelesse mirth" might instead suggest man's fickleness to a woman. Possibly the schism in their love affair has arisen from a difference in the couple's conception of this "harmelesse mirth," a not uncommon source of marital difficulties.

The opening poem of the sequence has set up a narrative out of which the sequence will grow. It has employed some crypsis— unfortunately for critical understanding. The poet has fallen in love, found his loved one perfidious to him, and been accused of unseriousness and too much attention to male escapades. He has reacted by rejecting his beloved, by wallowing in a sentimental rationalization of true love as the meeting of minds that the ancients proclaimed it, and by consoling himself with his poetry. At this point in the sequence we see the poet, deceived by self-pity, disparaging that which has been unattained. The poem represents, as Simmonds notes, the thwarted suitor's retreat into masculine convivialities, but it also serves a double function: it posits the supposed dialectic of love—the body or sexual love and the mind or spiritual love—and introduces a sequence, which concerned with dialectic, will culminate in the poet's—not the mistress's—encompassing of both. It is the poet who changes. His opposition of the world of men to his personal world will be shown, as it was in the first poem, to be in error, and only then, mind-set changed, can he enjoy "His usuall Retyrement" at Priory Grove.

In the Elysian Fields, R. W. and the poet meet Ben Jonson, then Thomas Randolph.[9] The lines immediately follow "More of thy Genius, and my mind." Is the poet suggesting that R. W. writes more in the manner of Jonson than he, and he more like Randolph? What is cited for Jonson are "sacred Layes" and poems on so many topics that the spirits throng "To catch the subject of his Song." Neither seems apropos of Vaughan in the present sequence, although the nature of the poems is vaguely Jonsonian—for example, in the last poem's relationship to topographic poetry. We do not know who R. W. was, although it has been suggested that he was the person killed at Rowton Heath in 1645, for whom Vaughan wrote an elegy.[10] But the equation with Randolph, who was a Son of Ben, just as R. W. shows genius and the poet only mind, is carried out in the sequence. Vaughan cites Randolph's "Lovers" (his comedy, *The Jealous Lovers*), "Amyntas" (his pastoral of that name), and "Nightingale" (his poem "On the Death of a Nightingale"). Vaughan's sequence continues with an excursion into matter for jealous lovers, "Les Amours"; later with a poem appropriate to Amyntas, "Song," which begins "Amyntas *goe, thou art undone*"; then with "An Elegy" such as the nightingale is said to sing for itself; and finally with the nightingale in "Upon the Priorie Grove." That is, poems 2, 5, 9, and 13—a rather definite pattern of placement—present the poet of the sequence as one of Randolph's mind. As Simmonds has suggested, the unfavorable comparison of Vaughan with Donne has been misplaced because Vaughan should rather be compared with Jonson.[11] Indeed, as I read the sequence, it becomes a rejection of the Donnean pattern, for it employs motifs, language, and metaphor found in Donne's poems to epitomize the false view of love. The poet of the sequence must become more like Jonson, though he can attain only to kinship. This first poem, a kind of fountainhead for the sequence, employs imagery of supposed death which contrasts with a world free of care and discontent. Its devices of balance, symmetry, and reversals will appear in the other individual poems as well.

"Les Amours" follows the narrative of the first poem by envisioning that time when the thwarted lover is dead. He begins "Tyrant farewell," thus saying farewell to his beloved, but also to his body and bodily needs, as comparison with the first poem shows. Since the rest of the poem manifests that he is not really saying farewell to either, we are prepared to read the poem as a rhetorical ploy—a commonplace for the Petrarchan poet. The ultimate point is that the poet must learn to reject such a ploy and achieve sincerity by simplicity and directness. But at this point he still keeps to such Donnean attitudes as characterize "The Dampe," "The Prohibition," or "The Legacie." The attitude of a kind of martyrdom hinted at in the first poem is reprised in the "sacrifice to Heaven" of his heart. While his ardor has turned his body (heart) to ashes (or cold dust), a tear from her eyes, which have scorned him though they have made him her victim, will allow his heart's flames to partake new life. Her eye can be "quickning," and from his grave will arise "Crimson flowers" to curtain his head. The male-female imagery of fire and water, in this proposed emblematic intercourse, will beget a different kind of delight from the pregnancy of the first poem, and, since the flowers are crimson, they represent resurrection and immortality for the dead lover, but signify acknowledgment of sin and remorse for the woman. The poet in the bed-grave and his loved one's creation of flowers by her tears shed over him are symbolic of union, but reverse the sexual roles expected in a seductive poem. The nonloving situation between them is different from what we were led to believe in the first poem. In the first poem—appropriate to such rejection of female love as the poet hypothesized—we have been led to believe that he has been faithful—at least in his fashion—to her, and that she has been inconstant and has perjured herself. But the second poem makes it clear that he has only been thwarted in loving her, and that she has not shown love for him as he would wish it. Her former inconstancy has become only rejection of love for him, and thus her "perjur'd face" comes to suggest that she has said or implied only that she does not love him. The unnamed woman referred to in these first poems is the Amoret of the rest of the sequence.

The poem divides into six, twenty, six, and two lines. In the first six lines the poet sacrifices his heart as he prepares to die. The poem moves to a point beyond the first poem. While "To my Ingenuous Friend, *R. W.*" has talked about "When we are dead," this second poem has postulated a later time, "Yet e're I goe." The first poem shows a rather immediate reaction to the poet's love affair as one on which he supposedly can turn his back to adopt a surrogate relationship; in "Les Amours" he contemplates his loved one's reaction to his death, expressing underneath that vision the hope that she still can care for him, that in death at least they can be united. The central section of the poem (twenty lines) proposes such union in male-female imagery of fire and water with resultant flowers springing "o'er all the tombe." The next six lines, balancing the first six, describe the emblems that this union after death will achieve: two hearts, one hers which has withstood his love, one his which has succumbed to her allure. His heart will retain a drop of dew on it, though it is "washt in bloud" (thus pure in theological terms), and though it should give off heat. The drop of dew reprises the Petrarchan tears he has shed while it also suggests what a tear from her quickening eye will yield. The two six-line sections balance each other in imagery as well as in structure, and the central section proposes the result, through the bed-grave image, of what their union might be. A final couplet summarizes the poem: "Thus Heaven can make it knowne, and true, / That you kill'd me, 'cause I lov'd you." The common metaphor of "die" and "death" as sexual union determines the main image of the poem, and the final couplet, like that of the first poem, evidences that the fable of love-death is "true." This truth is made known by heaven's emblems on each crimson flower. Possibly he refers to the flower called "love-lies-bleeding"; it is the *Amaranthus caudatus*, one type of the flower symbolizing immortality. Or possibly he refers to the flower called "bleeding hearts." The bed-grave image in "Les Amours" is thus related to the context that the first poem has set up for the sequence. The poet has picked up the vision of his mortal death—death being his hoped-for end in sexual terms—and presented it now symbolically, so that it is both mortal death and a kind of sexual death at the same time. It develops and advances the sequence. His strategy is obviously to get her to feel sorry that she has treated him as she has, and accordingly the central lines of the poem are: "But blesse my ashes with a teare: / This influxe from that quickning eye." Man consumed by his passion becomes but ashes; he needs woman's love—the influxing tear of her eye (with its clear double entendre)—to compound those ashes (or dust) into the living "clay" which is man. This is not a contrivance but a meaningful metaphoric statement—commonplace though its imagery may be. The crimson flowers that their love will produce contrast with the delight of the new state in the first poem and with the flowery banks of Lethe.

Whereas the first poem divides into two and the second into three sections, the first and third of which are symmetric, the next poem,

"To Amoret. The Sigh," is stanzaic, seemingly an ordinary form. The sigh for the Petrarchan lover is standard and repeated. There are four stanzas of five lines each; the rhyme schemes of the first and fourth are identical, and those of the second and third vary. The lines vary between seven and eight syllables. Though there is a suggestion of regularity, the meter and rhyme scheme really move toward a kind of sighing which is enhanced by the fitful phrasing: "Take this Message, and depart, / Tell *Amoret*, that smiles, and sings / At what thy airie voyage brings, / That thou cam'st lately from my heart." In the previous poem he mentioned tears and sighs and went on to develop the imagery of tears. In this poem sighs are the subject. In the former poems death has been postulated; in this poem death is still to take place soon, but the time relationship is earlier than the death of the previous poem. He is not yet even in a symbolic grave. The first three poems move from a kind of real death to a symbolic death to a contemplated death. We therefore should expect that the sequence will continue to move toward a concept of life, and it does, the last poem ending with a concept of renewal.

There is a break between poems 3 and 4 (as implied in the pattern of Amoret/non-Amoret poems given in note 8). The fourth poem, "To his Friend Being in Love," introduces a section of the sequence that modulates from reaction against conventional attitudes toward love to a change within the poet. The poem divides into twelve and six lines: the first section gives his friend's words to him; the second section records his compliance with that advice. But his friend here is his other self, his reason, and his "real" self is his heart. The tone of the first section is arrogant, impatient, unkind, but its advice is worthwhile: Ask her whether she loves you, and don't keep your love bottled up inside. But in the crucible of the heart the words (or the metaphoric tears) become kind and warm and loving. The heart needs only half the space the mind does to express itself. The time of the poem seems to be that of the previous one. The poet has advanced well toward rejecting the arrogant male attitude, which underlies the sequence up to this point. This fourth poem is compounded of the imagery of the previous ones: death, sighs, his but not her love, her coldness, his warmth, the eye, tears, tyranny, his sacrificed heart, and her white bosom and tears falling on it. Fire, water, air, earth, and their supposed properties also appear in all four poems.

The fifth poem is a "Song" addressed to Amyntas, that is, to the poet; and, since its "origin" is not the poet himself, it is printed in italics. It is in unbroken quatrains and, as a song, consists of iambic tetrameters without variation. It contrasts with his own heartfelt lines, in the previous poem. There the lines are iambic pentameters, but phrasing and enjambment disallow an artificial feeling; the last six lines sound as if they are the true words spoken by the poet's heart. The speaker of "Song" is again the poet's other self, which is now more gentle, though it still berates the tyrant who has slain many servants in order to achieve glory in their pain. Though death is mentioned, the poet is not envisioning his being dead. Tying this poem to poem 4, the reason now counsels recognition that his loved one does not love him any more than others she has known, and it would be best, therefore, just to forget about it and her. Casting this advice as a song subtly suggests its own artifice and its lack of individuation.

In contrast is poem 6, "To *Amoret*. Walking in a Starry Evening." Here there are four stanzas of six lines, each in a varied pattern of two or three rhymes, and a frequently altered meter of 8, 6, 4, 8, 4, 6 syllables per line. The effect is one of walking and stopping without pattern. It suggests thought, a necessary transition from the colder reason of the previous two poems into the Fancy that accompanies the poet in poem 7. The thesis of the poem is that the poet and Amoret were destined for each other; thus the advice of the immediately preceding poem is rejected. There is no reference to his death, and time has caught up to the present when his love has been born. However, it really deals with a time before the present: it speaks of their destined love, and it uses imagery of the sun and the stars and their creation in the heavens. This second poem citing Amoret compares and contrasts with the first poem citing Amoret; it has four stanzas of six rather than five lines, and it varies rhyme schemes and metric patterns, but now the effect is a kind of external indecision rather than internal fitfulness. "Walking in a Starry Evening" effects an important change: the poet takes on hope (though not hope explicitly stated) that there is sympathy between the lovers' "two conspiring minds," that is, minds which are mutually inspiriting.

With the seventh poem, "To *Amoret* gone from him," we have reached the middle of the sequence. The poem is in twelve tetrameter couplets. The imagery of walking and the night reappears, and the poet again talks to another self, now Fancy. As hinted in the previous poem, Amoret is equated with the sun. Its descent symbolizes Amoret's leaving him; with its descent comes night, symbolizing unhappiness. The poem becomes the vehicle by which he will take the previous advice of reason and tell her of his love, but it must be done fancifully. The poet should not be arrogant, as we have seen him before; nor should he act the martyr. The fanciful image will grow to simpler expression as the remaining poems develop. The sequence we are reading is his fanciful recitation of his love.

"A Song to *Amoret*," in quatrains, supposes a time when he will be dead and Amoret will have a new lover ("some fresher youth"). He could not give "So rich a heart" or "true resolved minde," for the poet "not for an houre did love, / Or for a day desire," but with his soul "had from above, / This endles holy fire." Past the middle of the sequence, the poet now confesses his love and does not try to excuse it or accuse her of thwarting it. He has turned from arrogance and admits that she could find other men with more fortune and beauty, greater men than he. Those things which others may have in greater store than he possesses are held in high esteem by the world, but they are ephemeral and material; yet his love, endless and spiritual, balances all those other worldly "goods." Stanza 2 implies that the poet has not been so faithful as the sun in its orbit, or chaste in his passions, or temperate in his lament:

> Were he as faithfull as the Sunne,
>> That's wedded to the Sphere;
> His bloud as chaste, and temp'rate runne,
>> As Aprils mildest teare.

It affirms our view of the poet as the unfaithful one in this relationship, one who has repented like the sentimental hero of eighteenth-century comedy, a kind of reformed rake.

There are in this poem affinities with various poems by Donne, particularly "The Apparition," but Vaughan has begun to transcend the assault on woman as inconstant and mere "body" and to accept the fault for the lovers' amorous disruption. Donne's persona is most often (though not quite always) driven to philandering by woman's unfaithfulness and insincerity. The cold Petrarchan mistress only sometimes causes Donne's lover problems; Vaughan's lover at first tries to cast his mistress in that role, but reason, knowing better, is causing him now to begin to cast her in her true role.

The ninth poem is both a love elegy and a funeral elegy for the poet himself, dead from love melancholy. "An Elegy," in pentameter couplets, ends with an appended half-line, as if the poem were cut off before being completed. It is an effective stroke, as if the speaker is so overcome that he cannot go on. The Latin quotation from Martial says, "Oh, 'tis now enough." Reacting to the opening line of "Song," spoken by the poet's other self, the persona says in the elegy, " 'Tis true, I am undone." But not yet dead, he will write an elegy for all lovers like him, an elegy, however, which is a love elegy in praise of the mistress as well. His strategy here is to win her by letting it be known that when others scorned her he upheld her beauteous worth. It is he whom she owes for hyperbolic praise—and the similes, depicting her face, might be expected to have continued in a blazon, had not the poet broken off.

The fusion of elegies wittily replays the meanings of "die" and enhances the import of "the Metamorphosis of Love." For through death as through love man and woman are changed into other beings: through love will come "death," through (his) death will come love (hers for him, should his strategy here win her sympathy). Even though the poet's ruse is not very subtle, at least the poem continues not to accuse the woman. And, though no blame accrues to the poet in this particular poem of the sequence, at least he praises his loved one without moderation.

In a reprise of the first poem (the tavern is specifically identified as The Globe—in Fleet Street—whereas in the first poem only two of its rooms, The Moon and The Star, are mentioned), the poet envisions in poem 10 a meaningless life of carefree drinking and its concomitants—all because his love has not been fulfilled. But, unlike the first poem, this contains no bitterness, no I'll-show-you attitude. Rather, a sorrowful tone pervades the poem, one of regret and resignation. For he is not a "Rich, happy man! that canst thus watch, and sleep, / Free from all cares." One of the effects of sack is poetry (that which we are reading), but it is clear that this is not the kind of poetry he would prefer to write as an apostrophe to his love (those poems which we will read soon afterward, nos. 11–13). Doomed by his thwarted love, his world would become the London he sees before him, all "riotous sinful plush." And he progresses to another dish and another and still more, until he and his companions "After full cups have dreames Poeticall."

The last eight lines are separated from the preceding and printed in italics. Again, as in "Song," it is the poet's other self that speaks—again with irony:

> Lets laugh now . . .
> And in our merry, mad mirth run

Faster and further then the Sun;
. . . So we men below shall move
Equally with the gods above.

The poet has talked himself out of this kind of life, as we can realize when we remark: "*As though* the Pot, and Poet did agree, / Sack should to both Illuminator be" (my italics); the Painter's "fiery Nose" (an allusion to syphilis) and the phallic pun on "his pencill"; and the emphasis on the dreams with which the cup is pregnant, the only means of yielding for the drunkards "more soules, and nobler fire." In "A Song to *Amoret*" he has renounced popular, earthly achievement; the satanic lure of being one with the gods above is ironic. The poem aims at eliciting so much sympathy from his mistress that she will in no way let him lead such a life. And, as he proceeds to the final three poems, there being a definite break between "A Rhapsodis" and the next poem, we see that his strategy has worked.

The title (probably a misprint for "A Rhapsodie") indicates that the poem was intended for recitation—a colloquial and spontaneous tone is evident—and that it was conceived in some kind of heroic terms, as part of an "epic."[12] What is epic is the sequence, in that it represents the history of a man who has overcome adversary forces to achieve heroic dedication to his love. It is, as well, "narrative" presented episodically; this is one of the episodes, as "rhapsody" implies. There is in this poem little of the rapturous, another meaning of "rhapsody," except in ironic use as false rapture for the dissolute life.

"*To* Amoret, *of the difference 'twixt him, and other Lovers, and what true Love is*" has had few admirers. Marilla calls it "not the most effective poem," but Simmonds at least sees that the "slow, halting rhythm and abrupt shifts in line length" enrich the subject.[13] The poem confesses the poet's past indiscretions, which have engaged neither true passion nor loving spirit, and which have been but *ignes fatui.* The difference between him and other lovers is that they, base sublunary lovers, will continue to feed on "loose prophane desire," while he, "by pow'rfull Love, so much refin'd," cannot dismiss the loved one's powerful attraction, the elements that have given his life its course. A combination of Donne's "A Valediction: Forbidding Mourning" and others employing an alchemical metaphor,[14] the poem is an extended analogy: Now he is clearly not hypothesizing his death (as he was in "An Elegy"), but he has become emboldened by his mistress's alteration of attitude toward him. Not only has "A Rhapsodis" shown the mistress what the lover's unhappy life will be without her, but it has filled in a space of time during which the poet's former protestations have had their effect. "*To* Amoret" in turn sets up the situation out of which will come Amoret's weeping in poem 12. For the poem is mainly gauged to assert what love is: the conspiring of spirits and stars by winged beams and mutual fire. ("Conspiring" puns etymologically on the meaning "enspiriting each other at the same time.") Love must be mutual of both visualization and of directed looks of love. She, as the cold Petrarchan mistress, is like the polar north to which the lodestar and the enamored steel of the compass move. It is only through such guidance of her mutual love that he can steer his way through the sea of life. The poet's strategy of high-flown rhetoric borrowed from affective poetry probably well known to Amoret will, of course, be successful.

This is the one poem in the sequence in an odd number of lines, thirty-five, arrayed in seven five-line stanzas. It is built on pentameters and tetrameters, for the sets of two dimeters also combine into tetrameters. These are the two basic meters of the sequence, and thus the poem pulls together the sequence even metrically. It will be followed by a poem in pentameter couplets and by one in tetrameter couplets. But the number of stanzas—since 5 is the number of love, a "marriage" number—and the number of lines— since 7 is the number of creation—are significant. The golden mean or section of the poem occurs at line 22,[15] "Whil'st I by pow'rfull Love, so much refin'd." The line not only defines the basic thought of the poem, it also states the theme of the sequence.

The "tone of confidential intimacy" in "To *Amoret* WEEPING," poem 12, has suggested to various scholars since F. E. Hutchinson that the poem was written to Catherine Wise, who became Vaughan's first wife.[16] Whether that is true or not—and my reading of the poems does not depend on the answer—the poem indicates a further advance in the sequence, for the lovers have come to understanding and mutual love. The prior poem almost reached this point, but not quite. The courtship seems to be about at an end; the strategy of the previous poems seems to have been successful, and we can expect marriage to ensue. At least a mutuality of love seems to dominate lines 37 to 58, and it is Amoret who is weeping, in remorse for the way she has treated the poet in the past.

In another reprise, now of "A Song to *Amoret*," the poet revives statements of his poor estate and of the transcendence of his —now their—love over such material and mundane concerns. Their love gives "a blessing which no gold can buye." The poem begins by recapitulating imagery and ideas of the former poems: Amoret's eyes, fortune or treasure, stars and tenements in heaven (to be contrasted with the rooms upstairs at The Globe), the sun's beams, the loved one's speech. The second verse paragraph restates the lover's ability to conquer time through his love. The third speculates on the venal life he might have led. Not having led such a life makes his estate poor, but enables him, ironically, not to have sunk lower into the hell sustained by gold. The fourth verse paragraph credits the loved one with having let him avoid the mean life by her dispensing of real fortune, love. Through his love for her, he has had heaven breathed into him (compare "conspiring" in the earlier poem) and has achieved courage to "dare / What ever fate, or malice can prepare."

Marilla, and probably others, felt that the poem lacks organic intensity, although it is unified by its basic theme.[17] But this view is not justified, it seems to me, when we read the poem in sequence, when we see the relation of verse paragraphs to what has preceded (in imagery and idea, as well as in theme) and observe the progress that the poem itself makes, and when we examine its structure. The first verse paragraph (1–8) is balanced and completed by the last six lines of the poem (53–58).[18] The treasure of her eyes should not be shed for the past, since on earth such "pious streames" are of no avail; but the treasure that the lovers have found (their "purse" and "mines," with obvious sexual connotations) emphasize a future under "a blessing which no gold can buye." (Remembering, in this context, the first poem and the apparent philandering of the poet, we know what gold can buy.) The questions of the first part are made irrelevant.

The second verse paragraph, lines 9 to 20, is balanced by lines 43 to 52 of the last verse paragraph. In the latter the poet talks of "fate" and "providence," of wealth and wit, and of being armed with "a gallant soule and sense." The questions of the second verse paragraph are answered more firmly there than in lines 9 to 20, which set the proem to lines 43 to 52. The third verse paragraph, lines 21 to 36, is balanced by lines 37 to 42, the first lines of the last verse paragraph. The problem of birth and position is countered by an apostrophe for deliverance from what the tinsel world thinks is important. He has been delivered from a hell on earth, owing to the miracle of his loved one and his love for her. The point in Amoret's weeping is that she should not weep for his death (a main theme of the sequence), since through it has come life as the better person he now is. The "blessed pow'rs" have made him rich "by taking all away."

The turning point of the poem comes at line 37, after the thirty-six lines in the first division, with twenty-two in the second. This is the golden section of the poem. It is the artistic focal point, and the poem clearly must have been manipulated to achieve it and the inverse balances we have noted. The poem builds to this point and then returns to the beginning in terms of its content. The number of lines which sustain the poem likewise suggests numerical considerations:

verse paragraph		
1	8 lines	
2	12 lines	
3	16 lines	
4	22 lines =	6 lines
		10 lines
		6 lines

There is a steady progression in weight (that is, in the number of lines in each paragraph), with a greater step at the position of the golden mean, for the fourth verse paragraph balances the preceding verse paragraphs, and the fourth is itself symmetrically balanced. At its center (48–49) are "providence" and his "gallant soule." The indentation at line 58, along with that at line 37, frames the paragraph.

It should thus be apparent that the final poem of the sequence, "Upon the PRIORIE GROVE, His usuall Retyrement," will describe the further progress of this affair into marriage, into serenity and life (not the death emerging formerly), into a world of the two together, rather than the world of men and whores depicted in the first poem. To contrast with the tavern of the worldly man, which was strategically revisited in the tenth "episode" ("A Rhapsodis"), the scene must be bucolic, edenic. Like the previous poem, this one divides in two at lines 22 and 23, the golden mean or focus of the poem. The first verse paragraph of four lines greets Beacon Priory, where the poet first fell in love with his mistress. The imagery of treasure, repeated, makes clear that this foreshadowing of heaven, where his treasury lies, answers the injunction of Jesus that "where your treasure is, there will your heart be also" (Matt. 6:21). The past is renounced, never to return, in the second verse paragraph, and the images of sound and sun and moon and fancy merge in a consummate statement of this grove as the world he has been seeking.

Once the sequence is completed, its logical outcome is marriage. The last verse paragraph, signaled by the division of the poem as focus, immediately catches a sense of the future envisioned after marriage has occurred. Just as the grove will go on, though with signs of age, so shall the loving couple. The rhythm of their future life is caught in the last two lines as it will accrue, step by step, by natural episodes (like the stories of the poems of the whole sequence), though it seems finally to go on without decline:

> And in they shades
> as now,
> so then, /
> Wee'le kisse,
> and smile,
> and walke agen.

Each phrase is another step as they walk on; we should pause at the end of each line as we read. The frequent references to Adam and Eve in the sequence place Priory Grove as an Eden and the loving pair, their differences behind them and the lures of the world's gold and position rejected, as the populators of a new world. As symbol the poem transfigures the grove, as Simmonds has remarked, into an ideal natural order that expresses the power of love to transfigure a fallen world. But as we read the sequence we recognize that it is the poet who has "first betrayed" his "loves faire steps."

What Vaughan achieves in the sequence is an allegedly more honest appraisal of the poet's and Amoret's relationship, going well beyond the usual Petrarchan love sequence where the man is faithful and loving and the woman is inconstant and cold. If the sequence is truly autobiographical, it may tell us something more about Vaughan's occupation before 1646, when he seems to have studied law, clerked for Sir Marmaduke Lloyd, possibly engaged in medical practice, and served in the Royalist cause. He was only twenty-four in 1646, and we can surely expect him to have sown some wild seeds of carousing, whoring, and quick money and fame, in the world of men, prior to that date. But, aside from autobiographical considerations, the sequence has importance as a variation on a standard literary subgenre, and demands evaluation as art, not as biography or philosophy. The poet does engage in moral reflections on large general issues like the "proper" attitudes toward Fortune, Fate, and Adversity (I am citing Simmonds), and he does present classic arguments in favor of a middle station in life.[19] But the significance is literary: the lovers are placed above the personal world and the chaos of London, in comparison (or contrast) with the lovers, say, in Donne's "The Canonization," in William Habington's *Castara,* and in Milton's *Comus* (see the Attendant Spirit's epilogue). Literary comparison should lie at the root of evaluation. Vaughan has captured much that becomes associated with the Cavaliers as well, though his style is so far removed from Jonson's that most people have not seen the derivation. But his Donnean phrases—like "Sublunarie Lovers"—are not employed any more "metaphysically" than such echoes are by Carew or Suckling.[20]

What is particularly Jonsonian about the sequence is (1) that the nature of the sequence is social rather than private, despite the theme, (2) that Vaughan's is not conceited verse, despite his borrowings from Donne, and (3) that Vaughan's style is the basic plain style (for example, in "A Rhapsodis" with its overlay of allusion). Remarks which Summers and Pebworth make of Jonson's Elegy 38 apply equally to Vaughan's sequence: "The realism of such details serves further to particularize the dramatic context. It also places the celebrated love within a recognizble social setting, and it incorporates within that public milieu a space for the personal and the private."[21] The jocular parodying of Donnean Petrarchanism is not unlike Jonson's achievement in "A Celebration of Charis." But it is perhaps in the style, which increasingly becomes Jonsonian as we move through the sequence, that Vaughan's kinship is attested. There is nothing of the high style in "Les Amours"; yet even lines like these are to disappear: "O're all the tombe a sudden spring / Of Crimson flowers, whose drooping heads / Shall curtaine o're their mournfull beds." Such lines no longer appear as we reach "To *Amoret* WEEPING":

> Nay further, I should by that lawfull stealth,
> (Damn'd Usurie) undoe the Common-wealth;
> Or Patent it in Soape, and Coales, and so
> Have the Smiths curse me, and my Laundres too.

Further, the sequence is carefully managed to achieve variety of form and prosody. Couplets are used for poems 1, 2, 4, 7, 9, 10, 12,

13; stanzas are the basis for poems 3, 5 (although the quatrains are not separated), 6, 8, 11. The following scheme indicates the balance and yet variety achieved in prosodic terms, a main intention of the poet in the sequence:

Poem	Form	Meter	Form	Number of Lines
1	couplet	tetrameter		58
2	couplet	tetrameter		34
3			5-line stanza	50
4	couplet	pentameter		18
5			4-line stanza	24
6			6-line stanza	24
7	couplet	tetrameter		24
8			4-line stanza	24
9	couplet	pentameter		24
10	couplet	pentameter		78
11			7-line stanza	35
12	couplet	pentameter		58
13	couplet	tetrameter		36

In all, the foregoing demonstrates that there is neither an awkwardness in development of thought nor a heavy, turgid effect, that there is much here to have employed Vaughan's time *and ours*,[22] that Vaughan knew very well what he wanted to say, and that the individual poems and the sequence do not fall apart. To my way of thinking, what is going on calls for praise of Vaughan's craftsmanship. It is a craftsmanship so subtle that the concept of sequence, once demonstrated, first strikes one like a jolt, but then one recognizes that each poem is different from what has been one's view of it before, that Donne's poetry is used only as foil, and that the Jonsonian sequence is the key to Vaughan's form and content. The concept of sequence implies an authorial control, calling up Jonson's "maker," a craftsman as concerned with his literary creation as with his personal feelings and thought. And to follow well, but not imitate, the supreme maker himself, "Great *BEN*," calls for praise indeed.

NOTES

1. See particularly "The Secular and Religious Poetry of Henry Vaughan," *Modern Language Quarterly* 9 (1948) 394–411, and *The Secular Poems of Henry Vaughan*, Essays and Studies on English Language and Literature, vol. 21 (Uppsala, Sweden: University of Uppsala Press, 1958).

2. "The Secular and Religious Poetry," p. 395.

3. Pittsburgh: University of Pittsburgh Press, 1972, p. 82.

4. Other poems in the Jonson canon also tend toward sequence; note, for example, those in *The Forrest* and the "Poems of Devotion" in *The Under-Wood* (no. 1 in three poems); and see particularly the discussion of Elegies 38, 40, and 41, in Claude J. Summers and Ted-Larry Pebworth, *Ben Jonson* (Boston: Twayne, 1979), pp. 184–87.

5. Raymond B. Waddington, in his contribution to this volume, " 'A Celebration of Charis': Socratic Lover and Silenic Speaker," comments importantly on the songs and their placement in sequence, on the fusion of public and private modes, and on the tetrameter couplet, particularly in its influence from the Anacreontic odes. One should particularly compare Anacreontics with Vaughan's poem 10, "A Rhapsodis," which I shall discuss later.

6. *The Works of Henry Vaughan*, ed. L. C. Martin (Oxford: The Clarendon Press, 1957), 2nd ed., vol. 1. Citations from Donne follow *The Complete Poetry of John Donne*, ed. John T. Shawcross (Garden City, N.Y.: Doubleday, 1970).

7. For example, Joan Bennett believes "there are two peculiarities in these early poems. The first is that Vaughan never appears to be interested in his subject. He plays lovingly with an image and delays its application, which is finally huddled into a last stanza. The other is that he prefers to draw his images from the countryside even when his model was Donne, who seldom looked in that direction. The result is often that his own experience, which finds an outlet in the image, has no inevitable connection with the situation to which he applied it with a logic more painstaking than convincing." See *Five Metaphysical Poets* (Cambridge: Cambridge University Press, 1964), p. 72.

8. The pattern, with poems that specifically cite Amoret italicized; is: 1, 2, *3*; 4, 5, *6*, *7*, *8*, 9, 10; *11*, *12*, 13. The individual poems are: 1, "To my Ingenuous Friend, *R. W.*"; 2, "Les Amours"; 3, "To *Amoret*. The Sigh"; 4, "To his Friend Being in Love"; 5, "Song"; 6, "To *Amoret*. Walking in a Starry Evening"; 7, "To *Amoret* gone from him"; 8, "A Song to *Amoret*"; 9, "An Elegy"; 10, "A Rhapsodis"; 11, "*To* Amoret, *of the difference 'twixt him, and other Lovers, and what true Love is*"; 12, "To *Amoret* WEEPING"; 13, "Upon the PRIORIE GROVE, His usuall Retyrement."

9. For Simmonds's view of the poem, see *Masques of God*, esp. p. 204. About the tavern setting of this poem, it is interesting to recall a story told of Jonson and Randolph: Randolph came to a "Club" of wits, which centered around Jonson, at the Devil Tavern near Temple Bar. Lacking money and looking shabby, he only peeped into the room, but was spied by Jonson, who called him in. On the spot, the wits composed verses on his ill condition, and these prompted a quatrain from Randolph, which Jonson so approved that he said, "I believe this is my Son *Randolph*," and thereafter Jonson always called him his son. See Giles Jacob, *An Historical Account of the Lives and Writings of our Most Considerable English Poets, Whether Epick, Lyrick, Elegiack, Epigrammatists, &c.* (London, 1720), pp. 169–70, under "Randolph."

10. See the note in *The Complete Poetry of Henry Vaughan*, ed. French Fogle (Garden City, N.Y.: Doubleday, 1964), p. 7.

11. Simmonds, *Masques of God*, pp. 22–23 and ff.

12. This has been read only as a drinking song and has thus suggested to critics the poet's complete withdrawal from the world into a limited society; see, for example, Marilla, *Secular Poems*, p. 126, and Simmonds, *Masques of God*, p. 126. The world of the tavern does imply a

buffer to the violent world outside, a kind of satiric paradise. But it is not really desirable to the poet, we see on careful reading.

13. See Marilla, "The Secular and Religious Poetry," and *Secular Poems*, p. 135, and Simmonds, *Masques of God*, p. 64.

14. The poet has moved from the cynical Donne (implied in the "other Lovers") to the Donne of the second classification under which Helen Gardner prints the "Songs and Sonnets," those of mutual love. Vaughan has certainly engaged in derivativeness here, indicating continued role playing, now philosophic, to plumb the success of the emotional role playing of the three previous poems, where he admits his fault, where he becomes her champion, and where he envisions for Amoret his life without her.

15. That is, of the thirty-five lines of the poem, 0.618 lie before this point and 0.382 after it. The golden section, a principle in painting, means that focal interest lies in a ratio derived from the Fibonacci series, $1 + 2 + 3 + 5 + 8 + 13 + 21 + 34 + \ldots + 1597 + 2584 + 4181 + \ldots$, where the sum of two terms ($1597 + 2584 = 4181$) is divided into the greater (0.618) or the lesser (0.382) to determine the golden section. In painting (as, for example, in most of Turner's sea canvases), this means that the focal interest lies 0.618 from one side (length) and 0.618 from the other (width); there are, therefore, four such focal points. The principle has long been applied to literary composition, for example, in the *Aeneid*. In Vaughan's poem, 0.618 of thirty-five lines yields 21.63, thus placing the focal interest within line 22.

16. See Simmonds, *Masques of God*, appendix 2, pp. 203–07, for a discussion of the identification of Amoret and for disassociation with Etesia, who figures in seven poems in *Thalia Rediviva* (1678).

17. See Marilla, *Secular Poems*, p. 140.

18. The only repeated rhymes in this poem are couplets found in the third verse paragraph and in this section of the fourth verse paragraph. The structure can be seen best in this way:

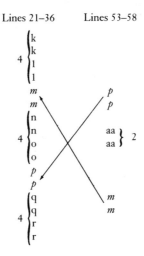

19. On ideal natural order, see Simmonds, *Masques of God*, p. 70; on Vaughan's moral reflections, see pp. 135–36.

20. While I have spoken of the Donnean form of love poem, since so many of the specific phrases can be traced to his poems, and many of the attitudes and images, I have intended the wide corpus of love poetry and sonnet sequence developed by the Elizabethan poet and his heirs. Among them are certainly Sidney and Giles Fletcher, Senior, Cherbury, and Alexander. The reactions of Donne to the Spenserian mold are carried on by such "Cavaliers" as Carew and Suckling; but Vaughan goes them one better by rejecting all of that for the poems of the plain style, numbers 12 and 13, "sincere" love poems which do not worry the minds of the addressee as Dryden thought Donne's did.

21. *Ben Jonson*, p. 184.

22. F. E. Hutchison commented that there is "little enough in it [*Poems*, 1646] to employ his time," except Vaughan's version of Juvenal's tenth satire; see *Henry Vaughan: A Life and Interpretation* (Oxford: The Clarendon Press, 1947), p. 50.

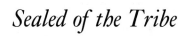

Sealed of the Tribe

THOMAS CLAYTON

‡

"At Bottom a Criticism of Life": Suckling and the Poetry of Low Seriousness

"*Natural, easy Suckling*"—with two lines of "Out upon it, I have loved / Three whole days together" and two of "Why so pale and wan, fond lover? / Prithee why so pale?"—is so apt and usual an opening for a discussion of Suckling that I have now used it myself, naturally. But the phrase is not my focus, though it is tempting. In fact, it is remarkable and somewhat disquieting how much functional—and often reductive—literary history and criticism can be effected by orotund phrases and obiter dicta. T. S. Eliot cramped Grierson's "metaphysical poets" into the planisphere of "the massive music of Donne" and "the faint pleasing tinkle of Aurelian Townshend," and F. R. Leavis had at Milton with such élan that his opening thrust has been serving in paraphrase for epitaphs and otherwise ever since: "Milton's dislodgement, in the past decade, after his two centuries of predominance, was effected with *remarkably little fuss*"—but Leavis's (and Eliot's) reports of Milton's demise were greatly exaggerated.[1] As for Suckling, Millamant's formula is ubiquitous, and so telling, as far as it goes, that it seems to tell all, and seeming often leads to misbelieving. But the spirit of the phrase, and Congreve's words for that spirit, are very meet and right, and they are welcome.

In identifying and placing any poet, the received contexts of literary history and interpretation include among others the primarily diachronic ones of sources and influences, the poet's place in the tradition or traditions, and "originality"; the synchronic ones of the poet's friendships and enmities, literary affinities and disaffinities, and relations generally with social and intellectual contemporaries at home and abroad; and the achronic or rather polychronic ones within the poems—matters of idea, scope, genre, form, style, and the like—and between poems and the other arts, and their audiences, contemporary and succeeding. All of these and other

217

contexts have their claims upon the attention of serious students of literature. But in the real world, where practical exigency and individual psychology compete with ideals and theoretical commitments, it is usual for these same students to cultivate plots—or undertake "projects"—of expediency or preference within the gardens of the whole, and cover their seeds and tracks with whatever soil they can muster. The plot I am primarily concerned with here is one in which many kinds of study begin and some end, within the poems and in the field of their interrelationships, where the primary engagement is between the poem and its readership, however delimited.

In particular, I want to say a few things that have not been said before, or said in this way, in favor of a poet usually treated condescendingly or with moralizing disapproval when addressed at all, and to comment on theoretical considerations as occasion arises. Rare indeed today is the temerity and spirit of Tucker Brooke, who wrote in 1948 that "of all the 'Cavalier' group Suckling had the most interesting mind and the largest potentialities for poetry." [2] I tend to agree with him, but invidious comparison of poets serves all ill, and I confine myself here to commenting on aspects of Suckling's art as a beginning of the end of extending appreciation of his range, not to try to make a major poet of a minor poet, but to let the minor be a poet in an age of such virtuosity that "minor" unfairly belittles achievements of some magnitude: the earlier seventeenth century was a peerless period for the lyric. This is a fact commonly lost sight of in the circumstances, almost exclusively academic, in which "we" today read—or, rather, often do not read—poets like Suckling, unless, eventually, as academic period-specialists, by which time some have become sufficiently accustomed to the mill that Suckling and others are only so much more grist to grin and bear. More's the pity, for reasons T. S. Eliot gives in "What Is Minor Poetry?" For "there are a great many casements in poetry which are not magic, and which do not open on the foam of perilous seas, but are perfectly good windows for all that"—and better than magic casements for some purposes, eminently close to home and ranging, too. [3]

In 1880, in "The Study of Poetry," Matthew Arnold characterized a poet as "a real classic, if his work belongs to the class of the very best," and "poetry" as "a criticism of life." He was surely right about "poetry" as "a criticism of life," and this formulation distinctly improved upon the one he had given in 1879 in his study of Wordsworth, where poetry was "at bottom a criticism of life." [4]

"At bottom" is idiomatic and innocuous, of course, but there is a hint of obliviousness in his failing to notice this potential double entendre, though it is as nothing to that in a recent exposition of sociobiology, where the author asks, "What is the essence of maleness? What, at bottom, defines a female?"[5] Still, the habitual heights of Arnold's later vision inclined him to presbyopia: he made "true classic" status depend entirely upon "high seriousness" and "absolute sincerity," and he denied the first rank to Chaucer and Burns. Burns's poetry, he wrote, has "truth of matter and truth of manner, but not the accent of poetic virtue of the highest masters. His genuine criticism of life, when the sheer poet in him speaks, is ironic." Arnold was a circumspect critic, and one can even concede secondary rank to Chaucer and Burns, in the context of his reasons; but both Chaucer and Burns are too good, taken all in all, to stand in the second rank, so there must be some weakness in the reasons: the depreciation of irony, perhaps, and still more the earnest insistence on "high seriousness" and its supposed source in "absolute sincerity," which can never be known but by appearances and God.

If Arnold had an attenuated appreciation of irony, his Victorian antitype, Oscar Wilde, did not. In "The Critic as Artist," Wilde declared that "the primary aim of the critic is to see the object in itself as it really is *not*." Furthermore, Arnold's annunciation of poetry's advent as the agency to succeed Christianity in the office of salvation was answered in effect in "The Decay of Lying," where Wilde prophesied the second coming of the archliar: "some change will take place before this century has drawn to its close. . . . Bored by the tedious and improving conversation of those who have neither the wit to exaggerate nor the genius to romance, tired of the intelligent person whose reminiscences are always based upon memory, whose statements are invariably limited by probability, and who is at any time liable to be corroborated by the merest Philistine who happens to be present, society sooner or later must return to its lost leader, the cultured and fascinating liar. . . . Whatever was his name or race he certainly was the true founder of social intercourse. For the aim of the liar is simply to charm, to delight, to give pleasure. He is the very basis of civilized society."[6]

Wilde was no less serious than Arnold, but their ways of seriousness are different, whether we prefer Arnold's lofty lectern or Wilde's playful Socratism. What *ever* would the mature Arnold have replied to the suggestion of Wilde's Cyril that we "go and lie on the grass, and smoke cigarettes, and enjoy nature"? Certainly something printable. Wilde noted that "in Falstaff there is something of Hamlet, in Hamlet there is not a little of Falstaff." He himself played Falstaff to Arnold's Hamlet, and Suckling played something of both to his court, his age, and his posterity. It is appropriate as well as variously significant that in the great Van Dyck portrait Suckling is holding a Shakespeare Folio open to *Hamlet*.

Suckling's art has seldom been denied, but his seriousness or sincerity is often in question, I think because it is rarely direct or obvious, never solemn or portentous, seldom conspicuous or high. If not to be high is to be low, if not to be Theseus is to be Bottom, then Suckling's seriousness is low; and, though not invariably, it is typically skeptical and ironic. Northrop Frye's low mimetic or ironic modes do not usefully accommodate him, but there is aptness in Frye's insistence that " 'high' and 'low' have no connotations of comparative value."[7] Suckling readily accepts—requires—ceremony, convention, decorum, circumstance, and sometimes even pomp. At the same time, he deplores—burlesques and ironizes—presumptuousness, affectation, vanity, and hypocrisy, violations of ethical and societal norms hardly confined to monarchies and aristocracies, or even "bourgeois democracies." The irony of manners of Suckling's muse is sui generis, and, if that phrase is audibly reminiscent of hog-calling, I cannot think his flexible wit would find it offensive or even impertinent, not least because country matters are among his proper business.

As a denizen of anthologies and literary histories, Suckling is customarily accorded the magisterial generalizations that put him in his place, and fleeting quotation of the odd couplet, quatrain, or stanza that keeps him there. The wages of restricted experience is a stereotype, one consequence of an anthology-tour of English literature without side trips or in-depth exploration: this is Tuesday, so it must be Herrick, Carew, Suckling, and Lovelace.[8] It seems to me both regrettable and a fact, especially recently, that premodern—even pre-"postmodern"—poems and poets have come to be little read and more overstood than understood, often for the worse part of "overstanding," a term recently used by Wayne Booth in defense of "Alien Modes" of criticism.[9] A corollary is a collective short shrift that is depriving even the major poets of their due—the seventeenth century's Donne, Herbert, Milton, Marvell, and Dryden, if one accepts the canon of twenty major English poets given by A. E. Dyson.[10] So much, or rather so little, for Ben Jonson *and* the Cavalier poets. Here, instead of offering a survey in little or a general, guided tour of Suckling,[11] I shall attend in some detail to four differently representative poems, each inviting a distinct critical perspective and treatment. It seems appropriate, too, to comment briefly on Suckling's two relatively "major" poems.

"A Ballad upon a Wedding" was probably written in 1637, the same year in which Suckling completed "The Wits" and *An Account of Religion*, when he was twenty-eight. "A Ballad" has been much praised and is among the most often discussed of his poems. Admired and often imitated in the seventeenth century, it belongs to a genre of Suckling's own invention that I have called the "rusticated epithalamion," a marriage poem that satirically rejects the received conventions of High Pastoral in favor of a (West Country) rural vision of nuptial events which concludes with a salty, invigorating, down-home emphasis on the mighty leveler, physical love:

> At length the candle's out, and now
> All that they had not done they do:
> What that is, who can tell?
> But I believe it was no more
> Than thou and I have done before
> With Bridget and with Nell.

A jocular dramatizing of a theme Herrick epigrammatizes as "Night makes no difference 'twixt the priest and clerk; / Joan as my lady is as good i' th' dark." "Rusticated" is useful also as the quasi-technical term for temporary banishment either from the city or, particularly, from university: to be rusticated is to be "sent down," and sending down is Suckling's characteristic mode of irony in sending up serious subjects, not to dismiss them but to reflect and refract them in comic and ironic perspectives.

"The Wits" is likely always to be better known as "A Sessions of the Poets," its almost certainly editorial title in *Fragmenta Aurea* (1646), published five years after Suckling's death. It has been appreciated and depreciated by turns, depending mainly on the *kind* of poem it is supposed to be. And it has been still more often quoted, especially by literary historians and biographers adopting Suckling's characters in little. Thanks to Suckling's gift for telling miniature caricatures, we have Carew's hard-bound muse, Davenant's lack of qualification for the laureateship in wanting a nose, the little Cid-ship of strong-lined Sidney Godolphin, and, best of all, Suckling himself, so finely sketched in consonance with the character—the *ethos*—of his fictions and with some of the facts of his life that the caricature is often taken for the whole historical person as well as the poet. If, as "all that were present there did agree, / A laureate's muse should be easy and free" (37–38), then in "The Wits" Suckling demonstrates his qualifications even as he declines to stake his claims, an artfully self-effacing gesture that identifies the wit as *poeta generosus:* Cavalier noblesse oblige and an instance of graceful presence in absentia.

Suckling's supple conjunction of "fixed" form and ostensibly spontaneous expression is found in these two "major" poems as in most others. In "A Ballad," a hearty rustic effortlessly expresses himself with the aid of the constraints of the *rime couée* supplied him. In "The Wits," bob-and-wheel stanzas fuse the looseness of four-stress lines with an epigrammatic wit that is at once acerbic and congenial, deflating and constructive: a graceful group-monumentalizing of a convocation of competing wits given narrative life with a master craftsman's articulation of individual figures, including his own (73–78):

> Suckling next was called, but did not appear,
> And straight one whispered Apollo in's ear,
> That of all men living he cared not for 't,
> He loved not the Muses so well as his sport;
> > And
> Prized black eyes, or a lucky hit
> At bowls, above all the trophies of wit.

It often goes unnoticed that Suckling is present in absence—he "did not appear," but here he is indeed—and also that his character is supplied by a whisperer in Apollo's ear, a telltale, a gossip. Nevertheless, one cannot resist the testimony, because it fits so well the identity or the stereotype we seek and find, conveying bonhomie and sprezzatura to some, and other qualities to others, often changing with the times—from "a gambler, wencher, and general reprobate in the court of Charles I" in the first edition (1962) of the *Norton Anthology* to "the prototype of the Cavalier playboy" in the fourth (1979), for example. The stereotype itself invites discrimination in assessing what Suckling rejects here, especially "all the *trophies* of wit," the tokens and memorials of vanity or vulgarity, or both. Suckling "loved not the Muses so well as his sport"—process, action, living, society, and play. He "*prized* black eyes," with the flash of vital attraction, and "a lucky hit at bowls," not the victory or the winnings, but the very moment of happy chance. There is no profundity in these synecdoches of sociable pleasure, engagement, and joie de vivre, but they have their charms, and the harm in them is slight enough.

Suckling is thrice-judicious in his absence from the sessions—the formal trial—of the wits, first because he has "better things to do," but also because, on a different plane, he can the easier *be* present in his absence. The narrator retails a whisperer's report, which gives credit even with detraction, not surprisingly, since Suckling the poet is characterizing Suckling the delinquent; the wink in the characterization invites a special recognition from the eye of the beholder. Finally, Suckling was right to absent himself on any account: an alderman ultimately wins the laurel, because Apollo—of all deities to sell out!—declared that " 'twas the best sign / Of good store of wit to have good store of coin" (107–08). So much for wisdom, wit, and art in the world's ways, a view not very welcome but abundantly in evidence throughout recorded history, as well as in literary reflections on lived experience. Suckling is often a keener observer of society and values than he is given credit for by persons more favorably disposed to Malvolio's garb than Feste's.

The first two of my four representative poems are scarcely given short shrift, let alone riddling shrift, by critics: "Upon St. Thomas's Unbelief" and "An Answer to Some Verses Made in His Praise." The first, a juvenile sestain (written c. 1626, when Suckling was sixteen or seventeen), is the first poem in the Oxford English Text; the second is #75 of the seventy-eight canonical poems.[12] One would readily associate neither poem with such standard anthology-pieces as "A Ballad upon a Wedding," "Out upon it," and "Why so pale and wan," by which Suckling is best or only known. But these two poems are equally though differently representative, perhaps especially so in being evidently lesser poems.

Upon St. Thomas's Unbelief

Faith comes by hearsay, love by sight: then he
May well believe, and love whom he doth see.
But since men leave both hope and charity,
And faith is made the greatest of the three,
All doctrine goes for truth; then say I thus,
"More goes to heaven with Thomas Didymus."

Suckling's abiding concern with religious belief is evident especially in eleven juvenile poems (about an eighth of the canon) and

An Account of Religion by Reason, which he wrote four years before his death at thirty-two, in 1641. Engaging and characteristic aspects of "Upon St. Thomas's Unbelief"—aside from the expression of a will to faith, which modern readers will take or leave as such—are its energy and ingenuity, its muted paradox and irony, its apparent sincerity and earnestness, and Suckling's self-identification with Doubting Thomas, implicit here and explicit in another poem, "Faith and Doubt," where it is said that

> Our faith, not reason, must us steer. . . .
> Each man is Thomas here, and fain would see
> Something to help his infidelity,
> but I believe; Lord, help my faithless mind
> and with St. Thomas let me pardon find.

From a modern perspective, the suggestions of existential angst are more evident and for most more compelling than the theological issues in the poem, but those issues are there, in the implied distinctions between "the faith believed in" *(fides quae creditur)* and "the faith whereby belief is reached" *(fides qua creditur)*, which figures prominently in "Faith and Doubt"; and between "unformed faith" *(fides informata)* and "faith formed by love" *(fides formata caritate).*

The address of "Upon St. Thomas's Unbelief" is closely related to the account of Thomas's doubting, seeing, and believing in John 20:24–29: Suckling's "Faith comes by hearsay" in part interprets the Gospel, where "the other disciples said unto" Thomas, "we have seen the Lord. But he said unto them, Except I shall see . . . I will not believe." And Suckling's "love [comes] by sight" reflects Thomas's response when the Lord reveals himself and says, in clear and present "hearsay," "be not faithless, but believing. And Thomas answered and said unto him, my Lord and my God," thus becoming the first explicitly to confess Christ's divinity. Suckling emphasizes the "eloquence" of sight, the primary sense proverbially associated both with truth and conviction and with love, for who ever loved that loved not at first sight? Thomas saw, believed, loved. But "since" the Ascension, willful men neglect two of the theological virtues, hope and charity; and make faith "the greatest of the three," like Lutheran believers in justification by "faith only" (the eleventh of the Thirty-Nine Articles without the twelfth, "Of Good Works"). By that reasoning, "All doctrine goes"—or passes current—"for truth," leading the young Suckling to the conclusion that "More goes"—that is, more go—"to heaven with Thomas Didymus" than with heterogeneous believers, many of whom must believe in vain, because those who differ in belief cannot all be right.

In fact, the poem seems to reach the same conclusion simultaneously by two different routes, using a striking duality of expression to make the case that they also deserve who only stand and wait in faithful doubt. One argument, that already paraphrased, concludes that faithful doubt is superior to dubious credence. The other has it that, if "All doctrine goes for truth" indeed, and "faith only" is acceptable to God as truth, then Thomas "More goes to heaven with Thomas Didymus"—the More who was no martyr for Suckling and his Anglican contemporaries, much less for the "true" believers in "faith only." [13] St. Thomas almost displaces St. Paul as guide and model here, and if any was patron saint to Suckling's skepticism it was Thomas Didymus the Doubter.

Second, "An Answer to Some Verses Made in His Praise."

> The ancient poets and their learned rhymes
> We still admire in these our later times
> And celebrate their fames; thus though they die,
> Their names can never taste mortality:
> Blind Homer's muse and Virgil's stately verse,   5
> While any live, shall never need a hearse.
> Since then to these such praise was justly due
> For what they did, what shall be said to you?
> These had their helps: they writ of gods and kings,
> Of temples, battles, and such gallant things,   10
> But you of nothing; how could you have writ
> Had you but chose a subject to your wit?
> To praise Achilles or the Trojan crew
> Showed little art, for praise was but their due.
> To say she's fair that's fair, this is no pains: 15
> He shows himself most poet that most feigns.
> To find out virtues strangely hid in me,
> Ay, there's the art and learned poetry.
> To make one striding of a barbed steed
> Prancing a stately round (I use indeed   20
> To ride Bat Jewel's jade), this is the skill,
> This shows the poet wants not wit at will.
>   I must admire aloof, and for my part
>   Be well contented, since you do't with art.

"An Answer" is a pleasing disavowal of self-importance, with a skeptical eye on current celebrity by contrast with posthumous renown, whose evergreen laurels are secure. Suckling offers one solution to "the problem of nothing," [14] too, celebrating the poet as both maker and liar, and reconciling Aristotle and Plato in effect, though this is not an explicitly philosophical, much less weighty, poem—a modest kind one can appreciate in our own age, over-stocked as it sometimes is with theory and Sir Oracles ("when I ope my lips, let no dog bark").

Homer and Virgil live by their own celebrations of "Achilles or the Trojan crew" and by encomiums extolling them; yet they showed "little art," because they "had their helps" in "gods and kings" and "gallant things," whose "praise was but their due." By contrast, Suckling's encomiast has made something of nothing and shown himself the greater poet, because "he shows himself most poet that most feigns," a tautological truism that resolves a problem of great antiquity with a flourish of paradox and ambiguity—or, if one likes, duplicity and polysemy. Sidney had written that the poet "nothing affirms, and therefore never lieth," as a poet. So Suckling's encomiast does, since he "writ . . . of nothing," thus affirming it. Again according to Sidney, "it is that feigning notable images of virtues, vices, or what else . . . which must be the right describing note to know a poet by," a Renaissance redaction of mimesis notably Aristotelian in identifying poetry not with verse but with mimesis and poesis. In *As You Like It* Touchstone favors Audrey with the tidings that "the truest poetry is the most feign-ing, and lovers are given to poetry; and what they swear in poetry may be said as lovers they do feign" (3.3.19–22).

Unlike Sidney's, Suckling's formal purpose is not to argue in defense of poetry, but to contribute a witty poetical instance in the apothegm applied: "To find out virtues strangely hid in me, / Ay, there's the art and learned poetry." And "to *make* one striding of a barbed steed / Prancing a stately round (I use indeed / To ride Bat Jewel's jade), this is the skill, / This shows the poet wants not wit at will." It is hard to imagine when or where Suckling's customary mount would have been "Bat Jewel's jade," with its amusing rus-tication of the Cavalier, nor do I know who, if anyone out of this fiction, that worthy, Bat Jewel, was: perhaps an otherwise unsung competitor of Thomas Hobson, the Cambridge carrier, offering choices even worse than Hobson's. The point is that the poet has *made* a noble equestrian figure of Suckling on a draft horse. LeSueur's statue of Charles I on horseback (1633) now at the top of

Whitehall and Van Dyck's painting in the National Gallery (c. 1635) come to mind, whether they came to Suckling's or not; the nobility of horsemanship had its antiquity long before Suckling's day. The genial last couplet wittily and gracefully asserts Suckling's prescribed role as admiring spectator—"I must admire aloof, and for my part / Be well contented"—together with the accomplished fact of performance in his own artful expression of "artless" appreciation: he is audience articulate; the last word is his *and* his encomiast's, "since you do't with art," the art of the poet's showing through Suckling's telling, text and performance two in one.

"An Answer" merges aesthetic and philosophical concerns with colloquial familiarity through the intermedium of a social genre tinged with shades of Great Tew, where John Earles "would frequently profess that he had got more useful learning from his conversation . . . than he had at Oxford." [15] It is a formal mimesis of a spontaneous conversational expression of gratitude and admiration; refined into graceful informality, it complements the praised work of translating rustic equitation into Cavalier urbanity, giving to airy nothing a knightly bearing and a place.

Not surprisingly, "Why so pale and wan, fond lover?" has received its meed of analysis and praise, most substantially in L. A. Beaurline's well-known essay, " 'Why So Pale and Wan': An Essay in Critical Method." [16] Beaurline's study differs considerably from the other two major studies of Suckling of the past two decades, though all three belong to critical analogues of seventeenth-century analytical and poetical modes. Raymond Anselment's essay on "The Love Poetry of John Suckling" is an instance of what could be called "promenade" criticism, an appreciative survey of sundry flowers—about seventeen, to be specific.[17] Charles L. Squier's volume, by contrast, is an example of the "topographical" survey, which is naturally more extensive and aims at summary comprehensiveness.[18] Beaurline's analogues would be found rather in the sphere of natural philosophy and scientific investigation, and the scrutiny of telling detail, as "Critical Method" in part suggests. The essay is—happily, I think—less methodological than critical, an invaluable study that is the only detailed close reading of a poem by Suckling I know of. Does anyone *not* know the "Song,"

> Why so pale and wan, fond lover?
> Prithee why so pale?
> Will, when looking well can't move her,

Looking ill prevail?
Prithee why so pale?   5

Why so dull and mute, young sinner?
Prithee why so mute?
Will, when speaking well can't win her,
Say nothing do't?
Prithee why so mute?   10

Quit, quit, for shame, this will not move,
This cannot take her;
If of herself she will not love,
Nothing can make her:
The Devil take her.   15

Beaurline's central "contention is that the term *elegant facetiousness*
['defined historically,' after Quintilian's *facetus*] best illuminates this
poem, for it fits the peculiar tone of the song, the air of the speaker,
the quality of the language, and the color of our emotional reaction." He goes on to argue that the poem's meanings and effects
depend prominently on its identity and place as a song sung within
a play, *Aglaura*, where it has special dramatic significance. There
the song has a "double audience":

it is sung in Act IV . . . by a gallant named Orsames, a young "anti-
platonic" lord . . . who . . . does not sing the song to a fond lover; rather he
sings it to the platonic ladies, Semanthe and Orithie. . . . After he sings,
he says that this was a bit of advice given ["foure or five yeares agoe,"
4.2.32] to a friend fallen into a consumption, and Orithie says that she
could have guessed it was the product of Orsames' brain. . . . To be sure,
most Elizabethan plays use songs strictly for ornament, but in this play
Suckling explicitly connects the song with the dialogue; the rhetorical
situation, therefore, presupposes the presence of the ladies. . . . The
doubleness of the rhetorical situation is one of the reasons why this poem
is so charming and playful. It gives us, the general readers or *third audience*,
a special detachment, and it probably contributes to the conventional
character of the speaker. The whole of the reader's relation to the poem is
like a window-peeper watching an eavesdropper hearing a conversation—

a witty way of characterizing the regresses that would lead eventually to "we are such stuff as dreams are made on."
   One would like to see left *in* what Orsames says in full in
4.2.31–32, that this song was "a little foolish counsell (Madam) I

gave a friend of mine *foure or five yeares agoe*, when he was falling into a Consumption" (italics mine).[19] Willa McClung Evans interpreted Orsames's lines to mean that "the musical setting . . . would appear to have been written several years previous to the performance of the play and was already familiar to the audience,"[20] and Beaurline himself had earlier referred to Orsames's lines as perhaps being "Suckling's way of apologizing for using an older piece of his verse."[21] What is in question is the literary identity—or identities—of the "Song," and its history bears on its poetical, dramatic, and critical status. It is reasonable for Beaurline to emphasize "the whole of the reader's relation to the poem" as it is apprehended in and through the play, but it is somewhat misleading to imply that the poem takes its primary if not sole identity from this relation. "Suckling explicitly connects the song with the dialogue," or rather the reverse, but the connection identifies the poem as a "dramatic lyric" only when it occurs *within* the play. Suckling could have provided the contextualizing dialogue long after he wrote the poem, and there is nothing *in* the poem that spells *Aglaura.*

Whenever "Why so pale and wan" was written, it appears in *Fragmenta Aurea* as a poem (and "Song") in its own right, and it *is* an autonomous poem when so presented and received. Set to music, sung, and heard, it becomes an art-song. And it acquires—and may have first acquired—its identity and place as part in a dramatic nest of spheres within spheres when written into a play and sung to an audience within the play that is beheld by an audience witnessing the play. This state of artistic affairs it shares in part with Jonson's poem—and "Volpone's"—"Song to Celia" ("Come my Celia, let us prove"), a case still more complicated by its intimate relationship with Catullus 5, "Vivamus, mea Lesbia." In his edition, William B. Hunter, Jr., implicitly emphasizes the treble identity by giving Ferrabosco's music together with the poem and noting that "this song appears in *Volpone* III.vii.155–83, where *Volpone uses it*" (italics mine).[22] Ian Donaldson notes in his edition: "Sung to Celia by Volpone . . . ; *in dramatic context*, a more sinister invitation than its Catullan model" (italics mine).[23]

Both editors suggest the distinction that needs to be made between the poem as poem, as art-song, and as song within a play. Suckling's song and Jonson's are made to be "dramatic lyrics" by their incorporation in a special context: neither poem in itself implies an ontologically distinct world beyond the rhetorical situation, or "heterocosm," of the poem-in-itself, *except* by the wisdom of hindsight, which purports to find "in" the poem external referents due not to its content but to its location. As Claude J. Summers and Ted-Larry Pebworth have noted, "even without knowledge of its original dramatic context in *Volpone*, readers cannot fail to grasp Jonson's satiric mode here."[24] Jonson's poem may *seem* more explicitly related to Volpone's than to an anonymous speaker's situation, but details within the poem take on particular reference in relation to the surrounding context that they do not have—or need—without it. For example, "Or his easier ears beguile" requires no antecedent for "his" because it is obvious from the poem's other details that "he" is "the husband"; the lyric monodrama makes its own necessary and sufficient sense.

The "root level" is the poem itself—within reason "the object as in itself it really is," subject to understanding, "overstanding," and misunderstanding by readers, *sine quibus non*. The other elements entering into combination with the poem are external and theoretically incidental, however different a poem's meanings and effects may be when it ceases to be the "whole" of a reader's experience and becomes a *part* of another whole, combining with music to make a song, or with a variety of elements to make a dramatic lyric *in* Suckling's *Aglaura*. In relation to song, a type of such combinations of elements, the issues have been treated in depth in Elise Bickford Jorgens's essay "On Matters of Manner and Music in Jacobean and Caroline Song": "at every level—meter and rhythm, versification and syntax, and formal and thematic structure—when there is a conflict between the formal and the semantic organization, a musical setting directs the listener's perception toward one or the other and lessens his awareness of the artful interplay between them designed by the poet. . . . The 'song-like' state for a poem, then, is one in which a single line of development serves both matter and manner and can be formalized in music."[25]

This is the case, she says, with Jonson's "Still to be neat" *(Epicoene)*, which is "clearly song-like," and with Shakespeare's "Sigh no more, ladies, sigh no more" *(Much Ado):* "if Sidney, or Jonson, or Donne" or Suckling "calls a poem 'Song,' whether it was designed for or ever appeared in a musical setting or not, we expect it to conform in some identifiable way with the conventions of the musical lyric." This generalization is no doubt sound enough even if many poems' titles were not supplied by the poets themselves, as seems to have been the case. By contrast, Jonson's poem in *Cynthia's Revels*, "Thou more than most sweet glove," is not songlike. "Although Jonson calls it 'Song,' that title must surely be taken as a conceit"; it "could of course be sung. But it breaks as many of the conventions as it embodies." Likewise, Carew's "Parting, Celia Weeps" is "simply not a suitable poem for musical setting. A through-composed setting could make rational sense of it, but only at the expense of its formal poetic structure. And since the poetic conventions of the period dictate that those features of formal structure remain as a visible and audible frame, as Carew obviously intended that they should, a setting that cannot do both is missing a significant feature of the poem"; Henry Lawes's "musical setting has virtually destroyed the poet's tenuous but altogether appropriate balance between versification and syntax." In short, the qualities of a *poem*, whether "song-like" or not, begin—and end—in the poetic art of the poem as "creation through words of orders of meaning and sound." [26]

In his "Essay on Critical Method," Beaurline gives a detailed exposition of the dialectic of the poem as an expressive mimesis centering on "the strategy of the speaker," whom he characterizes as a worldly-wise, formally "libertine" exponent of "playful cynicism," whose counsel in the third stanza he describes thus: "At that point where force is needed, Suckling's" poem "has force. When speaking well will not 'take' (i.e. charm) a lover or a friend, a man must change and speak bluntly. The gallant [speaker] not only recommends 'speaking well,' but his own words are a model of how to speak well and a demonstration of when to be blunt. Both his words and his actions show the value of ease, brevity, urbanity, agreeableness, elegant facetiousness, and all the other ornaments of wit." Beaurline gives an admirable exposition of the qualities of the poem in itself and its modes of operation in *Aglaura*, but he leaves the force and wit of the conclusion to interpret as well as speak for themselves, as indeed they do. But they also invite comment, first to the effect that the speaker does *not* say that "a man must change and speak bluntly"; it would be odd if he did, since doing so would almost certainly prove as inefficacious as ungracious. This seems to rest on a misunderstanding of the last line of the second stanza— "Prithee why so mute?"—which is concerned not with a need to speak out but with the futility of silence (like *pale*ness in the first stanza) as a gambit; in fact, in the third stanza the would-be lover is urged to give up, move on, and leave her—not, with Gertrude, to heaven, but—to hell.

The argument of the master of experience to his novice is this: when neither the "fond lover" 's "looking well" *or* "ill" and "pale" can "move her" (stanza 1), nor the "young sinner" 's "speaking well" *or* "saying nothing" and staying "mute" can "win her" (stanza 2), then he should

> Quit, quit, for shame, this will not move,
>> This cannot take her;
> If of herself she will not love,
>> Nothing can make her,
>> The Devil take her.

The redoubled "quit," each "quit" for an antecedent stanza and inquiry, as it were, is rhetorically felicitous as well as forcefully imperative, and the final three lines epitomize the whole poem. If "Why so pale and wan" were a freshman essay, one might admonish Suckling for a vague use of "This," but it refers, plainly enough, to the entire game of courtship epitomized by typical moves in the first and second stanzas. "When" (3 and 8) and "If" (13) hold the identical "linear" as well as dialectical position within stanzas, as temporally and conditionally emphatic expressions of the cause. The conclusion is certain: "Nothing can make her," an elliptical locution frequently *mis*understood in recent years through the application of current colloquial usage, but perhaps an occasion for "overstanding" that both William Empson and Wayne Booth might countenance, though one would hope not.

"The Devil take her" is the poem's pièce de résistance. If "nothing can make her" love, may she go to the devil: let "the Devil take her"—bear her away to have her as the subject of his nether reign and to hold as the object of his rude affection, *le droit sinistre du seigneur*. Or simply and keenly as Suckling has it: may "the Devil take her" to hell and "take her" himself, enjoying the love she selfishly withholds from the persistent but unsuccessful suitor addressed by the speaker in and of the poem.

There are many ways of interpreting and evaluating the ethics, politics, and sociology, as well as the aesthetics, of the relationships and situation, but most would agree that the fictionalized sentiment is consistent with "normal" and "natural" frustration in analogous circumstances: if one can't have her, him, it, whatever—to hell with the same; the perennial case of the fox's grapes, Aesopically speaking.

Sonnet 2 is also a standard anthology-piece, but one that often draws fire for its supposed cynicism, ugliness, brutality, licentiousness, and crudity—bad enough qualities, but not so bad as

Suckling fares in a Puritan assault upon him as "a scum of ungodliness from the seething pot of iniquity."[27] The poem is frequently compared invidiously with its partial source, Donne's "Community," which Charles L. Squier finds "hardly any less brutal" in concluding, "Changed loves are but changed sorts of meat, / And when he hath the kernel eat, / Who doth not fling away the shell?" Here is Suckling's poem:

> Of thee, kind boy, I ask no red and white
>   To make up my delight,
>   No odd becoming graces,
> Black eyes, or little know-not-whats, in faces;
> Make me but mad enough, give me good store   5
> Of love, for her I court,
>   I ask no more:
> 'Tis love in love that makes the sport.
>
> There's no such thing as that we beauty call,
>   It is mere cozenage all;   10
>   For though some long ago
> Liked certain colors mingled so and so,
> That doth not tie me now from choosing new;
> If I a fancy take
>   To black and blue,   15
> That fancy doth it beauty make.
>
> 'Tis not the meat, but 'tis the appetite
>   Makes eating a delight,
>   And if I like one dish
> More than another, that a pheasant is;   20
> What in our watches, that in us is found,
> So to the height and nick
>   We up be wound,
> No matter by what hand or trick.

If a poem like this is to be given a fair hearing, it helps to recall that it *is* a fiction and to make due adjustments in perspective: it is neither a hymn for the sons of Belial nor a versified slice of autobiography. David Hume supplied appropriate guidance, mutatis mutandis, over two centuries ago in "Of the Standard of Taste": "every work of art, in order to produce its due effect upon the mind, must be surveyed in a certain point of view, and cannot be fully relished by persons, whose situation, real or imaginary, is not conformable to that which is required by the performance. . . . A critic of a different age or nation . . . must place himself in the same situation as the audience, in order to form a true judgment," and should place "himself in that point of view, which the performance presupposes." Dr. Johnson wrote to much the same purpose in his *Preface to Shakespeare:* "Every man's performance, to be rightly estimated, must be compared with the state of the age in which he lived, and with his own particular opportunities." With respect to the ethics of art and the politics of sin in real life and history, I am content to invoke Elizabeth Burton, who notes in *The Jacobeans at Home* that "the pleasures of whoring, wantonness, and drink, contrary to popular belief, do not cause nations to fall." [28]

Sonnet 2 was addressed initially to a coterie of literate and literary wits well acquainted with libertinage in poetry and life, whether as practicing libertines, philosophizing platonics, or otherwise: an audience of variously behaved sophisticates—who were arguably much less "decadent," especially in relation to their Jacobethan predecessors and Restoration successors, than literary historians have often made them out to be. A. J. Smith has written, for example, "that in mid-seventeenth-century England sexual love had become categorically distinct from the love that holds the universe in sway, and that a choice compelled itself between a fashionable amorousness and the imperative search for truth"—a view that sounds rather like an extrapolation from poetry read under the influence of *The Elizabethan World Picture* and Eliot's notion of the "dissociation of sensibility." [29] According to Lawrence Stone, by contrast, "after about 1590 . . . there developed general promiscuity among both sexes at Court," though "the real break-through into promiscuity at Court . . . occurred under James. The popular reaction was that of Simonds D'Ewes, who spoke of 'the holy state of matrimony perfidiously broken and amongst many made but a May game . . . and even great personages prostituting their bodies to the intent to satisfy and consume their substance in lascivious appetites of all sorts'. As early as 1603 Lady Anne Clifford said that 'all the ladies about the court had gotten such ill names that it was grown a scandalous place.' " [30] Indeed, "it was not until the reign of Charles I and Henrietta Maria that a serious effort was made to sublimate this sensual promiscuity in the ideal of neoplatonic love, which rose above both animal lusts and the turbulent passions of love, to enter the calm arena of a spiritual union of souls"! [31]

The disparity between received and recent revisionary views of the Caroline social ethos—together with extraordinarily diverse estimates of our own—points up more than one shortcoming of negative critical judgments made prominently on moral grounds— the Moral Majority's or which Other's, for example? The evidence also leads to the reasonable inference that Charles I's courtiers were not exceptionally vicious—and perhaps that "we," taken all in all, are not preeminently virtuous, however sparing of cakes and ale. All "absolutes" as well as relativities include the beholder as well as the object beheld, perhaps *especially* the former, as subject, as her-meneutic theorists are wont to emphasize. And all critical observa-tion has need not only of historical, ethical, aesthetic, and, I should say, sociobiological circumspectness, but for due allowance to be made for such significant variables as time past, time present, the poet and his medium, the idiosyncrasies of readership, and the nature of human nature, whatever it is or might be.[32] It seems quite possible that such "brutality" as there is in Sonnet 2, which is first of all fictional and otherwise relative, is in part the subjective prod-uct of anachronistic attitudes and unsuspended disbeliefs, credible and even creditable in themselves but variously applicable to the case.

As I read it, Sonnet 2 wittily blends ethology, philosophy, tech-nology, insouciance, and joviality in a "natural, easy" fictional address every bit as "courtly writ" and reflective of "the conversa-tion of a gentleman" as Dryden's Eugenius found Suckling's lyrics when he pronounced them superior to those of the "last age." And it is not easy to find "ugliness" in a witty monodramatizing of the truism that affectional beauty is in the eye of the beholder. This, I take it, is what Suckling is talking about "at bottom," not as a jaded sexual gourmet but as a robust culinary realist: a case of *haute cuisine vis-à-vis cuisine bourgeoise;* or, one person's McDonald's is another's Tour d'Argent; or, as Suckling (or someone else) puts it in a poem not certainly by him, "this each wise man knows: / As good stuff under flannel lies as under silken clothes" ("Love and Debt Alike Troublesome"). The principle is of course not gender-bound.

Sonnet 2 is likely to be distorted by overlaid resonances of late-twentieth-century usage, semitechnical, colloquial, and vulgar, in respect especially of "meat," "appetite," "dish," "watches," and "trick." But what might most offend some modern sensibilities must have afforded Suckling's audience a mild shock of recognition tempered with amusement and delight. Because instinctual human responses are spontaneously reflexive, they can be aptly expressed in terms of mechanism; thus the clock or watch is a fitting figure, even a pleasing one, for, "in the seventeenth century, when the

Scientific Revolution exploded in all its exuberance and vigour, the champions of the new science manifested an avid interest in horological matters," and "in their eyes the clock was the machine *par excellence* and it fascinated them."[33] Indeed, "in the course of the sixteenth and seventeenth centuries the clock as a machine exerted deep influence on the speculations of philosophers and scientists. Kepler asserted that 'The universe is not similar to a divine living being, but is similar to a clock,' " and God Himself was spoken of as a master clockmaker.[34] "Portable" clocks, or watches, were relatively new, fashionable, costly, and intriguing.

It is this ambience that informed Suckling's poem in its origins, not that of *A Clockwork Orange*, Jan Kott's Grand Mechanism, or even that cybernetic Adam and Eve of the media, the Six Million Dollar Man and the Bionic Woman.[35] The effect was to convey provocative empirical observations on instinctual drives and behavior through the vehicle of a would-be precision instrument of certain design but—in Suckling's day—still variable working and performance. It is not farfetched to say that the essential analogy of the watch, not as used but as analogy, is the technologically attuned Caroline counterpart of "what a piece of work is a man" in *Hamlet*, where the Prince says he is Ophelia's "evermore, whilst this machine is to him" (2.2.123–24), and whose pulse "doth temperately keep time" (3.4.140). In this connection, "trick" itself is a quasitechnical term for "the mode of working a piece of mechanism, etc., the system upon which a thing is constructed" (*OED*, *sb*.1.8c), with specific application to clockworks. A clockwork popperin pear is perhaps how Suckling thought of his amorous watch-man, quite without depreciation or depreciability.

In the round, Sonnet 2 is an urbane wit's dramatic monologue about nature, art, attraction, appetite, pursuit, and play. It opens dramatically in mid-conversation, as it were, and the "kind boy" so familiarly and genially addressed is a compound of confidant, Eros, quartermaster, huntsman, apothecary, and procurer, of whom the speaker seeks nothing special, least of all affected, in the *object* of his love—no fashionable cosmetic arts and coquettish mannerisms, but only "good store / Of love," a simple, homely, but generous provision, "for her I court, I ask no more: / 'Tis *love* in love that *makes* the sport." This is a psychologically astute observation expressed appropriately in terms of the dual sports of venery: amour and the hunt. All the attractions the speaker rejects either are or involve fashionable artificialities, the first reducing the traditional "rose and lily" of the conventionally attractive complexion to the mere colors of makeup, "red and white." The commonplace of love as madness figures, too, but the emphasis of sense and meter falls on love as maker of the sport: the primary agency is the will to courtship, not the arty-crafty movements and appearance of the courted.

The second stanza deprives beauty of objective existence by dividing the *verbum* from the *res* in good Baconian form: "There's no such *thing* as that we beauty *call*" briskly dismisses an ancient and vermiculate question. "Cozenage" sums up the kindred tricks of the trade, and the claims of custom and precedent are next denied, making a bridge from the currently fashionable "red and white" of the first stanza to the blank "so and so" of any age's arbitrary fashion, by contrast with the exercise of individual preference given primacy here. "Black and blue" has an emblematic force more dramatically vital than that of "red and white," because it is natural, whereas the latter is merely abstract and conventional. It is a whimsically apt paradox for expressing the subjectivity of beauty that one *might* prefer the natural "black and blue" of bruises to an artfully "perfect" complexion. (There could be shades of "S&M" in "black and blue," but I doubt it.) The stanza's last line parallels its fellow in the first stanza, and "That *fancy* doth it beauty *make*" intensifies the creative force of the wit and will by repeating "make" and placing it here as the emphatic last word: beauty is the creature of the fancy.

The first quatrain of the last stanza realizes the field side of "sport," and the second abruptly technologizes the poem with the unexpected image of the lover as timepiece, an image we may see as darkened by our own spectacles, anachronistically, as I have already suggested.[36] Within the poem, however, the controls are such that emphasis falls not on the tenor or the negative aspects of the vehicles but on the speaker and the positive aspects: the "appetite" here is the counterpart of "love" in the first stanza and "fancy" in the second. It, too, "*makes*"—"makes eating a delight"; and "if I like one dish / More than another" reinforces, in the gustatory sphere, "if I a fancy take / To black and blue" in the visual. Taste expressed as a function of the imagination, "that we beauty call," materializes here as a source of true delight in a gustatory delicacy: "If I *like* . . . , *that* a pheasant *is*." This is the art of the heart's desire. Suckling was probably not thinking of Sir Edward Dyer's famous poem "My mind to me a kingdom is" when he wrote this line, but thematic similarities suggest the appropriate paraphrase: "My bird to me a pheasant is, however fowl."

The concluding quatrain is a miniature masterpiece of combined analogy, anatomy, physiology, phenomenology, horology, tech-nology—*and* apt and harmless ribaldry. The first twenty lines of the poem have conversationally explained the facts of human attrac-tion and the conclusions to be drawn from them. These four now explain *why* they are as they are, with focus on the phenomenon of desire aroused. The fusion of tenor and vehicle in itself validates the analogy of man and watch, and the terms apply almost equally to both, without alternation or transference: "height" and "nick" as "point, stage, degree"; "wind up," meaning in part "to excite" (*OED*, *sb.*1.22f)—the effect of which is conveyed also by the idiomatically strenuous inversion, "up be wound"; the technically horological along with the amatory senses of "trick," read even without resort to its current cottage-industrial association with the piecework of the oldest profession. The poem ends with a variation on the theme of the whole of Suckling's poem, "Love's Clock": "What in our watches, that in us is found" is the technological *fons et origo*, the *mainspring*, of course, a term applied also to the spring that drives the hammer in a gunlock, a sense used with cheerful grossness by Massinger ("né" Beaumont) and Fletcher in *The Cus-tom of the Country*,[37] and akin to the force that through the green fuse drives the flower and drove Dylan Thomas's green age. Thus Sonnet 2 concludes as it began, on a strikingly upbeat note.

A speculative point just possibly worth adding about the last stanza is that there may be an implicit unifying allusion to the "jack" as a *Jack-of-the-clock*, "the figure of a man which strikes the bell on the outside of a clock" (*OED*, *sb.*1.6), itself said to be "wound up," and "a machine for turning the spit in roasting meat" that was "wound up like a clock" (*OED*, *sb.*1.7). That there should be a subliminal poet's signature for Jack Suckling, Norfolk Londoner and man of parts, in a poem also concerned with every man-jack and woman-jill is appropriate enough, but this may be to consider too curiously. If there are no such Suckling-jacks in the poem, a couple of them could nevertheless have been at the back of the poet's mind, prompting him by mechanical association when he moved from the image of a meal's meat to the temporal measure of amorous man and woman.

Remember the words of Henry Vaughan, how he said, "How brave a prospect is a bright backside."[38] The seriousness and sincerity in Suckling require surgical removal from their vital and engaging poetic incorporation if they are to be seen as such, but they are there with the manifest criticism of life, and they are fundamental, keeping a low profile in an art the brighter and the better for its irony and wit. All work and no play would make Sir Jack not only a dull boy but never an inch of Suckling: that he is Sir John Suckling, let him a little show it, even in this. In fine, one may well be reminded of Duke Theseus's terminal directive to the hempen-homespun players, "let your epilogue alone," and be glad of twenty words in conclusion from one of James Howell's Epistles: "Be pleased to dispense with the prolixity of this discourse, for I could not wind it up closer, nor on a lesser bottom." [39]

NOTES

1. Eliot, "The Metaphysical Poets" (1921), in *Selected Essays* (New York: Harcourt, [1951]), p. 250. Leavis, "Milton's Verse," first published in *Scrutiny* 2, no. 2 (1933–34); quoted here from *Revaluation* (1947; rpt. New York: Norton, 1963), p. 42.

2. Tucker Brooke and Matthias A. Shaaber, *The Renaissance (1500–1660)*, 2nd ed. (New York: Appleton-Century-Crofts, 1967), p. 658.

3. *On Poetry and Poets* (New York: Farrar, [1957]), p. 47; the essay was first published in 1944. If Eliot has lost the authority he was accorded until a decade or so ago, he has his moments still; Brian Lee notes the positive side of "the conditions of self and society which co-operated to make Eliot a critic of high classical standing, a possessor of the intuition of genius, . . . exactly those which at the same time disable him from the *consistency* which would raise his criticism even higher in future estimation" (italics mine), in *Theory and Personality: The Significance of T. S. Eliot's Criticism* (London: Athlone, 1979), p. 103.

4. *Poetry and Criticism of Matthew Arnold*, ed. A. Dwight Culler (Boston: Houghton, 1961), "Study," pp. 307, 309, and "Wordsworth," p. 339.

5. Richard Dawkins, *The Selfish Gene* (New York: Oxford University Press, 1976), p. 151.

6. *The Artist as Critic: The Critical Writings of Oscar Wilde*, ed. Richard Ellmann (New York: Random House, 1968), p. 305. Comes the revolution, of course, there will be no "civilized society," no Wilde, *and* no Arnold—"sans Wine, sans Song, sans Singer and—sans End."

7. *Anatomy of Criticism* (Princeton: Princeton University Press, 1957), p. 34. All positions beget their opposites (and others) terminologically as well as dialectically, and I am hardly the first to write of "low seriousness." In 1975, for example, Dona F. Munker wrote of "That Paltry Burlesque Style: Seventeenth-Century Poetry and Augustan 'Low Seriousness' " in *SCN* 33, 14–22, using the phrase in a generic application that inevitably overlaps with my own use of it.

8. Whether nodding acquaintance en passant is better than none is a serious question in the literary curriculum and elsewhere; in many cases I think it is, despite the real disadvantages implied by the analogy.

9. See *Critical Understanding* (Chicago: University of Chicago Press, 1979); responding to a review by Jonathan Culler, Booth stresses that "the book in fact defends critical 'improprieties' " (*TLS*, April 25, 1980, p. 468), quoting his own page 335: "Neither the nature of art works nor our own legitimate interests will allow us to reject whatever improper questions promise to lead us to new territory." I am not wholly in sympathy with the note of cheery neofrontiersmanship here.

10. *English Poetry: Select Bibliographical Guides* (New York: Oxford University Press, 1971).

11. Charles L. Squier helpfully provides this service in *Sir John Suckling* (Boston: Twayne, 1978).

12. All citations follow *The Non-Dramatic Works of Sir John Suckling*, ed. Thomas Clayton (Oxford: The Clarendon Press, 1971), pp. 9, 78–79.

13. I have my own doubts about these converging lines of coalescent meaning, but the syntactical and semantic ambiguities work together too well to seem fortuitous, including "since," whether taken as "from then till now," as in my paraphrase, or as "because." In the manuscript (Cranfield Papers MS.U.269.F.36, no. 37), which provides the sole text of this poem, there are no handwriting distinctions, of the type italics allow in print, to set off proper names; worse, "More" is the first word in the line, so the capital, too, is ambiguous. It is at least interesting that *The Mirrour of Vertue in Worldly Greatnes, or The Life of Syr Thomas More Knight* (written in 1556) was printed (in "Paris") for the first time in the same year, 1626, in which the poem was quite probably written; from the scaffold on Tower Hill More "desired . . . all the people about him to pray for him, & to beare witnesse, that he should now there suffer death in, & for the fayth of the Holy Catholique Church" (facsimile rpt. Menston, Yorkshire: Scolar Press, 1970), p. 167.

14. See Rosalie L. Colie, *Paradoxia Epidemica: The Renaissance Tradition of Paradox* (Princeton: Princeton University Press, 1966), chap. 7.

15. *The Life of Clarendon by Himself* (1759), quoted from *Clarendon: Selections from "The History of the Rebellion and Civil Wars" and "The Life by Himself,"* ed. G. Huehns, The World's Classics (London: Oxford University Press, 1955), p. 38.

16. First printed in *Texas Studies in Literature and Language* 4 (1962–63), 553–63; rpt. in W. R. Keast, *Seventeenth-Century English Poetry: Modern Essays in Criticism*, rev. ed. (New York: Oxford University Press, 1971), pp. 300–11, the source of quotation here.

17. " 'Men Most of All Enjoy, When Least They Do': The Love Poetry of John Suckling," *Texas Studies in Literature and Language* 14 (1972), 17–32.

18. Nothing definitive can be inferred from elementary statistics, but it is not without interest that the ratio of discussion to poems is quite similar for Anselment and Squier, as it is, I suspect, for many treatments of many poets. In 53 pages Squier discusses 49 poems (according to the index) of the canonical 78 (63%, 1.08 pp. per poem). Anselment discusses 17 poems in 16 pages (22%, .94 p. per poem), which would have been 18 pages on Squier's scale.

19. Text from *The Works of Sir John Suckling: The Plays*, ed. L. A. Beaurline (Oxford: The Clarendon Press, 1971), p. 72.

20. *Henry Lawes, Musician and Friend of Poets* (London: Oxford University Press; New York: MLA, 1941), p. 260.

21. "The Canon of Sir John Suckling's Poems," *Studies in Philology* 57 (1960), 515.

22. *The Complete Poetry of Ben Jonson* (Garden City, N.Y.: Doubleday, 1963), p. 86.

23. *Ben Jonson: Poems* (London: Oxford University Press, 1975), p. 97.

24. *Ben Jonson* (Boston: Twayne, 1979), p. 162.

25. *ELR* 10 (1980), 239–64 (quotation, 258). For following quotations, see 239–40 and 262–64. Also see her book, *The Well-Tun'd Word: Musical Interpretations of English Poetry, 1597–1651* (Minneapolis: University of Minnesota Press, 1981).

26. "A typical contemporary definition of poetic art might run" thus, Reuben Brower wrote in 1952. The title, "The Heresy of Plot," identifies this as a piece of New Critical polemic, in one aspect, but it remains a thoughtful and provocative essay, nevertheless. The "definition" is hardly adequate for "poetic art"—as Johnson wrote in his life of Pope, "to circumscribe poetry by a definition will only show the narrowness of the definer"—but it has the right emphasis for the distinctions concerned here. The essay was first published in *English Institute Essays, 1952* (New York: Columbia University Press, 1952), pp. 44–69; rpt. in Elder Olson, ed., *Aristotle's Poetics and English Literature* (Chicago: University of Chicago Press, 1965), pp. 157–74 (quotation, p. 172).

27. *A Mappe of Mischiefe* (1641), p. 5.

28. London: Secker and Warburg, 1962, p. 286.

29. "The Failure of Love: Love Lyrics after Donne," in *Metaphysical Poetry*, ed. Malcolm Bradbury and David Palmer (1970; rpt. Bloomington: Indiana University Press, 1971), p. 52.

30. *The Crisis of the Aristocracy, 1558–1641* (Oxford: The Clarendon Press, 1965; corr. rpt., 1966), pp. 664, 665.

31. Lawrence Stone, *The Family, Sex and Marriage in England, 1500–1800* (New York: Harper, 1977), p. 504.

32. Marxist theorists tend to dismiss any reference to "(human) nature" as a specious bourgeois universalizing of the historically contingent, but there are psychobiological laws and facts of life and transcultural continuities of community to which Marxists, too, are subject.

33. Carlo M. Cipolla, *Clocks and Culture, 1300–1700* (London: Collins, 1967), p. 57. In "The Apotheosis of Faust: Poetry and New Philosophy in the Seventeenth Century," in Bradbury and Palmer, *Metaphysical Poetry*, pp. 149–79, Robert B. Hinman remarks acutely that "the notorious opposition between poets and new philosophers appears to be a largely modern construct projected backwards from a sense of separate cultures," whereas "the same ordering, synthesizing, all-encompassing imaginative surge towards 'reality', towards as much truth as man can express, seems evident in such achievements as *The Temple* and *Principia Mathematica*" (p. 156), and many a lesser work. "Science" was not a four-letter word in the seventeenth century.

34. Cipolla, *Clocks and Culture*, p. 105.

35. Suckling dramatically updated it, but he did not invent this eminently eligible analogy. Over two centuries earlier, for example, *Li Orloges amoureuses* of Jean Froissart the chronicler (1337–c.1404) devoted 1174 verses to the clockwork movements of the lover's heart. Later, there is a particularly choice use in *Tristram Shandy* (1.1): "*Pray, my dear*, quoth my mother, *have you not forgot to wind up the clock?*———*Good G–!* cried my father, making an exclamation, but taking care to moderate his voice at the same time,—*Did ever woman, since the creation of the world, interrupt a man with such a silly question?*" This "was a very unseasonable question at least," Tristram observed—with unfortunate consequences, according to Walter Shandy, who thought that "Tristram's misfortunes began nine months before he ever came into the world" (Professor Judith Herz of Concordia University, Montreal, reminded me of this at the Classic and Cavalier conference).

36. The theme of the "decadence"—quite aside from the hazards—of "smoking, drinking, and the like" is persistent. If the line between decorum and debauchery is drawn so near, there is not much breathing room for sociable indulgences *or* the licenses of fiction, even in its wish-fulfilling capacity. The appropriate lapel-button legend would seem to be "Thank you for ceasing to exist," perhaps adding in fine print, "Join me—at a distance. Whoever can tell which side of the grave is whose wins a custom-written epitaph by the immortal Saint Ben."

37. 3.3.8–10 in *Custom*, ed. R. Warwick Bond, in *The Works of Beaumont and Fletcher: Variorum Edition*, ed. A. H. Bullen (London: Bell, 1904–13), vol. 1, p. 532.

38. "Looking Back" (15), in "Pious Thoughts and Ejaculations," *Thalia Rediviva* (1678). French Fogle's edition retains the capital in "*Back-side*," Alan Rudrum's does not. See *The Complete Poetry of Henry Vaughan*, ed. Fogle (Garden City, N.Y.: Doubleday, 1964), p. 415; *Henry Vaughan: The Complete Poems*, ed. Rudrum (Harmondsworth, Middlesex: Penguin, 1976), p. 367.

39. Howell to the Earl R[ivers] from Hamburg, October 20, 1632, 1.6.3 in *Epistolae Ho-Elianae, The Familiar Letters of James Howell (1737)*, ed. Joseph Jacobs (London: D. Nutt, 1890–92), vol. 1, p. 300.

MICHAEL H. MARKEL

Perception and Expression
in Marvell's Cavalier Poetry

As Marvell's major lyrics have become better understood, commentators have turned their attention to his later, satirical poetry, in search of the balance and paradox that characterize his more famous works.[1] In his curious evolution from encomiast of Lovelace to Restoration satirist, Marvell is the greatest enigma of all English poets. Finding a private man who makes sense as Marvell the poet is likely to pose the ultimate scholarly riddle; his bloodless newsletters from Parliament to his constituents in Hull are as bizarre, in their own way, as the unbridled invective of the satires. In response to the current tendency to categorize the poet, Elizabeth Story Donno argues that he was not a Cavalier, a Puritan, or a satirist, but "the ultimate Renaissance poet," that is, a poet interested in literary traditions and uninterested in justifying his work on any but aesthetic grounds.[2] In a more Marvellian statement that makes essentially the same point, William Empson writes that, around 1650, Marvell "immediately stopped being in love with dead Cavalier heroes; he fell in love with Nature and mixed farming."[3]

In discussing his Cavalier poetry I take for granted that Marvell was familiar with his contemporaries. Margoliouth's edition makes clear that he was an avid reader who freely incorporated echoes of lines and ideas he admired.[4] And J. B. Leishman comprehensively traces Marvell's literary antecedents.[5] It is time now to analyze not whether, but in what ways and to what end, he read such contemporaries as Suckling, Waller, Cowley, Lovelace, and Carew.

Modern readers have rightly suggested that Marvell's interest in the Cavaliers was not simple and enthusiastic. Leah Sinanoglou Marcus, for example, writes that "The Unfortunate Lover" is a "mocking answer to the flocks of dilute Petrarchanists of his day who strained hard to express the torments of their passion."[6] To John Dixon Hunt, the conclusion of Marvell's commendatory

243

poem to Lovelace's *Lucasta* demonstrates the poet's "not entire identification with the Cavalier mode in either costume or verse."[7]
Most readers would probably agree about the difficulty of finding
any mode of verse with which Marvell entirely identifies. Indeed,
one of the poet's chief characteristics is his ability to freeze a moment in time and then casually stroll through his fictional world,
pointing out inherent paradoxes, conflicts, and ambiguities, without ever denying its beauty. Louis L. Martz writes accurately that
Marvell "looks back upon the remains of courtly culture with
attraction and regret."[8] Barbara Everett, discussing pastorals such
as "Daphnis and Chloe," comments that the poet makes the conventions "seem dated beyond belief . . . yet these same conventions
still exert power over the mind."[9]

Four of Marvell's poems about love—"The Gallery," "Mourning," "Daphnis and Chloe," and "The Fair Singer"—analyze Cavalier poetic conventions by focusing on the twin issues of perception
and expression. In the four poems, Marvell investigates the extent
to which a poet's awareness of multiple perspectives affects his
ability to define his subject accurately. These Cavalier exercises
constitute Marvell's playful definition of the limitations inherent in
contemporary social poetry.

A favorite Cavalier topic—the relationship between natural
beauty and artifice in women—is the subject of "The Gallery," a
poem based on the conceit of a lover's envisioning his beloved in
various pictures that make up a gallery in his mind. The lover
depicts Clora in alternately benign and malignant poses, as "an
Inhumane Murtheress," "Aurora in the Dawn," a cannibalistic
"Enchantress," and "Venus in her pearly Boat." The final stanza
describes the favorite pose:

> Where the same Posture, and the Look
> Remains, with which I first was took.
> A tender Shepherdess, whose Hair
> Hangs loosely playing in the Air,
> Transplanting Flow'rs from the green Hill,
> To crown her Head, and Bosome fill.

Critical attention given this poem has focused on the relationship
between the woman and the pictures, especially the one described
in the last stanza. Bradbrook and Thomas, for example, refer to the
"last and natural picture of the 'tender Shepherdess' which she was
at first."[10] Such readers as Rosalie L. Colie see even this last picture

as only another affected pose: "She is artificial, and she is his artifice." [11] Both explanations are plausible, but Clora's essence remains enigmatic. As A. J. Smith points out, the poem does not allow us to decide what she is. [12] In fact, the reader cannot tell even if Clora "exists" within the fictional confines of the poem. Colie writes that "The Gallery" has about it "a curiously aseptic quality . . . , as if the situation were in fact only mental, as if there were no real lady, no real love affair." [13] Nothing in the poem rules out this list of "as if's." On the contrary, Marvell's extraordinary subtlety makes the idea of an imaginary Clora just as persuasive as any other reading of the poem. But this equivocation is merely the beginning; the performance culminates when the reader realizes that the speaker too remains unknowable. The wit of "The Gallery" is that Marvell invites us to ask one question as we read the poem—What is Clora?—and then quietly suggests that we might reexamine whether we are inquiring about the right character.

In one deft stroke, Marvell has raised an interesting and troubling point about a common Cavalier strategy. Carew's excellent poem "Ingratefull Beauty Threatned," about a poet whose verse has turned the common beauty Celia into something of a celebrity, offers a characteristic instance. In threatening to destroy her fame if she does not remain faithful, the speaker reminds her that "Wise Poets that wrap't Truth in tales, / Knew her themselves, through all her vailes." [14] Marvell's "The Gallery" poses two simple questions: What is the truth? How do we know? Carew's truth might be that he created her through his artistry; Celia's truth might be that she created the poet.

In "Mourning," Marvell complicates the issue of nature and artifice by adding an uninvolved speaker, a poet whose task is to evaluate the relationship between the lamenting woman and those with whom she interacts. His poem about Chlora and her response to the death of her lover, Strephon, is probably based on Cowley's "Weeping." Cowley's four-stanza poem elaborates the idea he introduces in his first thought: "See where she sits, and in what comely wise, / Drops *Tears* more fair then others *Eyes!*" [15] In the first three stanzas of the poem, he elaborates the idea of her beauty. In the last stanza, we see what Cowley has been leading up to: her tears are so cold "that I admire they fall not *Hail.*" We suspect that the highly embellished praise in the first three-quarters of the poem has been mere scaffolding for his final witticism. Clearly, the poem conveys no emotion beyond the speaker's admiration of her beauty, and it completely ignores the question of context. Why is the woman weeping? We do not know; the speaker apparently does not know. He certainly does not care.

The first stanza of Marvell's poem immediately demonstrates what interests him about the kind of situation developed by Cowley:

> You, that decipher out the Fate
> Of humane Off-springs from the Skies,
> What mean these Infants which of late
> Spring from the Starrs of *Chlora's* Eyes?

Asking what Chlora's tears mean, Marvell asks several questions at once: What caused the tears? What are the speculations of the observers? What, if anything, can we know by watching the interplay between Chlora's behavior and public reaction to it? Adding a speaker who is completely uninvolved with the situation he is viewing enables Marvell to isolate and portray that situation effectively. Each of the poet's character groups is assigned a different mode of communication. The woman does not speak; she merely acts. The onlookers self-confidently interpret her actions. The speaker, through his use of ambivalent phrases and metaphors, only suggests possible meanings.

The woman weeps over the death of Strephon; her role is simple. One group of onlookers is sure that she is weeping "Only to soften near her Heart / A place to fix another Wound." Another group has a more cynical explanation for her tears: "That whatsoever does but seem / Like Grief, is from her Windows thrown." The last two stanzas of the poem are the speaker's:

> How wide they dream! The *Indian* Slaves
> That sink for Pearl through Seas profound,
> Would find her Tears yet deeper Waves
> And not of one the bottom sound.
>
> I yet my silent Judgment keep,
> Disputing not what they believe
> But sure as oft as Women weep,
> It is to be suppos'd they grieve.

The first of these two stanzas contains one of Marvell's finest word plays. If "sound" is a verb, her behavior reflects a profound grief; if it is a predicate adjective, she is an actress. In an excellent essay about "Mourning," Paul Delany points to the ambiguity of the final couplet of the poem: it can mean either that gentlemen respect women's tears, or that women's grief is artful dissimulation.[16]

What do Chlora's tears mean? We cannot know, and that, again, is Marvell's whole point. One group of onlookers might be correct; perhaps neither is correct. It is logically possible, as well, that Chlora genuinely grieves at the loss of Strephon. The closest we can come to the ultimate meaning of Chlora's tears is a careful articulation of the possible meanings, and, beyond that, we must preserve a wise reticence. As A. J. Smith describes the poet's tactic at the end of the poem, Marvell "will coolly leave the conflicting possibilities unresolved in the interest of a more wisely perceived equivocalness."[17] Marvell's "Mourning" is thus a brief epistemological essay.[18]

By raising these simple but fundamental questions about the nature of perception, Marvell suggests the limitations of the Cavalier compliment poem and, by implication, of any work which assumes that perceptions are necessarily accurate. In "Daphnis and Chloe" and "The Fair Singer," he goes one step further in his analysis of the complexity of artistic expression by investigating the dangers inherent in trying to describe what we think we see.

In "Daphnis and Chloe," Marvell's mode—and subject—is the seduction poem typified by "Love turn'd to Hatred," a comic sonnet attributed to Suckling.[19] That poem comprises thirteen and a half lines of exquisite raillery against women, men who love women, even the minuscule element of goodness that—not to their credit, of course—women possess. The remaining half-line— "what, wilt thou love me yet?"—economically demonstrates the Cavalier mating dance. The lady's ritualistic surrender must be delayed until the gentleman has wooed her long and well. The words are a prerequisite to the action. In "Daphnis and Chloe," Marvell orchestrates a similar encounter between two dull-witted sophisticates.

Chloe "neither knew t'enjoy, / Nor yet let her Lover go." And Daphnis

> came so full possest
> With the Grief of Parting thence,
> That he had not so much Sence
> ' s to see he might be blest.

This is Marvell's beautiful irony: Daphnis does not realize that he is only supposed to *threaten* to leave Chloe, that a skillfully delivered threat will prevent his having to leave. But he has worked himself into such a frenzy that he cannot deal with her acquiescence. Instead of enjoying her favors, Daphnis runs on for thirteen stanzas filled with frantic and sometimes incoherent references to executions, cannibalism, necrophilia, the wandering Hebrew tribes, and the magical properties of ferns.

The last two stanzas, by contrast, are the speaker's:

> But hence Virgins all beware.
> Last night he with *Phlogis* slept;
> This night for *Dorinda* kept;
> And but rid to take the Air.

> Yet he does himself excuse;
> Nor indeed without a Cause.
> For, according to the Lawes,
> Why did *Chloe* once refuse?

Like the poet-persona in "Mourning," the speaker here simply repeats Daphnis's understanding—or, rather, misunderstanding—of "the Lawes." It is illogical for Chloe's cavalier to leave *now*. Daphnis's real confusion is suggested by his hectic promiscuity after the debacle with Chloe. For any self-respecting cavalier, such behavior would be infra dig. And the speaker's warning to "Virgins all" is of course ironic, for it is unlikely that the clumsy Daphnis could pose a threat to any real fort. Phlogis and Dorinda are not innocent victims; they just capitulate quickly.

The irony of the poem is reinforced by its title. Marvell chose not to call the female character Chlora only because he wanted to allude to Longus's Greek romance *Daphnis and Chloe*. In the original, Daphnis receives instruction in the art of love from a libidinous woman who takes an interest in him; he then goes on happily to consummate his marriage to Chloe. Marvell's allusion to the romance reinforces his witty comment on the relationship between words and action. The poem does not stretch the pastoral "quite out of shape," as Rosalie L. Colie suggests; instead, it simply parodies big talkers. To assert that "Daphnis and Chloe" is "emotionally anti-pastoral and anti-love"[20] is to overburden the poem with excess philosophical baggage. Games shouldn't be taken so seriously.

Suckling would have enjoyed this poem, for he knew that the

game whose rules he codified requires a good deal of native intelligence and verbal dexterity. An unintelligent cavalier confuses the thing and its expression and, consequently, cannot achieve the goal for which he has been preparing so earnestly.

Perhaps Marvell's most interesting examination of the relationship between perception and expression is "The Fair Singer," which demonstrates that, in the process of describing something, one can learn that it is in fact quite different from what he had thought it to be. Whereas in "Daphnis and Chloe" Marvell explores the idea that words can forestall action, in "The Fair Singer" he suggests that words can actually engender action, for they lead his speaker to a new and disquieting understanding of his situation.

The speaker seems initially to seek a rather innocent goal: he wants to join the large group of poets who have immortalized their ladies through hyperbolic and ingenious verse. Rather than settle for the most tired metaphor of all—the man ensnared by the woman's physical beauty—he decides to fuse to it a second idea—the man captivated by her beautiful voice. One close parallel to this strategy of combined metaphor is Waller's "Of Mrs. Arden":

> Behold, and listen, while the fair
> Breaks in sweet sounds the willing air,
> And with her own breath fans the fire
> Which her bright eyes do first inspire.
> What reason can that love control,
> Which more than one way courts the soul?
>
> So when a flash of lightning falls
> On our abodes, the danger calls
> For human aid, which hopes the flame
> To conquer, though from Heaven it came;
> But, if the winds with that conspire,
> Men strive not, but deplore the fire.[21]

Another close parallel is Carew's "Song. Celia Singing":

> You that thinke Love can convey,
>   No other way,
> But through the eyes, into the heart,
>   His fatall Dart:
> Close up those casements, and but heare
>   This Syren sing;
> And on the wing

Of her sweet voyce, it shall appeare
That Love can enter at the eare:
    Then unvaile your eyes, behold
      The curious mould
Where that voyce dwels, and as we know,
      When the Cocks crow,
      We freely may
      Gaze on the day;
So may you, when the Musique's done
Awake and see the rising Sun.

Despite their superficial differences, these two poems share the same graceful artificiality. Waller's conceit of the wind conspiring with heavenly lightning is decorously imaginative: it praises the lady by assigning her divine powers. Carew's version, with Cupid's darts entering the lady's ear, is less felicitous; still, it directs its praises toward the lady, especially in the final image of the rising sun.

"The Fair Singer" is by far the best of the three poems:

> To make a final conquest of all me,
> Love did compose so sweet an Enemy,
> In whom both Beauties to my death agree,
> Joyning themselves in fatal Harmony;
> That while she with her Eyes my Heart does bind,
> She with her Voice might captivate my Mind.
>
> I could have fled from One but singly fair:
> My dis-intangled Soul it self might save,
> Breaking the curled trammels of her hair.
> But how should I avoid to be her Slave,
> Whose subtile Art invisibly can wreath
> My Fetters of the very Air I breath?
>
> It had been easie fighting in some plain,
> Where Victory might hang in equal choice,
> But all resistance against her is vain,
> Who has th' advantage both of Eyes and Voice,
> And all my Forces needs must be undone,
> She having gained both the Wind and Sun.

The traditional reading holds that the poem is "a well calculated mixture of gallantry and wit." [22] Certainly, it has an intellectual unity that Waller's and Carew's similar poems lack; the sea battle logically extends the traditional idea of the battle between the sexes. Compared to this conception, the ideas of heavenly lightning and Cupid tie for a weak second place.

Marvell's strategy in "The Fair Singer" exploits his metaphor-referent cluster to suggest the possibility that love is in fact a battle, that the figure of speech tells literal truth. Whereas the metaphors in the first stanza are used in a traditional way, as hyperbolic expressions of the lady's ability to keep the speaker enthralled, the imagery in the second stanza establishes a distinctly different mood. Gone are the musical terms that gave balance to such phrases as "fatal Harmony." In their place are such terms as "subtile Art," whose ambivalent connotations suggest the woman's contrived, even covert tactics. When we finish reading the second stanza's relentless images of entrapment—"dis-intangled," "trammels," "fetters"—we share the speaker's feelings of claustrophobia; the first stanza's "bind" and "captivate" begin to take on their more ominous connotations. This in turn contributes to the almost realistic tone of the second stanza, which now clearly opposes the more hyperbolic first stanza.

The speaker's tired resignation in the final stanza further reinforces our impression of his uncertainty. When he finally admits that "all resistance against her is vain," he seems to surrender not to a lovely lady with beautiful eyes and voice but to a deliberate and calculating military force. The speaker's concluding the poem with references to the military metaphor rather than to the lady herself implies that, on one level at least, he has begun to understand the ironic aspect—or at least the possibility of an ironic aspect—of his relationship with the woman: despite her great beauties, she might not be fair. The poem concludes without a definite statement. Marvell will not say that love is sweet surrender, or that it is literally a kind of warfare. What he has demonstrated, however, is the process by which his speaker has grown to realize the complexities of poetry and the integral relationship between an idea and its articulation.

The phenomenon traced in "The Fair Singer" relates to what William Empson has called a self-inwoven simile or a short-circuited comparison. Using Empson's terminology, Christopher Ricks has written of Marvell's characteristic use of the figure of speech "which goes beyond saying of something that it *finds* its own resemblance, and says instead, more wittily and mysteriously, that something *is* its own resemblance."[23] Ricks concludes his essay by demonstrating Lovelace's successful use of this figure of speech in his snail poems, and by implying that Marvell, who admired him, might have learned this technique from him.

Whether this is so cannot, of course, be determined. Balachandra Rajan writes that "The Garden" is "another one of those poems which must be resignedly described as 'elusive'. That word in Marvell criticism has come to connote exasperation as well as admiration."[24] But Rajan argues convincingly that, in Marvell, "controlled uncertainty is the objective of the poem rather than its enmeshment."[25] The Cavalier world that Marvell explored in some of his early lyrics was rife with simple truths that he saw as neither simple nor true: that lovers act consciously and meaningfully, that they send clear signals which are received and interpreted accurately, that in describing these lovers poets say what they mean and are never entrapped by their own words. The Cavalier social ritual was a perfect subject for Marvell's exercises because it enabled him to explore the behavior of art while chronicling the art of behavior. The phrase "controlled uncertainty" might be revised to "controlled, limited certainty." In his Cavalier poems, Marvell was absolutely precise in defining the limits of human perception and expression. Unlike the Cavaliers, he frequently insisted on the right to keep his silent judgment.

NOTES

1. See, for example, Warren L. Chernaik's "Marvell's Satires: The Artist as Puritan," in *Tercentenary Essays in Honor of Andrew Marvell*, ed. Kenneth Friedenreich (Hamden, Conn.: Archon Books, 1977); Barbara Everett's "The Shooting of the Bears: Poetry and Politics in Andrew Marvell," in *Andrew Marvell: Essays on the Tercentenary of His Death*, ed. R. L. Brett (Oxford: Oxford University Press, 1979); and Annabel M. Patterson's *Marvell and the Civic Crown* (Princeton: Princeton University Press, 1978).

2. "The Unhoopable Marvell," in *Tercentenary Essays*, ed. Friedenreich, p. 44.

3. "Natural Magic and Populism in Marvell's Poetry," in *Andrew Marvell: Essays*, ed. Brett, p. 40.

4. *The Poems and Letters of Andrew Marvell*, ed. H. M. Margoliouth, 3rd ed., comp. Pierre Legouis and E. E. Duncan-Jones, (Oxford: The Clarendon Press, 1971), vol. 1. All quotations follow this edition.

5. *The Art of Marvell's Poetry* (London: Hutchinson, 1966).

6. *Childhood and Cultural Despair: A Theme and Variations in Seventeenth-Century Literature* (Pittsburgh: University of Pittsburgh Press, 1978), p. 214.

7. *Andrew Marvell: His Life and Writings* (Ithaca: Cornell University Press, 1978), p. 57.

8. *The Wit of Love* (Notre Dame: University of Notre Dame Press, 1969), p. 153.

9. "The Shooting of the Bears," in *Andrew Marvell: Essays*, ed. Brett, p. 97.

10. M. C. Bradbrook and M. G. Lloyd Thomas, *Andrew Marvell*, 2nd ed. (Cambridge: Cambridge University Press, 1961), p. 30.

11. *"My Ecchoing Song": Andrew Marvell's Poetry of Criticism* (Princeton: Princeton University Press, 1970), p. 109.

12. "Marvell's Metaphysical Wit," in *Approaches to Marvell: The York Tercentenary Essays*, ed. C. A. Patrides (London: Routledge and Kegan Paul, 1978), p. 58.

13. *"My Ecchoing Song,"* p. 108.

14. *The Poems of Thomas Carew with His Masque "Coelum Britannicum,"* ed. Rhodes Dunlap (Oxford: The Clarendon Press, 1949; rpt. 1970), p. 18. All other quotations in the text derive from this edition.

15. *Poems*, ed. A. R. Waller (Cambridge: Cambridge University Press, 1905), p. 136.

16. "Marvell's 'Mourning,' " *Modern Language Quarterly* 33 (1971), 35.

17. "Marvell's Metaphysical Wit," p. 58.

18. Thomas Clayton, in " 'It is Marvel He Outdwells His Hour': Some Perspectives on Marvell's Medium," in *Tercentenary Essays*, ed. Friedenreich, p. 68, calls "Mourning" "an anamorphic study in poetical epistemology."

19. In his edition of *The Works of Sir John Suckling: The Non-Dramatic Works* (Oxford: The Clarendon Press, 1971), Thomas Clayton writes that the poem is "probably not by Suckling" (p. lxxxix).

20. *"My Ecchoing Song,"* p. 48.

21. *The Poems of Edmund Waller*, ed. G. Thorn Drury (London: George Routledge and Sons, 1905), vol. 1, p. 91.

22. Michael Craze, *The Life and Lyrics of Andrew Marvell* (New York: Barnes and Noble, 1979), p. 51.

23. Ricks, " 'Its own Resemblance,' " in *Approaches to Marvell*, ed. Patrides, p. 108. Empson created the phrase in *Seven Types of Ambiguity* (London: Chatto and Windus, 1930; 2nd rev. ed., 1947), pp. 160–61.

24. "Andrew Marvell: The Aesthetics of Inconclusiveness," in *Approaches to Marvell*, ed. Patrides, p. 168.

25. Ibid., pp. 160–61.

ROBERT B. HINMAN

"A Kind of a Christmas Ingine": Jonson, Milton, and the Sons of Ben in the Hard Season

Most modern critical guidebooks locate Jonson's "Forrest" about as far from Milton's Eden as connoisseurs of hospitality might place Penshurst's "liberall boord" from the paradisal table "Rais'd of grassy turf" for Adam and Eve. The distance seems even greater—in either poetic or culinary measurement—from Lewis Pemberton's "laden spits, warp't with large Ribbs of Beefe," to Eve's "fruit of all kinds, in coat, / Rough, or smooth rin'd, or bearded husk, or shell." And the hearth where Lovelace hopes to pledge his friend Cotton "with an o'erflowing glass" (or decanter) "of old Greek" seems—poetically, politically, potationally—about as remote as it can be from the "Silvan Lodge" where Eve prepares "inoffensive must, and meaths / From many a berry."[1]

It is not that—though separated from Milton in poetic geography—Jonson has no place in his poetic genealogy. In *Arcades*, says W. R. Parker, "Milton proclaims himself now one of the 'Sons of Ben.' " In the poet of "L'Allegro" and "Il Penseroso" Parker thinks "Jonson had found a sturdy son." If Jonson never had the opportunity to recognize or acknowledge him, still the family traits seem plain enough. Milton's "Epitaph on the Marchioness of Winchester" shows "the careless elegance and polished irregularity of a Cavalier poem; it might have been written by Lovelace or Suckling in one of their better moments." "On May Morning" has "the freshness and simplicity, the artful spontaneity, found in the poems of Jonson's disciple, Robert Herrick."[2]

But no one numbers Milton, "sealed" or "unsealed," of the Tribe of Ben. To the extent that the tribal affiliation represents (or represented) marked or felt affinities of temperament, interest, style, mode, attitude, and/or conviction, modern readers seldom note significant resemblances later than *Comus* between Milton and members of the tribe—unless perhaps in shared friendship with

255

Henry Lawes, who evoked tributes from Waller and Herrick as well as from Milton, or with Samuel Hartlib, whom both Cowley and Milton praised, or perhaps in a shared publisher like Humphrey Moseley, whose list for 1645 included Milton and Waller. Except for his well-known allusion to Jonson in "L'Allegro," in his writings Milton never mentioned any "tribesman" by name, and —though he is supposed to have ranked Cowley very high—Cartwright's *The Complaint of Ariadne* (and this not by title) seems to be the only "Cavalier" work about which Milton expressed admiration in print. If, as is probable, Milton interceded on behalf of Davenant in 1652, and if his respect for Davenant as man of letters is the explanation, this intercession seems to be the only instance of Milton's sympathetic personal involvement in the affairs of even a collateral heir other than Marvell. Although there are traditions that Waller accompanied Dryden on a visit to Milton in the last year of Milton's life, and that Denham greeted the publication of *Paradise Lost* with superlatives, Davenant's probable reciprocal intercession on Milton's behalf in 1660 and Milton's subsequent tutorial assistance of Davenant's son are the only likely indications of interest shown Milton even by an erstwhile Cavalier.[3]

No, for all Milton's undeniable classical learning and for all the unmistakable traces of Jonson in some of Milton's early work, Milton's name does not rush into our minds when we consider the theme "Classic and Cavalier: Jonson and the Sons of Ben." And yet most of us probably agree that interpreting "Sons of Ben" to include all poets who were influenced by Jonson unquestionably admits Milton to the group.[4] Does it, however, admit only the young Milton, or is there a significant sense in which—among Milton's English forebears—Jonson is, if not "onlie begetter," vigorously "progenitor german" of the poet of *Paradise Lost*, and Jonson's acknowledged "Sons" Milton's foster (or even his half-) brothers? Perhaps Parker suggests some such relationship when he says of the Jonsonian quality of Milton's work in 1631: "It is not pure imitation, such as one might expect from a new and ardent disciple. It is a subtler thing." Parker detects that subtlety in "rhythms," "simplicity and economy of diction," even in "a tone of whimsy or of courtly gallantry."[5] But perhaps, though it is this, it is also more profound than this and more pervasive than the hints of it in 1631 and a few years thereafter. What do we imply when we say, quite correctly, I think, that Milton's later, "new and serious poetry . . . had itself absorbed the most interesting poetry of the early part of the century," certainly, even especially, including Jonson's poetry?[6]

I think that—besides those skills, techniques, and devices all poets appropriate from their predecessors and contemporaries, sometimes simply to copy but more often to transform, improve, or even to reject conspicuously—what Milton absorbed or experienced was perhaps not so much "influence" (though, in addition to the modern critical sense, we might think, more or less metaphorically, of the seventeenth-century astrological sense) as "sympathy," in several seventeenth-century senses, one now entirely obsolete, except historically, and the other either obsolete or assimilated into a still current meaning: "(1) A (real or supposed) affinity between certain things, by virtue of which they are similarly or correspondingly affected by the same influence, affect or influence one another (esp. in some occult way), or attract or tend toward each other"; "(2) Agreement, accord, harmony, consonance, concord; agreement in qualities, likeness, conformity, correspondence."[7]

Such "sympathy" did not necessarily always include for Milton the meaning still current: "Conformity of feelings, inclinations, or temperament, which makes persons agreeable to each other; community of feeling, harmony of disposition."[8] However, it could certainly have included what most readers might consider the sense of being "affected . . . in some occult way." That is, Milton need not have found all persons in Jonson's "family" agreeable in order to have had something akin to family feeling, some "consonance" or "correspondence" with them as at least would-be adepts in what Cowley called the "Divine Science," the "Heav'enliest thing on Earth."[9] It is reasonable to assume that Milton was familiar with Jonson's *Discoveries*, and that he was in sympathy with what Jonson says there about the origin, nature, and role of poetry, that it

is the habit, or the Art: nay, rather the Queene of Arts: which had her Originall from heaven, received thence from the *'Ebrewes*, and had in prime estimation with the *Greeks*, transmitted to the *Latines*, and all Nations, that profess'd Civility. The Study of it . . . offers to mankinde a certaine rule, and Patterne of living well, and happily; disposing us to all Civill offices of Society. . . . it nourisheth, and instructeth our Youth; delights our Age; adornes our prosperity; comforts our Adversity; entertaines us at home; keepes us company abroad, travailes with us; watches; divides the times of our earnest, and sports; shares in our Country

recesses, and recreations, insomuch as the wisest and best learned have
thought her the absolute Mistresse of manners, and neerest of kin to
Vertue.   (2381–96)

Milton did not have to read Jonson's *Discoveries* to be convinced
that the "holy fire" with which a poet may be "timely rapt" is a gift
from "that eternal Spirit who . . . sends out his seraphim with the
hallowed fire of his altar, to touch and purify the lips of whom he
pleases." [10] But, in *Discoveries*, Jonson is as ready as Milton to confess that the unaided poet cannot reach "the highth of . . . higher
Argument," to insist with Ovid "Est, Deus in nobis," that the
genuine "*Poetical Rapture* . . . riseth higher, as by a divine Instinct,
when it contemnes common and knowne conceptions. It utters
somewhat above a mortall mouth." [11] When Jonson asserts that
poets may "With *Japhets* lyne, aspire / *Sols* Chariot for new fire, / To
give the world againe," or that poets are priests who strive to utter
about "that bright eternall Day / . . . Such truths, as [they] expect
for happy men," and to express in "bright *Asterisme*" as much of
"that full joy" as possible, he shares Milton's faith in the power of
"pledges of Heav'n's joy, / Sphere-born harmonious Sisters, Voice
and Verse," to animate "Dead things with inbreath'd sense . . . , /
And to our high-rais'd fantasy present" the concert of the morning
stars singing together in which we once joined. [12]

Perhaps, like most of his "Sons," "this while exil'd from" God,
Jonson more often felt himself cut off from the "happy-making
sight" than Milton did when he invoked "Celestial Light" by which
to "see and tell / Of things invisible to mortal sight"; but Milton,
too, even at the peak of youthful enthusiasm, acknowledged that
time, for the moment, dams up the full flood of eternal beatitude,
and, much later in his career, imagined Adam, though at the very
height of vision, still on the edge of an abyss, "Eternity, whose end
no eye can reach." Though Jonson yearned toward "The gladdest
light, darke man can thinke upon," he seldom sought to penetrate
that abyss, and—however much he longed to see and celebrate
"three / All coeternall in . . . Majestie"—he never "presum'd"
poetically, as Milton did, "Into the Heav'n of Heav'ns" to sing the
invisible "Fountain of Light" made visible in the countenance of
"Divine Similitude" on whom has been transfused "his ample
Spirit." Jonson usually settled for seeking, invoking, and finding
God "ever, here," in this mortal "Native Element"; yet surely the
earth-bound, heaven-reaching, middle-aged poet who, "so he had
written [Southwell's] *The Burning Babe* . . . would have been con-

tent to destroy many of his [own poems]," who himself sought to
utter the mystery of the Incarnation whereby "The Author both of
Life, and light; . . . made himselfe the price of sinne, / To make us
heires of glory," would (had he known him) have felt some degree
of sympathy with Milton. He would have imparted some sense of
spiritual kinship, not only to the young poet who envisioned "that
far-beaming blaze of Majesty" in "darksome House of mortal
Clay," but also to the elderly poet for whom God's union with man
meant divine endurance of "reproachful life and cursed death,"
obedience assimilated into love, and promise of stricken earth and
time healed into "far happier place / Than this of *Eden,* and far
happier days." [13]

Of course, neither the doctrine nor the discipline of these
Jonsonian and Miltonic words necessarily bespeaks either parent or
child. Here, if ever, we observe the impossibility of distinguishing
effects of nature from those of nurture. However, as we note in
Milton's work what might be attributed to one or the other or both
or neither, we may reflect that no poet could have transmitted to
Milton more vigorously, or made more readily accessible (and
perhaps acceptable), what Jonson seems to have implied about
poetry when (though topically, jocularly, even a little sardonically)
he described a poet as "a kind of a *Christmas* Ingine" and provoca-
tively permitted a cook to claim identity between the arts of poetry
and of cookery. [14] And no "family" of poets could have provided
more diverse instances of the truth of the parental precept, more
occasions for demonstrating, testing, and vitally reinforcing it in
Milton's experience, than Jonson's heterogeneous offspring.

Whether the purport of Jonson's witty wisdom reached Milton in
Jonson's or in other words, he seems to have comprehended it and
made it his own. Although, if he read or heard it, Milton doubtless
responded to Jonson's metaphor selectively and exemplified it
rather differently, more soberly and loftily, than any one else in the
family, Jonson's description of a poet (even perhaps including some
of its playful or ironic denigration) might aptly characterize
Milton's view of a poet's potential and power. Much in Milton's
mature poetry is consonant with some of the best work by Jonson's
progeny that suggests the Jonsonian dictum, except that Milton has
that unaccountable aura of authority which sets the very greatest
scion almost a species apart even from the general excellence and
occasional prodigiousness of an impressive family.

At a level beyond the occasional in Jonson's masque, his calling
the poet "a kind of a *Christmas* Ingine" links the poet's wit, his

creativity, his capacity to be a poet, to ultimate creative power, to what "In the beginning," and since the beginning, has breathed life into dead things. That power causes "Zephirus . . . with his sweete breeth" to inspire "in every holt and heeth / The tendre croppes" and enables Favonius to "re-inspire / The frozen earth, and clothe in fresh attire / The Lily and Rose, that neither sow'd nor spun."[15] To seventeenth-century poets, that ultimate creative power is the only true Christmas engine. Although Jonson and/or Milton might have resisted as blasphemous the unqualified vehicle of the metaphor applied to this particular tenor, both would probably have allowed the proportion: poet as animator or incarnator of a world of imagined phenomena (for example, Penshurst or Paradise) is to *the* Creator only as one might say a celebrator of the solstitial hope and meaning (that is, "a kind of a *Christmas* Ingine") is to Him (*the* Christmas engine) who continually directs the solstice and enacts the Incarnation. Or, to put the second half of the proportion another way, as an instance of Christmas celebration (the Nativity ode, "Star-Song," Twelfth Night revel, "showr's of old Greek" that restore his crown to "Dropping December," "Tuscan Air"—whatever wins "From the hard Season" and transforms it) is to the Christmas event itself.[16]

For Milton or Jonson, Herrick or Lovelace, however seasonably joyous each may often be, every mortal moment passes in "the hard Season," often experienced as "evil days," "the more loathesome Age," "times trans-shifting," or "frozen fate." Now "the bad season" has the chill of "the Cavalier winter," now the dearth of "so long a Lent." Though "with the Year / Seasons return," still "golden ears are cropped." "In darkness, and with dangers compast round" our "light is [often] spent"; "the dark hag" "is astride"; "Night hath no wings," and it often seems long "Till the bird of day / And the luckier lot betide" us.[17]

This is what it means to live in a fallen world, to know an order of nature brazen since Adam's "original lapse," denied the "more ample greatness" "agreeable to the spirit of man" but not to be found anywhere here since the Fall.

> 'Tis not, what once it was, the World
> But a rude heap together hurl'd;
> All negligently overthrown,
> Gulfes, Deserts, Precipices, Stone.[18]

But the poet's high vocation, answered as devoutly as Jonson and

Milton answered it, offers some moderation of the seasonal weather. Through precept and practice, Jonson taught his "Sons" that poetry—sent, like other manifestations of divine grace, for the relief of our estate—hailed and revered as a heavenly queen and served as such a queen deserves, may help us, not, indeed, to "regain the blissful Seat," for only the true Christmas engine does that, but to compensate, through "our erected wit," which "maketh us to know what perfection is," for the deficiencies of "our infected will," which "keepeth us from reaching unto" that pefection. [19]

Like Sidney, Jonson delighted in the poet as "maker" and in the dim but discernible likeness between the poet's heaven-bestowed making and God's. Unlike the true God, the true poet does not literally redeem and transform nature through incarnation, but—conceiving of his calling as God-given and of his creating as a sacred act that he is permitted, indeed, enjoined, to perform—he participates in the Redemption not only as all may, through faith and imputed righteousness, but also through his works. He participates as one who

so deliver[s] himselfe to the nature of the subject, whereof hee speakes, that his hearer may take knowledge of his discipline with some delight: . . . [who] so apparell[s] faire and good matter, that the studious of elegancy be not defrauded; [who] redeeme[s] Arts from their rough, and braky seates, where they lay hid, and overgrowne with thornes, to a pure, open, and flowry light: where they may take the eye, and be taken by the hand.   (*Discoveries*, 116–23)

The good poet (who for Jonson as for Milton is most successful if he is a good man)[20] may thus, both Jonson and Milton agree, also be a priest as well as (or because he is) "a kind of a *Christmas* Ingine." [21] Milton might not always have been willing to ordain the same figures as Jonson, or might have believed that some of them sometimes failed their office, but the poetic intelligence that perceived and praised the varied virtues of Shakespeare, Spenser, and Cowley would probably have conceded to Jonson and many of his "Sons" a share in the poet-priest's vicarious yet instrumental involvement in the restoration actually accomplished by "one greater Man." In the depths of "the hard Season," the poet-priest keeps his (and therefore, perhaps, our) attention fixed on that solstitial, incarnational moment and its promise of recovered Paradise.

When post-Edenic "Fields are dank and ways are mire," we "may live . . . many days, . . . though sad, / With cause for evils

past, yet much more cheer'd / With meditation on the happy end."
But, because of "our infected will," that end in "far happier place
. . . and far happier days" than Eden's days of "Graces and the
Hours in dance" and perpetual "vernal airs" is as difficult to realize
as the eternal spring of lost and long-obscured Paradise, about
which we know for certain only that it was (is) "Not that fair field /
Of Enna . . . nor that sweet Grove / Of Daphne by Orontes . . .
nor that Nyseian Isle / Girt with the River Triton, . . . Nor . . .
Mount Amara . . . enclos'd with shining rock." [22] What it was (or
perhaps will be) must be made. Poets must make it from fragments
of myth and memory, arduously gathering and combining scattered impressions of nature's cracked frame. Poets must make it as a
model of the "paradise within" that must not only suffice but be
"happier far," a world wherein "Time will run / On smoother"
"Till time stand fixt" and we discover what ultimately "may be won
/ From the hard Season," the reality of "Eden rais'd in the waste
Wilderness." [23]

No poet makes that model without "devout prayer to that eternal
Spirit," but neither does he make it without "industrious and select
reading, steady observation, insight into all seemly and generous
arts and affairs." He does not make it without acting to "redeeme
Arts from their rough, and braky seates." Poetry, Jonson says,
"offers to mankinde a certaine rule, and Patterne of living well, and
happily; disposing us to all Civill offices of Society." Poetry, Milton
believes, is the very soul ("subsequent, or indeed rather precedent")
of that learning which fits one for "all . . . offices both private and
public," which has as its end "to repair the ruins of our first parents
by regaining to know God aright, and out of that knowledge to love
him, to imitate him, to be like him, as we may the nearest by
possessing our souls of true virtue, which being united to the
heavenly grace of faith makes up the highest perfection." [24]

Of course, we will not become much like Him, except as He
transforms us. An "age too late, or cold / Climate, or Years," harsh
aspects of "the hard Season" defeat the would-be "*Christmas* Ingine"
"if all be [his]." But the essence of the mystery of the Incarnation,
even of that lesser mystery whereby the poet's vision is incarnated,
is that "God with man unites." [25] Powerless to perform the redemp-
tive role, paradoxically the mortal maker cooperates fully in it.
God, who transmutes materials far less promising than lead, can
make a saint out of Samson, divinity out of the most unpalatable
epigram (and presumably out of its subject) in Herrick's
Hesperides. [26] In a way that Satan can neither intend nor understand,
evil becomes God's good, for He brings forth good from it. The

Jonsonian/Miltonic poet does his best to "repair the ruins" and to be as like God as possible. Striving to make his own life a true poem in order to make a true poem, he seeks to bring forth the goodness of a work of art out of the evil of fallen life, knowing good and evil, knowing good *by* evil, yet in some sense innocent (as perhaps "negative capability" is innocent), "richer than untempted kings" in not wanting himself, since "he / That wants himself is poor indeed." If he can thus both lose and find himself, adding "Deeds to [his] knowledge answerable," he may possess not only that happier paradise but a shadow of the force that in "the hard Season" God opposes to "outrage from lifeless things," power to create and bestow "A genuine summer . . . And spite of this cold time and frozen fate, / Thaw us a warm seat to our rest." [27]

To dispense such warmth, one lucky enough to receive the hallowed flame must devoutly husband and tend it. The fire claimed by many poets is, Milton and Jonson agree, so far from being holy, so nearly *ignis fatuus*, that one "would never light his *Tobacco* with" their writings. Proper education, Milton says, would make us more aware "what despicable creatures our common rhymers and play writers be." But those worthy to imitate God (even, to a degree, to emulate Him as "*Christmas* Ingines") may reveal "what religious, what glorious and magnificent use might be made of poetry, both in divine and human things." [28]

Milton might have considered even some of the worthy too "cavalier" about their trust, too prodigal of the sacred fire. Francis Beaumont, for example, nostalgically rejoiced that "at the Mermaid" the gathering

> heard words . . .
> So nimble and so full of subtle flame,
> As if that everyone from whence they came
> Had meant to put his whole wit in a jest,
> And had resolved to live a fool the rest
> Of his dull life.

Beaumont and others at those tavern "services" recognized vocation when they heard it, even if none of the Mermaid priesthood made as "glorious and magnificent use" of poetry in divine things as Milton did; Jonson and some of his "Sons" joined Milton in making such religious use of "human things" that we may perceive how these things, too, have been touched by or reach toward divinity. "If Art could tell" how that garden where "Spring and Autumn . . . Danced hand in hand" still appears to God's all-encompassing, unwavering gaze, it might recall "Hesperian Fables true, / If true," true only in that garden; it might seek to replicate them as nearly as possible within "trans-shifting" time through "Brooks, . . . Blossomes, Birds, and Bowers," viewed in contiguity to Hell as well as Heaven, and it might call the whole *Hesperides* instead of *Paradise Lost*.[29] It might envision "A happy rural seat of various view" containing the elements of the fallen world, "But in more decent order tame," where, to be sure, "Nature boon" no longer "Wanton[s] as in her prime," but where

> The earely cherry, with the later plum,
> Fig, grape, and quince, each in his time doth come;
> The blushing apricot, and woolly peach
> Hang on [the] walls, that every child may reach.

Such a vision would call up Nun Appleton or Penshurst rather than Paradise, not precisely "A Heaven on Earth," but still "Heaven's Center, Nature's Lap. / And Paradice's only Map."[30]

When a human version of the prototypical Christmas engine works properly, he generates something akin to joy amid reasons for, even out of, despair. He can never, of course, deny or ignore "The flocking shadows pale" released nightly from "th' infernal jail." A "serpent river" winds through the peaceable kingdom where Sir Robert Wroth makes his "owne content" and the opportunity "to live long innocent," just as, amid all the frisking "Beasts of th' Earth, since wild," "the Serpent sly" insinuates himself, ready to become puppet of the thief in "God's Fold" who sits on the "Tree of Life . . . like a Cormorant . . . devising Death." And has devised it in "many shapes, . . . all dismal," whether with literal scythe a mower carves an unfledged rail in the meadow where "lowness is unsafe as Hight," or with figurative scythe Death "commands the Field" and "lays his icy hand on kings."[31]

But the poet can proclaim death "the gate of Life," even if, to incorporate all its forms into a pattern of redemption, he must weave the deaths of many creatures besides Lycidas into a pattern of sacrifice and atonement. At Penshurst, where "all come in, the farmer, and the clowne," exultantly bearing the local bounty, communal feasting has a faintly sacramental cast. "The painted partrich lies in every field . . . willing to be kill'd" to furnish the mess at which any guest may share the "lords owne meate." Where carp and pike swim eagerly into the net and eels leap into the fisherman's hand, there is a hazy recollection of a miraculous draught of fishes

that preceded an apostolic call and succeeded the Resurrection. At
Saxham the poor can survive the winter only because "the birds,
fearing the snow," have flocked there, "as to the Ark," and

> The willing ox of himself came
> Home to the slaughter, with the lamb,
> And every beast did thither bring
> Himself to be an offering.[32]

The infinite consequences of the sacrifice dimly figured here
attend the solstitial moment marked by each model of the *"Christmas* Ingine." "The Babe lies yet in smiling Infancy, / That on the
bitter cross / Must redeem our loss." Before "our bliss / Full and
perfect is" "the Winter wild" comes "arm'd with ice / And snow
and hail and stormy gust and flaw"; "sharp frosty fingers" top the
flowers, "And what scythes spared, winds shave off quite." From
the beginning of song, the mortal makers' burden has been the
brevity of mortal days, the evanescence of men "who are as leaves
are, and now flourish and grow warm / with life and feed on what
the ground gives, but then again fade away and are dead." "Surely
the people is grass," "For all flesh is as grass, and all the glory of
man as the flower of grass. The grass withereth, and the flower
thereof falleth away." "Take my tidings! . . . Snows descend /
Summer's end!" But the mortal maker never leaves it at that. The
Greek singer of tales, the Irish monk—each transforms the somber
fact into the joy of singing, through his song asserting life in the
presence of death. And, assimilating the Christian mystery into
that joy, the poet, as "a kind of a *Christmas* Ingine," reasserts that
life with the authority conveyed by conviction of his role in the
divine making.[33]

Paraphrasing Isaiah on our similarity to grass, Peter reiterates
that "the word of the Lord endureth forever." But he adds, "And
this is the word which by the gospel is preached unto you." Peter's
faith is the common fuel of the diverse "Christmas ingines" working
together in poetic sympathy, however strong their partisan or
sectarian antipathy. Such sympathetic souls, possessed "of true
virtue . . . united to the heavenly grace of faith," extract joy even
from the demise of a "poor verdant fool" that suggests the fate
common to king and minstrel. Incarnate in the song of the *"Christmas* Ingine," like the life breathed into dead things at the Sun's
Nativity, human joys become larger and more lasting than the
grasshopper's "perch of grass." If the song can imply that "green

ice" is the destined state of our grasslike flesh as well as of the grasshopper, it is also the power of such a song to animate that greenness "like the one warm spark in the heart of an arctic crystal," like a "green thought" waiting in the shade "till Favonius re-inspire / The frozen earth." [34]

In the Christmas song (or the Christmas-begotten song envisioning a latter-day Paradise in which to anticipate vernal breath, "New Heav'ns, new Earth, Ages of endless date"), "the Sun . . . , Curtain'd with cloudy red," always "Pillows his chin upon an Orient wave," warning away "the flocking shadows" and "Each fetter'd Ghost." Though "the mounted Sun" may no longer provide "more warmth than" Adam's children need, "fires shine bright on every hearth," uniting all elements in "cherishing flames . . . Through every room, where they deride / The night, and cold abroad; whilst they, / Like suns within, keep endless day," inviting toward shelter "all that wander in the night." [35] Whether in the "little house" where Herrick glows like the "living coale" on his "glittering Hearth" that God crowns "With guiltlesse mirth," or at the ample, hospitable chimney of Pemberton's "fat-fed smoking Temple which in / The wholsome savor of [its] mighty Chines / Invites to supper him who dines," the poet perceives and reveals "a God in man." "Content makes all ambrosia," both where Herrick's brother Thomas maintains "A Quire / Of singing Crickits by [his] fire" and where—if the weather does not permit "Il Penseroso" to wander out of doors—"glowing Embers through the room / Teach light to counterfeit a gloom, / Far from all resort of mirth / Save the Cricket on the hearth." Whether with Ben "at the Sun, the Dog, the triple Tunne," with Cotton at an "Etna in epitome," or by the fire with "Lawrence, of virtuous Father virtuous Son," the wine infuses "Lyrick Feasts," mingling with "immortal Notes and Tuscan Air" in noble wildness, "mirth that after no repenting draws." [36]

Reminiscence of the order of grace informs these human works shared with God and endows the human creations and conditions, also shared with Him, that each celebrates. Poet and king enjoy similar hospitality at Penshurst, where all is present as if the estate belonged to the poet or he "reigned there." No wish goes unfulfilled. The king finds the rooms, warmed as though by the zeal of the community, waiting to receive him as he might expect to find waiting one of those many mansions Jesus has departed to prepare. Other "lords have built," but Penshurst's "lord dwells" because *his* Lord dwells there. "Except the Lord build the house, they labor in vain that build it." No Raphael crosses the threshold where the

Fairfaxes practice "in doors so strait / To strain themselves through Heaven's Gate." He does not join the "mirth, and cheere" in Wroth's "open hall" or "conferre" at the "Shining Salt-seller" with Robin Herrick and his friend John Wickes. In "the hard Season," we should expect "No more of talk where God or Angel Guest / With Man, as with his Friend, familiar us'd / To sit indulgent, and with him partake / Rural repast." And yet the ancient concourse between heaven and earth seems scarcely broken. From "one Almighty . . . all things" still "proceed, and up to him return" with "A thankfull heart," as though never "deprav'd from good." When he dines, Herrick punningly confesses to God, all that came from Him in the beginning to make and sustain man as "a living soul" comes still: "The Pulse is Thine, / And all those other Bits, that bee / There plac'd by Thee," including "Wassaile Bowles to drink, / Spic'd to the brink." [37]

With "these delights," often interposed, "erected wit" in "a kind of a *Christmas* Ingine" acts to repair the ruins as it rejoices that God has chosen "with us a darksome House of mortal Clay." In the darkest recess of that house at the darkest moment of "the hard Season," deposed December regains his crown. If he be restored as "Christmas King," it is because *his* King, though "born / Barr'd of his right," is crowned by God, is proclaimed by "a Star / Unseen before in Heav'n." It is, of course, the proper wit and wisdom of the poet as "*Christmas* Ingine" to acknowledge that stellar coronation, to recognize and receive its miracle, like the Creation itself, as pure grace. Implicitly echoing Adam, the poet asks, "how came I thus, how here?" He implicitly answers, "Not of myself; by some great Maker then," and glorifies that supreme Maker, accepting and celebrating His gifts as readily and as unconcernedly as the lilies of the field, served—like the poet at Penshurst—as a king, indeed, exalted above "Solomon in all his glory." Finding himself, even amid "the grass . . . which today is, and to morrow is cast into the oven," unaccountably almost within the kingdom he seeks, the poet takes "no thought, saying . . . What shall we eat? or What shall we drink?" The "selfe-same wine, / That is his Lordships, shall be" the poet's, too. Being "not unwise," he spares the time to join the revel. In "the hard Season" he "disapproves that care, though wise in show, / That with superfluous burden loads the day, / And when God sends a cheerful hour," the poet does not refrain. [38]

But, since he seeks to be "a kind of a *Christmas* Ingine," the poet also *does* take thought—and action. Of course, the gift of life (and second life) is free. "One Celestial Father gives to all"; yet possession of that "paradise within" demands more than the faith that takes "no thought for the morrow." Such equanimity may serve the grasshopper, as it does the fowls of the air, who need not consider the harvest, and it contributes to the poet's power in "merry days" to make "merry men." But faith is also the "substance of things hoped for, the evidence of things not seen," and—though it abides—to it must be added the greater power of "Love, / By name to come call'd Charity, the soul / Of all the rest." In the poetic kingdoms where Milton joins Jonson and his "Sons" to "waste a sullen day" "with some delight . . . , Although the coldest of the year," such love is vigorously active. The threshold of Herrick's "doore / Is worn by th' poore." The open door of Appleton House is adorned by "A stately Frontispice of Poor." At the door of Saxham there is "no porter . . . t'examine or keep back the poor." Charity here is communal and reciprocal, not perfunctory and cold. The Appleton rooms are daily graced by "new Furniture of Friends." The neighboring farmers visit Penshurst, "no one empty-handed . . . , though they have no sute," simply to "expresse their love." Although even heaven and the world before the Fall are hierarchical, in the hall of Sir Robert Wroth "Freedome doth with degree dispense." Everyone participates in the revel, "As if in Saturnes raigne it were." At the home of Endymion Porter the ongoing festival encompasses the May-pole and the "Twelfe-tide Kings and Queenes; . . . And no man payes too deare for it." Lewis Pemberton, in whom "wise Poets" may discover all "Good men" together, leads "A House-dance neatly." Jonson allows Comus a considerably looser rein than Milton does, but even the austere Lady of Milton's Ludlow Masque seems to modify her judgment that in their harvest dances "the loose unletter'd Hindes . . . thank the gods amiss." In her father's hall, although the country dancers give way to the more stately figures she and her brothers perform, the shepherds are not banished, but only entreated to await the "next Sun-shine holiday." [39]

As Beaumont's recollections of the Mermaid and Jonson's *Leges Convivales,* testify, the "Sons of Ben" proclaim frequent "Sun-shine holidays," partake eagerly of these feasts of charity, and contribute richly to them as well. So do the sons of God, as Raphael does in Adam's "shady bower," where he expresses mutual esteem between angels and men and pleasure in earthly hospitality, and where the angelic poetry is as life-giving as the food, as endlessly thirst-quenching as an inexhaustible stream to one long parched. Raphael begins his epic of Satan's fall by recalling heavenly song and feasting "in communion sweet" to celebrate the birthday of God's Son, in whom all are born "as one individual Soul." The Muses are not strangers to the wassailing at Sir Robert's, and it is Herrick's poetry as much as his wine that restores their youth to him and his friend Wickes. Both elements of their conviviality combine to keep them "circular," that is, within the wholeness of God's creation. For the poet's creativity is the medium of his charity, and what he makes is his charitable act. The poor under Herrick's "humble Roof" "freely get / Good words, or meat." Like Peter, he has neither silver nor gold. Nor can he literally heal the crippled in Christ's name. But he can give each lyric in *Hesperides* as a legacy of his love "Left to all posterity." [40]

It is such a legacy, the light it shines on our darkness, that these "sympathetic" poets jointly bequeath. They not only acclaim the solstitial radiance, the Christmas star, but seek to set an image of it aloft "as clear Hesper." Though they may kindle no more than a candle, it focuses a little of the light of the first fiat and its power to drive night "From the light casements where we play, / And the dark hag from her black mantle strip / And stick there everlasting day." It is that day they entreat us to seize. We cannot reach the thornless rose or—with any map we can make—find the place where it grows. But, though "God doth not need / Either man's work or his own gifts," He expects His "Christmas ingines" to make the best maps possible, to gather such roses as (and while) they may, and to distill them into art. [41]

As Milton certainly knew, the rose is not the example Jesus offers of creatures that do not sow. In fact, the rose is every poet's example of what everyone should reap. Though it has served many a pagan poet, Milton accepts it because he knows that the fallen do not unite with God simply by being, as the lily does. They unite also through becoming, through plucking and cherishing the rose. Milton and Jonson are close relatives in this knowledge, and so are some Cavaliers, despite political and doctrinal divergences. There seems to be no way of coming very close to God, in poetry at any rate, except by trying to copy Him as a creator. And there seems to be no way of doing that, Marvell laments, except to "gather flow'rs . . . Dismantling all the fragrant Towers / That once adorned [his] Shepherdesses head." No way except to plunge deeply into mortal life, into the order of nature where "the serpent old" so entwines himself with even the loveliest festive garlands that they drop and "all the faded roses shed." [42]

Although God's "Omnipresence fills / Land, Sea, and Air, and every kind that lives, / Fomented by his virtual power and warmed," human arts falter in seeking "His bright appearances"; human artists tracing signs of His passing are glad to "behold though but his utmost skirts / Of glory, and far off his steps adore," skirts visible even to Seraphim only "dark with excessive bright." Ambitious beyond squaring "the mortal right-lined circle," human creators stretch toward the "circuit, undetermined square or round" of heaven and the uncircumscribed self-life of God in which the "Square grows [infinitely] Spherical." However, except for what—even at the rarely scaled "height of . . . great Argument"— is oblate or elliptical, poets must settle for something like "a country life" in which Thomas Herrick "ev'ry way lies square" and yet lives "round" in his "Rural Sanctuary" become "Elizium," or in which Sir Robert Wroth gratefully receives and renders back the life lent by God, to Whom

> man's dearer, then t' himselfe,
> And, howsoever we may think things sweet,
> He always gives what He knowes meet,
> Which who can use is happy.[43]

Although even the least promising member of the family of true makers may sometimes aspire "Above th' Aonian Mount," even the most illustrious knows that Parnassus and Helicon "made not poets, but the poets those," and that even delighting the Heavenly Muse with "Sion Hill," and aided chiefly by the Spirit present "from the first," the poet falls so far short of the Maker he hopes to resemble that his poetic "labor" can scarcely seem more than what Bacon calls "a pleasure or play of imagination," distinguishing such activity from "a work or duty thereof." Though Poetry is "the Queene of Arts, which had her Originall from heaven," when we compare it with God's art of actuality—even when we view His work in its fallen state—the poet's may seem no more than an art of cookery; "A Boyler, Range, and Dresser" in a kitchen such as Lewis Pemberton's may seem as likely as poetry to be "the fountaines / Of all the knowledge, in the *Universe*," the kitchen itself "that deep school, / That's both the Nource, and Mother of the *Arts*." The great poets (and the apprentice great) have claimed that poetry can lift "the deep transported mind . . . Above the wheeling poles," permitting it to peer through "Heav'n's door," to penetrate the zones of all the elements and all the spheres and to "sing of secret things that came to pass / When Beldam Nature in her cradle was." Jonson mockingly attributes such power to "a *Master-Cooke*," because he knows that the folly of the antimasque lurks within the noblest masquing, or within any other poetic vison figuring forth things as they are through things as they ought to be or might be or have been. In the most nearly perfect image of the unfallen world a poet can create, "th' unwieldy Elephant," to make mirth for the first parents, wreathes "His Lithe Proboscis." In such postlapsarian demiparadises as Penshurst and Saxham, the flora and fauna, acting *sponte sua* for human welfare, besides neither sowing nor spinning, vaguely recall the ludicrous or parodic beneficence of "Cockaigne" and "Lubberland" and dimly foreshadow "The Big Rock-Candy Mountain" and Al Capp's "Valley of the Schmoon."[44]

As "*Christmas* Ingine," presiding as Master of the Revels in "the hard Season," the poet can scarcely fail to create the role of fool of God. Herrick, with his jocund muse and his chaste life, of all the family most readily and frequently dons the motley, but all are quite prepared to wear it. Indeed, Milton says, however sober our intentions, we can scarce do otherwise, at least some of the time:

No mortal nature can endure, either in the actions of religion, or study of wisdom, without some times slackening the cords of intense thought and labor. . . . We cannot, therefore, always be contemplative, or pragmatical abroad, but have need of some delightful intermissions, wherein the enlarged soul may leave off a while her severe schooling, and, like a glad youth in wandering vacancy, may keep her holidays to joy and harmless pastime.

God encourages us in this joy, Milton believes, not concealing from us "his own recreations before the World was built: 'I was,' saith the Eternal Wisdom, 'daily his delight, playing always before him.' " But God's sobriety is one with His gaiety, His recreation the same as His labor: "to him, indeed, wisdom is as a high tower of pleasure, but to us a steep hill, and we toiling ever about the bottom." In becoming like God, "as we may the nearest," the poet seeks to make his poetic creation a form of that divine playing. Milton's Heavenly Muse "with Eternal Wisdom [did] converse, . . . and with her [did] play / In presence of th' Almighty Father, pleas'd / With [her] Celestial Song."[45]

But Milton knows that even the most "glorious and magnificent use . . . of poetry . . . in divine . . . things" must set forth folly, even if it is a form of *sancta simplicitas*. The poet's "good book," "the image of God, as it were, in the eye," preserves "the precious life blood of a master spirit" who is himself God's image.[46] But even the best fallen man the book can celebrate, epitome of all good men, as

Herrick's Pemberton is, or reflection of the attempted "true-poem" life of the man who made the book, as Milton's fallen Adam is, will still have a tincture of mortal folly. It is such folly to perceive any aspect of kingship in a "verdant fool" of a grasshopper or any evidence of divine care in the feeding of fowls which do not sow or reap, and which, then, to feed the company at Penshurst, are "willing to be kill'd." It is folly to perceive divine solicitude in the clothing of the lily or "the grass of the field, which to day is and to morrow is cast into the oven."

But such folly becomes the folly of God's fool when it shares in God's labor (inseparable from His revel), which overcomes the dark that He seems to contain and impose, or when it perceives and makes—and praises God for making—goodness out of the cold that God also seems to have made. It is good, Milton says, that God

> bid his Angels turn askance
> The Poles of Earth twice ten degrees and more
> From the Sun's Axle . . . to bring in change
> Of Seasons to each Clime; else . . . to those
> Beyond the Polar Circles . . .Day
> Had unbenighted shone.

It is good that "At that tasted Fruit / The Sun . . . turn'd / His course intended; else how had the World . . . Avoided pinching cold and scorching heat? " "God is so potent," says Herrick, "as His Power can / Draw out of *bad* a soveraigne *good* to man." When Michael pauses "As at the World's great period," Adam utters his well-known apostrophe to "goodness infinite, goodness immense! / That all this good of evil shall produce," and wonders whether, rather than repent of his sin, it would not be better to "rejoice / Much more, that much more good thereof shall spring, / To God more glory, more good will to men / From God, and over wrath grace shall abound."

Adam ponders such potential celebration after having witnessed and heard about the violence and viciousness of thousands of years of human history. Jonson and Carew and Lovelace knew, Milton knows as he writes, Marvell and Herrick know as they read, that there should be no reason for exultation here, any more than there should be on a bitter day at Saxham or on a bitter night in the Devonshire Herrick "loath[es] so much." But, "the more to increase [our] wonder," there is reason. The fools of God celebrate the birthday of the sun and feel its warmth even as "the north wind" spreads his "frost-stretched wings." Indeed, Aubrey tells us that "All the time of writing his Paradise Lost, [Milton's] vein began at the autumn equinoctial, and ceased at the vernal, or thereabouts."[47]

Although something precious and now unimaginable, except to God, disappeared forever when Paradise was lost, the "Christmas ingines" perform a kind of sympathetic magic that makes the Fall paradoxically fortunate, because—among other benefits—it gives birth to poetry, and to the community that fosters and appreciates it. Except in the inscrutable mind and unfathomable Being of God, until Satan or someone fell there was nothing *we* could know as poetry or communal celebration. After Satan spurned the heavenly feast, Raphael came to dinner in Paradise and made a poem. "At King Alcinous' feast" Demodocus later held "sad Ulysses' soul and all the rest / . . . with his melodious harmony / In willing chains and sweet captivity." Poets have been doing it ever since. At the Sidneys' table no one "tells [Jonson's] cups"; no waiter envies his gluttony, "But gives [him] what he call[s] and lets [him] eate." At Lewis Pemberton's, Herrick and the rest gorge themselves upon "Bullocks thighs, . . . Veales, . . . fat / Weathers, . . . Phesant, Partridge, Gotwit, Reeve, Ruffe, Raile, / The Cock, the Curlew, and the quaile." Thanking and complimenting their hosts, the poets enhance the revel to almost paradisal proportions by describing how, "though fall'n on evil days," foolishly happy holy sinners have come through "the hard Season."[48]

"The *Art of Poetry* was learnd, and found out . . . the same day, with the *Art of Cookery*," says the master cook in Jonson's masque. Not by angels, perhaps, but by men. When Raphael came to share a meal with Adam and Eve and to regale them with song that likened "spiritual to corporal forms," the food, though varied and plentiful, was raw. "From fireless Eden," says John Diekhoff,

> health food fads derive:
> Tree-ripened fruit, sweet herbs, and fresh raw green
> Whole grain and nuts and honey from the hive:
> A meatless, heatless, spiritless cuisine.
> "No fear lest dinner cool," his lines affirm;
> We owe the art of cooking to the Worm.

But, though Diekhoff's witty gloss on the felix culpa is the finest I know on the topos, it is a little misleading. To the extent that cooking and poetry represent alternative ways of attaining to the felicity God always intended, and fall short of what He still intends, the Old Dragon's fiery breath may be regarded as supervening, even efficient cause. But, as the "Christmas ingines" know, God is the first and final cause of both arts, which he bestows as helps meet for "the hard Season." Even before he has learned of the Incarnation and Redemption, Adam shoulders his burden of toil and trustingly anticipates the divine gift of fire,

> Which might supply the Sun: such Fire to use,
> And what may else be remedy or cure
> To evils which our own misdeeds have wrought,
> He will instruct us . . . ,
>   . . . so as we need not fear
> To pass commodiously this life, sustain'd
> By him with many comforts, till we end
> In dust, our final rest and native home.[49]

Thus, even when it does not look as though Favonius will ever "re-inspire" anything, the work of "a kind of a *Christmas* Ingine" reveals the possibility, with God's help, of creating "A genuine summer in each other's breast."[50] Such joyous confidence is folly, yet—as Milton and all the family seem to have realized—to put it into song is also the way in which to join Urania's converse with her "Sister Wisdom" in the pleased "presence of th' Almighty Father." Perhaps such communal realization and the sympathetic artistry it engenders simply place Milton, Jonson, and the other seventeenth-century poets discussed here in the family of common humanity. Or, at most, in the Tribe of Christ, seventeenth-century generation. However, by locating them all in close proximity on the "only Map" of Paradise available to them, perhaps their shared "not unwisdom" makes them not only congenial neighbors in "the hard Season" but also spiritual members of one poetic family of whom even Milton would have been proud to honor Jonson as earthly father—and as a master chef.

NOTES

Except as otherwise noted, poems are cited from the following editions. For the sake of brevity, page numbers are not given for these poems.

Herrick, Robert. *The Complete Poetry of Robert Herrick*, ed. J. Max Patrick. Garden City, N.Y.: Doubleday, 1963.

Maclean, Hugh, ed. *Ben Jonson and the Cavalier Poets.* New York: Norton, 1974.

Marvell, Andrew. *The Poems of Andrew Marvell,* ed. Hugh MacDonald. Cambridge, Mass.: Harvard University Press, 1963.

Milton, John. *Complete Poetry and Major Prose,* ed. Merritt Y. Hughes. New York: Odyssey, 1957.

1. Jonson, "To Penshurst" (59). Herrick, "A Panegerick to Sir Lewis Pemberton" (H-377, 9). Lovelace, "The Grasshopper" (20, 31). Milton *Paradise Lost,* 5.391, 341–42, 345–46, 377. Milton's epic is hereafter cited as *PL.*

2. *Milton: A Biography,* 2 vols. (Oxford: The Clarendon Press, 1968), vol. 1, pp. 83, 96, 103.

3. These references and possible or probable contacts are all documented in Parker, *Milton,* pp. 302, 419, 571–72, 584, 604, 610, 634, 929 (n. 35), 1017 (n. 13), 1084 (nn. 22, 23), 1096 (n. 76), 1115 (n. 38), 1129 (n. 16), 1148 (n. 62). It is possible that Cowley is one of the "more timely happy spirits" referred to in Sonnet 7. Although Marvell, with whom Milton did have personal connections, is surely in some sense an heir of Jonson and sometimes echoes such Cavaliers as Waller, we usually think of his mode and alignment as very different. For a recent treatment of Milton's literary relationship with him, see Judith Scherer Herz, "Milton and Marvell: The Poet as Fit Reader," *Modern Language Quarterly* 39 (1978), 239–63.

4. Hughes notes possible echoes of Jonson in "L'Allegro" (125–26), "Il Penseroso" (147–48), and *Comus* (963, 1018–23).

5. Parker, *Milton,* vol. 1, p. 91.

6. Herz, "Milton and Marvell," pp. 261–62.

7. *OED,* "Sympathy." "Sympathy" in sense 1 is of course not totally unconnected with "influence" in the astrological sense (*OED,* "Influence," *sb.* 2), but it excludes the implications of control of human destiny accepted by judicial astrologers. Nor is "influence," as critics use the term, totally unconnected with "sympathy" in sense 2, but this sense of "sympathy" excludes any implications of one party's or element's dependence on the other and any suggestions of domination/submission or superiority/inferiority.

8. *OED,* "Sympathy," *sb.* 3a.

9. Cowley, "The Preface of the Author" and "On the Death of Mr. Crashaw," *Poems,* ed. A. R. Waller (Cambridge: Cambridge University Press, 1905), pp. 12, 48.

10. "Holy fire" is Jonson's phrase in "On Lucy Countesse of Bedford" (*Epigrammes* 76). "Hallowed fire" is Milton's in *The Reason of Church Government;* see Hughes, p. 671.

11. Milton, *PL* 1.1–26 and 9.42–47. Jonson, *Discoveries* (2420–22).

12. Jonson, "An Ode. To himselfe" (27–29), "To the immortall memorie, and friendship of that noble paire, Sir Lucius Cary, and Sir H. Morison" (81–89). Milton, "At a Solemn Music" (1–5 ff.).

13. Jonson, "To Heaven" (13, 16), "To the Holy Trinitie" (35, 37–38), "A Hymne on the Nativitie of my Saviour" (2, 20–21), *Conversations* (180–82). Milton, "On Time" (13, 18), "On the Morning of Christ's Nativity" (9, 14), and *PL* 3.51–55, 375, 384–86, 389; 7.13, 16; 12.388–89, 402–06, 463–65.

14. *Neptune's Triumph for the Return of Albion* (34–35). On the occasional level, Jonson's poet is simply stating that, as a writer for the court, he is an instrument ("Ingine") employed each year during the Christmas season to use his wit ("Ingine") in devising a masque.

15. Chaucer, "Prologue," *The Canterbury Tales,* 5–6. Milton, Sonnet 20 ("Lawrence of virtuous Father . . . ," 6–8).

16. Milton, "Nativity," Sonnet 20 (5, 12). Herrick, "The Star-Song: A Caroll to the King; sung at White-Hall" (N-102), "Twelfe night, or King and Queene" (H-1035). Lovelace, "The Grasshopper" (29–32).

17. Milton, *PL* 3.40–41 and 7.25–27, Sonnet 19 ("When I consider"), "A Ready and Easy Way" (in Hughes, p. 880). Jonson, "Ode to Himselfe" (2), "The faery beame upon you" (9–10). Herrick, "The Argument of his Book" (H-1, 9), "The bad season makes the Poet sad" (H-612), "The Hag" (H-643, 1), "To his sweet Saviour" (N-77). Lovelace, "The Grasshopper" (13, 23, 35). Earl Miner, *The Cavalier Mode from Jonson to Cotton* (Princeton: Princeton University Press, 1971), p. 282.

18. Sidney, *An Apology for Poetry*, ed. Forrest G. Robinson (Indianapolis: Bobbs-Merrill, 1970), p. 15. *De augmentis scientiarum* 2, in *The Works of Francis Bacon*, ed. J. Spedding, R. L. Ellis, and D. D. Heath, 7 vols. (London: Longmans, 1857–74), vol. 4, pp. 315–16. Marvell, "Upon Appleton House" (761–64).

19. Sidney, *Apology*, p. 17. Sidney implies that he speaks of a mystery: "But these arguments will be by few be understood, and by fewer granted."

20. "A good life is a maine Argument" (*Discoveries*, 91–92). He "who would not be frustrate of his hope to write well hereafter in laudable things, ought himself to be a true poem, that is, a composition and pattern of best and honorablest things—not presuming to sing high praises of heroic men or famous cities, unless he have in himself the experience and the practice of all that which is praiseworthy" (Milton, "An Apology for Smectymnuus," in Hughes, p. 694).

21. Jonson, Cary-Morison ode (82). For Milton, the true poet's abilities "are the inspired gift of God rarely bestowed, but yet to some (though most abuse) in every nation; and are of power beside the office of a pulpit, to inbreed and cherish in a great people the seeds of virtue and public civility, to allay the perturbations of the mind and set the affections in right tune, to celebrate in glorious and lofty hymns the throne and equipage of God's almightiness, and what he works and what he suffers to be wrought with high providence in his church." See *The Reason of Church Government*, in Hughes, pp. 669–70.

22. Sonnet 20 (2); *PL* 12.602–05, 463–65, and 4.263–83.

23. *PL* 12.587, 555; Sonnet 20 (5–6); *Paradise Regained* 1.7.

24. Milton, *The Reason of Church Government* (in Hughes, p. 671), and "Of Education" (in Hughes, pp. 631, 632, 636–37). Jonson, *Discoveries* (2386–88).

25. *PL* 9.44–46 and 12.382.

26. Milton, *Samson Agonistes*, passim. Herrick, "His Prayer for Absolution" (N-2) and "To God" (N-113).

27. Cowley also conceives of life as "a well-order'd Poem" in "Upon Liberty," *Essays, Plays and Sundry Verses*, ed. A. R. Waller (Cambridge: Cambridge University Press, 1906), p. 391. In "Areopagitica," Milton suggests that "perhaps this is that doom which Adam fell into of knowing good and evil, that is to say, of knowing good by evil" (in Hughes, p. 728). *PL* 4.110. Lovelace, "The Grasshopper" (21–24, 37–40). Keats's phrase may, of course, be variously interpreted, but in defining it he does suggest one attribute of a sublime state of innocence: "being in uncertainties, mysteries, doubts, without any irritable reaching after fact & reason." See his letter to his brothers George and Thomas, December 21, 27 (?), 1817, in *The Norton Anthology of English Literature*, 4th ed., comp. M. H. Abrams et al., 2 vols. (New York: Norton, 1979), vol. 2, p. 867. *PL* 12.582 and 10.707.

28. Jonson, *Discoveries* (591–92). Milton, "Of Education" (in Hughes, p. 637).

29. Beaumont, "A Letter to Ben Jonson" (in Maclean, p. 422). Milton, *PL* 4.236, 250–51, and 5.394–95. Herrick, "Argument" (H-1, 1).

30. Milton, *PL* 4.208, 242, 247, and 5.295. Jonson, "To Penshurst" (41–44). Marvell, "Upon Appleton House" (766–68).

31. Milton, "Nativity" (232–33). Jonson, "To Sir Robert Wroth" (16–18, 65–66). Milton, *PL* 4.192–97, 340–50, and 11.467–69. Marvell, "Upon Appleton House" (395–424). James Shirley, "Dirge" from "The Contention of Ajax and Ulysses" (4, in Maclean, p. 196).

32. Milton, *PL* 12.571. Jonson, "To Penhurst" (29–62). Luke 5:6 and John 21:6. Carew, "To Saxham" (19–26).

33. Milton, "Nativity" (29, 151–53, 165), *PL* 10.697–98. Lovelace, "The Grasshopper" (15–16). Homer, *Iliad* 21.464–66, trans. Richmond Lattimore (Chicago: University of Chicago Press, 1951), p. 430. Ninth-century Irish song, trans. Alfred Graves, in *Medieval Literature in Translation*, ed. C. W. Jones (New York: David McKay, 1950), p. 120. Isaiah 40:6–8.

34. 1 Peter 1:24–25. Lovelace, "The Grasshopper" (17–18). Herman Melville, *Moby Dick*, ed. Charles Feidelson, Jr. (Indianapolis: Bobbs-Merrill, 1964), p. 87.

35. Milton, "Nativity" (229–34), *PL* 5.300–02. Jonson, "To Penshurst" (77–78). Carew, "To Saxham" (29–38).

36. Herrick, "A Thanksgiving to God, for his House" (N-47, 23–26, 37–38), "A Panegerick" (H-377, 6–8, 134), "A Country life: To his Brother, Master Thomas Herrick" (H-106, 116, 121–22), and "An Ode for him" (H-911, 1–10). Milton, "Il Penseroso" (77–82), Sonnet 20 (1, 12), and Sonnet 21 ("Cyriak, whose Grandsire," 6). Lovelace, "The Grasshopper" (28).

37. Jonson, "To Penshurst" (73–88, 102). John 14:2 and Psalms 127:1. Marvell, "Upon Appleton House" (31–32). Jonson, "To Sir Robert Wroth" (49). Milton, *PL* 5.469–71 and 9.1–4. Genesis 2:7. Herrick, "His Age" (H-336, 49–50), "A Thanksgiving" (N-47, 27–54). This last passage immediately follows that in which Herrick describes himself as glowing like a living coal.

38. Milton, "Nativity" (14). Lovelace, "The Grasshopper" (29–32). D. C. Allen discusses at length the links between grasshopper, kings, and the Christmas King, in *Image and Meaning: Metaphoric Traditions in Renaissance Poetry* (Baltimore: The Johns Hopkins Press, 1960), pp. 80–92 (reprinted in Maclean, pp. 570–77). Milton, *PL* 8.277–78. Matthew 6:28–33. Jonson, "To Penshurst" (63–64). Milton, Sonnet 20 (13–14), Sonnet 21 (12–14). See the discussion of these two sonnets by Anna K. Nardo, *Milton's Sonnets and the Ideal Community* (Lincoln: University of Nebraska Press, 1980), pp. 87–99; particularly note her discussion of the disputed meaning of "spare" in Sonnet 20 (pp. 91–92).

39. Milton, *PL* 5.403 and 12.583–84, Sonnet 20 (4). Matthew 6:34. Lovelace, "The Grasshopper" (11). Jonson, "To Sir Robert Wroth" (35–36, 48–50). Marvell, "Upon Appleton House" (65–68). Carew, "To Saxham" (49–50). Jonson, "To Penshurst" (49–57). Herrick, "A Thanksgiving" (13–14), "The Country Life, to the honoured Master Endimion Porter" (H-662, 47–61), "A Panegerick" (90–91, 135–36). Milton, *Comus* (174–77, 958–75).

40. Milton, *PL* 5.372–75, 451–55, 600–41; 7.66–69; 8.210–28. Jonson, "To Sir Robert Wroth" (52). Herrick, "His Age" (68–69 and passim), "A Thanksgiving" (15–16), "Lyrick for Legacies" (H-218). Acts 3:6. *Leges Convivales* are translated as "Ben Jonson's Sociable Rules for the Apollo" by Alexander Brome. See *Songs and other Poems*, 1661, in J. W. Hebel and Hoyt H. Hudson, eds., *Poetry of the English Rennaissance, 1509–1660* (New York: Appleton-Century-Crofts, 1945), p. 513.

41. Lovelace, "The Grasshopper" (33–36). Milton, Sonnet 19 ("When I consider," 9–10).

42. Marvell, "The Coronet" (6–8, 13–15). Milton, *PL* 9.893. The rose is mentioned only twice in the Authorized Version of the Bible, both times to designate flowers of entirely different species in the original. The rose is not mentioned at all in the Hebrew or Greek.

43. Milton, *PL* 2.1048, 3.380, 7.170, 11.329–38. Herrick, "A Country Life" (90, 135–38). Jonson, "To Sir Robert Wroth" (96–106). *Hydriotaphia, or Urne Buriall*, in *The Prose of Sir Thomas Browne*, ed. Norman J. Endicott (Garden City, N. Y.: Doubleday, 1967), p. 281. Marvell, "Upon Appleton House" (52). Cf. "Let others vainly strive t'immure / The Circle in the Quadrature" (45–46).

44. Milton, *PL* 1.10–20 and 4.345–47, "At a Vacation Exercise" (33–46). Sir John

Denham, "Cooper's Hill" (1–4, in Maclean, p. 293). Bacon, *Advancement of Learning* 2, in *Works*, ed. Spedding, Ellis, and Heath, vol. 3, p. 382. Jonson, *Neptune's Triumph* (42–87).

45. "Tetrachordon," in *The Student's Milton*, ed. Frank A. Patterson (New York: Appleton-Century-Crofts, 1946), pp. 656–57; *PL* 7.9–12.

46. "Areopagitica" (in Hughes, p. 720).

47. Milton, *PL* 10.668–91 and 12.466–78. Herrick, "Gods Power" (N-176), "Discontents in Devon" (H-51, 8). Lovelace, "The Grasshopper" (26–27). John Aubrey, "Collections for the Life of Milton" (in Hughes, p. 1024).

48. Milton, "At a Vacation Exercise" (48–52). Jonson, "To Penshurst" (67–69). Herrick, "A Panegerick" (63–66).

49. Jonson, *Neptune's Triumph* (71–72). John S. Diekhoff, "Felix Culpa," *Milton Quarterly* 10, no. 2 (May 1976), 63 (glossing *PL* 5.396). Milton, *PL* 10.1078–85. *OED*, "Commodious," 2.6: "Said of *life, living*: Endowed with conveniences, comfortable." Citing Cowley (1663), the *OED* notes that this sense is obsolete.

50. Lovelace, "The Grasshopper" (22).

Notes on the Contributors
Index to Works Cited

✝

Notes on the Contributors

ILONA BELL has published several articles on George Herbert and the English Reformation, one of which has been reprinted in *Essential Articles for the Study of George Herbert's Poetry*. A recent recipient of an ACLS research grant, she has taught at Smith College and at the Massachusetts Institute of Technology and is currently Assistant Professor of English at Williams College.

THOMAS CLAYTON, Professor of English at the University of Minnesota, earned his doctorate at Oxford University under the supervision of Dame Helen Gardner. A Rhodes Scholar, a Guggenheim Fellow, and a Danforth Associate, he has published numerous essays, primarily on Suckling and on Shakespeare, a monograph on *The Shakespearean Addition in The Booke of Sir Thomas Moore*, the definitive edition of *The Non-dramatic Works of Sir John Suckling* in the Oxford English Text series, and the anthology *Cavalier Poets* in the Oxford Standard Authors series.

MARTIN ELSKY is Assistant Professor of English at Brooklyn College, City University of New York, and has taught as Visiting Professor in the graduate division of the Department of English and Comparative Literature at Columbia University. He has published essays on George Herbert and seventeenth-century religious poetry and is currently working on a study of the relationship between Renaissance concepts of language and seventeenth-century prose and poetry.

RICHARD FLANTZ did his undergraduate and graduate work at Tel Aviv University and spent a year as a postdoctoral fellow at Yale. He is lecturer in the English Department of Tel Aviv University.

ROBERT B. HINMAN is Professor of English at the University of Pittsburgh. He has also taught at the University of Rochester, at Emory University, and, as Visiting Professor, at the University of Hull. A member of the editorial board of *Milton Studies* and an associate editor of *Seventeenth-Century News*, he has been especially interested in the relationship between science and literature in the seventeenth century and has published, among other studies, *Abraham Cowley's World of Order*, "The Apotheosis of Faust: Poetry and New Philosophy in the Seventeenth Century," and "The 'Verser' at *The Temple* Door: Herbert's '*The Church-porch*.' "

MICHAEL H. MARKEL is Assistant Professor of Humanities and Communications at Drexel University. He has written on Shakespeare, Suckling, Lovelace, and Housman, and has a book forthcoming on Hilaire Belloc.

RICHARD C. NEWTON is Associate Professor of English at Temple University, where he chairs the department. He teaches courses in Renaissance literature, writing, and the teaching of writing and has published essays on Donne and Jonson.

MICHAEL P. PARKER is Assistant Professor of English at the United States Naval Academy. A native of Washington, D.C., he received his undergraduate and graduate education at Yale University. He has published several articles on seventeenth-century poetry and is now doing preliminary research for a book on Caroline aesthetics.

C. A. PATRIDES is G. B. Harrison Distinguished Professor of English at the University of Michigan–Ann Arbor. He has authored *Milton and the Christian Tradition*, *"The Grand Design of God": The Literary Form of the Christian View of History*, and *Premises and Motifs in Renaissance Thought and Literature;* coauthored *Bright Essence: Studies in Milton's Theology;* edited Herbert, Sir Thomas Browne, Milton, Ralegh, and the Cambridge Platonists, as well as several collections of essays; and coedited *The Age of Milton: Backgrounds to Seventeenth-Century Literature.* An Honored Scholar of the Milton Society, he has been awarded the Guggenheim Fellowship twice.

TED-LARRY PEBWORTH, a principal organizer of the Biennial Renaissance Conferences at the University of Michigan–Dearborn, is Professor of English at that university. Author of *Owen Felltham* and coauthor of *Ben Jonson*, both in Twayne's English Authors Series, coeditor of *The Poems of Owen Felltham, 1604?–1668* and *"Too Rich to Clothe the Sunne": Essays on George Herbert*, and editor of *The Poems of Sir Henry Wotton* (forthcoming), he has also published critical and bibliographical essays on numerous seventeenth-century figures and subjects.

STELLA P. REVARD is Professor of English at Southern Illinois University, Edwardsville, where she also teaches Greek. She has published essays on Milton, Yeats, Shelley, Drayton, and other writers in leading scholarly journals and is author of *The War in Heaven: Paradise Lost and the Tradition of Satan's Rebellion.*

ROGER B. ROLLIN teaches courses in Renaissance literature and in the mass media and popular culture at Clemson University, where since 1975 he has been William James Lemon Professor of Literature. His most recent scholarship has focused on an affective classification of George Herbert's poems, a phenomenological approach to the poetry of John Donne, a psychoanalytic study of television heroes, and mythopoeia in popular culture.

JOHN T. SHAWCROSS, Professor of English at the University of Kentucky, is editor of *The Complete Poetry of John Milton* and *The Complete Poetry of John Donne* and has published widely on both seventeenth- and twentieth-century literature. He has contributed essays on Robert Herrick and George Herbert to prior Renaissance conferences at the University of Michigan–Dearborn. He is an Honored Scholar of the Milton Society of America.

CLAUDE J. SUMMERS, Professor of English at the University of Michigan–Dearborn and a principal organizer of that university's Biennial Renaissance Conferences, is author of books on E. M. Forster, Christopher Isherwood, and Christopher Marlowe, coauthor of the Twayne *Ben Jonson*, coeditor of *"Too Rich to Clothe the Sunne": Essays on George Herbert* and *The Poems of Owen Felltham, 1604?–1668*, and an associate editor of *Seventeenth-Century News*. His essays include studies of Marlowe, Shakespeare, Herbert, Herrick, Vaughan, Isherwood, Auden, and others.

RAYMOND B. WADDINGTON, Professor of English at the University of California, Davis, is author of *The Mind's Empire: Myth and Form in George Chapman's Narrative Poems* and coeditor of *The Rhetoric of Renaissance Poetry: From Wyatt to Milton* and *The Age of Milton: Backgrounds to Seventeenth-Century Literature*. He has held fellowships granted by the Guggenheim Foundation, the Newberry and Huntington Librar-ies, the Institute for Research in the Humanities, and the Humanities Center at Johns Hopkins University; he is currently working on a book-length study of Shakespeare's *Sonnets*.

JACK D. WINNER, Instructor in English at Louisiana State University, Baton Rouge, is a recent recipient of an ACLS grant. In addition to further work on Jonson, he is writing a study of the novelist Margaret Drabble.

SUSANNE WOODS, Associate Professor of English at Brown University and author of numerous articles on Renaissance poetry and stylistics, has just completed a book on English Renaissance versification. She has held Clark and Huntington Library fellowships, and she is a member of the MLA Executive Committee on Seventeenth-Century English Literature and a founding member of Lyrica, the Society for Words and Music.

✝

Index to Works Cited

This index includes only works by British writers of the sixteenth and seventeenth centuries.

Ascham, Roger
  The Scholemaster, 78–79
Aubrey, John
  Brief Lives, 172–73
  "Collections for the Life of Milton," 273
Bacon, Sir Francis
  The Advancement of Learning, 79–81, 270
  De augmentis scientiarum, 92, 101–02, 260
Beaumont, Francis
  "A Letter to Ben Jonson," 263, 268
Breton, Nicholas
  Britons Bowre of Delights, 33
Brome, Alexander
  "Ben Jonson's Sociable Rules for the Apollo," 277
Brome, Richard
  Five New Plays, 153
Browne, Sir Thomas
  Hydriotaphia, or Urne Buriall, 270
Burton, Robert
  The Anatomy of Melancholy, 48–49, 102–03
Camden, William
  Britannia, 95, 96–97, 104
  Remaines Concerning Britaine, 97
Campion, Thomas
  Observations in the Art of English Poesie, 82
Carew, Thomas
  Coelum Britannicum, 184, 188
  "A deposition from Love," 186
  "An Elegie upon . . . John Donne," 151
  "In answer of an Elegiacall Letter . . . from Aurelian Townsend," 184

"Mediocritie in love rejected," 49
"On a Damask rose," 191
"Parting, Celia weepes," 231
Poems (1640), 47
"A prayer to the Wind," 191
"A Rapture," 189, 191
"A Song ['Aske me no more where Jove bestows']," 50
"Song. Celia Singing," 249–50, 251
"To Ben. Johnson," 139, 144, 148, 151
"To my friend G. N. from Wrest," xvi, 171–91
"To my Mistresse in absence," 191
"To my Mistris sitting by a Rivers side. An Eddy," 189
"To Saxham," 171, 175, 176, 178, 185, 265, 266, 268
"To the King at his entrance into Saxham," 182
"Upon a Mole in Celias bosome," 178
"Upon a Ribband," 191
Cartwright, William
  The Complaint of Ariadne, 256
  "No Platonique Love," 50
Congreve, William
  The Way of the World, 217
Cowley, Abraham
  The Mistress, 193
  "On the Death of Mr. Crashaw," 152, 257
  "The Preface of the Author," 257
  "Upon Liberty," 276
  "Weeping," 245–46

285

Crashaw, Richard
"Out of Catullus," 7
Steps to the Temple, 47
Daniel, Samuel
Defence of Ryme, 82, 89
Whole Works (1623), 46
Davenant, Sir William
Salmacida Spolia, 177, 185
Denham, Sir John
"Cooper's Hill," 270
Donne, John
"Amicissimo, et meritissimo Ben.
Jonson. In Vulponem," 148
"The Apparition," 196, 203
"The Canonization," 122, 196, 210
"Community," 233
"The Dampe," 196, 199
"The Extasie," 127
"The Legacie," 199
"Loves Alchymie," 196
"A nocturnall upon S. Lucies day," 167
Poems (1633), 47
"The Prohibition," 199
"The Relique," 196, 197
"A Valediction: Forbidding Mourning,"
164, 167, 205
"A Valediction: Of Weeping," 167
Drummond, William
*Conversations with William Drummond of
Hawthornden*, xii, 4, 5, 61, 81–84, 108,
140, 141, 143, 144, 148–49, 258–59
Dryden, John
"A Discourse concerning the Original
and Progress of Satire," 144, 152–53
"An Essay of Dramatic Poesy," 235
"The Secular Masque," 189
Dyer, Sir Edward
"My mind to me a kingdom is," 237
Elyot, Sir Thomas
Boke named the Governour, 78
Fane, Mildmay
"He who began from brick and lime," 148
Gascoigne, George
Certayne Notes of Instruction, 89
A Hundredth sundrie Flowres, 34, 42
Godolphin, Sidney
"No more unto my thoughts appear," 50
"On Ben Jonson," 148
"Song ['Or love me less, or love me
more']," 49

Googe, Barnaby
Eglogs, Epytaphes and Sonnetes, 34
Greene, Robert
Groat's-worth of Wit, 147
Habington, William
Castara, 193, 210
Hall, Joseph
Works (1621), 46
Harington, Sir John
Epigrams (1618), 46
Herbert, George
"Affliction (I)," 165
"The Collar," 165–66
"Dedication," 158–60, 161, 162, 167
"The Flower," 166–67
The Temple, xvi, 47, 157–70
Herrick, Robert
"The Argument of his Book," 260, 264
"Art above Nature, to Julia," 50
"The bad season makes the Poet sad,"
260
"A Country life: To his Brother Master
Thomas Herrick," 266, 270
"The Country Life, to the honoured
Master Endimion Porter," 268
"Delight in Disorder," 50
"Discontents in Devon," 272
"Gods Power," 272
"The Hag," 260
Hesperides, 50, 262
"His Age," 267, 269
"His Prayer for Absolution," 262
"His Prayer to Ben. Johnson," 151
"Lyrick for Legacies," 269
"No difference i'th'dark," 221
"An Ode for him [i.e., Jonson]," 148
"A Panegerick to Sir Lewis Pemberton,"
176, 255, 266, 268, 270, 273
"The Star-Song: A Caroll to the King,"
260
"A Thanksgiving to God, for his
House," 266, 267, 268, 269
"To God," 262
"To his sweet Saviour," 260
"To the Rose. Song," 50
"Twelfe night, or King and Queene,"
260
"Upon Julia's Clothes," 50
"Upon Master Ben. Johnson. Epigram,"
139

Hobbes, Thomas
"The Answer . . . to . . . D'Avenant's
   Preface before *Gondibert*," 80
Hooker, Richard
   Of the Laws of Ecclesiasticall Politie, 78
Hoskyns, John
   Directions for Speech and Style, 92–93
Howell, James
   Epistolae Ho-Elianae, 144, 239
Jones, Inigo
   "To his false friend mr: Ben Johnson,"
   xii
Jonson, Ben
   "And must I sing?" (F. 10), 13
   Catiline, 39
   "A Celebration of Charis" (U. 2), xii, xv,
      3, 70–71, 121–38, 148, 193–94, 210,
      212
   *Conversations with William Drummond of
      Hawthornden. See* Drummond, William
   Cynthia's Revels, 35, 41, 43, 127, 230–31
   Discoveries, xii, xiii, 3, 4, 5, 11, 14, 60,
      82, 84, 92–94, 98–99, 101–02, 117,
      135, 139, 141, 143, 146, 148, 149, 150,
      151, 257–58, 261, 262, 263, 270, 276
   "The Dreame" (U. 11), 49
   "An Elegie" (U. 38), 13, 210, 212
   "An Elegie" (U. 39), 13, 16
   "An Elegie" (U. 40), 13, 212
   "An Elegie" (U. 41), 13, 212
   "An Elegie on the Lady Jane Pawlet"
      (U. 83), 12, 109
   The English Grammar, 92
   Epicoene, 50, 230
   Epigrammes, 38, 50, 59, 84, 97, 107, 109,
      110, 118, 161
   "Epistle. To Elizabeth Countesse of Rut-
      land" (F. 12), xiii, 47
   "Epistle. To Katherine, Lady Aubigny"
      (F. 13), 41, 100–01
   "An Epistle to Master John Selden"
      (U. 14), 62–64, 98, 145–46
   "An Epistle to Sir Edward Sacvile"
      (U. 13), 62–64, 98
   "Epitaph on Elizabeth, L. H." (E. 124),
      108, 109, 111–12, 161
   "Epitaph on S[alomon] P[avy]" (E. 120),
      108, 109, 110–11, 112, 113
   "Epode" (F. 11), 11, 41
   Every Man in his Humour, 38, 40, 42

Every Man out of his Humour, 35
"An Execration upon Vulcan" (U. 43), 11
"An Expostulation with Inigo Jones"
   (U. V. 34), 13, 86
"A Fit of Rime against Rime" (U. 29),
   85–86
The Forrest, 38, 47
The Golden Age Restored, 38
The Gypsies Metamorphosed, 260
Horace, His Art of Poetrie, 3, 12
Hymenaei, 5
"Inviting a Friend to Supper" (E. 101),
   165
Leges Convivales, 268, 277
Mercury Vindicated, 38
"My Picture left in Scotland" (U. 9), xii,
   133
Neptune's Triumph for the Return of Albion,
   259–60, 261, 270–71, 273–74
"A Nymphs Passion" (U. 7), 14
Oberon, 134
"Ode" (U. V. 6), 151
"An Ode" (U. 26), 94–95
"An Ode" (U. 27), 5
"An Ode. To himselfe" (U. 23), 59, 72,
   139, 258
"Ode to Himselfe" (*The New Inne*), 5, 28,
   144, 260
"An Ode to James Earle of Desmond"
   (U. 25), 5
"Ode. To Sir William Sydney" (F. 14),
   41, 96
"On Court-worme" (E. 15), 131, 163
"On Don Surly" (E. 28), 100
"On Lucy Countesse of Bedford" (E. 76),
   xii, 69–70, 162–63, 164, 165, 258
"On Margaret Ratcliffe" (E. 40), 97, 108,
   110
"On My First Daughter" (E. 22), xii,
   113, 116
"On My First Sonne" (E. 45), xii, xv,
   66–69, 107, 113–18, 150
"On Play-wright" (E. 100), 45
"On Poet-Ape" (E. 56), 45–46
"On Sir John Roe" (E. 27), 108, 110
"On Sir John Roe" (E. 32), 108
"On Sir Voluptuous Beast" (E. 25), 99,
   131
"On Some-thing, that Walkes Some-
   where" (E. 11), 163

"On the Townes Honest Man" (E. 115), 98

Pleasure Reconcil'd to Vertue, 73

"Poems of Devotion" (U. 1), 13, 212, 258, 259

Poetaster, 39–40

Sejanus, 34, 35, 37, 38

"A Song ['Oh doe not wanton with those eyes']" (U. 4), 49

"Song. To Celia" (F. 5), 5–6, 229, 230

"A speach according to Horace" (U. 44), 13

Timber. See Discoveries

"To All, to Whom I Write" (E. 9), 97, 118

"To a Weake Gamster in Poetry" (E. 112), xi

"To Benjamin Rudyerd" (E. 121), 139

"To Censorious Courtling" (E. 52), 99

"To Clement Edmonds" (E. 110), 40–41

"To Fine Grand" (E. 73), 46

"To Fine Lady Would-bee" (E. 62), 131

"To Francis Beaumont" (E. 55), 152

"To Heaven" (F. 15), 65–66, 68, 258

"To John Donne" (E. 23), xv, 141–42, 144

"To John Donne" (E. 96), xv, 140

"To King James" (E. 4), 140

"To Mary Lady Wroth" (E. 105), 100, 101

"To Mr. Josuah Sylvester" (E. 132), 152

"To My Lord Ignorant" (E. 10), 131

"To My Meere English Censurer" (E. 18), 109, 118

"To Old-end Gatherer" (E. 53), 45

"To Penshurst" (F. 2), xi, xii, 40, 49, 84–85, 165, 171, 175, 176, 178, 179, 188, 190, 255, 260, 264, 266, 267, 268, 273

"To Person Guiltie" (E. 38), 97–98

"To Pertinax Cob" (E. 69), 131

"To Proule the Plagiary" (E. 81), 45

"To Sir Henry Nevil" (E. 109), 96

"To Sir Robert Wroth" (F. 3), 46, 176, 183, 264, 267, 268, 269, 270

"To Sir Thomas Overbury" (E. 113), 152

"To Sir Thomas Roe" (E. 98), 139

"To the immortall memorie . . . of . . . Sir Lucius Cary, and Sir H. Morison" (U. 70), xii, xv, 17–29, 65, 70, 72–73, 86–88, 99, 101, 111, 133, 258, 261, 276

"To the Learned Critick" (E. 17), 39

"To the memory of . . . William Shakespeare" (U. V. 26), xv, 11, 144–54

"To the Reader" (E. 1), 51, 118, 158, 160–61, 162

"To the Reader" (U. V. 25), 143

"To the Same [i.e., Alphonso Ferrabosco]" (E. 131), 43

"To the Same [i.e., Benjamin Rudyerd]" (E. 122), 100

"To the Same [i.e., Celia]" (F. 6), 6–7

"To the Same [i.e., Sir Henry Goodyere]" (E. 86), 100

"To the Same [i.e., Sir John Roe]" (E. 33), 108

"To the worthy Author on the Husband" (U. V. 20), 139

"To Thomas Earle of Suffolke" (E. 67), 60

"To William Camden" (E. 14), 95–96

"To William Earle of Pembroke" (E. 102), 98, 118

"To William Lord Mounteagle" (E. 60), 118

"To William Roe" (E. 128), 163–64, 167

The Under-wood, 47

Volpone, xi, 5, 12, 41, 107, 115, 146, 229, 230

"Why I Write Not of Love" (F. 1), 41

Workes (1616), xiv, 37–40, 44, 59

Kendall, Timothy
Flowres of Epigrams, 33

King, Henry
"Sonnet ['Tell me no more how fair she is']," 50

Lovelace, Richard
"The Grasshopper," 137, 255, 260, 263, 265, 266, 267, 268, 269, 272, 274, 277
Lucasta, 244

Marvell, Andrew
"The Coronet," 269
"Daphnis and Chloe," 244, 247–49
"The Fair Singer," 244, 247, 249–52
"The Gallery," 244–45
"The Garden," 252
"Mourning," 244, 245–47
"The Unfortunate Lover," 243
"Upon Appleton House," 171, 176, 183, 184, 188, 260, 264, 267, 268, 270

Massinger, Philip, and John Fletcher
  The Custom of the County, 238
Milton, John
  "An Apology for Smectymnuus," 261,
    276
  Arcades, 255
  "Areopagitica," 271, 276
  "At a Solemn Music," 258
  "At a Vacation Exercise," 270, 273
  Comus, 210, 255, 268, 275
  "Epitaph on the Marchioness of Win-
    chester," 255
  "Il Penseroso," 255, 266, 275
  "L'Allegro," 255, 256, 275
  "Lycidas," 264
  "Of Education," 262, 263
  "On May Morning," 255
  "On the Morning of Christ's Nativity,"
    259, 260, 264, 265, 266, 267
  "On Time," 258
  Paradise Lost, 139, 255, 256, 258, 259,
    260, 261–62, 263, 264, 265, 266, 267,
    268, 269, 270, 271, 272, 273, 274
  Paradise Regained, 262
  "The Passion," 46–47
  Poems (1645), 46
  "A Ready and Easy Way," 260
  The Reason of Church Government, 258,
    262, 276
  Samson Agonistes, 262
  "Sonnet 19 ['When I consider']," 260, 269
  "Sonnet 20 ['Lawrence of vertuous
    Father']," 260, 261, 262, 266, 267, 268
  "Sonnet 21 ['Cyriak, whose Grandsire'],"
    266, 267
  "Tetrachordon," 271
Puttenham, George
  The Arte of English Poesie, 34, 79
Randolph, Thomas
  "Amyntas," 198
  "Answer to Mr. Ben Jonson's Ode," 148
  "A gratulatory to Mr. Ben. Johnson," xiv
  The Jealous Lovers, 198
  "On the Death of a Nightingale," 198
Selden, John
  Titles of Honour, 62, 104
Shakespeare, William
  As You Like It, 104, 226
  Hamlet, 157, 220, 236
  A Midsummer Night's Dream, 239

Much Ado about Nothing, 230
  Sonnets, 69, 138
  Twelfth Night, 223
  Works (1623), 46, 143, 145, 146, 147
Shirley, James
  The Contention of Ajax and Ulysses, 264
Sidney, Sir Philip
  An Apology for Poetry, 69, 73, 79, 81, 226,
    260, 261, 276
  Arcadia, 37
  Astrophil and Stella, 69, 73
Southwell, Robert
  The Burning Babe, 258
Spenser, Edmund
  The Faerie Queene, 33–34, 37, 42
  The Shepheardes Calender, 33, 42
Suckling, Sir John
  An Account of Religion by Reason, 221, 224
  Aglaura, 228–29, 231
  "An Answer to Some Verses Made in
    His Praise," 223, 225–27
  "A Ballad upon a Wedding," 221, 222,
    223
  Fragmenta Aurea, 221, 229
  "Love turn'd to Hatred," 247, 253
  "Love's Clock," 238
  "Out upon it! I have loved," 217, 223
  "A Sessions of the Poets" ("The Wits"),
    139, 221–23
  "Song to a Lute," 50
  "Song ['Why so pale and wan, fond
    lover?']," 217, 223, 227–32
  "Sonnet II ['Of thee, kind boy']," 232–38
  "Upon St. Thomas's Unbelief," 223–25
Tottel, Richard
  Miscellany (Songes and Sonettes), 49, 109
Vaughan, Henry
  "An Elegy," 195, 198, 203–04, 205, 210,
    211, 212
  "Les Amours," 195, 198–200, 210, 211,
    212
  "Looking back," 238
  Poems (1646), 193–214
  "A Rhapsodis," 195, 204–05, 206, 208,
    210, 211, 212
  "Song," 195, 198, 201–02, 204, 211, 212
  "A Song to Amoret," 195, 203, 206, 207,
    211, 212
  "To Amoret gone from him," 195, 202–
    03, 210, 211, 212

"To Amoret, of the difference 'twixt him, and other Lovers," 195, 205–06, 211, 212, 213

"To Amoret. The Sigh," 195, 201, 211, 212

"To Amoret. Walking in a Starry Evening," 195, 202, 211, 212

"To Amoret Weeping," 195, 206–08, 210, 211, 212, 213

"To his Friend Being in Love," 195, 201, 210, 211, 212

"To my Ingenuous Friend, R. W.," 194, 195–98, 199, 200, 210, 211, 212

"Upon the Priorie Grove," 194–95, 198, 208–09, 211, 212

Waller, Edmund
"Of Mrs. Arden," 249, 250, 251
"Song ['Go, lovely rose']," 50
"Upon Ben Jonson," 148

Wilkins, John
An Essay Towards a Real Character, and a Philosophical Language, 92

Wilson, Thomas
The Art of Rhetorique, 109, 114–15